An Illustrated History
of
# L. M. S.
## COACHES
# 1923–1957

# An Illustrated History

## of

# L. M. S.

## COACHES

# 1923–1957

by Bob Essery
and David Jenkinson

Oxford Publishing Co.

This is an enlarged and revised edition
based upon a book first published by Ian Allan Ltd in 1969.
SBN 902888 83 8

To Wynne and Sheila—as usual!

ISBN 0 902888 83 8

Reprinted 1984

Printed in Great Britain by:
Balding & Mansell Ltd., Wisbech, Cambs.


Published by:
Oxford Publishing Co.
Link House
West Street
POOLE, Dorset

# Contents

*Summary Tables of Vehicles Built &c.*

*Table Reference and Title*

# Foreword

THIS book was first published in 1969 as a companion volume to 'Locomotive Liveries of the LMS' and we were pleased when enthusiasts and historians began to regard both volumes as standard works of reference. Unfortunately, both books went out of print in the early 1970s and are now only available at highly inflated prices through the second hand market. We were, therefore, highly gratified when the Oxford Publishing Company sought our permission for a re-issue under their auspices.

We were even more pleased when we were invited to consider a major re-structuring to take account of changed techniques in the book publishing industry and to allow the incorporation of any additional facts which may have emerged since the first editions. In the case of 'Locomotive Liveries' therefore, we have decided to enlarge the work considerably to become, we hope, a more comprehensive illustrated history of LMS locomotives and the revision work is now being actively pursued. In the meantime, we felt that since 'The LMS Coach' was essentially complete as first published, having been compiled from the outset as a comprehensive history of the subject, a reprint was the simplest way of making the work available again. For this reason, the very few additional comments which we felt necessary have been added at the ends of the relevant chapters. However, we have been able to re-position the pictures closer to the relevant text and also add many more photographs and drawings. Nevertheless, the essential character of the work has not been altered. Our original aim was to present as complete a survey as possible of LMS coaching practice after 1922 and this is what we hope is still contained in the following pages.

Our starting point was the series of official LMS coaching stock diagram books which indicated precisely what sort of coaches were built, and how many of each type. From this primary source and by careful analysis the rest of the account has been constructed. We have been allowed free and liberal access to all the photographs, drawings and other data which British Railways could locate and no effort has been spared to allow us to investigate anything pertaining to the subject. In particular we are grateful for having been given permission to consult and quote extensively from the files relating to the building of LMS coaches, particularly those referring to articulated stock. Without this information we could not have embarked upon the venture and we would like to single out for our special thanks Messrs T. J. Edgington and R. E. Wilson of the London Midland Region for their kindness, tolerance and, above all, their astonishing ability to locate long-lost information!

Faced with all this data, the hardest problem to solve was the extent and depth of coverage we should attempt. Here, we have had to strike a balance between what could be said and the amount of space the publisher would give us in which to say it! If we have given too much attention to some areas and not enough to others, we crave the reader's forgiveness. However, we have tried to be guided by the general consideration that inclusion was justified if information was available, interesting and, most important, previously unpublished.

Our researches have brought us in contact with many coaching stock enthusiasts who have been able, by their own observation and record keeping to supplement our own and the official records; thus completing several gaps in the story. In particular we would like to express our very sincere thanks to Messrs John Alsop, Richard Casserley, John Cull and Roy Wells for their kindness in checking masses of data and for vetting the manuscript proofs of the book. It would be rash to claim that no mistakes have been overlooked but everything possible has been done to ensure their elimination.

Most of the photographs used in this book are the original LMS official series, initially made available to us by courtesy of BR(LMR) at the time of the first edition. The bulk of them have now been transferred to the National Railway Museum, York which has also made available some of the additional material incorporated in this second edition. To both organisations we acknowledge our continued indebtedness. The source of all non-official pictures used in this book is given with the caption concerned.

Lastly, but by no means least, we must acknowledge our indebtedness to the late Gavin Wilson of Wormit, Fife for the preparation of the colour panels used in the book.

RJE  
Solihull  
West Midlands  
1977

DJ  
Knaresborough  
North Yorkshire  
1977

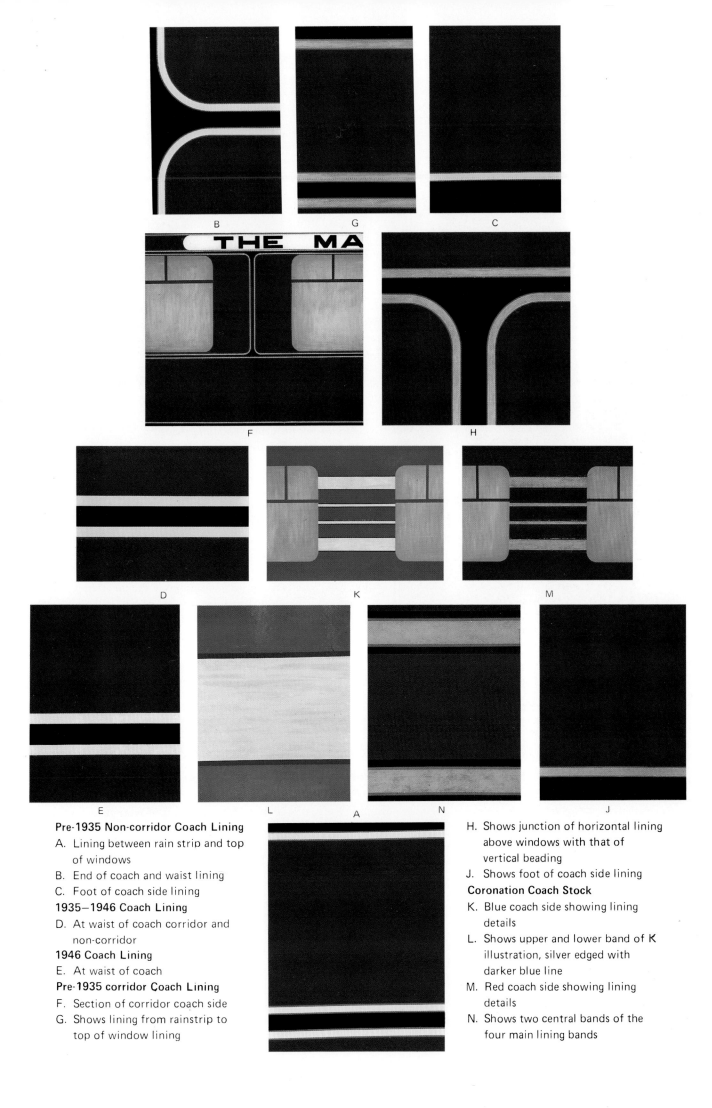

**Pre-1935 Non-corridor Coach Lining**

A. Lining between rain strip and top of windows

B. End of coach and waist lining

C. Foot of coach side lining

**1935–1946 Coach Lining**

D. At waist of coach corridor and non-corridor

**1946 Coach Lining**

E. At waist of coach

**Pre-1935 corridor Coach Lining**

F. Section of corridor coach side

G. Shows lining from rainstrip to top of window lining

H. Shows junction of horizontal lining above windows with that of vertical beading

J. Shows foot of coach side lining

**Coronation Coach Stock**

K. Blue coach side showing lining details

L. Shows upper and lower band of K illustration, silver edged with darker blue line

M. Red coach side showing lining details

N. Shows two central bands of the four main lining bands

O

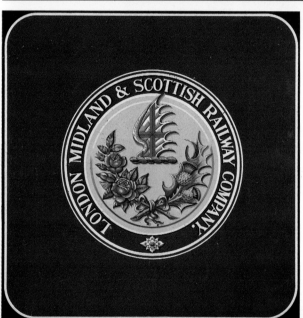

P

Q

O. Simplified coach livery (1934 onwards) showing waist lining and seriffed pattern 'LMS' in chrome yellow and fully shaded. The style of LMS lettering from 1923 onwards was of this type but before the adoption of the simple livery, the base colour was gold (gilt).

P. LMS 'Coat of Arms' as used on carriage stock. The version illustrated is the post-war variety with 'straw' coloured letters/ surrounds. Before the war, the same design had been provided with gold lettering &c (full livery) followed by chrome yellow lettering, &c (simple livery).

Q. Simplified livery showing fully shaded sans serif numerals in chrome yellow. This style of running number was used during the 1934–40 period.

# Introduction

THE passenger carrying vehicles bequeathed to the LMS at the grouping of 1923 must surely represent one of the most heterogeneous collections of coaches ever to be possessed by one railway company. They varied in kind from the opulence of the long distance coaches of the larger companies to the somewhat frugal accommodation provided on local trains in many parts of the far-flung system—not necessarily in those areas most removed from the centre of activities either! Tempting though it would be to reminisce in detail about these many and varied products of a by-gone age, it would be impossible to do all the designs full justice and, therefore, no such attempt has been made. Aside from which, much ground has already been covered by such authorities as C. Hamilton Ellis and G. M. Kichenside. This story is, therefore, concerned with the development of the passenger coach during the lifespan of the LMS and afterwards until its final supersession by BR standard designs in the 1950s.

As with locomotives, so too with coaches, the Midland Railway influence was soon to the fore in the LMS design offices. With Reid appointed as the first carriage superintendent, it was only to be expected that Derby ideas would soon be standard for the new company. However, although many criticisms can, with justice, be levelled at the policy of perpetuating the Midland's locomotive policy, it is less easy to quarrel with the basic principle of continuing with MR carriage design methods. The Midland was to the forefront of British railway companies in this respect and, apart from a select few vehicles from other pre-group constituents, it is probably fair to say that in terms of quality, the MR had the best overall stock of carriages of any of the pre-group constituents of the LMS.

At the same time, there was not quite the same rigidity of approach to carriage policy as there was in the locomotive field and several ideas from other companies were integrated into the LMS standard coaches. Thus one finds the 57ft underframe adopted as the norm almost from the start of things in preference to the MR 54ft length—although in fairness one should point out that the Midland had, latterly, adopted 57ft as its standard for corridor coaches. In fact, both 57ft and 54ft non-corridor coaches were built by the LMS depending on the area of operation. In some instances the early LMS coaches showed no real signs of Midland influence—for example the early 12-wheel sleeping and dining cars which except for the increased waist panel depth were of almost pure LNWR style, at least outwardly. However, most traces of pre-group individuality had gone from the construction scene within the first five or six years after 1922.

To avoid filling the text with sterile masses of figures, tabular presentation of all the important dimensional, running number and other details has been adopted in Part II while the Appendices contain certain other information which it is felt will be useful in completing the picture. It has been again thought desirable, for ease of reference, to adopt the technique of relating text to illustrative matter wherever possible, even at the risk of some interruption to the 'flow' of the account. Finally and in order to avoid undue repetition through the text, a brief explanation of terms has been included immediately following this introduction.

# Explanation of Terms

## DIAGRAMS AND LOTS

LMS coaches were built to various *Diagrams*. Basically the Diagram was a drawing which defined the precise type of coach which was to be built although not, in itself, a working drawing. The various Diagrams have identifying numbers, not necessarily in consecutive sequence through the years, and in this book will be referred to throughout as Dxxxx. Several Diagrams were current for a number of years and each separate batch of coaches built to a particular diagram was given an identifying *Lot Number*. In general, Lot numbers, while not always consecutively numbered on a particular Diagram, were in ascending order as the years went by. Thus Lot 954 of D1915 would represent later coaches than Lot 843 of the same Diagram.

Whenever a design was changed—even to a minor extent— a fresh Diagram was almost always issued. As far as can be ascertained there were very few exceptions to this policy and these have been noted in Part II. Several Diagrams have been used as illustrative material in this book.

## PLATING

This term will be used to refer to the LMS practice of putting works plates on the coach. These were carried on the solebar and on the coach end. The solebar plate generally gave details of the works where built and the date of building, including Lot numbers from 1934/5, while the plate on the coach end was a dimension plate giving length, width and tare weight, to the nearest ton. Sometimes the plates were slightly at variance with the official Diagram version. The policy in this book will be to give the Diagram version drawing attention where necessary to any discrepancies in the coach plating details as observed in traffic.

## DIMENSIONS

Unless otherwise stated, basic coach dimensions will be given as follows:

Height:   Rail level to top of roof, not counting roof ventilators.

Length:   Over Headstocks—with LMS coaches, which almost always had flat ends, this dimension was some 1in to 1½ins less than the body length of the coach.

Width:    Over projections—i.e. a coach with a 9ft 0in wide body but with projecting handles would be quoted as 9ft 3in if this dimension was the width over the handles.

## STRUCTURAL TERMS

The following definitions have been adopted as a standard for this work.

*Beading:*    Raised wooden strips covering the panel joints on wood panelled stock.

*Cantrail:*    The point at which the coach side meets the roof.

*Cornice:*    The moulding, often of slightly ornamental nature, which was frequently found along the line of the cantrail.

*Chassis:*    The complete underframe together with bogies, buffing and draw gear &c.

*Gutter:*    The rainwater channel along the top of the cornice.

*Headstock:*  The end section of the underframe which carried the buffing and draw gear.

*Light:*    A generic term for a carriage window, sub-classified as follows:

    Droplight:    An opening window which moves in the vertical plane—usually wood framed but there were aluminium frame and frameless variants.

    Fixed Light:    A window which will not open.

    Quarterlight:    The small fixed light flanking the doors of all compartments which had outside doors.

    Toplight:    A small window situated between the cantrail and the top of the main carriage window.

*Panelling:*   A generic term relating to the method of covering the exterior of the coach—e.g. wooden panelling, steel panelling, flush panelling &c. The following principal sub-classifications should be noted:

    Eaves Panel:    The section of the body panelling located between the window top and the cantrail.

    Flush panelling:    Used to refer to any coach which did not have any form of raised body projections in the form of wooden beading.

    Matchboarding:    The name used in reference to the type of coach end panelling which consisted of a series of tongue and groove boarding running vertically from roof level to headstocks. This was a technique generally confined to coaches with an 'all wood' exterior finish.

    Tumblehome:    The incurving portion of the bodyside panelling as it approaches the solebar.

    Waist Panel:    The portion of the body panelling situated immediately below the windows and on LMS coaches, having a depth of some 8in. Waist panelling was generally confined to high waisted fully beaded coaches of wood panelled style.

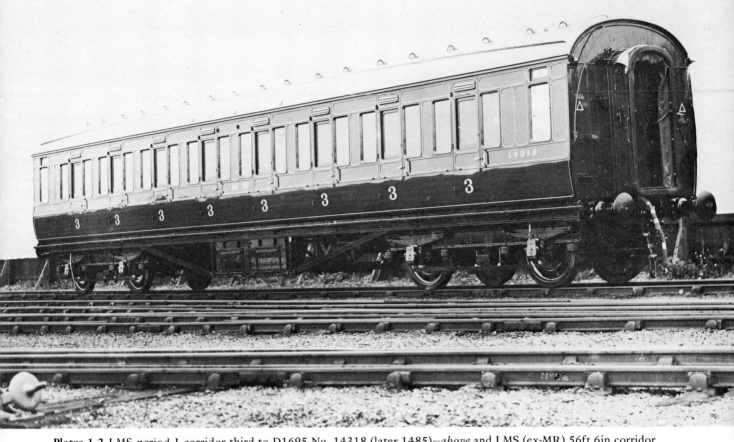

**Plates 1-2** LMS period I corridor third to D1695 No. 14318 (later 1485)—*above* and LMS (ex-MR) 56ft 6in corridor third No. 58 (later 3214)—*below*. Comparison of these two pictures reveals the almost total adoption of MR styling features in most early LMS standard stock. The MR coach was originally built as a World War 1 ambulance, converted to corridor in 1922. Note that it is carried on an older type of underframe, has beaded end panels and is fitted with recessed door handles.

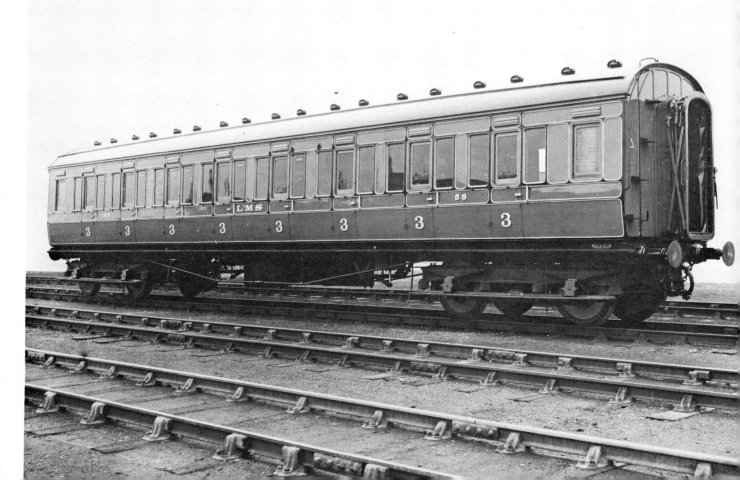

*Roof Types:* The LMS, for the most part, adopted two types of roof as follows:

| | |
|---|---|
| Rainstrip roof: | This was of wood and canvas construction with a continuous rainstrip from end to end and on each side of the roof. |
| Ribbed roof: | This was the Stanier pattern metal clad roof with a series of strengthening ribs from one side of the coach to the other, rainstrips if present at all, being generally confined to the section of the roof immediately above the doors. Some coaches had flush welded roof panels without external transverse ribs. |

*Semi-elliptical:* This is a term used to refer to the roof profile above the cantrail when in the form of a semi-ellipse.

*Solebar:* The heavy section forming the main side members of the coach underframe. On LMS design coaches this was a steel channel section, generally with the channel facing outwards.

*Truss-rods:* The angle section fixed underneath the underframe between the bogies, giving additional strength to the underframe itself and acting as a support for some ancillary fittings.

*Underframe:* The supporting frame of the coach on which the body was mounted, but not counting the bogies, buffers, ancillary fittings &c.

*Ventilators:* The following principal sub-classifications should be noted:

| | |
|---|---|
| Door ventilators: | These were the ventilators situated on outside doors above the droplight, either hooded or louvred. |
| Hooded ventilators: | External ventilators (generally on doors or above windows) which were covered by a plain metal 'hood'. |
| Louvre ventilators: | External ventilators (usually mounted over door drop-lights) which consisted outwardly of a series of horizontal wooden louvres, usually three. |
| Shell and Torpedo ventilators: | The two types of roof ventilator generally used by the LMS. Torpedo ventilators were of several styles and the differences are best appreciated by comparing pictures of the various types. |
| Sliding ventilators: | The type of ventilator used in the upper part of the big side windows of Stanier pattern gangwayed coaches. |
| Stones ventilators: | These were ventilators generally placed above the main windows of coaches in the eaves panel. They had swivelling glass vanes (six or nine elements) which could be adjusted by the passenger to 'face' or 'trail' the airstream past the coach. |
| Dewel ventilators: | Similar to Stones ventilators but even shorter (five moving vanes). |

## TYPES OF COACH

The following definitions will be adopted throughout:

| | |
|---|---|
| Corridor coach: | A coach with a side corridor for all or part of its length and with gangway connections to adjacent vehicles. |
| Dining Car: | A vestibule coach containing a kitchen as well as passenger seating accommodation. |
| Vestibule coach: | An open coach with gangway connections to adjacent vehicles. Note that a vestibule coach used exclusively for dining purposes but *not* having a kitchen was referred to as a 'vestibule dining coach' and was *not* called a dining car. |
| Non-corridor coach: | Any coach without gangway connections. |
| Lavatory coach: | A non-gangwayed coach with toilets serving individual compartments either directly or from a short side corridor. |

The nomenclature of other types of coaches is self explanatory.

## COACH CODING

Where it seems appropriate, the standard British Railways coach codes have been adopted for ease of reference. These are, in fact, based on the old LNER system but the familiarity of present day usage will, it is felt, make them easier to understand for most readers than the official LMS codes. Full details are given at Appendix I, together with the old LMS code letters.

## COACH NUMBERING

Until 1932, new standard LMS coaches were numbered somewhat haphazardly in the gaps available between the various batches of pre-group coaches which themselves, apart from the ex-MR vehicles, had been numbered in blocks in 1923. The ex-MR coaches retained their pre-group numbers except for the M&GSW and M&NB Joint Stock vehicles which were given vacant numbers in the ex-MR allocation, generally at the end of this series.

From 1933, the whole coaching stock (pre-group and standard) was renumbered systematically by generic vehicle types and these 1933 numbers are the ones which are used throughout this book. Details of the renumbering principles are given at Appendix II. At Nationalisation, LMS coaches generally retained their numbers and newly built coaches to LMS/LMR diagrams were given numbers in the appropriate LMS series. From 1948 until 1951, the LMS number was prefixed by a letter 'M' to denote the company/region of origin of the design. At about the time of the introduction of BR standard coaching stock, the prefix/suffix system was introduced. The prefix letter now denoted the region of allocation and the suffix letter was introduced as the identification of the vehicle's origin. Thus, for example, LMS coach No. 1234 would first have become M1234 in 1948 and then, if allocated to, say, Scotland, would have finally become Sc1234M. For the sake of consistency, it will be the policy in this book to omit the prefix/suffix letters in all references to LMS/LMR coaches—even those which entered service carrying such prefix or suffix letters.

# Part One

# A General Survey of LMS Coaching Stock

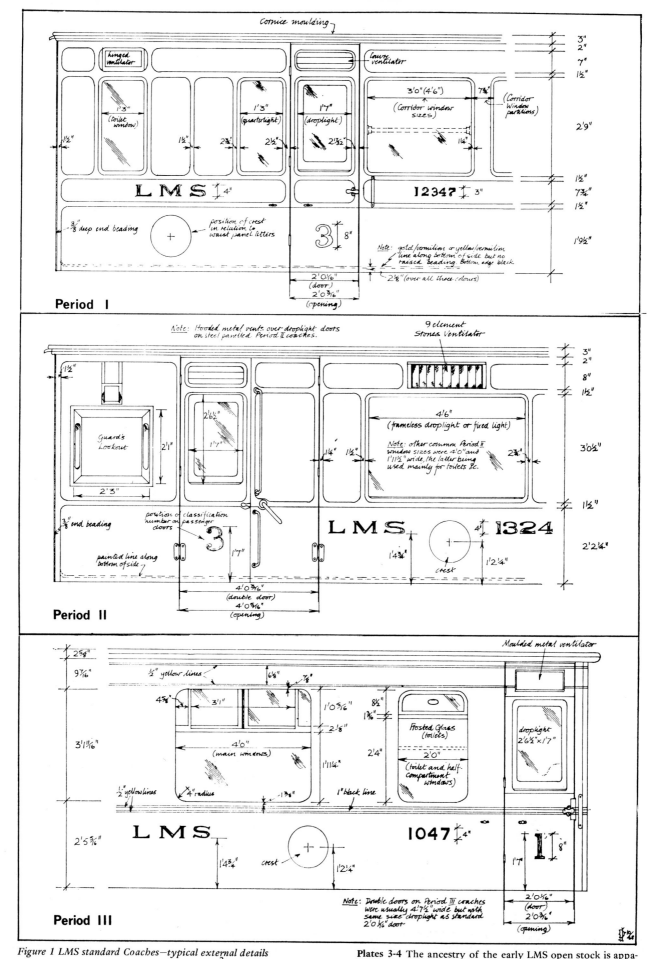

**Figure 1 LMS standard Coaches—typical external details**

These drawings reproduced approximately to $\frac{3}{8}$in—1ft scale, which are of no particular vehicles, are designed to illustrate typical external details of the three main periods of LMS standard coach design. They also show the location and size of insignia in relation to windows etc, but should only be taken as giving an approximate representation of the shape of LMS insignia. Period II steel panelled stock was the same as drawn but without the beading strips.

*(Drawn by D. Jenkinson)*

Plates 3-4 The ancestry of the early LMS open stock is apparent by comparison of these two pictures. LMS standard open third No. 4649 (later 7784) was built to D1353 and still retained the MR type recessed door handles, dimension plate on the solebar and hooded vents over the door lights.

M & GSW open third class dining coach No. 394 (1st LMS 4028, later 9617), designed by Reid c. 1917, exhibits the final version of the characteristic 'twin-window per bay' feature adopted as standard by the LMS. The underframe and bogie design also anticipated LMS practice but the reduced body width at the entrances was not perpetuated in LMS designs.

6

# Chapter 1 - The Design and Evolution of the LMS Coach

*Introduction; Period I—1923 to 1928/9; Period II—1929 to 1932; Period III—1933 onwards;*
*Post-nationalisation: Conclusions*

FROM almost the very inception of the LMS Railway, the design and building of coaches followed a very standardised pattern. There were very many types of coaches built to suit the various services and needs but, in general, the progression of design features was a logical one and is not unduly difficult to analyse. Three quite distinct periods of design can be recognised, the last of which continued until after nationalisation. For a variety of reasons it has been felt desirable to build the study of LMS coaches round these three periods, drawing attention to any departure from the normal practice at the time concerned.

## PERIOD I—1923 TO 1928/9

The characteristic Period I LMS coach was a wooden framed and panelled, high waisted vehicle. It was fully beaded on the outside with a wood and canvas roof, matchboard ends and mounted on a steel underframe derived from the final MR design. Corridor coaches had a full complement of external compartment doors and the door ventilators of all vehicles were generally of the louvre pattern. Roof ventilators were generally of the torpedo type. The coaches were fitted with non-automatic screw couplers and gangwayed stock made use of the British standard pattern corridor connection of scissors type (as used also on the GWR), rather than the Pullman type gangway. For inter-company working to the LNER and SR, gangway adaptors were fitted. Most coaches ran on two four-wheel bogies which were of a 9ft 0in wheelbase single bolster design which hardly changed for the whole of the company's life. Some special vehicles ran on twelve wheel chassis and the six-wheel bogie on these vehicles was of 12ft 6in wheel-base, based on the LNWR design. All coaches except kitchen cars were electrically lit and normally fitted with vacuum brake as standard. In this connection one might add that the general design of the LMS coach chassis scarcely changed at all once it was settled in the early post-grouping years.

In terms of general styling, early LMS coaches followed much the same ideas as were prevalent elsewhere in Britain. The wooden framed and panelled, fully beaded body with a semi-elliptical roof, doors to all compartments of corridor coaches, window ventilation mainly by droplight and mounted on a steel underframe was fairly typical British design. However, certain characteristic Midland Railway features were incorporated in the design of early LMS coaches which distinguished them from those of other lines. Most noticeable of these was the twin-window arrangement in each seating bay of the vestibule coaches. This took the form of two rectangular windows side by side (one fixed and one drop-light), rather than a single window or centre drop-light with two flanking quarterlight arrangement. There was generally a Stones pattern ventilator in the eaves panel above the fixed light of these window pairs.

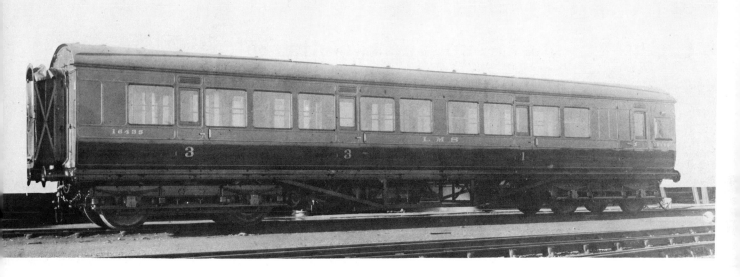

**Plates 5-6** These two pictures show the corridor side elevations of LMS standard corridor brake composite No. 16435 (later 6653) to D1755 and Midland Railway corridor composite No. 2811 (LMS 4904 after 1933). The similarities are too obvious to need additional comment. These pictures are not of the highest quality but, on the originals, lining can just be distinguished on the narrow pillars between the windows on the MR coach—a feature which was not perpetuated by the LMS which painted the whole of the pillar in black.

Other ex-MR features were also perpetuated to a limited extent for the first year or so in the form of countersunk locks and door handles. This gave an overall width of 9ft 1½in rather than 9ft 3in which latter dimension, however, rapidly became universal on all new construction. A 57ft underframe was also rapidly standardised for most general service stock although for certain areas (e.g. the LT&S Section), a 54ft length was preferred for non-corridor stock. Other lengths employed during this first design phase included a 68ft 12-wheel chassis for sleeping and dining cars and a 50ft chassis for full brakes and kitchen cars.

During this period, the new company introduced a considerable quantity of conventional coaches which were comfortable and well built but it cannot be denied that, although their comfort left little to be desired by comparison with other lines, the designs were not particularly revolutionary. Externally, of course, these early LMS coaches were extremely attractive in the fully panelled and beaded style and with the fully lined Crimson Lake livery; but in terms of interior styling and amenity, the time was, perhaps, getting a little overdue for a change.

The first indication of changing ideas were some very handsome corridor vehicles in 1927. For the first time, the LMS abandoned outside compartment doors in corridor coaches and introduced larger windows in their stead. At first there were two such windows in each compartment (one fixed and one frameless droplight) in the manner of the characteristic Midland pattern vestibule coaches already considered, but only the first class passenger could, initially, enjoy the privilege of having no draughty door. Furthermore, not many were built (25 BFKs to D1654 and ten FKs to D1748). They differed from the normal twin-window style in having frameless droplights and Stones ventilators over both windows and the style soon became adopted for other vehicles. By 1930 it had made its appearance in some composites (CKs to D1716 and BCKs to D1704), this time with but one Stones ventilator centrally over the window pair and with large 4ft 6in wide corridor side windows.

**Plate 7** Period I 'Two-window' 5½ compartment corridor first to D1748 No. 3499 (later 1013). Note the Stones ventilators over both compartment widows and the frameless droplights in the left hand windows of each pair. A corridor side elevation of the same type of vehicle is given at Plate 110 and the brake first version is at Figure 15.

All the same, except for these few composites and, of course, the vestibule carriages, the third class passenger, although enjoying a comfortably cushioned ride in the best Midland tradition, was still being provided with a full complement of compartment doors in the third class corridor coaches.

The next development in the somewhat tentative progression towards more up to date amenity was the development of a single window per bay design which was introduced in 1928 with the building of ten very palatial carriages for inclusion in the 'Royal Scot' and other prestige trains. Five of these coaches were semi-open firsts to D1707 and these had three compartments all finished in a different style with only four seats in each; each passenger thus had a corner seat. The open end was rather more conventional, seating 18 in two-and-one arrangement. These coaches were classed as dining vehicles and generally ran next to a kitchen car. The other five coaches were equally luxurious lounge brakes with accommodation for 10 first class passengers in eight individual armchairs and a settee (D1741). They again had large single windows instead of the two-window arrangement.

These 10 vehicles, beautiful examples of the coach builder's art, were closely followed in 1929 by a similarly styled batch of 25 neutral vestibule coaches for either first or third class passengers to D1706. These were 42 seaters with seven bays arranged two and one and again designated as dining vehicles. With these, the single window style could finally be said to have 'arrived' in LMS gangwayed coaches.

There were, however, snags. Although these 1928/9 coaches had single windows, they were still of the 'high waisted' design with full exterior beading—as indeed were most LMS coaches to this time—and there is some evidence that although the single window was more appreciated than the earlier arrangement, it was not always easy to see out of it because of the high waist. This was, apparently, particularly irksome in the lounge brakes which with their very low seated chairs were, seemingly, never very popular. Thus it was that the single window design was not perpetuated in the high waisted style.

At this point, mention ought also to be made of the introduction in 1925/6 of some all-steel coaches. These were open thirds and brake thirds, together with a large number of full brakes, which were built by outside contractors, probably to assist the steel industry at that time (TOs to D1745, BTOs to D1746 and BGs to D1715). Construction apart, however, their 'two window' style and interior layout showed no advance on the other coaches of the time while externally they were finished in pseudo fully beaded style.

**Plate 8** Period I 'All Steel' full brake to D1715 built by Birmingham C & W Co. in 1926/7 (No. 6996, later 30546).

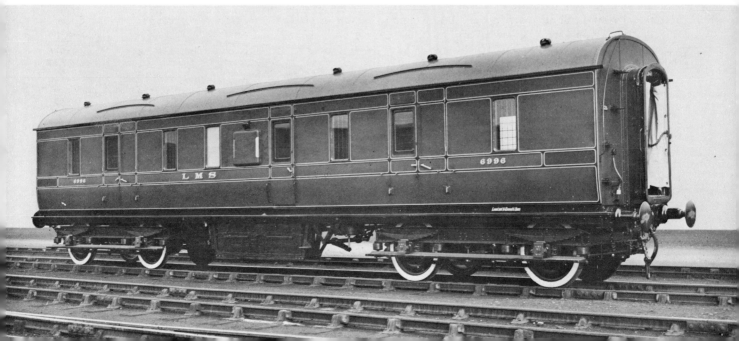

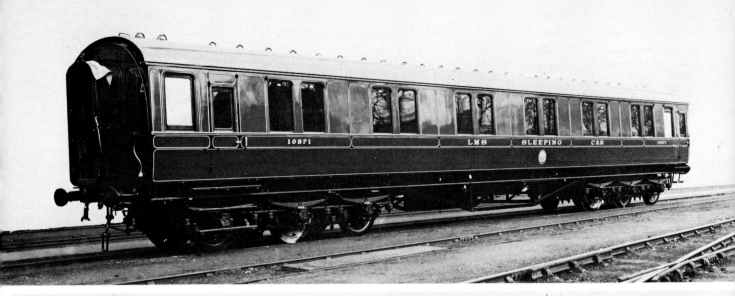

**Plates 9-10** *(above)* Early LMS 12-wheel stock owed much more to the LNWR than the MR, except for the angle-trussed underframe adopted by the LMS. These two pictures clearly illustrate the LNWR influence on sleeping car design. LMS standard car No. 10371 (later 323) is to D1705, additionally illustrated at Plates 65/69 and drawn at Figure 5. West Coast Joint Stock No. 445 (1st LMS 10323, later 485) represents the final pre-group style adopted by Wolverton. The slightly recessed doors were not adopted by the LMS and the waist panel was slightly shallower than on the LMS version.

**Plate 11** *(below)* The single window Period I styling appeared on a variety of coaches. This view shows the corridor side of the pioneer third class sleeping cars to D1709. Other illustrations of this type are at Figure 6 and Plates 83/4. This coach (No. 14247) became No. 522 in 1933.

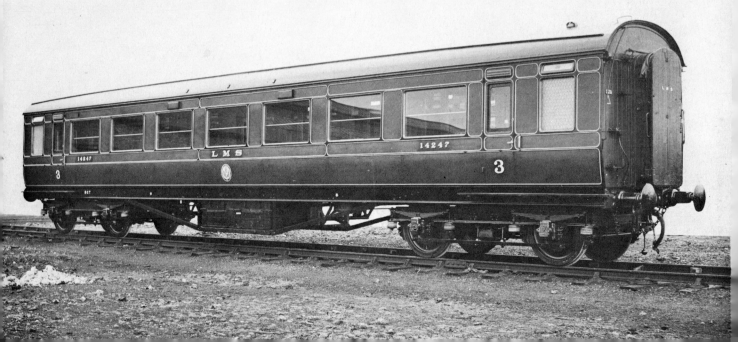

Meanwhile, the more specialised branches of coaching stock seemed of lesser importance. The LMS had inherited a considerable number of dining cars from its constituents, particularly the LNWR and MR, and few new ones were built for some seven years after grouping. Those that were (a batch of six RCs to D1743), largely followed LNWR practice in exterior styling. However, considerable numbers of kitchen only cars were built to run with the new vestibule dining vehicles so it is possible that the need at this time was for rather more dining accommodation than could be provided by a completely self-contained coach.

Sleeping cars were, however, needed and it is interesting to note that as with the first few dining cars, no real attempt was made to depart from pre-group policy—at least externally. The LNWR tradition was perpetuated in the first class cars to the tune of over 50 new 12 wheel sleepers between 1924 and 1929 (D1739 and D1705). The third class passenger, on the other hand had no sleepers until 1928 when the first of an eventual 85 convertible coaches was put into service to D1709. Externally these were pure LMS Period I standard coaches except for the absence of compartment doors. They were, however, mounted on 60ft underframes which introduced this length to LMS standard vehicles. The corridor side had the large 4ft 6in windows which were soon to become more familiar on the 'single window' stock of 1928/9 (see remarks above).

However, kitchen cars and sleepers were relatively few in number compared with the vast quantity of general service vehicles built in this first phase of LMS coach building. By the time of the first basic change in style, over 2000 new gangwayed carriages had been built of which no fewer than 851 were vestibule thirds, followed by 571 corridor composites and thirds—about equal numbers of each style.

This emphasis on the open carriage was very characteristic of the LMS and may possibly have been influenced by the long Midland Railway tradition of allowing passengers to travel all the way in the dining cars which probably led to a greater number of open carriages being needed. In fact, of the 1902 general service gangwayed coaches of all classes built during this first period, over 1000 were open vehicles and this proportion was to be exceeded even more noticeably during the next phase of coach design.

Meanwhile, a considerable quantity of non-corridor coaches had been put into service during this period. Most were on 57ft underframes for short distance stopping services and suburban use but a number were built on 54ft chassis (mostly for the LT&S Section). A number of 57ft non-corridor coaches were also built with lavatories for cross-country inter district services but all the coaches shared the characteristic Period I styling features. There were, however, some small batches of non-corridor coaches built with outside steel panelling but otherwise Period I characteristics. These were built by outside contractors and were of somewhat spartan nature—the composites being only 51ft long and with five a side seating in the first class section! They were built for use on the Cathcart Circle services in Glasgow and are interesting as representing the forerunners of the Period II non-corridor stock.

During the first design phase, the LMS also built new compartment type stock for the Euston—Watford and Liverpool —Southport electrified lines. These were 'all steel' in construction and, when new, were given full livery with imitation waist panelling.

**Plate 12** Third class trailer coach for the London-Watford electric suburban services built in 1929 to D1684. This vehicle, although steel panelled, was given the fully lined livery, including the waist panel.

## PERIOD II—1929 TO 1932

The start of the second phase in LMS carriage design was almost contemporary with the introduction of the previously mentioned high waisted single window designs and the new trend of thought was first exemplified by the appearance in 1929 of six luxury brake firsts with two-a-side compartment seating and somewhat palatial toilet accommodation. All the compartments were differently finished and the coaches seem to have been introduced in preference to repeating the earlier lounge brakes. These six were closely followed by 10 more of the luxury semi-open firsts of the kind already mentioned in connection with the single window designs at the end of Period I. These 16 new carriages all had single windows but the waist of the coach was much lower than hitherto. The principal external difference was the elimination of the waist panel consequent upon the deepening of the windows. The new coaches were, however, still wood panelled and fully beaded and with the full lining represented very handsome designs. As with their Period I predecessors, these coaches went to the more important trains like the 'Royal Scot' and 'Merseyside Express'. One more of each type was built with steel panelling and no raised beading as replacement for the similar coaches destroyed in the Leighton Buzzard crash of 1931.

This low waisted trend in design only partially set the pattern for new construction because corridor composites continued to come out in the fully beaded 'two window' style and the corridor thirds/brake thirds continued to have full compartments doors until 1930. Thus there was a certain amount of overlapping styles during the first part of the second period of LMS coach building.

It was again the vestibule coach which received the bulk of attention during this second phase. First were a series of spacious 60ft long 42 seaters. Some of these were built as firsts but downgraded a few years later on the advent of the Stanier 65ft firsts. These 42 seat coaches, of which 50 were initially built to D1721 and D1722, were classed as dining vehicles and were followed by a 56 seater for general service. More 42 seat coaches followed which, although identical to the original 42 seaters, were not classed as diners. All these 60ft coaches had the new low waist and were wood panelled with full outside beading. However, a much larger group of low waisted vestibule coaches was the 57ft, 56 seat version of which 300 were built to D1807. These were built in 1931/2 and differed from the 60ft version in that they were steel clad with simulated external beading in paint. They did, however, follow the Period II style in all other respects and retained the raised window edge mouldings.

Eventually in 1930/31, the new low waisted style was adopted for all corridor stock too. Although mainly confined to composites and brake composites, it was a batch of corridor thirds in 1930 that really set new standards (D1782). These coaches were but 10 in number but had only seven compartments on a 60ft underframe. Although the traditional four on each side seating was retained, the compartments were no less than 6ft 6in between partitions. They were again wood panelled and fully beaded and were, reputedly, extremely comfortable to ride in—presumably no more were built because they were a little extravagant of space and large numbers of the earlier designs had, in any case, been built between 1924 and 1928.

On the specialised coaching side, this second phase of design was represented mainly by dining cars of which 36 were built (24 RFs and 12 RCs). Mention has already been made of the relative lack of new dining cars during the first six years of the LMS but these new 68ft, 12 wheel coaches amply made amends. Like the above mentioned 57ft vestibule thirds, these diners were steel panelled with painted 'beading'.

There were also two batches of 12 wheel composite sleeping cars built at this time to D1781 which were rather in the nature of 'odd men out'. They retained a high waist and certain LNWR styling features but were flush clad with frameless droplights. They are fully described in Chapter 6 but must be regarded as distinctly outside the main trend of LMS coach design.

**Plate 13** (*below*) Period II BFK to D1717 from the corridor side—compare Figure 18. This coach, No. 5006, is shown running on experimental twin bolster long wheelbase bogies which give every appearance of having been derived from the standard six wheel type but without the centre pair of wheels. On this coach, the solebar appears to be red.

**Plate 14** (*opposite top*) Period II open third to D1807 No. 2744 (later 8737). A later example from the same diagram is shown at Plate 144 and exhibits detail differences.

**Plate 15** (*opposite centre*) Period II corridor composite to D1791 No. 14993 (later 3810) taken from the corridor side. This design is drawn and illustrated at Figure 20.

**Plate 16** (*opposite below*) Period II composite sleeping car No. 10637 (later 709). This design (D1781) still showed some residual LNWR influence and is additionally illustrated at Figure 7 and Plate 87.

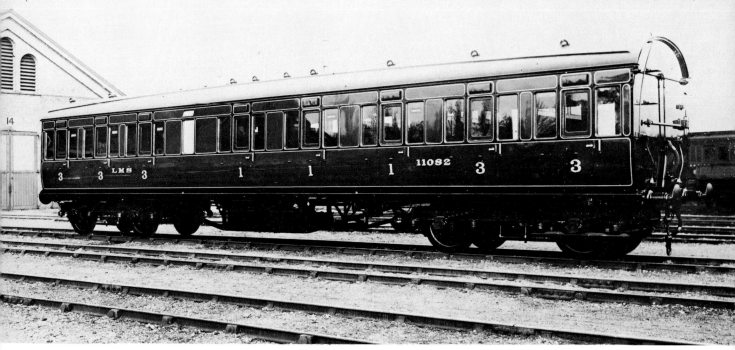

**Plate 17** A typical period II non-corridor coach. This is a lavatory composite to D1736 No. 11082 (later 19190). The fully panelled version of this design is drawn at Figure 32.

From the point of view of other changes, the most noticeable detail alteration from the Period I coach during this 1929—32 period was the change in window ventilation. Over the tops of the main windows almost exclusive use was made of the Stones or Dewel pattern glass vane ventilator. These features had always supplemented the droplight in the 'two window' and high waisted single window designs but did not become universal for all gangwayed coaches until the complete adoption of single window designs. There were some partial exceptions. Some of the 1932 built 57ft vestibule thirds had hooded ventilators over many of the windows while it was by no means unusual to find hooded ventilators or even no ventilators at all over the windows on the corridor side of non-vestibule coaches. Outside doors, of course, still retained droplights and top ventilators but, on steel clad stock, the latter were exclusively of the plain hooded pattern rather than the more usual louvre type on the wooden coaches.

With the Period II vestibule coach, most of the windows were of fixed light design with raised mahogany mouldings round the edges. There were, however, generally two or three frameless droplights incorporated in each side of the vehicle. The whole window could be partially lowered in its surround (usually made of aluminium) and from the outside could be identified by the lack of raised wood mouldings and the two hand grips which were fixed to the glass near the upper edge. Needless to say, compartment windows of Period II corridor stock were all of this type while corridor windows were mostly fixed lights.

Non-corridor Period II stock continued to have the high waist and was little different from its Period I predecessor except in the steel panelling and absence of beading. It retained the raised window mouldings and full livery but, unlike the Cathcart Circle and early electric stock mentioned did not have a pseudo waist panel in paint. There were no innovations at all in the design of Period II non-corridor coaches but it should be mentioned that the LMS did build a considerable quantity of electric stock of Period II style as well as the locomotive hauled variety.

Summing up the second phase of LMS coach design, it should be emphasised that, although steel panelling had occasionally been used before 1929, it was this second period of design which saw the genuine transition from wood to steel panelling and the abandonment of raised external beading. The design period itself was somewhat short lived, spanning less than four years. During this time, however, some very good coaches of more than normally handsome aspect had been built and, with the gradual introduction of outside steel panelling, the precedent had been well and truly established for the final change to completely flush exteriors which was to characterise LMS coaches for the rest of the company's lifetime.

## PERIOD III—1933 ONWARDS

In 1932, Mr. William Stanier took up his appointment as Chief Mechanical Engineer to the LMS and the first of the completely flush sided LMS coaches emerged soon enough after his assumption of office to lead to the coaches ever afterwards being referred to as Stanier stock. Just what real influence the CME had on external coach styling is rather conjectural but most sources refer to the flush sided designs as Stanier coaches and it seems less likely to confuse matters if this term is adopted.

The LMS flush sided coach, of which many examples still remained as late as 1967—8, differed in appearance from its predecessor mainly in the shape of its windows which now exhibited well rounded corners. All the earlier coaches had, of course, been built with slightly rounded window corner mouldings but by comparison with Stanier vehicles the Period I and II coach window was almost 'square' cornered. The second major visible difference was also in the window area. During Period I, the favoured method of admitting fresh air was the droplight which was frequently supplemented by and finally (in Period II) in large measure superseded by the Stones and Dewel pattern glass vane ventilator. With the Stanier stock was introduced the now familiar sliding ventilator incorporated in the upper part of the window. Initially this was quite shallow with only one section moveable but in 1934 this was replaced by the deeper ventilator with two wide sliding sections which remained almost until the end. From about 1947/8, the sliding portions were somewhat shortened and in this form were retained as a feature of the BR standard coach.

**Plate 18** *(above)* The first ever Stanier gangwayed coach design for the LMS was this corridor brake composite to D1850 No. 9318 (later 6784). Additional views of this very significant new type are at Plates 48-9, 68 and Figure 21. The picture here was probably taken when the coach was given luxury style seating to D1939 in 1933. Note the shallow window ventilators, pre-1933 series running number and fully lined livery.

**Plate 19** *(below)* Period III BTK No. 5518 to D1905. This was one of the batch which had the projecting lookouts removed for working on the 'Sunny South Express'. It was also one of the only batch of Period III BTK with the standard deep window ventilators to receive full livery.

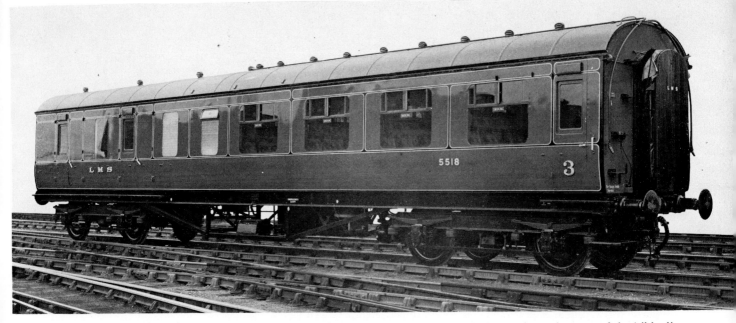

There were, however, other points of difference in the Period III coach. Firstly, the roof now became of the 'ribbed' pattern rather than the wood/canvas/rainstrip variety while almost from the start of construction, torpedo roof ventilation gave way to shell ventilators and side lamps were omitted above the guard's lookout on brake coaches. The torpedo ventilators returned after the second World War but in modified form as perpetuated on a great number of BR standard coaches. The Stanier coach also marks the general introduction of the 'suspended' type of British Standard corridor connection to the LMS. As this feature first seems to have made its appearance on some of the 1932 Period II 57ft vestibule thirds, one wonders if Stanier imported the idea from Swindon where it had been in use from about 1925. Since shell ventilators were also used at Swindon before Stanier came to the LMS, it seems quite possible that these detail changes were at the behest of the CME himself. Some Stanier ideas—e.g. the removal of the lamps above the guard's lookout—were applied retrospectively to older coaches.

The Stanier coach was still a wood framed vehicle; the total employment of flush steel outer panels and the ribbed roof being the main differences from the Period I/II coach as far as construction was concerned. The underframe changed but little except to develop a few more length variations. In general the 57ft length remained the standard where possible but the 60ft length, first introduced in 1928 with the convertible third class sleepers, was the common standard for open firsts, corridor composites and corridor brake composites. The extra 3ft of length was useful in giving the first class passenger a little more leg room while it was invaluable in the composites in helping to do away with the half, or coupé compartment which, as will be seen in Chapter 8, caused a certain amount of trouble to the design staff. Certain other coaches by virtue of their more specialised purpose were even longer and these mainly came in the following categories.

| | |
|---|---|
| 69ft long | 12 wheel sleeping cars |
| 68ft long | 12 wheel dining cars |
| 65ft long | Eight wheel third class sleeping cars and eight wheel vestibule first class dining vehicles |
| 62ft long | Later designs of corridor brake composites |

**Plate 20** Period III high capacity open third No. 9174 to D1915. This design, with 7½ seating bays, had the highest seating capacity of any LMS standard design of gangwayed open coach.

**Plate 21** LMS third class dining car No. 142 to D1923, typifies most features exhibited by the Stanier period coaching stock.

The final distinguishing feature of the Stanier coach was probably its livery. While the first year or so of new construction saw the perpetuation of a fully lined quasi-beaded style (in paint), the characteristic simplified livery was much more common with horizontal lining only, this variation being introduced only a short time after the introduction of the deeper window ventilators. As time went on, all coaches were, of course, finished in this simplified style but during the middle thirties, the difference of livery was also, more often than not, indicative of a difference in coach style too.

To many people, flush sided coaches are much of a muchness with little visible difference between those of Stanier, Thompson, Bulleid, Hawksworth or even the BR standard designs. While it is undoubtedly true that the flush sided style introduced a greater monotony into the external appearance of the coach, the differences were still there. It is, however, to the interior layout of the coach that one must look for changes and in this respect the full progression of interior design and layout and of detail changes in the Stanier coach is best appreciated by considering the detailed analysis of each type of coach in the later chapters. However, in this preliminary survey it *is* worth mentioning that the Stanier coach, amongst other things, introduced a general policy of three a side seating in the third class compartments of LMS corridor coaches for the first time.

In passing, it is interesting to note that in this respect the first BR standard coaches followed their regional predecessors. The LMS from 1933 was wedded to the three a side third class corridor coach whereas the GWR and SR tended to favour the more frugal four a side seating. This may have been to keep down dead coach weight per passenger but it was a source of some surprise to the writers to find the BR standard coaches built for the Western and Southern Regions long after 1950 still perpetuated this somewhat uncomfortable feature when otherwise identical vehicles built for the Northern main lines were given armrests. Possibly the heavier holiday traffic carried by the Southern and Western region was the main reason for the four a side policy.

As well as general service vehicles, the Stanier era introduced further examples of specialised coaches, all bearing the common house style. Possibly the most noteworthy *new* designs (at least as far as LMS standard coaches were concerned) were the first LMS fixed berth third class sleeping cars, the massive third class dining cars and the rather neat Engineers' saloons of the 1940s. Mention ought also to be made of the building of various articulated coaches mainly for general service and/or excursion use in the Central and Northern Divisions (see Chapter 12), but not forgetting the magnificent special vehicles built for the second Coronation Scot train—regrettably never to run as such in this country. During the Stanier period too, experiments were also conducted in lightweight design, welded bogie construction and so forth. From these experiments there stemmed a partial adoption of welded underframes and bogies from about 1935/6 onwards although the basic design of these features remained substantially unchanged and the riveted style continued to be used alongside the welded chassis.

Although the third period of LMS coaches introduced many desirable features into the gangwayed stock, sufficient indeed to make it compare more than favourably with almost anything built by BR until recent years, the same cannot be said about the non-corridor stock which remained of pretty nondescript character right to the very end. It is true, of course, that there is little scope in the non-corridor vehicle for large scale innovation but at the same time it seems a little

**Plate 22** Corridor side elevation of the pioneer Stanier first class sleeping car also illustrated at Plate 80. This makes an interesting comparison with the post-war version at Plate 81. Note the wider body profile.

surprising that a company which in its heyday produced some of the best riding and most comfortable corridor and vestibule stock in the country, did not do more for the stopping passenger services. One wonders, perhaps, why nothing was attempted along the lines of the ex-LNER semi-corridor cross-country coaches. On the other hand, it might be argued that as the LMS seemed more prone to use older corridor coaches on its cross-country services than did the other companies, there was less need for specialised cross-country sets.

Be that as it may, during the Stanier period, non-corridor coaches varied but little from the pattern laid down in the 1920s except for the flush clad exterior. The design was still high waisted and the seating arrangements never changed from the earlier years. No inter district lavatory sets were built during the Stanier régime and apart from a few lavatory composites for the LT&S Section, all the Stanier non-corridor stock was of the 'suburban' type. There was an interesting batch of articulated triplets made in 1938 but these do not seem to have been very popular. They were, perhaps, less flexible in the traffic sense than they were mechanically (see also Chapter 12).

The Stanier period is also interesting as witnessing the bulk of newly built LMS standard motor fitted (push-pull) stock. Again it is somewhat surprising that in view of the many GWR imports which Stanier brought to the LMS, there seems to have been no attempt to build an LMS equivalent of the GWR auto-trailer. Yet the LMS had need of a considerable stock of motor fitted vehicles and one can only conclude that reasons of standardisation at Wolverton and Derby were the main factors behind the appearance of LMS motor fitted trains which looked scarcely any different from their suburban contemporaries. For this reason, motor fitted coaches do not suggest themselves as topics for separate discussion in the LMS coach story and have been included with their associated non-corridor vehicles in Part II.

**Plate 23** Period III non-corridor third brake to D1735 No. 20609. This is a very typical Stanier period non-corridor type but has a few features which were not retained for long (torpedo roof ventilators, side-lights over the guard's lookout and full livery). This coach was actually built to a Period II diagram and the driving trailer version of it is illustrated at Figure 35.

**Plate 24** A train of Liverpool-Southport open stock seen in service c. 1946. Note the post-war type of insignia—compare Plate 197.

Apart from locomotive hauled stock, the third period did witness some changes in the type of vehicle provided for some of the electrified lines. In the Wirral and between Liverpool and Southport there were introduced some new open coach multiple unit sets rather reminiscent of the London Transport style. They had (and still have for most are still in service at the time of writing) sliding doors and other characteristic type features. Livery apart, they would look reasonably at home on the Circle Line! They do not, therefore, fit into the mainstream of LMS coach design and have been considered separately in Part II.

## POST NATIONALISATION

LMS design coaches continued to be built for several years after 1947 until the introduction of the BR standard designs. This short-lived period was, in fact, little more than a continuation of the Stanier era and was not really a new phase in the same sense that the flush sided stock itself was. Later corridor coaches have, however, been distinguished by the name Porthole stock by virtue of the circular toilet window feature which they introduced. This stock actually commenced building a year or two after 1947 and was, therefore, not strictly LMS stock as such but it was in the direct tradition of LMS coachbuilding practice and has, therefore, been included in this survey. It differed from the last versions of the Stanier stock proper (which themselves were built well into BR days) principally in the circular toilet windows which replaced the earlier rectangular ones, but also in having post-war torpedo ventilators and the final style of sliding window ventilators.

**Plate 25** Period III CK No. M4878M from the corridor side. This picture shows the first post-war D2117 version with two extra corridor doors. Note also the shorter sliding portions of the window ventilators. The picture was taken in 1962 to illustrate the newly introduced yellow band above the first class section of the coach.

Plate 26 'Porthole' BTK No. M26668 to D2161 built new in 1950 with BR crimson and cream livery. This is a compartment side view (compare Plate 129) and note the longer pattern of sliding window ventilators used on this example.

One batch of 'Portholes' was however, of particular significance. These were 'all steel' corridor composites to D2159 and although retaining many LMS features they saw the first real change from their predecessors in that the coach profile was changed. In these particular coaches, the profile was more clipper-sided with a slightly more accentuated tumblehome. Moreover the junction between sides and roof at the cantrail was sharper and the roof lost its pure semi-elliptical shape. As a final point of difference, the sides met the ends in a small radius curve rather than a sharp angle. One can presume that but for Nationalisation, these coaches, of which large numbers were still in use as late as 1967/68 would have probably set the pattern for subsequent design development at Derby. The drawings date from 1947 and they bequeathed their roof profile and rounded off side/end junction to their BR standard successors.

Another post-1947 innovation entirely in the LMS tradition was a batch of twin berth third class sleeping cars to D2169. These did not appear until 1951 and they perpetuated the more traditional LMS sleeping car profile in spite of being built after the above mentioned composites. Because of their twin berth arrangement, they looked more like the standard Stanier first class sleeper than their first class predecessors. However, they ran on LMS standard 65ft chassis.

On the non-corridor side, amongst the more interesting points to note is the fact that considerable numbers of LMS pattern motor fitted coaches were built after 1947, presumably to replace the outmoded conversions of pre-group coaches which were hitherto frequently used for motor train working. Another interesting batch was a group of fifteen non-corridor firsts built in 1951 to a Diagram issued in 1938 (D1997). These were amongst the last vehicles to be built to any LMS design and their late building may have been a contributory reason for the non-appearance of a BR standard non-corridor first. However, the oddest feature of all is undoubtedly the fact that the last general service coaches of all to be given LMS series numbers were actually built at Swindon to a pre-war GWR design. These were 59ft composites to D2189 and it is understood that they were built at Swindon because the need for them was urgent and the ex-LMS works were all fully occupied at the time building BR standard stock. Details have been included in Chapter 10 for the sake of completeness but the coaches were not, of course, LMS designs. In addition to these, LMS type TPO vehicles appeared until 1956/7 and a batch of LMS design Mersey/Wirral electric stock emerged in 1956/7.

Finally, after 1948, several ex-LMS coaches were converted for other uses. These included conversion to buffet cars, heating vans &c. and where it has been possible to trace these conversions, details have been included.

Plate 27 Period III CK No. M24623 as built new in late 1949 with BR crimson and cream livery. This coach was to the same diagram as those shown at Plate 131-132 and clearly illustrates the slightly altered end profile of the final LMS design corridor coaches.

**Plates 28-29** The above two views show how little the end profile of LMS coaches changed during almost the whole of its lifetime. On the left is a Period I gangway end exhibiting matchboard panelling. Period II was similar but from 1930 had steel sheeting. Coach 5403 was an ambulance conversion—hence the safety chains on the headstock. The right hand view shows a Period III gangwayed brake end. The coach was BTK No. 26321 of D1968, built in 1945.

## CONCLUSIONS

The high degree of standardisation of LMS coaching stock has been mentioned and this may well be one of the reasons why the company never seemed particularly anxious to build special vehicles for its glamour trains. Apart from the 1939 Coronation Scot stock, the nearest it came were probably such coaches as the already mentioned lounge brakes and semi-open firsts. Even the 1933 'Royal Scot' tour train to the USA was composed of standard stock and in this matter of special vehicles, the LMS came rather a poor third to the LNER and GWR whose streamlined and centenary stock respectively set new standards on their own lines.

All the same, when the LMS so wished, it *could* build extremely fine coaches and its supporters could argue with some justification that the general high standard of LMS coaches, together with the high replacement rate of sub-standard pre-group stock was sufficient not to warrant the provision of specially designed luxury vehicles. In any case, these would probably interfere with the mass production techniques of the works at Derby and Wolverton and, moreover, cost far more than the standard designs for which the works were laid out. This seems the only logical explanation for the lack of new coaches for the Coronation Scot train of 1937 which has often been unfavourably compared with its LNER rival. What seems generally to have been overlooked is that the 1937 train was itself a very fine set of coaches and it speaks volumes for the quality of the Stanier coach that a cheap refurbishment of three sets of standard vehicles could compare favourably, if not totally with a specially built prestige train. When the LMS did wish to build some special vehicles for the exhibition of the Coronation Scot in America in 1939, it showed itself more than capable of matching anything that the rest of British railways could produce. It seems a thousand pities that the three sets which were finally completed after the war were never reformed into full trains.

The first type of BR standard coach did not, superficially, owe much to its LMS predecessor as the length, gangways and couplers were all of a different standard and nearer to that of Bulleid than Stanier. Yet in some ways the coach owed as much to the LMS as any company for it should be viewed in relation to the last batch of 'Portholes' which, as suggested above, really represent the final expression of LMS design ideas. Experience of the early BR standard coach tempts the thought that in some respects it would have been better to perpetuate more LMS features. In particular, in preferring a narrow single sliding door to the compartment to the LMS arrangement of wider double doors, the BR coach seems to have taken a major step backwards.

Throughout the rest of this book, the above sub-division into Periods I, II and III will be adopted for convenience* since the design periods are also reflected in the non-corridor and other passenger stock built by the LMS, remembering, of course, that the low waist, first introduced in the Period II gangwayed stock was never adopted in non-corridor vehicles.

---

*In the above chapter, no mention has been made of certain non-standard coaching type vehicles which the LMS owned. Included among these were such vehicles as the Sentinal steam railcars and the experimental diesel articulated streamline train. These vehicles do not really form part of the mainstream of LMS standard coach development and have therefore, been confined to Chapter 16 where all are considered together. The same is also true of much of the non-passenger carrying stock (except full brakes and TPO coaches) which exhibited a considerable variety of exterior styling features which do not lend themselves to the Period I/II/III generalisations. These vehicles are included together in Chapter 17.

# Chapter 2 - Constructional Methods and Coach Interiors

*Introduction; Underframes; Body construction; All-steel coaches; Coach interiors (open stock, compartment and corridor stock, sleeping cars)*

## INTRODUCTION

THE technique of construction of LMS coaches varied but little throughout the company's existence and seems to have directly evolved from methods adopted by the Midland Railway. During early years, LNWR techniques were employed at Wolverton on a few specialised vehicles and an odd batch of non-corridor coaches was built at Newton Heath with slightly different compartment dimension (See Chapter 10, page 140, D1767). As well as constructional methods, body dimensions too became remarkably standardised within a very short space of time and although there were many superficial external differences between coach types, all exhibited standard panel, door, gangway, seat and other dimensions.

The LMS at grouping took over control of a considerable number of locomotive, carriage and wagon works but only three (Derby, Wolverton and Newton Heath) were ever involved in the building of LMS standard coaches. Of these, Newton Heath was only involved for a short period and to a limited extent and the vast bulk of LMS coaches were built at Wolverton and Derby. There were also batches of coaches built by outside contractors but the coaches thus supplied were of standard LMS type except, in some cases, for the all-steel constructional methods adopted.

## UNDERFRAMES

With very few exceptions, generally all-steel coaches built without conventional underframes—see page 27—all LMS standard coaches had separate, usually wood framed bodies mounted on a steel underframe. The underframe design first appeared in 1923 and hardly changed at all, except for developing different lengths as years passed by. It was directly derived from final MR style and is depicted at Figure 2.

The underframe itself was built from mild rolled steel channel sections and plates riveted together. The solebars had the channel section facing outwards and trussing was made of 'L' section rolled steel. Bogies were also made from rolled steel channels, angles and plates. They were of single bolster design fitted with laminated side bearing springs and had bolster springs of helical coil type. The four wheel bogie was of 9ft 0in wheelbase and the six wheel of 12ft 6in wheelbase. Slight changes in this general specification were to be found in the electric multiple unit coaches.

The underframe headstock was fitted with non-automatic screw couplings and generally had round headed buffers. Long coaches (62ft and above) had oval buffers. All LMS standard coaches except 50ft kitchen cars, were electrically lit and thus the underframes all carried dynamos and battery boxes. Most coaches were vacuum fitted only with two vacuum cylinders. However, some coaches were dual fitted with vacuum and Westinghouse air brakes for through working. Gas cylinders and other ancillary equipment were also fitted to the underframes of such vehicles as dining cars and kitchen cars.

In the middle 1930s, welded construction was introduced to save weight and increase strength. This technique initially appeared in the pioneer Stanier 69ft sleeping cars (D1926, page 67) and became an alternative standard method of construction. The underframe design remained basically the same but the welded construction made it possible to preserve a flush top to the underframe and enable the steel floor to be welded directly to it. By bringing the teak body pillars right down to this very strong substructure it became possible to dispense with the use of bottom side members for the coach body. The bottom of the teak pillar was bolted direct to a steel box bracket welded to the underframe.

The LMS standard underframe seems to have been all but identical to the final MR style—it being well nigh impossible to detect the difference between them in pictures. The four wheel bogie was probably also derived from the MR but the six wheel bogie was more of an LNWR speciality. However, MR and LNWR bogie design was so very similar by 1923, especially in appearance, that there was probably little to choose between the two sorts. What does seem clear is that LMS coach and bogie design seemed to owe very little to any of the companies except the LNWR and MR.* Like the underframe, the LMS standard four wheel bogie changed scarcely at all and in spite of its single bolster design it was an extremely good riding unit. Recent experience of riding in the residual survivors of LMS design coaches confirmed this latter fact.

The standard LMS underframe was built in a variety of lengths but the vast bulk of designs were made for the 57ft length which was the final LNWR standard and was also, latterly, a length which the Caledonian and Midland Railways had used. Regardless of length, all LMS underframes were substantially identical and shared common truss rod dimensions (Fig. 2). Longer chassis were adopted for more specialised stock and the following list summarises the principal utilisation of the various lengths, other than the 57ft standard variety:

| | |
|---|---|
| 69ft | Period III 12 wheel Sleeping Cars. |
| 68ft | All Kitchen/Dining Cars and pre-Stanier 12 wheel sleeping cars. |
| 65ft | Period III vestibule first dining coaches and third class sleeping cars. |
| 62ft | Later versions of Period III corridor brake composites. |

*It should, however, be recorded that the final Caledonian Railway coaches were 57ft vehicles with angle trussed underframes.

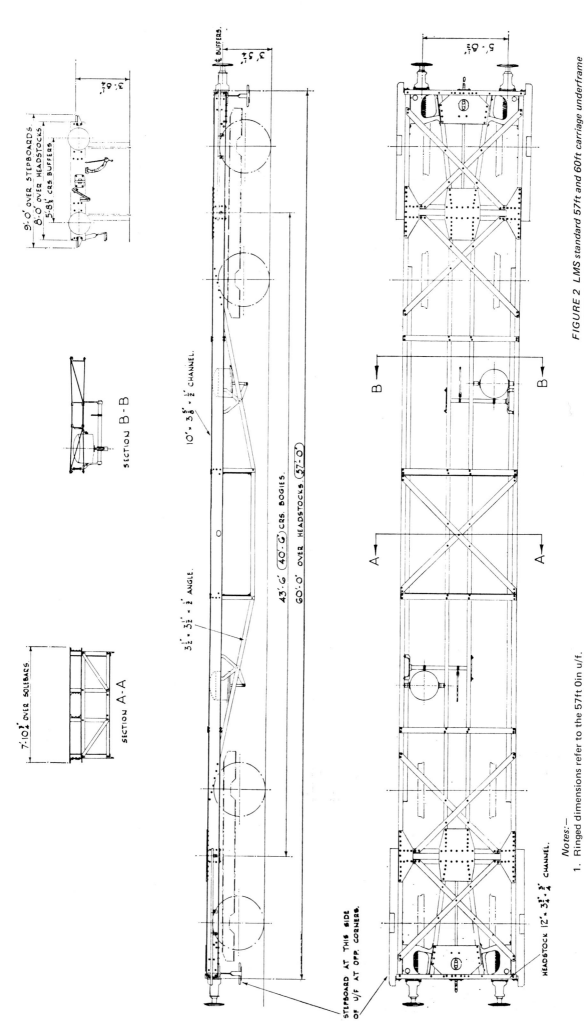

SECTION A-A

7'-10½' OVER SOLEBARS

SECTION B-B

10'× 3⅝'× ½' CHANNEL.

3½'× 3½'× ½' ANGLE.

43'-6' (40'-6') CRS. BOGIES.
60'-0' OVER HEADSTOCKS. (57'-0')

STEPBOARD AT THIS SIDE
OF U/F AT OPP. CORNERS.

HEADSTOCK 12'× 3½'× 3' CHANNEL.

9'-0' OVER STEPBOARDS
8'-0' OVER HEADSTOCKS
5-8½' CRS. BUFFERS

3'-6½'

₵ BUFFERS.

3'-5½'

5'-0½'

*FIGURE 2 LMS standard 57ft and 60ft carriage underframe*
These drawings reproduced approximately to 4mm—1ft scale show the main constructional features of the standard LMS underframe. Although the 57ft and 60ft versions are represented, all LMS standard underframes shared broadly similar structural features.
*(Drawn by L. G. Warburton)*

Notes:—
1. Ringed dimensions refer to the 57ft 0in u/f.
2. Lot 1041 and later—bogies fitted with 5ft 0in laminated springs.

22

| | |
|---|---|
| 60ft | Period I third class sleeping cars, Period II vestibule third class dining coaches, most designs of corridor composites and brake composites (except for the earlier Period I all-door designs) and many TPO vehicles. This was the most common alternative length for gangwayed coaches after the 57ft variety. |
| 59ft | Some electric driving motor coaches. |
| 58ft | Some electric multiple unit stock. |
| 54ft | Non-corridor stock for the LT&S and Cathcart Circle services plus a few batches for general service. |
| 51ft | One batch only of non-corridor composites for the Cathcart Circle services. |
| 50ft | Most passenger full brakes and kitchen cars. |

The LMS also built some articulated coaches and for the gangwayed vehicles, Stanier designed a centrally trussed lattice type underframe. This was first tried out as far as is known on corridor third brake No. 5844. The 1937 general service coaches were articulated by a single pivot 'male and female' joint, but for the experimental diesel articulated train (p. 201) and the 1939 'Coronation Scot' stock, the 'LMS type' of articulation was utilised. This basically made use of a double pivot and enabled a slightly longer distance between bogie centres to be achieved without the throw-over on curves exceeding the loading gauge although still within the maximum distance between wheels permitted by points locking bars. Three basic kinds of articulated locomotive-hauled stock were built. In 1937 there were introduced some gangwayed open articulated pairs in the Central Division—mainly for excursion use—and at the same time there was built a batch of three coach units of non-corridor stock. These were articulated on the same principle but had conventionally trussed underframes. Finally there were the 1939 'Coronation Scot' coaches which had centrally trussed frames like the 1937 vestibule pairs but had the later type of articulation. The full history of the LMS articulated experiment has survived in contemporary documents and is given in Chapter 12 and 13.

## BODY CONSTRUCTION

Apart from the all-steel vehicles, LMS coaches were generally built with wood frames. From grouping until 1930, coach bodies were timber framed (usually teak) and timber panelled in mahogany. Panel joints were capped by raised wooden beading strips on the outside of the coach while coach ends were made from tongue and groove matchboarding arranged vertically from roof to headstock. Coach roofs were teak framed and covered with longitudinal boards which were then concealed with canvas and fitted with longitudinal end to end rainwater strips. All external mouldings, cornices and so forth were also made from timber.

The later method of construction involved a change to steel outside panelling. From 1930, steel took the place of wood for sides and ends but roofs, window framing, cornices and so on remained as they had always been. However, metal framed or frameless droplights entirely replaced wood framed droplights except in the outside doors. From the start of the Stanier period, steel panelling was introduced for the roof and cornices while outside window mouldings ceased to be used. However, the coaches retained their timber framing except that, as already remarked, when welded underframes came into general use, the bottom side member was omitted. Little further change seems to have taken place except that increasing use seemed to be made of steel components for other parts of the coach such as cantrails, corner pillars and so forth.

It was in 1923 that the celebrated Derby mass-production technique was introduced into the building of coaches and, fortunately, full details of its principles have survived. It was later introduced at Wolverton. Although materials changed during the 1930s, the basic method of assembly remained fairly constant and the great majority of Wolverton and Derby built coaches were constructed to these principles.

Fundamentally, the building of an LMS coach depended on the prefabrication in quantity of all the standard basic coach units (sides, ends, roofs &c.). This was first made possible by the introduction of limit gauges into Derby Works by R. W. Reid, the Midland and then LMS carriage superintendent, in 1923. By this means and the overhauling of the saw mill, it became possible to use jigs for cutting out components instead of laboriously marking out each one separately. All components were machine-cut, then inspected and gauged for accuracy. The use of well-seasoned timbers all but eliminated shrinkage problems and the main task became to ensure that the design of components was such that they could be incorporated into as many different varieties of coach as possible. This enabled numerically larger production runs of components to be made before setting up the jigs and tools for a different unit. It was the use of this method that enabled the LMS to dispense with all its other carriage works although the number of coaches built was considerably greater than anything either Wolverton or Derby had tackled before.

Once the pre-cut units had been checked for accuracy, they were fabricated with a minimum of hand tools into basic coach units—sides, ends, roofs, doors, partitions, seats and so forth. The fabrication process took place simultaneously on a variety of different components in various parts of the works so the final coach assembly involved little more than the fitting together of a minimum number of finished units. In the assembly of the units themselves, extensive use was made of power tools such as jig drills, magazine fed screwdrivers, compressed air cylinders for forcing tenons onto mortices and the like. All doors were fitted into standard cast iron openings. By this means, complete sides and ends could be assembled simultaneously.

Roof construction was equally mechanised. The roof was built on a floor level jig with adjustable pillars for the various coach sides. The cantrail was dropped on to the jig, the roof profile timbers—already pre-drilled &c.—were fixed and the roof boards, canvas, water strips and cornices added.

The main floor framing was built on the underframe direct. One bottom member was fixed to a solebar, the cross bearers clamped into it and then the other bottom side member fixed to the cross bearers. This was clamped tight by means of a portable ball bearing clamp which ran along the full length of the underframe and was fitted with handwheels to enable the second bottom side member to be pulled up tight. Pre-cut floor boards were then fitted and the whole time for a single coach floor assembly was one working day.

**Plate 30** Wooden bodied coaches under construction at Wolverton Works during the 1920s. Note the number of mass-produced standard components assembled on various parts of the shop floor.

**Plate 31** Interior view of a pre-war Stanier coach under construction—type of vehicle unidentified. The coach visible through the window is the Duke of Sutherland's private saloon—now preserved at the National Railway Museum.

**Plate 32** A post-war side corridor coach at Derby Works with the framing erected on the underframe but before the addition of side panels. The vehicle is typically Period III in style, being of composite timber and steel construction. The end framing and each of the sections of side framing between the door openings were prefabricated before erection on to the frames. The coach was a corridor brake third to Lot 1448 (D2123).

The coach erection was simplicity itself. Erection roads had platforms round them at coach floor level to dispense with scaffolding. The underframe was brought in and the coach floor laid as described. The prefabricated ends were then fitted into the endboard tenons by compressed air cylinders. The complete side units, minus bottom panelling, were similarly added and finally the complete roof was lowered onto the coach by means of two hand cranes running the length of the erecting roads. Power clamps were applied inside the cantrails to pull the roof down onto the tenons. The whole operation after the floor had been laid took about one hour.

Interiors were similarly mass-produced using jigs and standard patterns for each and every component even down to picture frames on the compartment walls. Little if any handwork was done on any of them and the work was of a high order.

As far as has been ascertained, few significant changes in assembly procedure were made when steel panelling was first introduced. However, as has been stated, increasing use was made of steel for other parts of vehicles too as time went by and this led to a common policy of prefabricating and erecting the complete coach framework before adding outside panelling.

**Plate 33** The method by which steel panelling was applied to Period III stock. The vehicle is one of the 1937 vestibule articulated coaches—see Chapter 12.

**Plates 34-35-36** Various stages in the erection of the pioneer Stanier 69ft 12-wheel sleeping cars to D1926. Note particularly the steel box brackets, welded direct onto the underframe, thus dispensing with the need for a bottom side member for the coach body. Note also the continued use of prefabricated sections of side framing as during the wooden bodied period. The main difference in body erection during Period III was that the whole of the framework was erected before the side sheeting was applied.

**Plate 37** Detail view of the welded version ▶ of the LMS standard six-wheel bogie. Note the heavy framing above the centre axle linking the two swing planks of the bolster, thus enabling it to function as a single unit but effectively doubling the amount of springing available. Coaches fitted with this bogie were supremely comfortable to ride in.

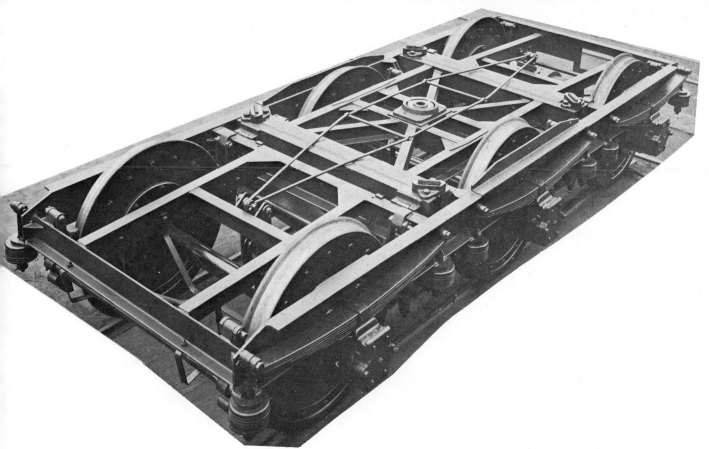

## ALL-STEEL COACHES

The principal exceptions to conventional coaches were the various 'all steel' vehicles. For the most part these were built by outside contractors and in the case of the Period I vestibule coaches and full brakes (see p. 167), they were almost certainly ordered to assist the steel industry at the time. The open coaches were designed principally for use on long distance weekend trains and excursion workings.

The coaches were built in the form of a long tubular girder. The underframe formed the bottom boom and the cantrails, purlins and roof sheets the top boom. The body side plates formed webs connecting upper and lower booms and were stiffened by pressed channel section pillars riveted to them. The whole structure was very light but extremely rigid. The coaches were practically fireproof and much stronger than the equivalent wooden vehicles. None of them had conventional truss rods but all carried a somewhat rudimentary support for the battery boxes and electric light regulator.

The coaches were built by various outside contractors (see Tables 9 and 14b, pp. 130 and 174) and the designs varred in detail between the batches. Some were heavily riveted; others were of a more flush sided nature. Some had rounded side/ end corners—as on modern BR stock but less emphasised—and so on. These variations in detail were, according to the surviving records, devised to gain practical experience in this country of the methods adopted by the various contractors in the construction of similar vehicles for use overseas. Thus, all had insulating lining material except the Cammell-Laird coaches which were given a free-air space between the inner and outer lining of the coach.

Most vehicles were finished inside in the standard LMS style utilising mahogany veneers but some were steel throughout in which case special colour schemes were used. Seats were covered with black or fawn York velvet and the brass fittings were finished in Venetian bronze.

Following on these twin-window vestibule coaches and full brakes, the next steel coaches were some corridor brake firsts and brake thirds during Period II. They could be identified from their Period II contemporaries by the deeper than normal eaves panelling and the lack of conventional truss rod framing. The coaches were again built in the form of a hollow box girder using both roof and floor as strengtheners—hence the presence of the rather deeper eaves section which was an essential part of the structural form. These coaches too had metal roof panelling.

The final pre-war steel coaches were the 1939 'Coronation Scot' trains but these were specialised vehicles and are considered in detail in Chapter 13.

During the war, virtually all coach construction ceased and a considerable backlog of overdue vehicle replacement had to be cleared immediately hostilities ceased. This left little time for further experimental work and the LMS embarked on a massive coach construction programme utilising basically pre-war patterns and ideas—not that the coaches were in any way inferior because of this fact. However, by 1949 the immediate shortages had been overcome and Derby works presumably felt free to experiment again with steel construction. Although no recorded evidence has been located, the experiment was presumably encouraged by the Railway Executive since one must assume that consideration was being given at this time to the designing of new BR standard stock. The outcome was the appearance of the 60ft corridor composites to D2159, the design for which had appeared in 1947, and these vehicles may safely be stated to be the last expression of pure LMS design ideas although not the last LMS pattern coaches to be built. The slightly altered profile has been alluded to on page 19 but the construction too had several points of interest, especially since it more or less established BR standard coach construction methods.

The steel body shell was welded directly to the underframe which was carried on standard LMS pattern welded bogies. However, the underframe, although similar to the LMS pattern was designed with slightly lighter section solebars and truss rods. Furthermore, the truss rods, although still of the conventional angle section were also fitted to the central longitudinal chassis members as well as to the solebars. Sides, ends and roof were prefabricated units of light skeleton structure to

**Plate 38** The construction of the 'porthole' CKs to D2159 at Derby in 1949. These vehicles were of 'all steel' construction and the side, end and roof sections were prefabricated before erection on to the underframe. This picture gives a good impression of the changed profile of this batch with the rather sharper radius between side and roof.

which were welded the steel outer panels. All the main body assembly was welded together and the timber floor was fixed direct to the underframe. Interior finishing was of conventional woodwork and veneered surfaces but in order to reduce corrosion from interior condensation, circulation air spaces were left between the interior finishing panels and the steel structure of the coach. An innovation inside the coach at least from the LMS/LMR point of view, was the elimination of sharp corners from the compartment and corridor ceilings by introducing ceilings of an arch type. These blended at the corridor partition into a common through pocket in which the coach wiring was carried. Many of these vehicles remained in service until at least 1967/8.

**Plate 39** Period I 'two-window' FO No. 3716, later 7414. This coach exhibited a transitional seat end design from the Midland style to the LMS standard pattern of Figure 3. The ornate panel decoration between the windows did not last long after Grouping.

**Plate 40** Interior of 56-seat open third No. 6260, later 8071. This was a member of the Metropolitan C & W batch to Lot 185 and was given all metal interior finishing. The seat end design, although rendered in pressed steel is still of standard LMS pattern—see Figure 3. Note the 'cranking' of the seat end to provide more gangway width at shoulder level—a feature of all LMS open coaches with two-and-two rather than two-and-one seating.

## COACH INTERIORS

Regrettably, less information has survived about LMS coach interiors than one would have liked. Nevertheless, it is possible to reconstruct an abbreviated story of the development of ideas. Figures 3a/3b give some of the more common interior designs.

At all times the LMS made extensive use of timber finishing. Throughout its history the company laid strong emphasis on the use of 'selected Empire timber' and this may have had suitable patriotic overtones for the publicity department. However, the important point seems to be that timber finishes lent themselves admirably to the mass-production technique. Interior panels, window frames, tables, seats and the like could all be mass produced. In consequence, the interiors of LMS coaches, especially the Period II examples, showed far less change than one might expect from the outside styling.

### Vestibule stock

Early vestibule stock was particularly consistent. Kitchen/dining cars, vestibule dining coaches and general service open stock all had common seat designs, variations being principally in the width of the seat depending on whether the coach seated two-and-one or two each side of the gangway. First class seats were generally a little softer (!). The seat end design remained unchanged for almost 10 years (Fig. 3a/b) and its wing ended style owed a great deal to its Midland predecessors. In centre gangway coaches, the seat-ends were shaped to give a greater width to the gangway at seat back level than at the seat itself. This gave extra elbow room for passengers walking through the coach but enabled the widest possible seat to be achieved.

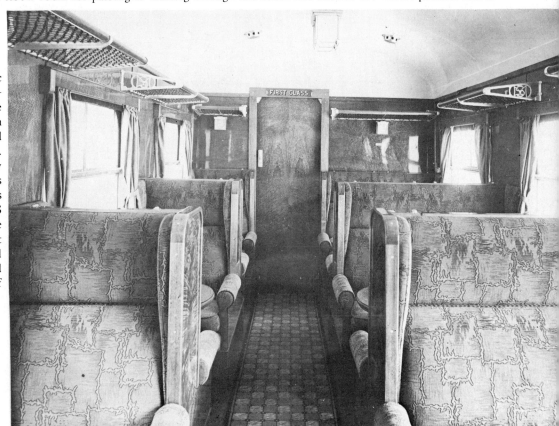

**Plate 41** The characteristic Period III open first style— see Figure 3. The picture is of the first class portion of the vestibule articulated coaches—see Chapter 12. The offset gangway is very clear and the doorway is surmounted by a class indicator board. The LMS monogram in the luggage rack supports was not always present in Period III coaches, being replaced by a plainer design of support—see Figure 3.

Tables were fitted between the seats in all open coaches and a reading lamp was often located on the wall over the table. Pullman type table lamps were occasionally used in dining cars. Three bulb 'electroliers' or single unit fixtures were spaced down the centre of the ceiling which was enamelled white for greater reflectivity. Interior veneers were generally mahogany stained to a very dark shade, although first-class coaches often had silver grey wood veneers instead. The double floors were felt insulated and had a strip carpet down the gangway.

Upholstery was provided in various patterns. Unfortunately the contemporary accounts do not give much idea about the colours adopted. It would seem that traditional red and black velvet was very popular but fawn and blue patterned moquettes were increasingly used as time went on. Seat antimacassars in the first class cars were unbleached holland embroidered with the LMS monogram.

The Stanier coaches witnessed little change in seat size but the general styling was modernised to the typical 'boxy' style so favoured in the 1930s. Both classes of accommodation retained wooden seat ends—presumably for their harder wearing properties—but open firsts became much 'softer' in appearance (Fig. 3a/b). From the many black and white pictures of LMS interiors it seems that there was little standardisation in upholstery colour but that patterned moquette, sometimes of rather bold design, had, by this time, become almost universal. The shade of wood veneering was also lightened and the lamps and other fittings were somewhat more 'streamlined' in their styling.

**Plate 42** (*left*) The typical Period III open third finish—again an articulated coach. Extra width at shoulder level in Period III coaches with 2 + 2 seating was gained by inclining the whole seat end from the armrest level rather than 'cranking' the end as was the case in pre-Stanier coaches.

**Plate 43** (*below*) When Period III third class coaches had 2 + 1 seating, as in the case of this composite dining car No. 241 (see Plate 98 for exterior view of same type), the seat end supports were vertical.

These cross-sections reproduced approximately to $\frac{3}{8}$in–1ft scale are typical of most LMS coaches of the periods concerned but the diagrams to which the original works drawings relate are quoted in brackets:

I   Period I non-corridor first class compartment (54ft Lavatory Composite D1765, Lot 130).

II  Period I non-corridor third class compartment (57ft Third Class Brake D1703, Lot 356).

III Period I/II vestibule stock (first or third)—centre gangway types had 'cranked' seat ends—see plate 24d (60ft vestibule dining coaches to Lots 491/519 of D1721 and D1722).

IV  Period III vestibule Stock showing third class seat desing (LHS) and first class seat design (RHS). Centre gangway thirds had the seat end angled-in above the armrest level—see Plate 27c (68ft composite kitchen dining cars D1938, Lot 905).

V   Period I corridor first class half compartment showing the partition arrangement opposite the sets (57ft corridor first D1747, Lot 246).

VI  Period II corridor third class compartment (60ft corridor third D1782, Lot 551).

*(Drawn by D. Jenkinson)*

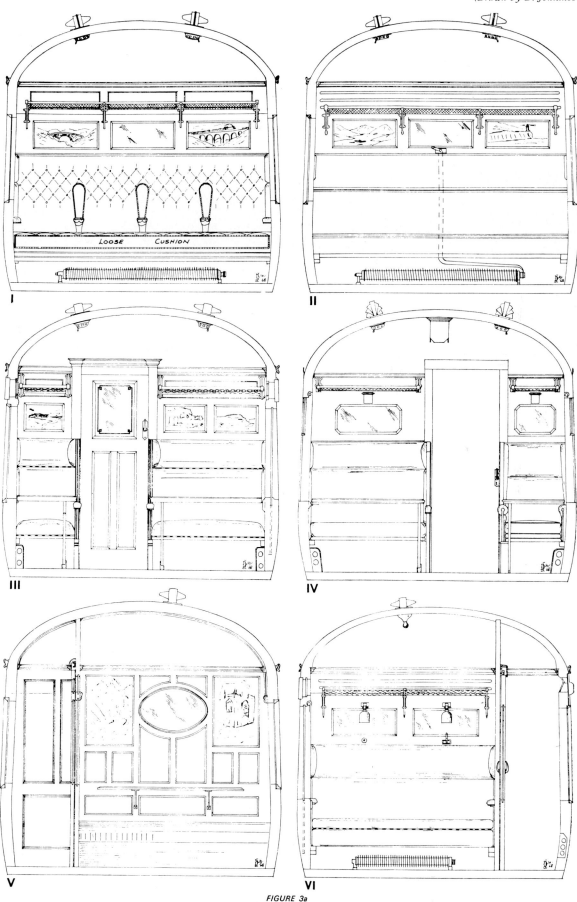

FIGURE 3a

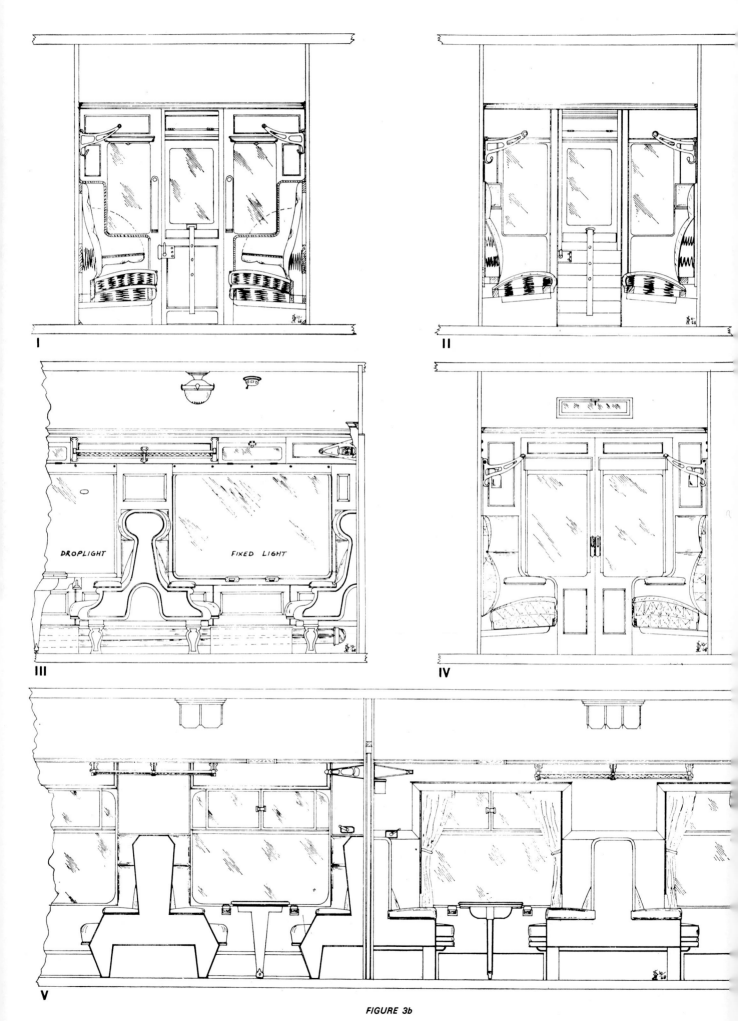

I

II

III

DROPLIGHT  FIXED LIGHT

IV

V

*FIGURE 3b*

32

These sections also at $\frac{3}{8}$in—1ft
scale match the cross sections in
Figure 3a except for the corridor
first which is omitted in order to
include both types of Period III
seat end design:

I  Period I non-corridor first
   class.
II  Period I non-corridor third
   class.
III  Period I/II vestibule stock
   (first or third class).
IV  Period II corridor third
   class.
V  Period III vestibule stock
   showing third class seat
   design (LHS) and first class
   seat design (RHS).
        *(Drawn by D. Jenkinson)*

**Plate 44** Interior of 'two-window' style Period I coach. Note the difference in framing between the fixed light (LHS) and the drop-light (RHS). The scenery through the window is a fake as is proved by the Midland clerestory coach just visible through the Stones ventilators!

Most LMS open carriages were designed to carry luggage as well as passengers. There was a considerable space beneath the seats which was achieved by fitting the steam radiators close to the sides of the coaches beneath the windows and covering them with perforated brass guards. The system hardly changed for over 30 years except for the less ornate guards over the radiators by the time of the BR standard coaches which used the system. Supplementary net racks for smaller luggage were also fitted inside the coaches and these mostly made use of supports in whose design was incorporated the LMS monogram.

Large racks for heavier luggage were fitted inside the entrance vestibules which also contained toilets with hot and cold water supply. Later Stanier pattern excursion coaches tended to dispense with the luggage shelves, even though the coaches were often used for main line work as well.

## Compartment and Corridor stock

During early years, third class compartments were characterised by the extensive use of crimson and black figured velvet upholstery and mahogany veneers. Fittings were brass. First class compartments were generally trimmed with blue cloth on the top sides and American cloth on the under surfaces. They were usually panelled in walnut and had Venetian bronze fittings. First class compartments were also fitted with carpets—often with the letters 'LMS' incorporated in the design.

There does not seem to have been any real difference between the furnishing of corridor and non-corridor stock at this time. Third class compartments had no armrests in either case but the first class areas did, frequently with headrests as well. Seating was six a side in non-corridor thirds and four a side in the corridor equivalents; first class compartments were four and three respectively. There was, however, one batch of non-corridor coaches (Cathcart Circle stock—pp. 147/8) which was given five a side first class seating without armrests.

All compartments were electrically lit, first class compartments usually rather better than the thirds—for example four 12 candle power lamps per compartment instead of three. Extra courtesy lights were often placed over the first class seats, and ceilings in both types of compartments were enamelled white. Steam heating was generally employed but electric stock was, of course, electrically heated.

When the LMS introduced its twin-window style corridor firsts and first brakes in 1927, many improvements were made, quite apart from the obvious one of improving the outlook and eliminating the outside compartment door and its attendant draughts.

**Plates 45-46** Two contrasting compartment interiors of LMS 15933—see also Plate 140, the first design of semi-open coach to D1707. All three compartments were, in fact, slightly different in upholstery, veneers and decorative motifs. Note the very wide double doors to the compartments. In both cases, the view through the window is a fake.

**Plate 47** Corridor view inside Period II coach No. 15556 (Figure 18). The compartments of these coaches seated two per side and were very similar to those on the 1928 luxury stock.

The first change was to increase the compartment size from 7ft 3in to 7ft 6in between partitions and this gave more leg room. Inside panelling was now rendered in silver/grey wood veneering relieved by olive green mouldings. Upholstery was in Persian pattern moquette and seats were fitted with embroidered antimacassars with the company monogram. Specially made Wilton rugs were fitted in the coaches and the floors were covered with thick felt to deaden the sound. Removable tables were also provided and all compartments had bell pushes to summon the attendant. Fittings were satin brass.

This more opulent trend was continued in the single window first class coaches of 1928/29 with two a side seating. These were the semi-open firsts and the Period II first brakes. In these coaches, all compartments were differently finished both in upholstery and in the wood veneer employed. In photographs these coaches look to have been supremely comfortable and seem also to have been of less sombre appearance than earlier vehicles. These coaches appear to have introduced the double sliding door to the compartment.

By the time Period III corridor coaches appeared, first class compartment design seemed to have reached its ultimate expression except for the increasingly varied nature of upholstery materials, the more modern fittings and the generally paler shades both of wood and upholstery. Seats became a little softer and deeper and were built both two a side and three a side.

The former were regarded as 'luxury' finish and confined to the more important trains. After the war, the compartment size was reduced from 7ft 6in to 7ft 2in in order to fit six into a 57ft body length. One wonders why the LMS did not use a 60ft length for its full firsts as it had long done for its composites.

**Plate 48** First class half-compartment of LMS BCK No. 9318, see Plate 18, Figure 21. Note the luxury two per side seating and the still very dark wood veneers of this 1932 coach. Ash trays and luggage racks both display the LMS monogram and the seating is 'softer' than earlier first class compartments.

**Plate 49** Third class half-compartment of 9318, see Plate 18, Figure 21. These coaches set the style for

Stanier-pattern third class corridor coach compartments, and apart from lighter wood finishes, the design remained largely unchanged until after Nationalisation.

**Plate 50** Interior view of a typical Period III first class compartment in a side corridor coach. Interestingly, the coat hooks on either side of the window seem to be of an almost pure Midland Railway pattern.

**Plate 51** Corridor view of Period III coach No. 4298 (picture dated 1939). By this time, wood finishes had become lighter in shade. Note the corridor carpet at the first class end only.

**Plate 52** This typical Period III third class compartment is of coach M4858 of the 1947/8 batch to D2117. It shows the shorter element sliding window ventilators but otherwise little changed from the pre-war version.

Until 1930, third class passenger accommodation in compartment and side corridor stock seems to have been rather neglected. Not until 1929 were outside doors abolished and even this was only in a few 'two-window' composites. It was the advent of Period II coaches that saw the final abolition of outside doors to all compartments and this went with an increase in length of third class compartment from 6ft 0in to 6ft 6in between partitions. At the same time, the Period II third class compartment retained its traditional four a side seating (Fig 3a).

With the advent of the Period III coach, the third class passenger was given a completely new standard of travel—comparable in many ways with the emancipation of the third class passenger in the 19th Century by the Midland Railway in the person of James Allport. Stanier is justly remembered for his magnificent stock of locomotives but the third class LMS passenger had equal cause to remember the LMS CME of the 1930s.

From 1932 onwards, all side corridor third class compartments were built with three a side seating with armrests, courtesy lights and single large windows. Apart from the slightly firmer springing of the seats and the folding nature of the armrests, they were little different from their contemporary three a side firsts. By the time of the 1939—45 war, the Stanier corridor third was so widespread that one could claim that the LMS almost certainly led the field as far as the British scene was concerned. Moreover, many of the more modern Period I and II coaches were converted to three a side seating and generally refurbished to match the Stanier coaches. So good, in fact, were the LMS thirds that after the war, some of the 'Coronation Scot' cars were actually *upgraded* to first class when they re-entered service!

The design of third class compartments changed little from 1933 onwards. The only major alteration was to reduce the size from 6ft 6in to 6ft 3in which allowed slightly improved toilet facilities to be provided. This remained the standard dimension apart from the 1939 'Coronation Scot' coaches which reverted to 6ft 6in and were the ones which were temporarily upgraded. These coaches are considered in greater detail in Chapter 13.

One wishes that one could be equally enthusiastic about the non-corridor stock. Right until the end, LMS non-corridor stock remained virtually unchanged. In fairness, however, it became increasingly confined to short distance suburban working where maximum seating capacity was of the essence. Inter-district and medium distance workings were increasingly handed over to older gangwayed coaches.

Upholstery in Stanier compartment and corridor coaches seems to have been as varied as it was in the open stock. No specific details can be given beyond the general statement that colours became lighter and patterned finishes more common.

## Sleeping Cars

The design of LMS sleeping cars seems to have derived from that of the LNWR and, of course, the first 50 or more first class coaches were basically LNWR designs brought up to date. The first 10 were slightly more old fashioned than the remainder which were the vehicles which initially established the post-group trend. However, both types set the style, as it were, for the LMS Sleeping Cars.

To reduce vibration and noise, India-rubber body blocks were fitted between body and underframe and hair felt was inserted between the double floors. Inside the compartments, walls above the dado, together with the ceilings, were enamelled in white, while wood veneers were mahogany or walnut. All wall angles were rounded for ease of cleaning and beds were metal framed with loose spring mattresses and separate hair stuffed mattresses.

**Plate 53** Interior of 'porthole' brake first No. M5077 (Plate 123). These coaches had several features similar to the later BR standard coaches—upholstery material (bluish grey), ash trays, window ventilators. The letters BR (M) appeared on the carpet in succession to the LMS of pre-1948 vehicles.

Particular attention was paid to those small ancillary details calculated to make a good impression on the class of passenger for which the coaches were designed. Apart from hot and cold water supplied to each compartment wash basin, drop writing tables, mirrors, brush and comb racks, glass holders and shelves were additional fittings. All compartments were single but eight could be utilised to form four twin berth compartments by unlocking the interconnecting doors. Windows were fitted with rolling shutters which gave rather a snug appearance when they were lowered. Other fittings included bedhead lights and electric fans, both of which could be regulated from a switchboard near the bedhead, and loose bedside rugs were provided as a finishing touch. Not surprisingly, these very fine coaches lasted for many years, not becoming extinct until 1962.

Until 1928 the third class railway traveller in this country had to take what rest he could in his compartment if he was misguided enough to wish to travel at night. In that year the LMS, LNER and GWR pioneered third class sleeping cars, the LMS vehicles being 60ft coaches to D1709. There was nothing particularly revolutionary about the design itself, the coaches being rather like a corridor third and styled inside to match. However, above the seats was a fold-away top bunk which enabled each compartment to be converted for night use into a four berth sleeping area. Full bedding was not provided but pillows and rugs could be obtained. The idea was basically that of a modern European couchette coach. For through coach working, this convertible idea was combined with six orthodox first class sleeping compartments in the composite sleepers of 1930/31.

By the middle 1930s the older sleeping cars were thought to compare unfavourably with the newer Stanier types then being built. As a result of this, the third class compartments of many of the third class and composite sleepers were converted to a fixed berth arrangement while the LNWR styled 68ft first class coaches were modernised. The LMS records refer to this as being an air conditioning operation but it is felt that the 'air conditioning' was of the type to be described below, rather than the more generally understood present day interpretation of the term.

The Stanier sleeping cars again set new standards of comfort much as their contemporary day coaches had done. The first class cars were built to the maximum dimensions allowed by the loading gauge (9ft 2¼ins over the body). They were fitted with recessed door handles to allow for this extra width and were made a foot longer than the earlier coaches, thus becoming the largest non-articulated coaches ever built by the LMS or any of its constituents. The interiors retained all the conveniences of the earlier cars but the extra width enabled the provision of a slightly longer bed. They were also given much brighter interiors in which considerable use was made of plated metal fittings.

**Plate 54** First class compartment of non-corridor composite coach No. 16502 (D1849). This was one of the first Stanier non-corridor coaches. Note the 'LMS' woven into the corner panel of the carpet.

**Plate 55** Third class compartment of 16502.

**Plate 56** Interior view of the 1951 built non-corridor first class coach No. M10124 (Plate 157), again featuring certain BR style details.

Plate 57 This picture shows the interior of a compartment in first class sleeping car No. 350 (D1705) which went to America with the 'Royal Scot' tour train in 1933. Compared with the earlier LNWR and LMS sleeping cars, this vehicle exhibited considerably brighter decor, albeit still with plenty of polished wood-work. Note the use of the 'air conditioning' control above the bedhead, replacing the wall fan of earlier cars (see also Plate 77).

Plate 58 Close-up view, showing panel and other detail, of Period I BFK No. 18564, later 5035, to D1654. This is a corridor side view of the coach later fitted with LNER type bogies—see Table 8.

A further innovation in these cars was the provision of a combined heating and ventilation system under the individual control of the passenger. This seems to have been referred to by the LMS as air conditioning. All the compartments were fitted with a punkah louvre type air vent which enabled the passenger to adjust the volume, direction and temperature of the incoming air. The post-war batch of these coaches with slight further improvements, was with the odd exception, still in service as late as 1968, many being finished BR Blue/Grey. Several are now privately preserved.

Stanier also introduced the first fixed berth third class sleeping cars to the LMS which may have been a GWR inspired importation. These singularly handsome cars again represented a major step forward in passenger amenity and the earlier versions were altered to match them as nearly as possible. As with the earlier sleeping cars, the basic principle of the Stanier pattern first and third class cars were combined in the 69ft composites.

The final improvement in sleeping cars came after the war when, in 1951/2, the first twin berth sleeping cars for third class use were built. They were mounted on the 65ft chassis of the pre-war thirds but were given the wider body of the Stanier 12 wheel sleeping cars. They were pure LMS designs and most were still in service as late as 1968. Apart from the twin berth arrangement they were every bit as well equipped as the matching firsts sharing such features as carpeted floors, reading lamps, passenger controlled heating/ventilation and so forth. They were additionally interesting as being, with their Eastern Region contemporaries, the first British third class sleeping cars to be provided with fully made up beds.

LMS design sleeping cars tended to be less standardised in their furnishings than did day coaches and almost every batch exhibited some changes or innovations compared with their predecessors. The above general outline of sleeping car interiors only covers the main trends and additional details for individual batches of cars are given in Chapter 6.

# Chapter 3 - Livery, Painting and Finishing

*Introduction; body colours; lining details; insignia styles; insignia placing; summary of styles;*
*special liveries; painting methods; paint specifications; interior finishing*

UNLIKE that of locomotives, LMS coach livery was very standardised and for the most part, generalisation is readily possible. Coaches were usually repainted every six or seven years, except during the war, so it is also possible to make reasonably accurate deductions as to the probable repainted styles of various coach types from the building dates and the known style of painting at the time when coaches were due for shopping. With the exception of obsolete and obsolescent pre-group stock due for early scrapping, the following livery summary applies equally to all the coaches taken over by the LMS in 1923.

## BODY COLOURS

The standard LMS body colour was crimson lake, being basically the ex-MR shade. This colour has been discussed at length elsewhere so the argument will not be repeated here. The shade may have become a little darker as the years went by but until 1946 the nomenclature never changed. In this year, the LMS changed the name to maroon although whether there was any noticeable change in the actual colour is conjectural.

In 1956/7 when BR adopted an all-red coach livery, a definite attempt was made to revert to the pre-war MR/LMS shade and careful matching of painted panels indicates that this was achieved, especially when BR coaches were newly ex-works. At the same time, BR never reverted to calling the shade 'crimson lake' and it was always referred to as 'BR locomotive hauled stock maroon'. However, as the shade is more recent in history than LMS red, it will probably help readers to visualise the colour more readily.

Coach ends were painted crimson until about the close of 1936 when, except for the driving ends of motor driving trailers, black ends were adopted and remained standard from that date. Chassis and all ancillary details were black but the roof colour varied a little. Until the Stanier period, roofs were generally painted in MR style which was lead grey between the rainstrips and black between rainstrips and cantrail. All-steel coaches often had a metallic roof finish. From 1933 to the outbreak of war, new Stanier pattern coaches generally had a metallic aluminium type paint finish on the roof and this treatment was also specified for repainted pre-Stanier coaches (see p. 50). Unfortunately, roof tops quickly became dirty in service assuming an overall muddy grey shade and it is not, therefore, possible to be more precise about their colour. Most available pictures are of ex-works new coaches so these do not assist greatly in assessing the colour for repaints.

The post-war painting drawings specify grey as the roof colour but its introduction cannot be exactly date. It probably started during the war years and continued until the abandonment of LMS coach livery some two years after nationalisation. The final batches of LMS design coaches were usually turned out from new in BR crimson and cream, or plain crimson livery, although a few coaches were, at first, given some of the early experimental BR liveries (other details not known).

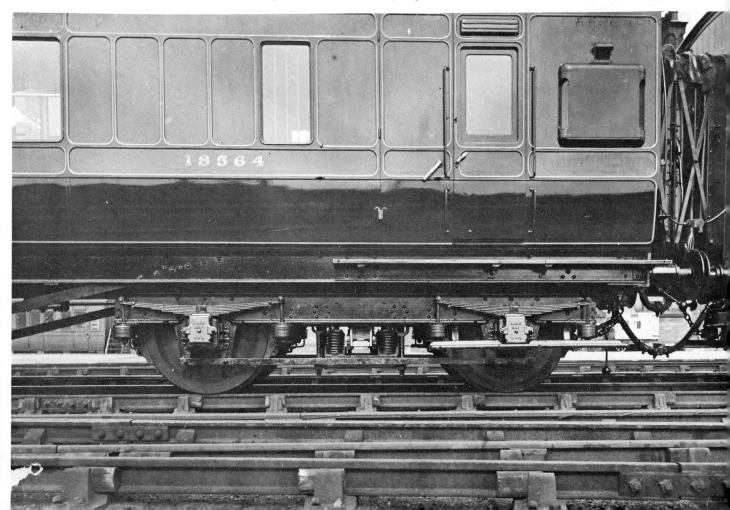

**Plate 59** Unidentified Period I 'twin window' open third to D1692 (fitted with experimental American type equalised beam bogies) showing Period I panel and lining detail.

## LINING DETAILS

Until the close of 1933/early 1934, all coaches were fully lined out in Midland style. All raised beading was painted black and was edged in 3/8in gold (gangwayed stock) or 3/8in pale yellow (non-gangwayed stock). The gold or yellow lines were edged each side with 1/16in vermilion lines. The lining followed the physical outline of the beading (square cornered in the case of pre-group stock with this variety of beading) and all three colours appeared on the beading itself and not on the main body panels. Coach ends were unlined but detail work (steps, pipework etc) was generally picked out in black. Pre-group coaches were fully panelled and beaded ends (as opposed to the LMS type matchboard ends) usually had the end beading painted black without lining which was the old MR practice.

This fully lined livery continued in use during the whole of Period II and the first year or so of Period III and was thus applied to many coaches with steel panelling and no beading. In this case, pseudo 'beading' in paint was applied to the coach side and appeared in two main variants; high and low waisted.

**Plate 60** Kitchen side elevation of kitchen car No. 312 (see also Plate 101). Note the very slightly altered panelling and insignia placing compared with that shown on Car No. 262 (Figure 13). These cars all showed typical Period I "pseudo" panelling on a steel clad vehicle. They also typify the pre-1928 insignia placing, with the running number repeated twice. Car 312 became 30002 in 1933.

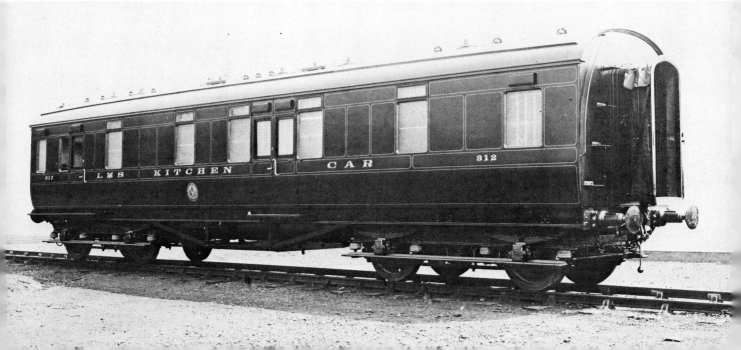

**Plate 61** Period II non-corridor composite to D1734 No. 3096 (later 16363). This shows the Period II livery style (without waist panel) and the post-1928 insignia placing with only one running number. In this view, the running number is in the enlarged 'stretched scroll' figures.

Steel panelled stock with high waist built before the end of 1928 was given imitation waist panelling in order to match the fully beaded orthodox Period I coaches. It was generally given rounded corners further to simulate raised beading but one or two batches of coaches were given a slightly simplified style with square corners (e.g. some 'all steel' open thirds).

With the introduction of low waisted stock in 1929, waist panelling was abandoned and this was also reflected in the imitation 'beaded' livery of flush clad Period II and early Period III coaches. Even when the coach type retained a high waist—e.g. some sleeping cars and all non-corridor stock—the coaches were not given painted waist panelling after 1928 if they were flush clad. Needless to say, high waisted *wood* panelled stock, which continued to be built in small quantities until 1930, retained waist panelling and full lining.

Examples of the lining shades and some of the dimensions during the full livery period are depicted in the Panels on page ix and in Figure 1 (page 6).

From 1934 onwards, the LMS adopted a simplified lining scheme. This took the form of a single horizontal ½in yellow line just below the cantrail, a similar ½in line above the tops of the windows and two ½in yellow lines separated by a 1in wide black line just below the windows. The yellow shade was changed to a darker chrome yellow hue and with this simplified livery, there was no distinction in lining colour between gangwayed and non-gangwayed stock, yellow being universal.

During the war, all lining was discontinued if coaches were fully repainted but this practice was not common, retouching of existing paintwork being the more usual procedure. The simple lining was reintroduced from 1945 onwards and from 1946 the colour was changed from yellow to straw—an even paler shade than the 1923-33 pale yellow lining colour.

The simplified livery was applied to all repainted stock and in the case of wood panelled, fully beaded coaches, the single yellow lines were applied centrally along the upper and lower beading strips of the eaves panel and the yellow/black/yellow line was applied along the upper beading strip of the waist panel. This livery with straw lining continued in use until about the end of 1949. Panel E (page ix). and with Figure 1, (page 6) illustrate the simplified livery and insignia placing.

**Plate 62** Period III open third No. 8929 to D1904 shows the fully lined livery as applied to some early Stanier coaches. Note particularly the post-1933 running number rendered in unshaded gold sans-serif figures.

**Plate 63** Standard 60ft open first to D1917 illustrates the typical Period III simple livery in its earliest form with unshaded sans-serif figures and the coach end still painted red with details picked out in black. The post-war version of this livery with full sans-serif insignia is illustrated on a coach of similar design at Plate 146.

## INSIGNIA STYLES

### Lettering

From 1923 until Nationalisation, the letters LMS and any other descriptive wording—KITCHEN CAR, SLEEPING CAR &c. —were applied to the coach side in somewhat elongated serif characters, 4in high. The basic colour was gold leaf until about 1934/5 and chrome yellow after this date. At all times the letters were shaded in pinkish white to the left blending to dark red/brown below the characters. They were shadow shaded to the right and below in black. From 1946 onwards, a very few coaches were given block style lettering 6in high in straw paint edged with black. This was not widespread but would, presumably, have become the standard treatment. At the same time, the branding of dining cars was changed to 'RESTAURANT CAR' if given this block style of letter.

The lettering 'ROYAL MAIL' on GPO vehicles was in 10in high serif characters, coloured as for the letters LMS (Fig 4). *Note:* Smaller lettering about 3in high, was used on many pre-group coaches with shallow depth waist panels but not often, as far as can be ascertained, on LMS standard vehicles.

### Numbering

Several styles of running number were adopted by the LMS but the changes generally coincided with coach styling changes as well.

*1923-28* Small scroll figures in gold leaf some 3in high were employed, shaded to match the serif 'LMS' described above. They just lasted to the start of Period II designs.

*1929-32* During Period II, a stretched out scroll type figure the same height as the serif 'LMS' was employed, retaining the same colour scheme as before. Wolverton Works refers to this design as the 'bastard' style and claims that the figures were handpainted not transferred. These figures remained in use only until the 1932/3 renumbering and were, in consequence, confined mainly to Period II coaches and the few Period III coaches which were built before the renumbering. They were also placed on the coaches of the 'Royal Scot' train which toured America in 1933. These latter coaches were renumbered before the tour and are thought to be the only vehicles which had their post-1932 numbers in the 'stretched' scroll style of figure.

**Plate 64** Period III non-corridor third No. 12194 to D1906, illustrates the simple LMS livery in perhaps its most common form with shaded sans-serif numbers (now in chrome yellow) and black painted coach end. On this example, as with many coaches, the insignia were placed well in from the coach ends.

I **THE COMET**

**THE MANCUNIAN**

**LONDON (EUSTON)**

**EUSTON**

III

10 inch letters (exclusive of all shaded areas)

body colour yellow or gold        shading white, blending through        black shadow
                                  pink and crimson to brown

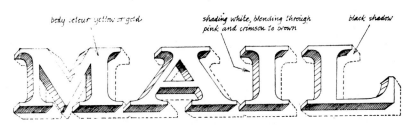

IV

pillar box red background colour to letter box

LMS
30204          ROYAL    G⚭R    G⚭R    MAIL    ← 10 inch letters        LMS
                                                                       30204

Position of crest

4 inch letters and figures

Upper inscription on letter box reads: POST OFFICE        Lower inscription on letter box reads: LETTERS POSTED
                                       LETTER BOX                                                HERE MUST BEAR
                                                                                                 AN EXTRA
yellow/black/yellow line along waist                                                             HALFPENNY STAMP

2¼" capital letters        1¾" capital letters        1½" capital letters        ½" yellow lines
1⅝" ordinary letters       1⅛" ordinary letters       1" ordinary letters

                                                                          Note: The cypher between 'ROYAL' and 'MAIL'
                                                                          changed to ℟ with the accession of
                                                                          King George VI.

LMS          G⚭R                    ROYAL    G⚭R    MAIL                              LMS
30204                                                                                30204

       lamp            Position of crest            lamp

FIGURE 4 *LMS coaches—miscellaneous livery drawings*
I   Coach headboards—1935 and later:—These boards reproduced at ½in—1ft scale were 12ft 6in long, 6in deep and carried 5in high letters
    in black on a white ground. The width of the letters was adjusted to suit the name of the train or service. The boards were either mounted
    on the roof (Period I/II and early Period III stock) or on the eaves panel (later Period III stock). Some Period III coaches had mounting
    brackets in both locations.
II  *Coach destination boards*: Upper: 1923-33 pattern; black letters on white ground
                               Lower: 1933 and later; black letters on deep cream ground
    These boards were 2ft 4in long and usually fixed to brackets on the eaves panel close to an entrance door.
III *Lettering 'Royal Mail'*:—¾in—1ft scale. These letters were 10in high but the drawing also gives the correct general shape, colour and
    shading details for all types of serif LMS coach lettering. The shading detail is also generally accurate for carriage running numbers. The
    original from which this drawing was prepared is the only official LMS insignia drawing which has been located by the authors.
IV  Layout of lettering etc., on Royal Mail vehicles c. 1935/6 Scale ⅛in—ft.

*(Drawn by D. Jenkinson)*

**Plate 65** This view of a D1705 sleeping car No. 3792 (later 342) shows the full livery and pre-1928 layout of the descriptive wording. After 1928, coaches with a proper waist panel still carried the descriptive wording over the LMS emblem but the 'LMS' itself moved to the position of the left hand running number in this view.

**Plate 66** Typical insignia layout on a Stanier 12-wheeler. Note the descriptive wording flanking the emblem. The diner is to D1900 and externally was all but identical to the D1923 version at Plate 21.

**Plate 67** Period III FO No. M7544 to D1917 shown in close-up. Note the post-war pattern of insignia and the large figure '1' on the window. The date of this picture is probably 1948.

*1933-40* The 1932/3 renumbering introduced new sans-serif coach numbers still 4in high. For a year or so they were applied in plain gold figures but from about 1934/5 onwards they became chrome yellow and were shaded to match the serif pattern 'LMS' and remained thus. In general the shaded style of block figures seems to have been introduced at or shortly after the time of change to simple livery and the change from gold leaf to chrome yellow colour approximately coincided with the similar change in lining shade. Vitually all new coaches and renumbered pre-1933 coaches received this style of sans-serif number and the style itself may have been introduced to enable the operating staff, during the renumbering period, to distinguish more readily between the renumbered coaches and those with original numbers. There were, of course, odd exceptions like the case of the 1933 'Royal Scot' train (page 44).

*1940 onwards* From this period, reversion was made to scroll type figures generally similar to the 1923-28 type but about 4in high, chrome yellow in basic colour and having flat topped '3s'. For economy reasons, residual supplies of sans serif numerals were probably used up on repaints but most, if not all newly constructed vehicles were given scroll pattern figures. They continued in use after Nationalisation until the onset of BR livery, frequently being given an 'M' prefix in 1948/9. In 1946 a sans-serif style of figure, 4½in high in straw edged with black was introduced to match the 6in high straw coloured 'LMS' mentioned above but only saw limited use, being confined to the few coaches given the experimental 1946 sans serif insignia.

Full colour samples of the shaded sans-serif numbers are incorporated in Panel Q, (page x).

## Passenger Class Numbering

Most LMS coaches carried the figure '1' or '3', as appropriate, on the outside of carriage doors. These were always 8in high and again rendered in gold (changing to chrome yellow in about 1934/5), with blended red shading, shadow shaded black. Throughout the 1923-47 period these figures were of scroll pattern but in 1940, or thereabouts, the 's' was changed to a flat topped version. In this form it was applied to all new and repainted coaches. As with lettering and numbering, there was a short-lived 1946 sans serif version in straw with black edging which again only saw limited use.

After the war, it was general to affix a figure '1' centrally on the windows of all first class compartments (including the appropriate corridor side windows). The colour of this figure was white or cream and it seems to have been a sort of adhesive label some 6in–8in high (details uncertain).

Very few LMS coaches were placed in service without class branding. Those that were turned out minus figures on the doors were usually 'neutral' vehicles (i.e. for first *or* third class use) and included such coaches as composite diners, unclassed vestibule coaches and so forth. There were not very many of them. After Nationalisation, of course, the present practice of labelling only the first class areas of the coach was introduced.

## The LMS Emblem

The circular LMS emblem—it was not a true coat of arms in the heraldic sense—was used continuously on coaching stock from 1923 to 1947. It was nominally 14in in diameter and the lettering and surrounds were gold until 1934/5 when they became yellow coloured. There was also a post war 'straw' version (Panel P). The principles underlying the use of the device do not seem to have been at all clear but the following observations are correct as far as they go.

The emblem was never used on non-corridor stock (except for some open electric stock) or on corridor coaches with a full complement of compartment doors. It was always applied to vestibule stock and specialised gangwayed stock (Kitchen Cars, Dining Cars, Sleeping Cars &c.). It was generally used on the later types of side corridor stock which had no compartment doors but there were numerous exceptions to this practice, generally third class coaches.

## INSIGNIA PLACING

The placing of the insignia on the coach side was relatively straightforward and only two methods were adopted, most details of which are incorporated in Figure 1 (page 6).

From 1923 to 1928, the letters 'LMS' appeared in the coach waist panel as near to the centre of the vehicle as possible. The exact configuration of the vertical beading dividers in the waist panel rarely affected the insignia placing and often the 'LMS' was off-centre in relation to the specific panel in which it appeared. The LMS emblem, if present, was located immediately below the LMS and midway between the lower waist beading, or pseudo beading, and the solebar.

During the same period, the running number appeared twice on the coach side, located towards each end of the vehicle and always in the waist panel—real or simulated. The precise placing of the numbers was a little variable. They were rarely located at the extreme end of the coach side, there generally being at least one compartment, or equivalent, 'outside' the running numbers. Running numbers were almost invariably placed 'inside' the end doors of vestibule coaches.

Descriptive wording during 1923-8 appeared in full in the waist panel thus:'LMS SLEEPING CAR' and was located so that the whole inscription was as near central as possible. The emblem was placed centrally beneath the descriptive wording.

From 1928 onwards, slight changes were made in this scheme. These coincided with the first Period II coach designs with low waists and this revised placing remained unaltered for the rest of the company's lifetime. The 'LMS' was now placed towards the left hand end of the coach and the running towards the right hand end. In fact, they occupied much the same places as had the two running numbers during 1923-8. With Period II and III coaches, the insignia was placed just below the waist lining—full or simplified—but it remained in the waist panel of coaches which had this feature, whether or not the livery was simplified or full.

The LMS emblem was still located as near to the centre of the coach side as possible. On Period II and III coaches it was placed midway between windows and solebar but the descriptive wording, if any, now flanked the emblem. At the same time, high waisted Period I and pre-group specialised vehicles continued to carry their descriptive wording in the waist panel surmounting the LMS emblem. This was also true of the Period II high waisted steel panelled composite sleeping cars which had no waist panel.

At all times, passenger class figures were placed centrally on the lower door panels, midway between lower waist beading and solebar on Period I coaches and usually midway between door handles and solebar on the remainder (see Figure 1).

## SUMMARY OF STYLES

As can be seen, most changes in livery approximately coincided with changes in coach styles and although there are exceptions to this pattern which are duly noted in the relevant chapters, it seems useful to give the following generalised summary of the livery of *new* coaches. Repainted pre-group coaches generally followed the same principles as far as possible.

*Period I*          Full livery, red ends, grey and black roofs, original insignia placing, small scroll type running numbers.

*Period II*        Full livery, red ends, grey and black roofs, final insignia placing, 'stretched' scroll type running numbers.

*Period III (1933—4)* Full livery, red ends, metallic roof finish, final insignia placing, unshaded sans-serif running numbers.

*Period III (1934—9)* Simple livery, red ends (1934-6), black ends (late 1936 onwards), metallic roof finish, final insignia placing, shaded sans-serif numbers. Insignia shade changed from gold leaf to chrome yellow.

*Period III (1940—9)* Simple livery (with straw lining from 1946 onwards), black ends, grey roof finish, final insignia placing, small scroll numbers with flat topped '3', flat topped '3' on outside doors, figure '1' on first class windows.

Wartime repainting was unlined and after Nationalisation, the LMS lettering and circular emblem were omitted but an 'M' prefix was often added to the running number, often in matching style.
*(below)

## SPECIAL LIVERIES

The LMS employed few special coach liveries. The most well known were the 'Coronation Scot' liveries of 1937 and 1939. The 1937 style was blue and silver and the 1939 style was red and gold, each version with its own lettering style.

The other distinctive livery was that applied to the three-car diesel articulated unit (see page 200). This was cream above the waist and bright red below the waist, the two colours being separated by a black line.

No evidence has been located of any other LMS coach liveries nor of any experimental liveries during 1923. It seems that, as with locomotives, so with coaches, Derby would brook no argument about their colour! The decision to adopt the MR coach livery as the LMS standard was taken early in May 1923 and actually *preceded* the decision to adopt the Midland Railway locomotive livery as well.

## PAINTING METHODS

The painting and finishing of LMS coaches was a somewhat complicated procedure and, perhaps surprisingly, involved rather more stages and considerably more time in shops than the procedure for finishing locomotives. The technique varied with the type of coach (steel or wood panelled) and, accordingly, the two will be considered separately. It should be noted that the details given below apply to new and fully repainted coaches *only*. In many other cases, coaches were given an intermediate 'rub down and re-varnish' between general repaints. The details given also apply to fully repainted pre-group coaches except for old vehicles with a limited life expectancy of up to four years. The latter, if due for repaint, were painted to a rather similar but less thorough specification. The details given are those issued by the Carriage and Wagon Department at Derby in September 1935. Paint mixes are referred to by numbers, the full specifications being given on pages 50 and 51.

### Steel Panelled Coaches (New or completely repainted)

Before assembly of the coach and prior to painting, all body and roof panels had the oil and grease removed with cotton waste and were then 'washed' with a 4:1 mixture of Methylated Spirit and Phosphoric Acid. Galvanised steel panels were similarly washed but with a rather more sophisticated mixture (Mix 1). The following day, all panels were painted with steel primer (Mix 2). Steel details (e.g. roof struts) were painted with bauxite (Mix 3) and wooden body framing was painted with lead colour paint (Mix 4). All key sheeting for floors was given two coats of Venetian Red bitumastic paint.

The backs of plywood panels which formed the ceilings of the compartments were painted with protective white paint (Mix 5) as was the back of the deal lagging which formed the interior surface of brake vans.

Pre-assembly work on the underframe and bogie consisted of the removal of rust and mill scale from the components by scraping or wire brush which process was immediately followed by coating the part concerned with bauxite (Mix 3) and a second coat of bauxite (Mix 3A). All parts of the underframe of non-welded coaches were painted before assembly but painting was not carried out before assembly in the case of underframes of welded construction. After welding, the weld itself was thoroughly cleaned and then coated with a primer for welded joints (Mix 6). After this, the complete underframe was painted in similar manner to the individual components of the non-welded underframe.

After assembly the insides of body and roof panels were painted with bauxite (Mix 3). Any new panels fixed to repaired coaches were, in addition, given two coats of steel primer (Mix 2) before fixing.

The exterior finishing procedure laid down in the paint schedules assumed that for repainted vehicles, the whole of the earlier paint coat had been burnt off or other 'suitable arrangements' made for the areas not so treated. Emphasis was also laid on the importance with steel coaches of removing all rust, scale &c. before repainting—using panel 'wash' if need be. Once the vehicle was prepared for painting/repainting, the daily sequence was as follows:

*Note

The authors have, regrettably, been unable to locate many usable drawings of LMS insignia. The little information which has survived is appended at Figure 4. Fortunately, the heights and placement of the various insignia *were* recorded and the perusal of photographs in this book together with Figure 1 will clarify this chapter. In addition, Panel O gives a good idea of the colour of the LMS insignia shading.

| Day 1 | One coat of steel primer (Mix 2). |
|---|---|
| Day 2 | Brush filling (Mix 7) applied over joints and screw holes, stopped up with hard stopping (Mix 8) when the brush filling was dry. |
| Day 3 | Repeat Day 2. |
| Day 4 | Faced down with stone blocks and water. Stopped up with hard stopping where necessary. |
| Day 5 | Faced down with composition rubbing blocks and water, left for at least four hours and afterwards given one coat of lead undercoat (Mix 9). |
| Day 6 | One coat of brown undercoat (Mix 10). |
| Day 7 | One coat of undercoat for lake (Mix 11) |
| Day 8 | One coat of standard LMS lake (Mix 12). |
| Day 9 | One coat of lake glaze (Mix 13). |
| Day 10 | Lined in black, yellow and red*, (Mixes 14–16) and transfers applied. |
| Day 11 | One coat of exterior finishing varnish over the whole body. |
| Day 12 | Coach allowed to harden. |
| Day 13 | Varnish flatted with pumice dust and water, second coat of varnish applied over the whole body. |
| Day 14 | Coach allowed to harden. |
| Day 15 | Varnish flatted again with pumice dust and water, third coat of varnish applied over the whole body except the ends. |
| Note: * | It is not known why red lining colour was specified in 1935. All available evidence indicates that this colour was omitted when the fully lined style of painting was terminated in 1933/4—but see note at end of chapter. |

During the above painting process, the roof was, after treating with steel primer, given two coats of metallic roof paint (Mix 17). At the same time, the complete chassis (including bogies and wheels) was painted with black enamel, lettered in white and then varnished. Battery boxes were painted with acid resisting black varnish. Door droplights were painted lake and varnished after being treated with wood primer (Mix 18).

Finally, the coach was allowed to harden for at least two more days after completion of all painting and before entering service was sparingly wax polished.

**Plate 68** This view of BCK No. 6792 (formerly 9485) was almost certainly taken at the time the vehicle was renumbered. Both numbers are painted (temporarily) on the right hand compartment window. The picture also shows one of the many locations adopted on LMS coaches for the short destination boards (see Figure 4-II). The coach itself is to D1850.

## Wood Panelled Coaches

By 1935, the LMS had ceased to make wood panelled coaches so the 1935 paint schedules refer solely to repainted vehicles. However, the procedure used was in all probability very little different to that employed during the building of wood panelled coaches. As far as can be deduced, the chassis was treated exactly as described for steel coaches and the differences apply solely to the body treatment. The schedules again assume that the whole of the previous paint was burnt off before repainting:

| | |
|---|---|
| *Day 1* | One coat of wood primer (Mix 18) over the whole body. |
| *Day 2* | One coat of a mixture of equal parts of brush filling (Mix 7) and lead undercoat (Mix 9) over the whole body. |
| *Day 3* | Two coats of brush filling (Mix 7) over the whole body except the ends. The coach was stopped up with hard stopping (Mix 8) at a convenient stage. |
| *Day 4* | Rubbed down with stone blocks and water. |
| *Day 5* | One coat of lead undercoat (Mix 9) plus further hard stopping (Mix 8) as necessary. |
| *Day 6* | Faced down with composition rubbing blocks and water, left for at least four hours and then given one coat of undercoat for lake (Mix 11). |
| *Days 7—14* | As for steel coaches Days 8—15. |

With wooden coaches, repainted roofs were given two coats of metallic roof paint (Mix 17) which represented a change in colour for many coaches from their original black/grey scheme (see page 41). If the roof needed repairing, the old canvas was removed, any repairs to the wood completed and all bare wood then treated with wood primer (Mix 18). Jointing paste was then applied and the new canvas stretched on. It was treated with a 50/50 mixture of boiled linseed oil and jointing paste and then covered with *three* coats of metallic roof paint (Mix 17). Presumably, when new, wood/canvas roofs had been similarly finished (except for the colour of the roof paint itself) during the 1923-32 period.

## PAINT SPECIFICATIONS

**Mix 1—Zinc Wash for galvanised panels**

| | |
|---|---|
| Methylated Spirits | 6gal |
| Toluol | 3gal |
| Spirits of Salts | ½gal |
| Carbon Tetrachloride | ½gal |

**Mix 2—Steel Primer**

| | |
|---|---|
| Oxide of iron in oil, type R, red shade | 88lb |
| Zinc Oxide white in oil | 2lb |
| Aluminium powder (fine varnish powder) | 10lb |
| Raw linseed oil | 10lb |
| Mixing varnish | 26lb |
| Genuine Turpentine | 16-20lb |
| Liquid Drier | Not more than 4lb |

**Mix 3—Bauxite Paint**

| | |
|---|---|
| Boiled linseed oil | 8lb |
| White Spirit | 6-10lb |
| Liquid Drier | 2-4lb |
| Bauxite residue in oil | 82lb |

**Mix 3A—Bauxite Paint (2nd coating)**

| | |
|---|---|
| Mixture No. 3 | 100lb |
| Black in oil | 6lb |

**Mix 4—Lead Colour**

Note: This mixture was the standard LMS lead colour for wagons and was intended to match British Standard Colour No. 32. Slight adjustments were permissible for matching purposes.

| | |
|---|---|
| Zinc White, composite pigment in oil | 112lb |
| Boiled linseed oil | 60lb |
| Black in oil | 3-4lb |
| Liquid Drier | 2-5lb |
| Mixing Varnish | 19lb |
| Ultramarine blue in oil | 3-4lb |

**Mix 5—Protective White Paint**

| | |
|---|---|
| Protective white paint paste | 112lb |
| Paste Driers in oil | Not more than 4lb |
| White Spirit | 4-8lb |
| Boiled linseed oil | 8-12lb |

**Mix 6—Primer for welded joints**

| | |
|---|---|
| Mixture No 2 | 80lb |
| Aluminium powder (fine varnish powder) | 10lb |
| Mixing varnish | 10lb |

**Mix 7—Brush Filling**

| | |
|---|---|
| Enamel filling | 112lb |
| Gold size, type A (dark) | 4-7lb |
| Mixing varnish | 4-7lb |
| Genuine Turpentine | 14-18lb |
| Raw linseed oil | Not more than 4lb |

**Mix 8—Hard Stopping**

| | |
|---|---|
| Enamel filling | 112lb |
| Gold size, type A (dark) | 4 parts  This to be added to the filling to bring to required consistency |
| Genuine Turpentine | 1 part |

**Mix 9—Lead colour undercoat**

| | |
|---|---|
| Protective white paint paste | 112lb |
| Liquid Drier | 9-12lb |
| White Spirit | 26-30lb |
| Black in oil | 9-10lb |
| Raw linseed oil | 4lb |

**Mix 10—Brown undercoat**

| | |
|---|---|
| Oxide of iron, in oil, type R, red shade | 100lb |
| Liquid Drier | 4-6lb |
| Mixing varnish | 26-30lb |
| Genuine Turpentine | 12-14lb |

**Mix 11—Undercoat for Lake**

| | |
|---|---|
| Mixture No. 10 | 95lb |
| Black in oil | 5lb |

**Mix 12—Standard LMS Crimson Lake**

| | |
|---|---|
| Standard LMS Lake (paste form) | 12lb |
| Mixing varnish | 4lb |
| Genuine Turpentine | 3-5lb |
| Liquid Drier | 1-3lb |

**Mix 13—Lake Glaze**

| | |
|---|---|
| Mixture No. 12 | 75lb |
| Exterior finishing varnish | 25lb |

**Mix 14—Black lining colour**

| | |
|---|---|
| Drop black in turpentine | 78lb |
| Gold size, type B (light) | 18-20lb |
| Genuine Turpentine | 6-8lb |
| Raw linseed oil | 8-10lb |
| Liquid Drier | Not more than 4lb |

**Mix 15—Yellow lining colour**

Note: This mixture was intended to match British Standard Colour 56 and adjustments to quantities were permissible for matching purposes.

| | |
|---|---|
| Lemon Chrome in oil | 18-20lb |
| Orange Chrome in oil | 2-3lb |
| Zinc White, composite pigment in oil | 15-20lb |
| Genuine Turpentine | 2-5lb |
| Liquid Drier | 6-10lb |

**Mix 16—Red lining colour**

| | |
|---|---|
| Vermilion substitute in oil | 100lb |
| Gold size, type B (light) | 8-12lb |
| Genuine Turpentine | 6-8lb |
| Liquid Drier | Not more than 4lb |

**Mix 17—Roof Paint**

| | |
|---|---|
| Protective white paint paste | 56lb |
| Thickened linseed oil | 4lb |
| Boiled linseed oil | 7lb |
| Mixing varnish | 7lb |
| White Spirit | 8-12lb |
| Black in oil | 8lb |
| Aluminium powder (fine varnish powder) | 7lb |
| Liquid Drier | Not more than 4lb |

**Mix 18—Wood Primer**

| | |
|---|---|
| Mixture No. 9 | 80lb |
| Aluminium powder (fine varnish powder) | 10lb |
| Mixing varnish | 10lb |

## INTERIOR FINISHING

The ceilings and compartments of new coaches were painted white, receiving three coats of undercoat and one finishing coat of gloss white enamel or eggshell gloss white enamel, depending on the type of coach. Repainted ceilings varied from receiving a simple touching up coat to a complete repaint involving burning off the old coat.

Interiors of brake vans, when new, were given one coat of knotting prior to any painting. Ceilings and sides down to 14in from the ceiling were then painted white as for compartment ceilings. The remainder of the interior was painted terra cotta (two coats) followed by terra cotta varnish. The terra cotta shade was mixed as follows:

| | |
|---|---|
| Zinc White, composite pigment in oil | 112lb |
| Venetian Red in oil | 38lb |
| Vermilion substitute in oil | 14lb |
| Yellow ochre in oil | 38lb |
| Orange Chrome in oil | 28lb |
| Liquid drier | 9lb |
| White Spirit | 8-12lb |
| Boiled linseed oil | 16-20lb |

The terra cotta varnish shade was a 9:1 mixture of the above paint and Mixing Varnish. Repainted coaches were given the same colour scheme, the number of coats depending on the state of the vehicle.

The interior finishing of compartments was mostly concerned with the preparation and finishing of the various wood veneers involved. The type and colour of the wood filler used varied according to the nature of the veneer, but could generally be obtained by a judicious blending of the three standard fillers, brown, walnut and white. The schedules laid down that only three types of wood *stain* were to be used, namely Vandyke crystals or Mahogany crystals (both water soluble) and Acid Brown (spirit soluble). Sanding down of the wood finishes was always done with grade 0 or grade 1 sandpaper. New work underwent the following stages of preparation and finishing:

| | |
|---|---|
| *1st Process* | Water stain applied to the bare wood and allowed to dry thoroughly. |
| *2nd Process* | Sandpapered, treated with wood filler and allowed to stand at least six hours. |
| *3rd Process* | Where matching up was necessary, a second coat of water stain was applied. |
| *4th Process* | One coat of spirit stain followed by sandpapering. The stain was mixed as follows: |

| | |
|---|---|
| Methylated Spirit | 1gal |
| Acid Brown | sufficient to produce the required shade. |
| Genuine Orange Shellac | 4 oz |

| | |
|---|---|
| *5th Process* | First coat of cellulose lacquer applied and allowed to stand overnight. |
| *6th Process* | Sandpapered and matched if necessary with a further coat of spirit stain. |
| *7th Process* | Second coat of cellulose lacquer applied and allowed to stand overnight. |
| *8th Process* | Third coat of cellulose lacquer applied and allowed to stand overnight. |
| | *Note: First class compartments had a fourth coat of cellulose lacquer applied.* |
| *9th Process* | Bodied up with levelling solution mixed 3:1 with cellulose lacquer and a small amount of thinners added. |
| *10th Process* | Finished with the mixture described in the ninth process. |
| *11th Process* | Burnishing carried out as and when necessary, using reviver obtained from the Derby paint laboratory. |

In general, interiors of repaired coaches were cleaned down with a weak solution of soda water and then brought back with reviver. Sometimes, if a finish had been damaged or had 'sunk' it was brought back with a 4:1 mixture of levelling solution and cellulose lacquer. If it was necessary to strip wood right down, the area had to be treated as new wood.

Finally, toilets were treated in yet a different way and the following procedure was employed:

| | |
|---|---|
| *Day 1* | One coat of wood primer for Scumblegrain, Duck Egg Green shade, applied by spray. |
| *Day 2* | One coat of Buffer Coat, Duck Egg Green shade, applied by spray. |
| *Day 3* | One coat of Scumblegrain, Duck Egg Green shade, applied by brush and stippled. |
| *Day 4* | Two 'mist' coats of cellulose lacquer, applied by spray. |
| *Day 5* | Finished by flatting with soap and water, using a mild abrasive if necessary. |
| | Note: Polished wood in toilets was treated as for the wood veneers in compartments. |

*Addenda*

Since this work was first published, evidence has been examined which proves that a fourth variety of the circular LMS emblem was provided for use with the blue painted 'Coronation Scot' sets of 1937. This emblem was identical to the normal version but with lettering and surrounds rendered in silver. Very few transfers could have been made—almost certainly one batch only—for only 27 coaches were painted in this style.

We have also established that with the advent of the simple livery in 1934, first class sleeping cars and dining cars continued to have the new style lining rendered in gilt with vermilion edging. This would undoubtedly explain the presence of red lining colour in the 1935 schedules—see page 49. On these coaches, the gilt version of the circular emblem continued in use, as did the use of gilt insignia.

# Chapter 4 - Train Formations and Coach Working

*Express Workings; Dining Cars; Sleeping Cars and Mail services; The coaches used;*
*Medium Distance and Excursion workings; Suburban and Local workings*

WHEN analysing the formation of LMS passenger trains, it is important to remember that the company was never particularly addicted to the operation of set train formations for long distance working. Set formations were more common for suburban working and short distance inter-district operation but there was little sacrosanct about even this class of traffic. Thus when describing LMS trains one can only discuss the matter in general terms.

## Express Workings

LMS express workings varied from massive regular formations of 16 coaches or more to quite lightly loaded trains. In general, the pre-group picture altered surprisingly little. Thus, for example, the heaviest tasks were usually to be found on the ex-LNWR lines while the Midland Division tended to perpetuate the shorter and more lightly loaded formations. The nature of the workings changed little in the early years and it was some time before rationalisation of services such as the running of Heysham boat trains to Euston instead of St. Pancras, began to be seen. The West Coast Joint Stock became wholly LMS owned as did the M&GSW element of the Midland-Scottish Joint Stock. Only the M&NB stock remained in shared ownership and this perpetuated the anomalous M&NB designation until 1928 when the coaches were divided between the LMS and LNER. However, since only two coaches (both SLFs) had been built after 1922 specifically for the M&NB services and both of them eventually came to the LMS, the effect of the division of the ex-M&NB stock was negligible as far as the LMS was concerned.

**Plate 69** This nostalgic view of the 'Royal Scot' dates from the early 1930s and illustrates the variety of types of coach to be seen even on the most prestigious LMS trains. From the foreground backwards can be identified the following types before the detail becomes unclear: Period II BFK to D1717; Early Period III BTK to D1851; RC to D1743 (LNWR styled); Period II Semi-RFO to D1719. The picture also shows the very characteristic carriage headboards—see Figure 4-I.

# TABLE 4a  SELECTED LMS EXPRESS TRAIN FORMATIONS

*Note:* The formations given below are only a representative sample of pre-war LMS trains as it would be impossible to give a complete coverage. Most of them have been extracted from the LMS passenger train marshalling books of the 1930s but some are based on the personal observation of enthusiasts. All formations are given in the down direction (where applicable) with locomotive to the left. The numbers adjacent to the name of the train refer to the footnotes.

| Train | Approx Date | Formation |
|---|---|---|
| The Royal Scot [1] | c. 1938 | BTK/TK/TO/RTO/RK/Semi-RFO/BFK/TO to Glasgow<br>RTO/RK/Semi-RFO/TO/BTK to Edinburgh |
| The Coronation Scot | 1937-9 | BTK/RTO/RK/RTO/RTO/RK/RFO/FK/BFK |
| The Night Scot [2] | 1938 | BG/SLF/SLF/SLF/RF/RCO/SLT/SLT/CK/TK/TK/BG |
| The Mid-Day Scot [3] | 1934 | BG/TK/RTO/RT/Semi-RFO/BFK/to Glasgow<br>BTK/Semi-RFO/RT/BTK/to Edinburgh<br>CK/BG to Aberdeen<br>TK/BFK to Whitehaven |
| The Royal Highlander [4]<br>Key: a. Glasgow<br>Key: b. Aberdeen<br>c. Inverness<br>d. Dundee<br>e. Oban(FO)<br>f. Crewe only | 1934 | BG/ /CK/SLC/BG/ /TK/CK/SLC/BG/ /BG/ /SLC/ /RC<br>   a       b              c              d      e      f |
| The West Coast Postal [5]<br>Key: a. Liverpool<br>b. Manchester<br>c. Preston<br>d. Stranraer<br>e. Perth(SO)<br>  Aberdeen(SX)<br>f. Aberdeen (one only<br>  to Perth (SO))<br>g. Glasgow | 1934 | BG//BG/POT//BG//POT/POT//POS/POS//POS/POS/POS/POT<br>a   b   c    d    e        f          g |
| Thames-Clyde Express [6] | 1938 | BTK/TK/TO/RTO/RK/RCO/CK/BFK |
| Thames-Forth Express [7] | 1938 | BTK/TK/TK/RTO/RF/CK/BTK |
| St Pancras-Glasgow [8]<br>night express | 1938 | BG/BG/CK/SLF/SLT/TK/TK/BG |
| The Irish Mail [9]<br>Key: a SO<br>b SX<br>c MFO | 1934 | BG/POS/POT/POS/POS/BG/BG/SLF/SLT/BTK/CK/<br>   a   b       b   a   a<br>CK/BTK/TK/BG/BG . . . . all to Holyhead<br>   c   b   b<br>plus: BG(SX) for Birkenhead<br>TK(SO) for Crewe<br>BG/BG(SO) for Manchester and Hereford |
| The Comet (Down) [10] | 1934 | BTK/TK/RTO/RF/CK/BFK to Manchester<br>BTK/CK/CO/RTO/RK/RFO/BFK to Liverpool<br>BCK to Birkenhead |
| The Comet (Up) [11]<br>(ex-Manchester) | 1934 | TK/RTO/RF/CK extra coaches<br>BFK/CK/RF/RTO/TK/BTK the main set<br>TK/BCK to Birmingham |
| The Merseyside Express [12] | 1934 | BTK/CK/BFO(lounge)/RFO/RF/CK/CK/RTO/RK/RTO/<br>BTK to Liverpool<br>TK/BFK to Southport |
| The Pines Express [13]<br>Key: a extra coaches<br>b Manchester—<br>  Birmingham set<br>c Main train<br>d Through coach<br>e GWR through coach | 1939 | TK/TO//BTK/CK/BTK//BCK/RCO/RT/BTK//BCK//BCK<br>          a            b                 c             d     e |
| The Peak Express [14]<br>The Palatine | c. 1937 | BTK/TK/TK/RT/RFO/BFK |
| 1005 Glasgow-Aberdeen<br>(1520 return) | 1938 | BTK/TK/CK/RT/RCO/CK/TK/BTK to Aberdeen<br>BTK/CK/BTK to Perth (northbound only) |
| 0800 Glasgow-Oban [15]<br>(1715 return) | 1938 | BTK/CK to Callander<br>RT/RCO/TK/BTK/CK/BTK to Oban |
| 1015 Inverness-Kyle<br>of Lochalsh [16]<br>(1735 return) | 1938 | CK/CK/RU/TO/TO/BG |

*Footnotes*

1. Standard formation—strengthened when necessary.
2. The RF/RCO inserted at Carlisle (northbound only). Often loaded heavier than this.
3. Formation given ex-Euston. The Aberdeen and Whitehaven coaches came off at Crewe and were replaced by through coaches from Plymouth to Glasgow. The train also carried a TK for Barrow (FSO), detached at Crewe.
4. This train ran in very similar formation for many years. There was no southbound 'Royal Highlander' at the time as the balancing workings of the coaches were too complex.
5. Formation given ex-Euston. During the journey there was considerable re-marshalling by addition/detachment of coaches.
6. The standard set, augmented by extra TKs on Saturdays. Conveyed through coaches for Leeds only (northbound) and for Bristol (southbound). There was also an extra BG(southbound) from Glasgow. Train reversed at Leeds so the BTK was always at the leading end when departing from either London or Glasgow.
7. The standard set. Up to four extra TKs (SO) in summer. Train reversed at Leeds (see note 6).
8. This was the 2130 St Pancras-St Enoch train. The leading BG was for Kilmarnock. During the journey the train picked up various through sections from Bristol and Leeds. The 2115 St Pancras-Edinburgh train was somewhat similar except for the replacement of the SLF/SLT by a single SLC.
9. This was the down train. The SLT contained facilities for serving light refreshments. The Birkenhead coaches came off at Chester and the Manchester/Hereford coaches at Crewe. The passenger carrying portion of the up train was identical but the complement of vans was slightly different.
10. Extra TK(SO) for Manchester and extra TK(MFO) for Birkenhead.
11. The up Comet did not carry a Liverpool portion.
12. This was the down train and carried an extra TK(FO). At times of peak traffic this train loaded to 15 or even 16 coaches. The up train ran less the leading BTK/CK and had a modified Southport section viz: BCK(SO)/BFK/TK/TK(MFO). The lounge brake was replaced by a BTK during Christmas and Easter weeks and the BTK/CK pair did not run on Saturdays.
13. An observed southbound formation at Birmingham (New Street) in March 1939.
14. Typical lightweight Midland Division trains—often with through sections added.
15. BCK added at Callander from Edinburgh to Oban. In the reverse direction, the Oban-Edinburgh portion was BCK/TK/BCK(SX) and the Callander-Glasgow section was two TKs(SO).
16. Usually carried odd vans (outward). The coaches seem to have been remarshalled for the return trip thus: TO/CK/RU/CK/TO/BG.

**Plate 70** This view of a southbound express at Oxenholme c. 1934 shows a typical LMS cavalcade of the inter-war years. There are examples of Period I, II, and III coaches, not to mention an 'all-steel' open third and an ex-LNWR double ended brake composite fourth from the rear. There do not appear to be any catering vehicles in the twelve coach train. Another interesting feature is that half the coaches are brake ended and at least four of the brakes are composites. The locomotive is Royal Scot 4-6-0 No. 6138 'The London Irish Rifleman'.

The most noticeable post-1922 change was the increasingly widespread use of open stock for third class passengers on express services. Until 1939, the LMS built open gangwayed stock almost on a 'one for one' basis with side corridor types and in so far as anything typified an LMS express train, the greater proportion of open coaches vis à vis that found on other lines might well be said to be the main characteristic. This matter is considered in more detail in Chapter 9.

The LMS laid down precise marshalling instructions for all its passenger services. These filled quite substantial sized booklets and space permits only a few examples to be given. They are listed in Table 4a.

From the details in the Table, a few generalisations can be drawn. First class accommodation tended to represent some 20—30 per cent. of the capacity of the train in terms of vehicles (not counting diners) and was usually marshalled towards one end of the formation. This was generally the London end for those trains operating from the capital city. The dining cars were usually positioned between the first and third class areas of the train, although in several instances, e.g. the 'Royal Scot', some of the bigger formations were, in effect, two trains in one with two sets of diners, first class sections &c. Short through portions attached to the major trains were located at whichever end was more convenient from the point of view of traffic working. For the most part, these through sections contained the only first class seats which were located away from the main first class areas.

A study of contemporary working instructions reveals that the LMS, in its heyday, provided a considerable number of through workings to smaller traffic centres off the main trunk routes, although the company did not favour the 'slip' coach method of operation. A single through coach would almost invariably be a corridor brake composite of which the LMS built very many (see Chapter 8). Typical through portions consisting of more than one coach might be CK + BTK or TK + CK + BTK or, possibly even TK + BCK. It seems to have been somewhat more rare for open stock to have been utilised on these through portions than on the main train itself.

**Plate 71** This train leaving St. Pancras behind 4-6-0 No. 5570 'New Zealand' is composed mainly of Stanier coaches in simple livery, but the first vehicle, probably a strengthener, is a Period II open third in full livery. The date of the picture is probably 1938/9, but may just be post-war.

**Plate 72** This impressive shot taken at Bushey troughs c. 1939, shows a 17 coach train headed by a red streamlined 4-6-2 No. 6225 'Duchess of Gloucester'. The train itself is 'The Royal Scot' and the leading seven coaches are the Edinburgh portion. The ten coach Glasgow section at the rear is wholly made up from Period III coaches but as can be seen, the Edinburgh section, apart from the Period III kitchen car, is formed from Period I and II coaches. The leading two vehicles are a BFK to D1717 and a semi-RFO to D1707. Behind the kitchen car are marshalled a Period I unclassed open diner (D1706) and three Period II fully panelled 60ft coaches. The Glasgow formation cannot be identified. (Photomatic)

## Dining Cars

Little generalisation can be made about the use of dining cars. The LMS was the greatest user of dining cars in Britain and built a considerable variety of vehicles in order to satisfy the various different needs of its patrons. The simplest form of refreshment vehicle was the Tea car for light corridor service and the like. These coaches were not LMS-built vehicles but were generally similar to pre-group corridor thirds. A small number of LMS standard Buffet Cars was, however, built (see page 80). These seem to have been somewhat experimental and were not widespread; the growth of buffet type facilities being more of a post-nationalisation phenomenon. The most common LMS type of single-unit dining vehicle was the composite kitchen dining car. The LMS built some 30 of these coaches in addition to the many pre-group examples of the genre such as the handsome ex-LNWR and ex-MR coaches or the equally distinctive ex-Pullman vehicles taken over in Scotland. Many of the pre-group coaches were originally first class cars but by the 1930s had become classified as 'common' diners—i.e. for first *or* third class use (BR code RU). They were in particular demand at weekends and in holiday periods.

Where the services demanded more than one vehicle, there was a little more consistency in approach. First class kitchen diners, of which the LMS built very many, were almost always marshalled with a 42 seat vestibule third class diner and, sometimes, with two of these coaches. Third class kitchen diners generally ran with a vestibule composite or, somewhat more rarely, a full vestibule first diner. The respective seating capacities of these combinations were usually as follows: RF + RTO: 24F + 42T; RT + RCO: 18F + 48T; RT + RFO: 42F + 30T.

Continuing up the scale, where even more meals were envisaged, the full kitchen car was employed. This type of vehicle was very rare before the grouping but the LMS built very many of them. This policy was probably allied to the building of large quantities of open stock already mentioned on page 55. The kitchen car was marshalled between, at the very least, a full vestibule first and a full vestibule third diner. Sometimes two vestibule third diners would be provided while in many instances the semi-open firsts (see page 9) were marshalled next to a kitchen car. Typical kitchen car formations and seating capacities would therefore include the following: RTO + RK + RFO: 42F + 42T; Semi-RFO + RK + RTO + RTO: 18F + 84T. Kitchen cars were also used widely in excursion trains which, when formed as they often were from open stock, lent themselves readily to the insertion of one or two kitchen cars somewhere in the formation.

For a more detailed account of LMS dining car services of the 1930s, readers are referred to the *Railway World* for January/February 1968 and February/June 1969.

## Sleeping Cars and Mail services

Sleeping car and mail services were fairly straightforward. Apart from the notable example of the 'Night Scot' (Table 4a), there seems to have been no other regular LMS train composed mainly of sleeping cars. The most usual policy was to provide a certain number of sleeping cars (probably one or two each of first and third class) supplemented by side corridor third class accommodation. It was, however, somewhat rare to find much first class accommodation, other than the sleeping cars themselves, in LMS sleeping car trains. Composite sleeping cars seem to have been used almost exclusively on an individual basis as single through coach workings to various small centres or as the sole sleeping car in an otherwise fairly normal train. As through coaches they would generally run attached to a convenient main line overnight service for the bulk of the distance involved.

The third class sleeping cars were first introduced on September 24, 1928, on the following routes: Euston to Aberdeen, Edinburgh, Glasgow, Holyhead, Inverness and Stranraer; St Pancras to Edinburgh and Glasgow. The charge for berth reservation was 6/- (30p) (between England and Wales) or 7/- (35p) (between England and Scotland). Compartments were reserved for ladies only if necessary—and where this was possible by grouping four bookings for ladies together—and preferences for upper or lower berths were granted as far as possible.

Turning now to mail services, a few points can be made. The celebrated "West Coast Postal' service (Table 4a) was, of course, an entirely non-passenger train comprised of mail vans and full brakes. However, it was not entirely typical of mail workings on the LMS. A much more common solution seems to be that represented by the 'Irish Mail' (Table 4a), where the train formation was a combination of passenger and mail coaches. Of course, a considerable mail traffic was also handled by normal trains—generally utilising luggage compartments or by adding an extra full brake or two to the normal formation (particularly overnight services). It should be noted that only where TPO facilities were necessary, were specially designed mail coaches incorporated in the formation. Even so, these vehicles ranged pretty far and wide, penetrating well into the more remote areas of Scotland and Wales.

## The coaches used

With regard to the vehicles used on LMS express services, it was, as has been mentioned, somewhat rare for the LMS to build coaches for a specific service and the most usual policy for the newest vehicles to be rostered immediately to the most important services. Thus, for example, the palatial Period II corridor thirds to D1782 were immediately put in service on the 'Royal Scot' train as had been the luxury lounge brakes and semi-open firsts (page 9) a year or so before. However, as these coaches were superseded by later stock, they became more widely scattered through the system. Similarly on the Midland Division, as new dining cars were built during the 1930s so the older Midland cars were either scrapped or relegated to lesser workings. In general, Scotland seemed to get less than its share of new gangwayed coaches, especially diners, but this may have been because many of the services operating into Scotland were formed from vehicles based south of the border.

The LMS only introduced complete set trains for the 'Coronation Scot' services of 1937 and afterwards. These were of unusual interest and are covered in detail in Chapter 13. However, in 1933, the company sent a set of coaches on exhibition to North America which seems to have escaped much notice. It was a collection of vehicles assembled for the Chicago World Fair of 1933 and was aimed at showing off LMS locomotive and coaching practice. The engine was a member of the Royal Scot class while the train, masquerading as the 'Royal Scot' set, was in fact made up from typical examples of LMS type coaches. Being purely an exhibition train, its formation in terms of vehicle types bore little resemblance to a typical LMS express least of all the 'Royal Scot' itself! The coaches themselves were an interesting mixture of all three periods of LMS design, the Stanier era having just commenced, and the details were as follows:

| | |
|---|---|
| Period II | 57ft Corridor brake first No. 5005 (D1717) |
| Period I | (LNWR styled) 68ft First class sleeping car No. 350 (D1705) |
| Period III | 65ft Third class sleeping car No. 585 (D1863) |
| Period I | (Single window) 57ft First class lounge brake No. 5003 (D1741) |
| Period II | 57ft Corridor/vestibule Car No. 1030 (D1719) |
| Period III | 60ft All-electric kitchen only car No. 30073 (D1855) |
| Period II | 60ft Vestibule third class dining coach No. 7764 (D1795) |
| Period III | 57ft Corridor brake third No. 5465 (D1851) |

All the coaches were, of course, in fully lined livery and carried their new (i.e. 1932/3 series) running numbers in the 1930-32 stretched scroll type characters. As far as is known, no other LMS coaches were renumbered using this style of figure.

## Medium Distance and Excursion workings

Between the extremes of long distance express and short distance local and suburban workings was a range of medium distance services and excursion workings of such variety that it almost defies analysis in the space available. Basically, these services made use of short sets of gangwayed stock formed into what the company called 'Inter-Corridor' sets. These were generally formed either BTK/CK/BTK or BTK/CK/TK/BTK although in many cases two composites or an odd open coach would find their way into the set. Such three- or four-coach sets would also be used—possibly in pairs— to provide, say, an additional express train, often with a dining car set inserted for good measure. Alternatively, one such inter-corridor set might form a through section attached, intermediately, to some other long distance working. For example, the Lancashire-Scotland services via the Midland route frequently utilised a three- or four-coach set which was attached at Hellifield to the main train—except on summer Saturdays when it expanded to a full train of somewhat indeterminate formation.

Excursion workings often employed open stock throughout, although some examples included the odd side corridor composite or composite brake. Kitchen cars could be inserted if necessary in such excursion sets. There were also, however, many excursion workings which employed non-corridor stock, often without either lavatory or refreshment facility.

It is not readily possible to generalise about the coaches used in these intermediate services. Both pre-group and LMS standard coaches of side corridor type were to be found in the inter-corridor sets, sometimes a mixture of both. It was, however, more usual to find the older stock in such sets rather than the very latest coaches, although the latter did sometimes appear. Most vestibule excursion sets were of mainly LMS standard stock since open stock was more of an LMS development than a pre-group feature. Table 4b gives some fairly characteristic examples of LMS medium distance workings of the 1930s.

## TABLE 4b SELECTED LMS MEDIUM DISTANCE WORKINGS

*Note:* The English trains listed are based mainly on contemporary observation by enthusiasts during the 1930s. The Scottish details have been extracted from official records. In some cases pre-group coaches can be identified. These are indicated thus:

(W) — LNWR coach
(M) — Midland coach
(S) — N. Staffs coach
(Y) — LYR coach

| Train Type | Formation |
|---|---|
| Typical Euston-Wolverhampton sets: | BTK/CK/RF(W)/TO/CK/BTK |
| | BTK/TK/FK/RCO/RT/TK/BTK |
| | BTK/RTO/TO/RK/RFO/FK/BTK |
| | BTK/CK/FK/RFO/RT(W)/TO/BTK |
| Typical Western Division 'Inter-Corridor' sets: | |
| Holyhead, Manchester & Liverpool | BTK(W)/CK(W)/BTK(W) |
| London and Rugby | BTK/CK(W)/CK(W)/BTK |
| Crewe and Llandudno[1] | BTK/CL(W)/CL(W)/BTK(W) |
| Typical Western Division 'Extra Trains' for | BCL(W)/TL(W)/TL(W)/FL(W)/TL(W)/BCL(W) |
| excursion and other work: | BT(S)/4 × T(S)/C(S)/BT(S) |
| | BCK(W)/4 × TO/BTO |
| | BCK(W)/3 × TK(W)/2 × CK(W)/BTK(W) |
| | BTO/7 × TO/BTO |
| Typical Central Division Extra or | BTO/4 × TO/RK/4 × TO/BCK(Y) |
| Excursion sets: | BT(Y)/C(Y)/6 × T(Y)/BT(Y) |
| Typical 'London Rd & Buxton' set: | BTO/CO/FO/FO/CO/BTO |
| Typical Midland Corridor sets: | BTK/CK/TK(W)/BTK(M) |
| | BTK(M)/TK/TK (W)/BFK(M) |
| | BTK/TK/CK/BTK(M) |
| | BTK(W)/CK/TO/BTK |
| Typical Midland Division Excursion sets: | BCL(M)/4 × TL(M)/BCL(M) |
| | BT(M)/4 × TL(M)/BT(M) |
| | BCK(M)/6 × TO/BTO |
| | BCK(M)/4 × TO/TO(M)/2 × TO/BTO |
| Typical Scottish sets: | |
| Carlisle-Perth | BTK/TK/TK/CK/CK/TK/BTK |
| Carlisle-Stranraer[2] | RU/BTK/CK/BTK |
| Dundee-Glasgow/Perth | BTK/CK/BTK to Glasgow plus non-corridor |
| | Inter-District set to Perth |
| Edinburgh-Perth | TK/BCK/BTK/BCK/TK |
| Glasgow-Stranraer[3] | BTK/CK/BTK/BG |
| Inverness-Aberdeen | TK/CK/TK/BG |
| Perth-Inverness[4] | RU/TK/CK/BG via Carr Bridge plus CK/BG |
| | via Forres |
| Wick/Thurso-Inverness[5] | TK/CK/BG from Wick plus BCK/TK from Thurso |

1. The mixture of corridor/non-corridor stock was not uncommon.
2. This would often be added to a through boat train working from England.
3. Sometimes an Inter-Corridor set plus diner would be used, depending on the time of service.
4. Such a set would almost always run with through coaches from further south to supplement the seating.
5. A dining car would often run attached to such a train between Helmsdale and Inverness.

## Suburban and Local workings

LMS locomotive-hauled stopping services were operated by a variety of non-corridor coaches together with older pattern (usually pre-group) gangwayed vehicles. Non-corridor stock was generally of suburban type but the LMS built a reasonable quantity of lavatory stock for the longer distance inter-district workings. This was a direct continuance of pre-group practice where the non-corridor lavatory type vehicle was a favoured type for services other than for purely suburban commuting purposes. With the exception of the London, Tilbury & Southend line, the North London services and the Cathcart Circle services of Glasgow (see Chapters 10 and 11), little effort was made by the LMS to introduce standard non-corridor coaches in set formations. Thus, local trains tended to be a somewhat indiscriminate mixture of pre- and post-group stock. Nevertheless, it was quite common to assemble 'sets' of coaches in the various districts and brand them as such on the coach ends. Euston-Bletchley-Northampton sets were unaccountably branded as 'Euston and *Watford* set No. X'. However, locally formed sets were frequently made up from non-matching stock of various ages, sometimes including gangwayed coaches. Suburban formations varied considerably from area to area. Many of the Midland Division London area services were formed of three-coach sets often in Paris, while at Euston six, later seven, coach sets were the rule. In contrast, 11 coach sets were used on LTS services.

The non-corridor LMS standard lavatory stock was, theoretically, introduced as an attempt to provide new inter-district sets but the coaches themselves rarely ran in set trains, often being used as one-for-one replacements of roughly comparable pre-group vehicles. This one-for-one replacement of old stock was quite a common feature of LMS operating practice, noticeably so in the case of first class and composite coaches. This was to ensure that the first class passenger was given the first benefit of better accommodation and often resulted in local trains formed basically from pre-group third class coaches but with LMS standard first class or composite coaches in place of the older type equivalents.

By the 1930s, non-corridor stock seems to have started to go out of favour for the longer distance inter-district services. No non-corridor lavatory coaches were built by the LMS after 1930, except for four vehicles for the LT&S services, and the use of older inter-corridor sets on medium distance stopping services gradually increased. Even so, the mixture continued as before and one could often see even non-lavatory stock in quite long distance workings. Non-corridor stock was also extensively used for excursion working (because of its carrying capacity) and was often mixed indiscriminately with vestibule stock.

The actual formation of local trains was equally variable. The main differences were found between the Divisions. Thus, the Midland Division tended to employ a basic two-coach unit of brake third plus composite and augment it where necessary. The Western Division and many districts in Scotland, preferred slightly more third class space in their basic

**Plate 73** A 15 coach Euston-Manchester train approaching Tring c. 1946 behind 4-6-0 No. 5552 'Silver Jubilee'. The train itself is two-thirds composed of Period III stock, but among the earlier coaches can be identified a Midland clerestory corridor, a Period I 'twin-window' vestibule and, probably, at least one ex-LNWR coach.

**Plate 74** The 10.25 a.m. Euston-Windermere train ascends Camden bank in 1946 behind rebuilt Royal Scot No. 6116 'Irish Guardsman'. In spite of the fact that the LMS was then 23 years old, the first ten coaches are a really interesting mixture viz: LNWR corridor composite c. 1910; LNWR corridor brake c. 1910; LMS Period I composite; LMS Period II vestibule third; LMS Period I vestibule third; LMS Period I composite (or third); LNWR full brake; two LNWR corridors of 1913 vintage and a Period III brake!

formations and tended to utilise a three-coach unit of brake third, composite, brake third. The ex-LYR areas preferred even more third class seats and it was by no means rare in this division to have a first/third ratio of something like one composite to every six or seven third class coaches.

Of course, much variation reflected the nature of the districts in which the trains were operating and one should not assume that the Midland Division had no services with a high proportion of thirds or that in Lancashire there were few first class travellers. Quite the contrary, in fact, since the Central Division was responsible for running some of the high class Club trains as well as its predominantly third class suburban services. Thus, as might be expected, the proportion of third class accommodation bore a strong correlation to the amount of industrialisation in the operating areas of the LMS.

For branch services, the LMS, like other companies, often employed push-pull trains, referred to by the company as motor-fitted trains. Many of the vehicles used were of pre-group origin but the company also built its own motor-fitted stock. Apart from the extra vacuum fittings and the windows in the driving ends of the coaches, the vehicles were all but indistinguishable from conventional non-corridor stock. The usual formations, involving two coaches, were driving trailer third and composite or driving trailer third and third. Many services were operated by a single driving trailer third and locomotive.

The LMS did not have a large network of electrified lines but for the London Suburban (ex-LNWR), Liverpool-Southport and Mersey/Wirral lines, there were built several sets of electric multiple-unit stock. The electrified Manchester, South Junction and Altrincham lines were also operated by LMS-pattern vehicles. All the electric coaches and their associated set formations are considered together in Chapter 16.

**Plate 75** This BR vintage picture taken at Carlisle towards the end of steam services still shows a typical LMS local train. It is composed of three Period III corridors (two brake thirds and a composite) but with a non-corridor third as a strengthener. This type of working was very characteristic of later LMS and early BR practice for stopping trains, other than purely suburban services.

# Part Two

# Coach Types Analysed

# Chapter 5 - Basic Dimensions and Assumptions

IN the chapters following this, the various generic types of coach built by the LMS are described and listed. Because of the high degree of standardisation of LMS coaches it is possible to take as read many basic features of the designs and thus confine the description of the types and the tabulated data to those aspects peculiar to the coaches under discussion. It is hoped that this will simplify the understanding of the subject.

## Dimensions

The following basic table of dimensions can be taken as standard for all coaches of the lengths specified:

| Length over Headstocks | 69' | 68' | 65' | 62' | 60' | 58' | 57' | 54' | 51' | 50' |
|---|---|---|---|---|---|---|---|---|---|---|
| Bogie Type | 6wh | 6wh | 4wh | 4wh | 4wh | 4wh | 4wh | 4wh | 4wh | 4wh |
| Bogie wheelbase | 12'6" | 12'6" | 9'0" | 9'0" | 9'0" | 9'0" | 9'0" | 9'0" | 9'0" | 9'0" |
| Bogie centres | 46'0" | 45'0" | 48'0" | 45'6" | 43'6" | 41'6" | 40'6" | 37'6" | 34'6" | 33'6" |
| Buffer type Oval (O) or Round (R) | O | O | O | O | R | R | R | R | R | R |

Because of this standardised pattern, the only dimensions quoted in the summary tables will be length over headstocks, width over projections and height from rails to rooftop.

Typical window and panel dimensions of all three periods of design are given at Figure 1, page 6.

## Assumptions

Unless stated otherwise it may safely be assumed that the following styling and other features were common to all LMS coaches to be described:

*Period I coaches:*

Body: High waisted, wood panelled, fully beaded sides and matchboard ends.

Roof: Wood construction with canvas covering and carrying an end to end longitudinal rainstrip at each side.

Roof vents: Torpedo pattern.

Door vents: 3-element louvre type, but hooded metal on coaches built with MR locks/handles &c.

Corridor connections: British standard (scissors type).

Livery when new: Fully lined out, original insignia styles and placings, grey and black roof, red coach ends.

*Period II coaches:*

Body:
a. Gangway stock: Low waisted, 'square windowed', wood or steel panelled. The type of panelling and presence or absence of beading will be specified in the narrative.
b. Non-corridor: High waisted, steel panelled, 'square' windows.

Roof: Wood/Canvas/Rainstrip.

Roof vents: Torpedo pattern.

Door vents: Hooded metal (steel panelling), louvre type (wood panelling).

Corridor connections: British standard (scissors type).

Livery when new: Fully lined out but without waist panel, stretched scroll figures and later insignia placing, grey and black roof, red coach ends.

*Period III coaches:*

Body: Totally flush clad without raised window mouldings, rounded window corners, steel panelled.

Roof: Metal clad 'ribbed' pattern.

Roof vents: Shell pattern.

Door vents: Hooded metal.

Window vents: Sliding type with *two* moving elements.

Corridor connections: British standard (suspended gangway type).

Livery: Simplified lining, shaded block style figures and later insignia placing, metallic roof finish (pre-war), grey roof finish (post-war), black ends from late 1936, 'straw' lining from 1946.

The principal exceptions to the above summary were the early Stanier coaches. Some of these came out in full livery and some had the earlier sliding ventilator with one moving element. A few had torpedo ventilators and there were other slight points of difference. All these aspects are covered in the summary tables. Stanier coaches in full livery generally carried unshaded block style figures.

In all subsequent chapters, the various coaches are listed in the form of standardised summary tables at the end of the narrative. These give all details supplementary to those which may be deduced from the above list of assumptions. The tables themselves are, in most cases, supplemented by diagrammatic plans of the coaches themselves to show the interior layout of the vehicle.

In most summary tables, the first and last withdrawal dates for each coach 'lot' are given. The dates are London Midland Region four-week periods and relate to the normal planned coach withdrawals. They do not generally take account of premature withdrawals due to accident or wartime enemy action.

# Chapter 6 - Sleeping Cars

*First Class coaches; Third Class coaches; Composite coaches; Summary Table*

IN numerical terms, sleeping cars were among the less common standard coaches, only 253 being built to LMS designs and this total includes quite a number built after 1947. At the same time, the design phases are interesting especially since the early first class cars represent what might be called the 'final flowering' of the LNWR design ideas. Moreover, the first two varieties of third class coach were each responsible for introducing a new length of vehicle to the LMS.

## FIRST CLASS COACHES

There were but four types of LMS first class sleeping car and only two really different styles. The first two types perpetuated the LNWR styling except for the depth of waist panel, while the last two types were Stanier pattern coaches. All were 12 wheel vehicles, the Period III coaches being 69ft long and the earlier ones 68ft long.

Towards the end of the pre-group era, the LNWR had built for itself and for the West Coast Joint Stock some massive 68ft long semi-elliptical roof sleeping cars (see Frontispiece) and the first two LMS types were logical developments of this final LNWR design. They were built in various batches between 1924 and 1930. Ten were to D1739 while the remainder were to D1705. There was little difference between the two diagrams but the distinguishing aspects may have been significant. Both versions had 12 berths but the earlier coaches had the attendant's and the lavatory compartment both at the same end and 'outside' the entrance vestibule. In D1705, the attendant was placed 'inside' the vestibule entrance adjacent to the sleeping compartments and at the opposite end of the coach to the lavatory, which remained 'outside'.

**Plate 76** This is the pioneer LMS first class sleeping car to D1739 from which the more numerous D1705 was derived. Coach No. 10389, later No. 308. Note the smaller than usual descriptive lettering.

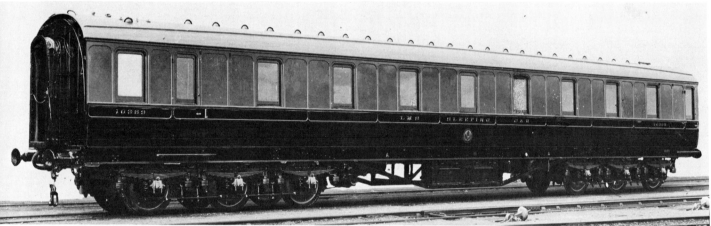

**Plate 77** Passenger compartment of the pioneer LMS first class sleeping car, No. 10389 to D1739. Note the heavy timber veneers and the hinged toilet fixture against the right hand wall of the compartment.

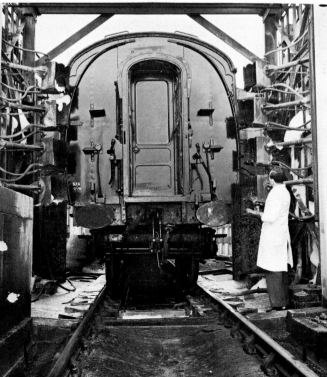

**Plate 78** First class sleeping car from D1739 under the washing plant at Willesden in 1956. This shows the non-standard end panelling given to the early post-grouping 12-wheel stock.

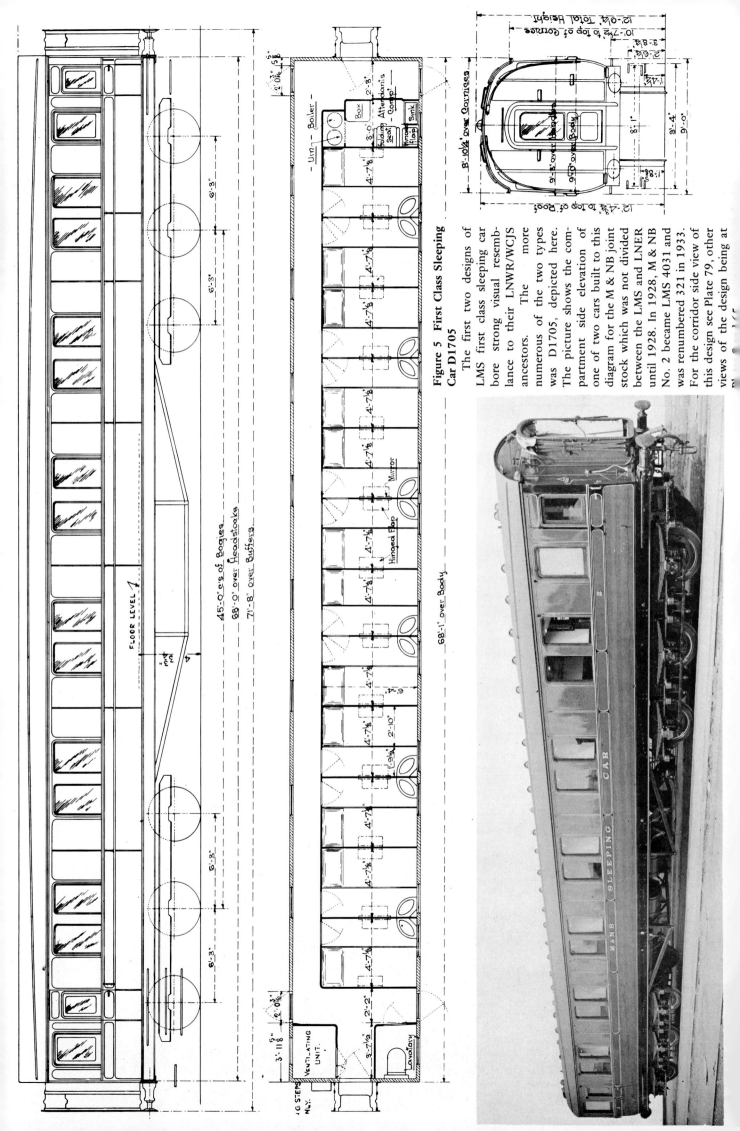

**Figure 5  First Class Sleeping Car D1705**

The first two designs of LMS first class sleeping car bore strong visual resemblance to their LNWR/WCJS ancestors. The more numerous of the two types was D1705, depicted here. The picture shows the compartment side elevation of one of two cars built to this diagram for the M & NB joint stock which was not divided between the LMS and LNER until 1928. In 1928, M & NB No. 2 became LMS 4031 and was renumbered 321 in 1933. For the corridor side view of this design see Plate 79, other views of the design being at

**Plate 79** LMS Car No. 10370. This picture also shows a D1705 car but note that between the windows the panels are now of double width compared with M & NB No. 2. This coach became LMS 351 in 1932/3.

This re-positioning of the service areas seems to have represented a partial reversion to LNWR practice since this company, of course, always placed everything 'inside' the entrances. This policy was, as many will appreciate, traceable back to the original LNWR 12 wheel sleeping cars with very narrow vestibule entrances which left room for little more than the corridor connections. It is possible, therefore, that the predominantly LNWR staff of the early LMS sleepers objected to the new position of their compartment. It separated them from their passengers and, being over the bogie, may have given a less comfortable ride. Moreover, the 'outside' location of the attendant was more of a Midland idea which may, in the circumstances have given rise to its own particular problems—Wolverton exterior styling notwithstanding! At all events, D1705 went back to the earlier LNWR arrangement as far as the attendant was concerned. Many more of these were built than the D1739 version and the design remained current for some five years or more.

The detail differences between the two types were more subtle. Both had fully beaded exteriors but later examples of D1705 introduced a single panel of double width between the windows rather than the characteristic double panels of the earlier coaches. Neither type had door ventilators but D1705 did have a small panel above the droplight which suggests that a door ventilator may, originally, have been intended.

Inside the coaches there were again small differences. Both had heavily wood panelled interior finishings, probably mahogany, and contemporary illustrations reveal the ornate finish of these elegant sleeping cars. The sleeping berths themselves were alternately right and left handed when entering via the corridor door and the bedheads were positioned against the corridor wall. Within the compartments, the later versions were fitted with corner handbasins below the window as opposed to the combination toilet cabinets against the compartment wall in the D1739 cars. The later cars also had hinged flap shelves above the berths and extra luggage shelves adjacent to the vestibule entrance.

These coaches represented almost exactly half the total of LMS design first class sleeping cars. Lot 341 was additionally interesting as its cars were built for the M&NB joint stock in 1927. After this stock was divided between the LMS and LNER in 1928, both the cars eventually came to the LMS but during the first year or two of their life it must have seemed a little strange to observe an almost pure Wolverton coach in M&NB livery.

These early sleeping cars were robust coaches. They were refurbished inside to Stanier standards of comfort in the 1930s and in this form lasted well into BR days, ultimately succumbing to BR designs in 1962. Car 350 went to America in 1933 with the 'Royal Scot' train while car 342 achieved a certain amount of immortality by being used in the Prime Minister's train during the second world war—it was still in fully lined livery at the time.

Stanier pattern first class sleepers were introduced in 1935 to D1926 and saw an increase in length from 68ft to 69ft. Their interior arrangement was very similar to the earlier cars except that they went back completely to the old LNWR

**Plate 80** LMS Car No. 352, the pioneer Stanier first class sleeping car to D1926, shown in simple livery. A similar car (377) was modified and repainted for the 1939 Coronation Scot tour of America. Note the recessed door handles to allow for a slight increase in body width.

**Plate 81** LM Region Car No. M387M, the post-nationalisation development to D2166 of the Period III sleeping car. This view was taken at Wolverton in 1968 and shows the BR blue/grey livery which most of this batch acquired. Note, compared with Plate 80, the absence of hooded door vents, completely flush roof, BR type vents and roof top air conditioning apparatus.

**Plate 82** This picture shows a typical Stanier first class sleeping compartment. The upper berth was added in 1942 but other than this, the style of compartment hardly altered between 1935 and the final versions in 1952. The upper berth was removed in about 1949/50. The interior layout of post-Nationalisation twin berth thirds was very similar.

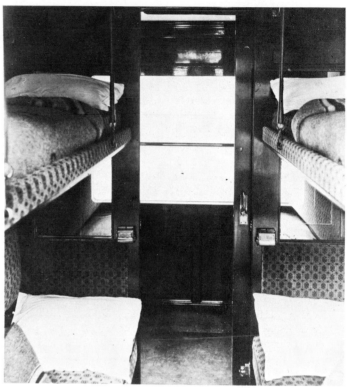

**Plate 83** A compartment of the convertible third class coaches (D1709) as made up for night use. The arrangement of berths in the fixed four-berth coaches was similar except there was no window to the corridor behind the heads of the berths.

**Plate 84** LMS Car No. 8617 represents the later, steel-panelled version of D1709 from the corridor side. Note the single waist lining at the 'low waisted' level, the changed insignia placing and the 'stretched' scroll running numbers. The coach was renumbered 580 in 1932/3.

arrangement and the entrances were at the extreme ends of the car. Externally they were typical Stanier vehicles but, as with all Stanier sleepers, the lower edges of the compartment windows were at a higher level than those on the normal Stanier gangwayed coach. Door handles were recessed to enable a little extra body width to be obtained within the limits of the loading gauge. In relation to their size, they were not unduly heavy coaches, being of welded construction.

The LMS clearly regarded these new Stanier cars as the last word in sleeping car luxury. Special attention was paid to smooth and silent riding. The underside of the floor was sprayed with almost half an inch of asbestos to act as an anti-noise blanket, while the floors themselves were covered with layers of cork, felt, linoleum and carpet.

The usual compartment fittings were provided (hot and cold water, towel rails, clothes hangers, luggage racks, shelves and mirrors) and much use was made of plated metal fittings. The whole interior decor was considerably brighter than the earlier cars and four decorative schemes were utilised. Each compartment had a distinctive colour scheme (yellow, green, blue or beige) with rugs and bedcovers to match, the object of the designer being to make the compartment conform, within the limits of space, to the standard first class hotel bedroom. Timber finishes used were teak, sycamore or walnut.*

The compartment heating and ventilation was of the passenger controlled 'Thermotank' type with punkah louvres for each berth. These were of the 'Thermo-Reg.' pattern which gave passengers control, not only of the volume and temperature of the incoming air, but also the direction of discharge. They were located over the bed head.

The LMS seems to have referred to this system as 'air conditioning' and, as far as can be ascertained, fitted it to the earlier sleepers in place of the old rotary electric fans.

In 1939, car 377 of the first Stanier series was refurbished and fully air conditioned and went to the USA with the 'Coronation Scot' special train to act as an accommodation car for the staff. For this visit it was repainted in the Crimson/Gold livery and given the streamlined fairings to conceal the underframe and match the special set of coaches. It returned to this country in December 1946.

From May 1942, some of these Stanier cars were experimentally converted to a two-berth arrangement in the end compartments. This was in order to increase the passenger accommodation to 14 without increase of train weight. A second berth was installed above the existing bed and access was via a short ladder. The LMS converted further coaches to this pattern in 1943 and the surviving records indicate that at least 36 cars were scheduled for this operation. If so, clearly it must also have involved some of the earlier cars, but which ones are not known. The first class twin berth arrangement was new to LMS sleeping cars and probably provided the idea for the post-war twin-berth thirds described on page 69. All reverted to single berth c. 1949/50.

The final design of first class sleeping car was to D2166 of which 25 were built. These did not appear until 1951/2, were almost identical to D1926, but were considerably heavier than their predecessors. The interiors were similar to D1926 and they represent the last complete batch of 12 wheel coaches to run in general service in this country. They were also the only first class sleeping cars to last long enough as a class to receive the latest BR blue and grey livery—but see remarks column of Table 6 (D1926).

## THIRD CLASS COACHES

Third class sleeping cars were introduced to the British railway scene in 1928, by which time the single window design of coach was beginning to make its appearance on the LMS system. This design trend resulted in the externally rather attractive coaches to D1709 of which 85 were built at Derby between 1928 and 1931 in four batches. These cars introduced a 60ft underframe to LMS standard coaches and they were true Period I vehicles owing little to pre-group ideas.

They had a symmetrical end to end layout containing seven compartments with diagonally opposed toilets and lavatories at the four extreme corners of the car. The entrance vestibules divided these facilities from the compartment area. The corridor side exhibited the large single window styling of the 1928/9 period but the compartment windows were almost unique—at least for the LMS. They were of a triplet arrangement with two quarterlights separated by a single frameless droplight and without external door. There was a nine-element Stones pattern ventilator in the eaves panel above the droplight.

Inside the coaches the upholstery was in fawn velvet, the wood finish was mahogany and compartment floors were covered with grey mohair carpet. The compartments were, in essence, conventional four-a-side thirds but were convertible for night use. The lower seats were used as berths, being provided with a spring mattress, while an additional spring mattress, used as a daytime seat, provided the sleeping mattress for the upper berth. The seats were arranged to pull forward to give a wider berth for sleeping. The top berth was hinged to the compartment partition and in the lowered position was supported by brackets and fitted with two safety straps. When folded out of use, the underside of the top berth displayed mahogany panels with the usual pictures and mirrors, thus rendering it difficult to distinguish the coach from a normal day vehicle. Access to the upper berth was by a combined fold-away table and ladder. For night use, the four berths were provided with pillows and blankets only. They were illuminated by a dim blue light which was automatically switched on when the main lights were turned out.

The first 75 cars to this design were fully beaded with a high waist and matchboard ends in orthodox Period I style. The last 10, however, post-dated the change to steel panelling and came out with this style of treatment. They did, however, retain the high waist of the wood panelled version and were given a fully lined livery. However, this livery was applied without a waist panel and the waist lining was placed at the, now standard, low waisted level of the Period II coaches. This put the lining some 3in below the window level and, in consequence, made the coaches look rather peculiar.

None of the D1709 cars carried the legend 'Sleeping Car' since this branding seems to have been reserved by the LMS for single purpose sleeping coaches. In fact, the coaches were very similar to, if rather more spacious than the orthodox LMS corridor third of the day. They went into service on all the principal LMS overnight services in September 1928 (see page 57) and the charge to passengers was 6/- (30p) per berth.

*A fine model of one of these coaches is displayed in the National Railway Museum.

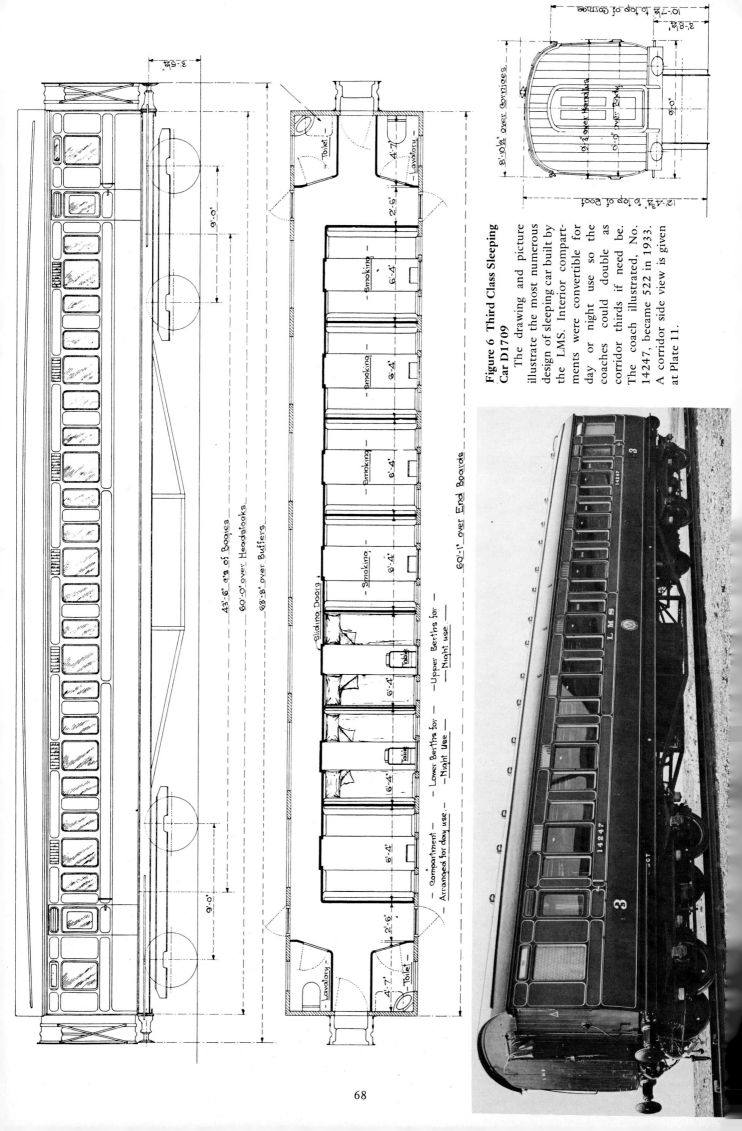

**Figure 6 Third Class Sleeping Car D1709**

The drawing and picture illustrate the most numerous design of sleeping car built by the LMS. Interior compartments were convertible for day or night use so the coaches could double as corridor thirds if need be. The coach illustrated, No. 14247, became 522 in 1933. A corridor side view is given at Plate 11.

68

At a later stage, during the 1930s, many of the cars were altered to fixed berth although still, as far as is known, without the wording 'Sleeping Car' on the exterior. Some 40 of them were further converted into ambulance vehicles during the war and later still, after nationalisation, 17 re-appeared as cafeteria and buffet cars (see page 86), the remainder being reconverted to sleeping cars, some of which retained the convertible berths.*

Because of the large number of sleeping cars to D1709, the LMS itself only built 15 more third class coaches of the type. These were all Period III vehicles to D1863. Again there was introduced a new length of underframe, this time 65ft and the outcome was a more than usually handsome looking vehicle. Along with some 65ft open first (see page 123), they were the longest eight-wheel locomotive hauled coaches to be built by the LMS.

The coaches were built in one batch at Derby in 1933 and thus had the early Period III shallow window ventilators. They were also the first modern LMS thirds, having fixed berths from the outset. This may have been a Swindon-inspired Stanier importation from the GWR where fixed berth thirds had for some time superseded the convertible type. There were again seven compartments with corner sited toilets and lavatories. The extra length over the earlier cars was used to provide an attendant's compartment—at the right hand end of the compartment side. The exterior elevations of the coach presented a 'mirror' image with single windows on the corridor side exactly the same size as and directly opposite to those on the compartment side. All the batch had the fully lined livery when new. However, car 585 was given its number in the 'stretched' scroll figures for its trip to America with the 'Royal Scot'. It was probably the only one to have this particular livery variation.

Inside these 65ft sleepers, the compartments were finished in stippled brown rexine with mouldings and frames in matching finish. Ceilings were pale cream rexine, upholstery was fawn and brown shaded rep and mattresses were one of two types, either spring interior or rubber latex. Mirrors, racks and coat hooks were provided and there was a baggage recess over the corridor ceiling for the upper berth occupants. Window blinds were fitted with 'Zip' Flexide fasteners. The blue night light was again present but, in addition, each berth had a bell push and reading light. Ventilation was by 'hit and miss' floor level ventilator slides under passenger control and the floors themselves were covered with rubber mats.

Toilets and lavatories were duck egg blue with mahogany mouldings. They included water filtering equipment and drinking cups were provided to supplement the pantry facilities available in the attendant's compartment. To cut down noise, the floor was of 1¼in cork sheet laid over a dovetail steel sheet with a blanket of insulating material fitted to the underside of the floor.

These cars represented pretty lavish provisioning for the 1933 third class passenger and give further evidence, were such needed, that the LMS was making more than a little effort to cater well for this class of traveller on its long distance trains of that period.

The third and final design of LMS pattern third class sleeping car was to D2169 and post-dated nationalisation by some four years. The cars themselves were, however, very much in the LMS tradition, even more so than the corridor composites alluded to on page 19. British Railways built 25 cars of this pattern and, like both preceding third class types, they introduced a whole variety of new features, later developed for the standard BR-type cars. In this case it took the form of a standardised twin-berth compartment of the kind first introduced as a wartime expedient on the first class cars. These twin-berth third class cars retained the 65ft eight-wheel chassis of their predecessors but were rather more massive looking because the body width was increased to the first class dimension to take full advantage of the loading gauge. For the same reason they were fitted with recessed pattern commode handles. The new profile and exterior details, together with

*One or two survived in departmental stock as staff dormitory coaches into the 1970s and have been preserved for posterity, including one in almost original condition for the National Railway Museum collection.

**Plate 85** LMS Car No. 585 was the first example of the 65ft Stanier pattern fixed berth third class sleeping cars to D1863, with the shallow window ventilators and full livery typical of very early Stanier vehicles. This coach went to America in 1933 with the 'Royal Scot' tour—hence the 1932/3 series running number in obsolete stretched type numerals. These coaches were the first fixed berth LMS thirds and the first third class sleeping cars to be so branded.

**Plate 86** LMR Car No. M603 one of the post-nationalisation twin berth third class cars to D2169. Note the general similarity in style to the Stanier 12-wheel sleeping cars. The 65ft underframe was little changed from the earlier coaches but note the self-contained, double acting buffers, a post-LMS innovation, retrospectively applied to some of the pre-war 65ft sleeping cars.

the 'paired' arrangement of the compartment windows consequent upon the twin-berth interior, gave the cars a very strong resemblance to their contemporary 12-wheel first class partners.

In construction, there were one or two other new features for third class sleeping cars. Integral body structure was adopted, considerable use being made of welding in both body framing and outside panelling. The sound insulation was generally to the now standard first class specification, while the coaches were fitted with self-contained double acting buffers with rubber springs and strengthened heads. LMS standard screw couplings were fitted but the coaches had gangway adapters from the outset.

Apart from the double deck arrangement of the twin berths and the fact that there were only eleven instead of twelve compartments, the general layout and amenity of these cars was all but identical to the first class version. All the usual Period III luxury features were present and, for the first time, third class passengers were given the individually adjustable 'punkah louvre' type ventilation for each berth. Air ducts for these fitments were carried above the corridor ceiling.

The resemblance to first class cars went through to the corridor side where, instead of the full complement of windows of their third class predecessors, they had small windows in the manner of the orthodox Period III 12-wheel sleeping cars.

Finally, these coaches introduced fully made up beds into third class sleeping accommodation and the supplementary charge for their use was some 50 per cent greater than for the four berth third. In effect, they provided what might be termed 'second class' sleeping accommodation by comparison with the previous single and four berth variety.

The twin berth thirds (now seconds) remained in service to the mid-1970s.

## COMPOSITE COACHES

Only two varieties of composite sleeping car were built by the LMS. The first were to D1781 and were introduced during Period II. As explained on page 12, these coaches were distinctly atypical of LMS designs in general except for their overall dimensions. Their exteriors indicated that LNWR influences predominated in the styling but, not being built until 1930/31, they post-dated the change to steel panelling. Thus, apart from the heavy waist moulding strip, the exteriors were, to all intents and purposes, flush sided. They did not even have the normal Period II raised moulding round the window apertures.

Inside the coaches there was a marriage of style between the Period I first and third class sleeping cars. There were six single berth first class compartments in the centre, flanked each side by two convertible four berth thirds arranged like those of D1709. The similarities continued to the outside in that the thirds had Stones ventilators above the centre droplight which was flanked by quarterlights while the external windows in the first class area were of the normal 'paired' type

**Plate 87** This view shows the corridor side of SLC No. 10637 (later 709) to D1781 as built. Note that the full livery was not applied symmetrically in relation to the windows in each 'panel' although there was an end-to-end symmetry on the whole vehicle.

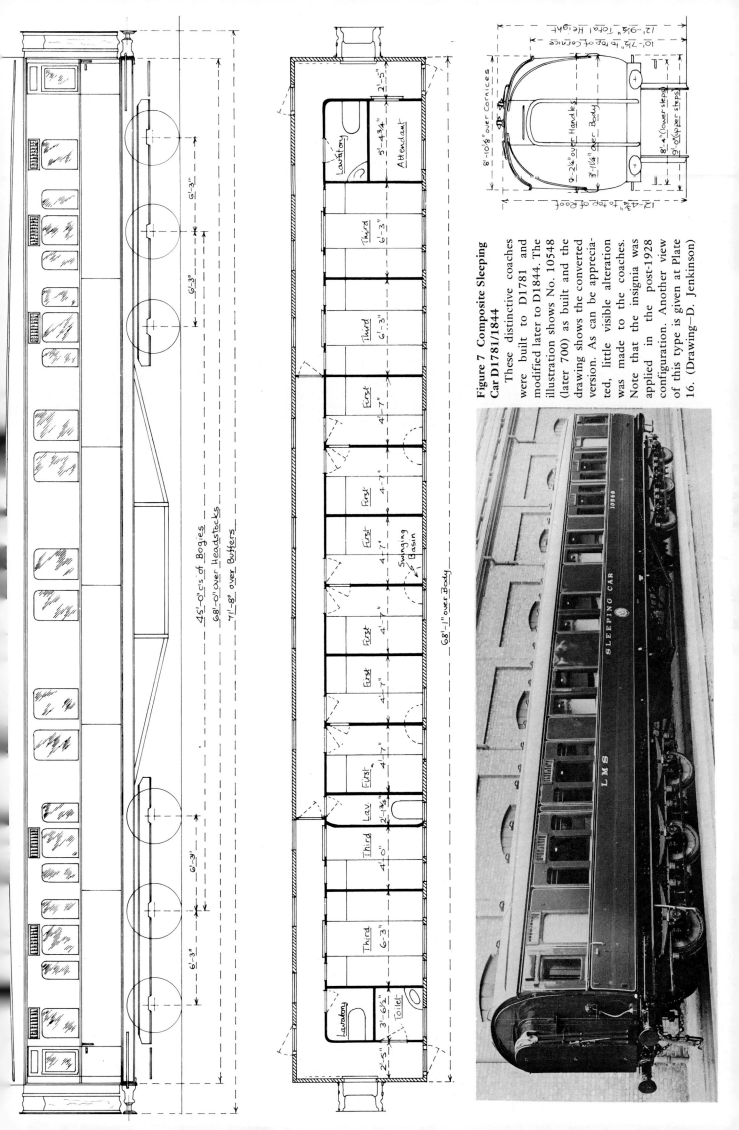

### Figure 7 Composite Sleeping Car D1781/1844

These distinctive coaches were built to D1781 and modified later to D1844. The illustration shows No. 10548 (later 700) as built and the drawing shows the converted version. As can be appreciated, little visible alteration was made to the coaches. Note that the insignia was applied in the post-1928 configuration. Another view of this type is given at Plate 16. (Drawing—D. Jenkinson)

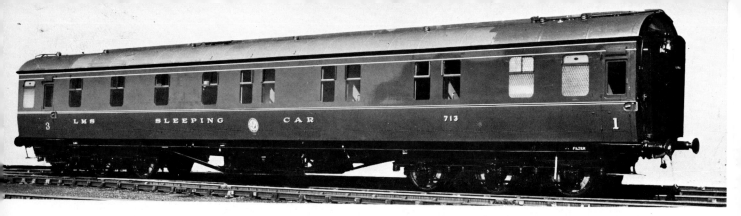

**Plates 88-89** The Stanier composite sleeping cars to D1947 were very similar to their contemporary first class companions but, unlike the earlier composites, had all the third class compartments at one end. This pair of pictures shows both sides of the first vehicle of the type to be built, No. 713.

extended to cornice level. All the external windows had rather rounded top corners—again reminiscent of the LNWR—and there was the prominent waist moulding along the outside of the car to add to the effect. There was, however, no waist panel either real or simulated.

There were one or two internal details worthy of further comment in these cars. The wash basins in the first class compartments were of the 'swing out' type, being housed out of use under a glass top shelf. Metal fittings were oxidised silver. First class compartments were panelled in walnut and the thirds in mahogany. Third class upholstery was exactly as described for the 1928 built third class sleepers.

During the 1930s, the third class accommodation was reduced to 14 from 16 and the cars converted from convertible third class to fixed berth third class. The reduction in accommodation was effected by turning one third class compartment into a twin berth and altering the area occupied by the other two berths into a narrow lavatory compartment serving the first class section. This converted compartment was immediately to the left of the first class section when viewed from the compartment side. The conversion was to D1844 and at the same time it is thought that the first class compartments were refurbished to Stanier standards of comfort. In this form they lasted until the end of 1963.

The remaining composites were Stanier pattern cars to D1947. Like their first class equivalents to D1926, they were 69ft coaches. However, whereas the Stanier first class cars were little changed in layout from the earlier pattern, the Stanier composites showed a number of changes from the D1781 coaches just described. All the third class compartments were now brought together at one end of the coach and were of the fixed-berth type from the outset. There were three four-berth and one two-berth third class compartments. Outside windows were of the familiar 'paired' style at the first class end while the thirds had a single window, slightly larger than that of the firsts, between the pairs of berths rather in the fashion of the Stanier 65ft third class cars of 1933. The corridor side was very much like the first class sleeping cars except that the third class toilets were 'outside' the entrance vestibule.

All six first class compartments were arranged in inter-connecting pairs and were fitted-out in the same fashion as the contemporary full first sleeping cars. Three colour schemes were used, blue, beige and green, one for each pair of compartments. Wood finishes were either sycamore or walnut. The third class berths were similar to those described for D1865. They were finished in patterned rexine with cream rexine ceilings. Wood panelling was Philippine Walnut (upper panels) and mahogany (lower panels). The ventilation arrangements, however, showed an improvement over the pioneer Stanier third class sleepers.

The first class 'Thermo-Reg.' system was adopted but with louvres on the ceiling and arranged to diffuse the air so that no currents were perceptible by passengers. Air was extracted by a louvred opening at the foot of the compartment door and there was no recirculation, all incoming air being drawn from outside. The ducting for the ventilation was carried on top of the roof in order not to encroach upon the luggage space provided over the corridor ceiling at the third class end of the vehicle. The roof ducts were protected by a long external cowl which was carried the full length of the vehicle. From the outside, this cowl was a further distinguishing identification feature of these coaches.

Each third class berth had an attendant's bell push which, via a corridor mounted indicator, showed the attendant from which berth the call had originated.

*Addenda*

It eventually turned out that the longest lived passenger carrying vehicles to LMS design (other than special and Royal Saloons) were the post nationalisation sleeping cars. The twelve wheel firsts ran on well into the 1970s and the twin berth thirds (later seconds) were not finally withdrawn until the turn of 1975/6. Some of these cars have, happily, been privately preserved.

# TABLE 6: SUMMARY TABLE OF LMS STANDARD SLEEPING CARS

*Note:* This table should be read in conjunction with the list of standard dimensions and details on page 62.

| Type | Diag | Lot | Qty | Date | Built | Dimensions (L × W × H) | Weight | Period | Running Numbers | Withdrawals First | Withdrawals Last | Remarks |
|------|------|-----|-----|------|-------|------------------------|--------|--------|-----------------|-------------------|------------------|---------|
| SLF | 1739 | 62 | 10 | 1924 | Wolverton | 68' × 9'1½" × 12'4¾" | 41T | See remarks | 300-309 | 5/58 | 10/59 | The first LMS version of the LNWR style —plated 9'2". |
| SLF | 1705 | 140 | 10 | 1926 | Wolverton | | 42T | See remarks | 310-319 | 10/59 | 2/60 | The standard LNWR styled version with slight detail changes and more modern fittings. Lot 341 were built for the M&NB joint services later being absorbed into LMS stock. Car 350 went to America in 1933 with the Royal Scot train. Car 342 was used in the Prime Minister's train during the second world war. Car 347 plated 42T. |
| | | 297 | 10 | 1927 | Wolverton | | 41T | | 322-331 | 8/58 | 2/60 | |
| | | 341 | 2 | 1927 | Wolverton | | 41T | | 320-321 | 2/59 | 6/60 | |
| | | 381 | 5 | 1928 | Wolverton | 68' × 9'3" × 12'4¾" | 41T | | 337-341 | 12/60 | 1/61 | |
| | | 401 | 5 | 1928 | Wolverton | | 41T | | 332-336 | 12/60 | 6/62 | |
| | | 441 | 5 | 1929 | Wolverton | | 41T | | 342-346 | 4/61 | 1/62 | |
| | | 489 | 4 | 1929 | Wolverton | | 41T | | 348-351 | 6/60 | 11/62 | |
| | | 521 | 1 | 1930 | Wolverton | | 41T | | 347 | — | 12/60 | |
| SLF | 1926 | 876 | 20 | 1935/6 | Wolverton | 69' × 9'3" × 12'4⅞" | 42T | III | 352-371 | 8/64 | 11/66 | Underframes were built at Derby. Car 377 to America in 1939 with 'Coronation Scot' train. One very late survival (376) because of a premature withdrawal of car 397 of D2166. 376 was given BR blue/grey livery, the only pre-war LMS coach to be so finished, except for odd departmental coaches. |
| | | 935 | 6 | 1936 | Wolverton | | 42T | | 372-377 | 8/64 | see remarks | |
| SLF | 2166 | 1570 | 5 | 1951 | Wolverton | 69' × 9'3" × 12'4⅞" | 47T | III | 378-382 | — | — | The post-nationalisation version of D1926. Much heavier cars and slight detail differences eg, no hinged ventilators above lavatory windows. All given crimson/cream livery when new. Postwar torpedo type ventilators. All withdrawn in mid-1970s. |
| | | 1584 | 20 | 1951/2 | Wolverton | | 47T | | 383-402 | 8/66 | — | |
| SLT | 1709 | 418 | 25 | 1928 | Derby | 60' × 9'3" × 12'4¾" | 29T | I | 500-524 | 4/59 | 12/60 | Convertible sleepers styled as for a Period I TK but no compartment doors. Lot 579 was flush clad and had no painted waist panel. Cars later converted to fixed berth and probably heavier on conversion. Many later conversions to RB &c—see p.86. |
| | | 428 | 25 | 1928/9 | Derby | | 29T | | 525-549 | 11/55 | 8/61 | |
| | | 469 | 25 | 1929 | Derby | | 28T | | 550-574 | 11/55 | 11/61 | |
| | | 579 | 10 | 1931 | Derby | | 30T | | 575-584 | 11/60 | 10/61 | |
| SLT | 1863 | 699 | 15 | 1933 | Derby | 65' × 9'3" × 12'4⅞" | 37T | III (Shallow ventilator) | 585-599 | 11/61 | 13/63 | Full livery when new. 585 to America with Royal Scot in 1933. First LMS fixed berth SLTs. |
| SLT(T) | 2169 | 1574 | 10 | 1951/2 | Derby | 65' × 9'3" × 12'4⅞" | 40T | III | 600-609 | 12/65* | — | Twin berth sleepers built after nationalisation. All BR crimson/cream when new and fitted Torpedo ventilators (postwar style) Pressure heating/ventilation. *Accident withdrawals—most others withdrawn 1975/6. |
| | | 1628 | 15 | 1952 | Derby | | 40T | | 610-624 | 8/67* | — | |
| SLC | 1781 (later D1844 —see remarks) | 543 | 6 | 1930 | Wolverton | 68' × 9'2¼" × 12'4½" | 42T | see remarks | 700-705 | 2/61 | 12/63 | Period II vintage but LNWR type styling. Third class compartments were originally convertible for day use but the cars were later altered to fixed berth losing two third class berths in process becoming 6F + 14T. Conversion to D1844. |
| | | 571 | 6 | 1931 | Wolverton | | 42T | | 706-711 | 7/61 | 12/63 | |
| SLC | 1947 | 934 | 13 | 1936 | Derby | 69' × 9'3" × 12'4⅞" | 43T | III | 712-724 | 5/63 | 1/64 | Bogies built at Wolverton. Fitted thermostat heating equipment. |

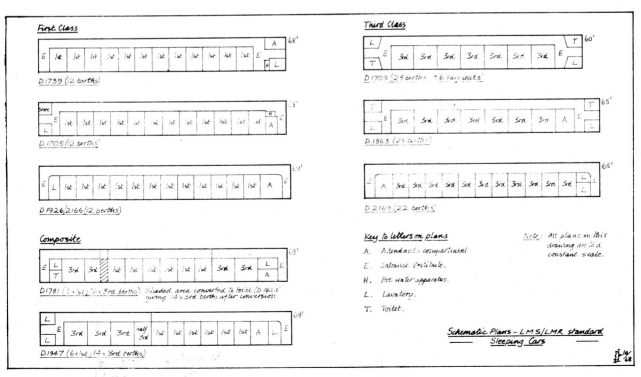

*FIGURE 8 LMS standard sleeping cars—sketch plans* (Drawn by D. Jenkinson)

73

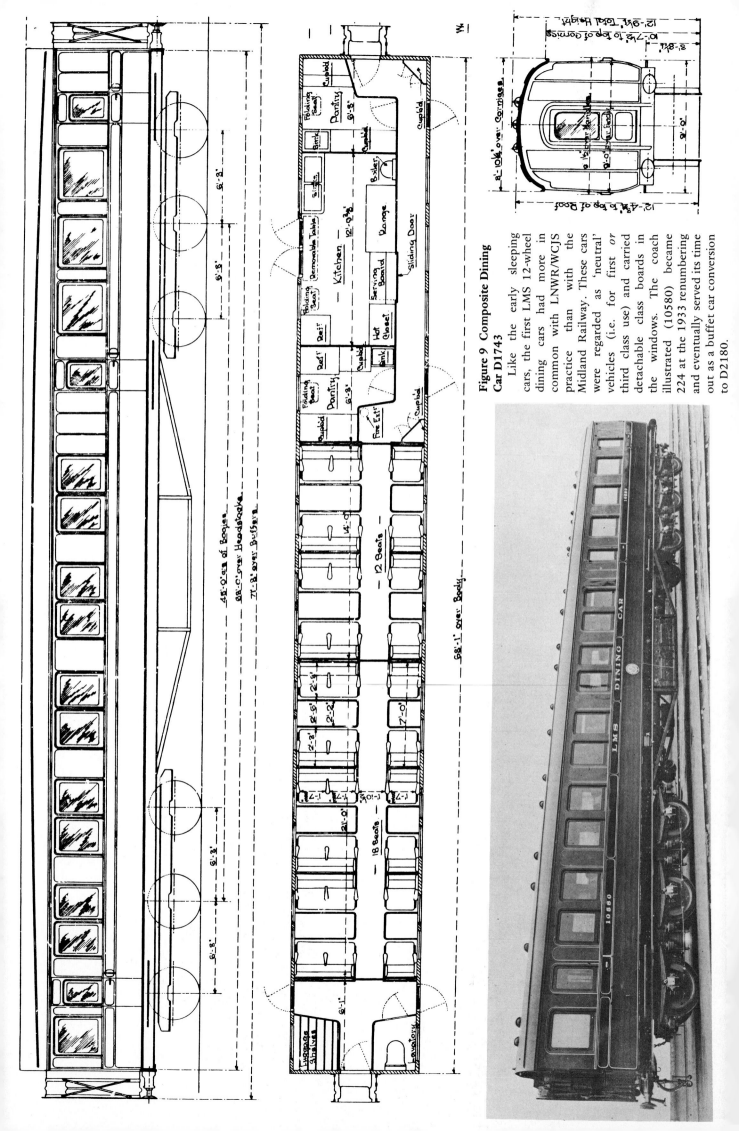

**Figure 9 Composite Dining Car D1743**

Like the early sleeping cars, the first LMS 12-wheel dining cars had more in common with LNWR/WCJS practice than with the Midland Railway. These cars were regarded as 'neutral' vehicles (i.e. for first or third class use) and carried detachable class boards in the windows. The coach illustrated (10580) became 224 at the 1933 renumbering and eventually served its time out as a buffet car conversion to D2180.

# Chapter 7 - Dining, Kitchen and Buffet Cars

*Kitchen/Dining coaches; Buffet cars; Kitchen only cars; Post Nationalisation conversions; Summary Tables*

THE LMS in 1923 assumed responsibility for the continuance of the strong dining car traditions established by the pre-group companies—particularly the LNWR and MR. True to these traditions, the new company continued to lay emphasis on good refreshment services and built a considerable number of comfortable and well-equipped dining vehicles. They can be conveniently divided into those with some form of cooking facility and those without. The latter were nearly all of the full open type, very similar in style to the general service open stock and as such, they are dealt with in Chapter 9.

## KITCHEN/DINING COACHES

LMS design combined Kitchen and Dining coaches, hereafter referred to simply as dining cars or diners, were built during all three periods of LMS coach design, eventually totalling 119 vehicles of all three classes. All were 68ft, 12 wheel cars.

The first to appear were six rather ornate cars to D1743 in 1925. These were styled in LNWR fashion and can be compared with the contemporary sleeping cars to D1739. They seated 30 passengers in two saloons (12 plus 18) arranged in five seating bays. The seats were arranged singly on the corridor side of the coach and in pairs on the kitchen side. This 2 + 1 seating arrangement was universal in all LMS dining cars and will not, therefore, be alluded to again. The D1743 diners were regarded as being for first *or* third class passengers—nominally 12 first and 18 third—but variable by the dining car staff to suit the needs of the traffic. They were numbered into the composite series in 1932/3.

Why LNWR styling was preferred for these cars is no clearer than in the case of the contemporary sleeping cars. There seems no good reason why these six coaches could not have been given orthodox Period I features but they were not and, moreover, they were the only dining cars to appear during the first design phase. After nationalisation, they were converted as kitchen/buffet cars to D2180 and ran for several more years in this new role.

The relative lack of Period I dining cars was amply compensated in Period II when the LMS introduced 36 palatial cars in the short space of two years between 1930 and 1932. Of these, 24 were first class cars with four seating bays

**Plates 90-91** These two pictures give an interior impression of the D1718 first class dining cars. The kitchen was a fairly typical LMS arrangement with the gas cooking range prominent in the foreground (car No. 2592, later 4). The passenger interior view is car No. 3129 (later No. 7) of the same batch. The elegant styling is reminiscent of contemporary Pullman Car design and the non-standard seat end design compared with most other LMS open stock is worthy of note.

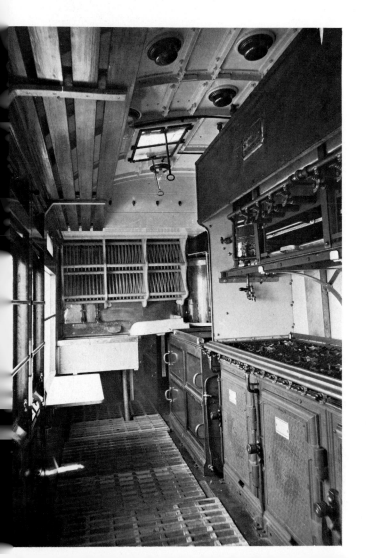

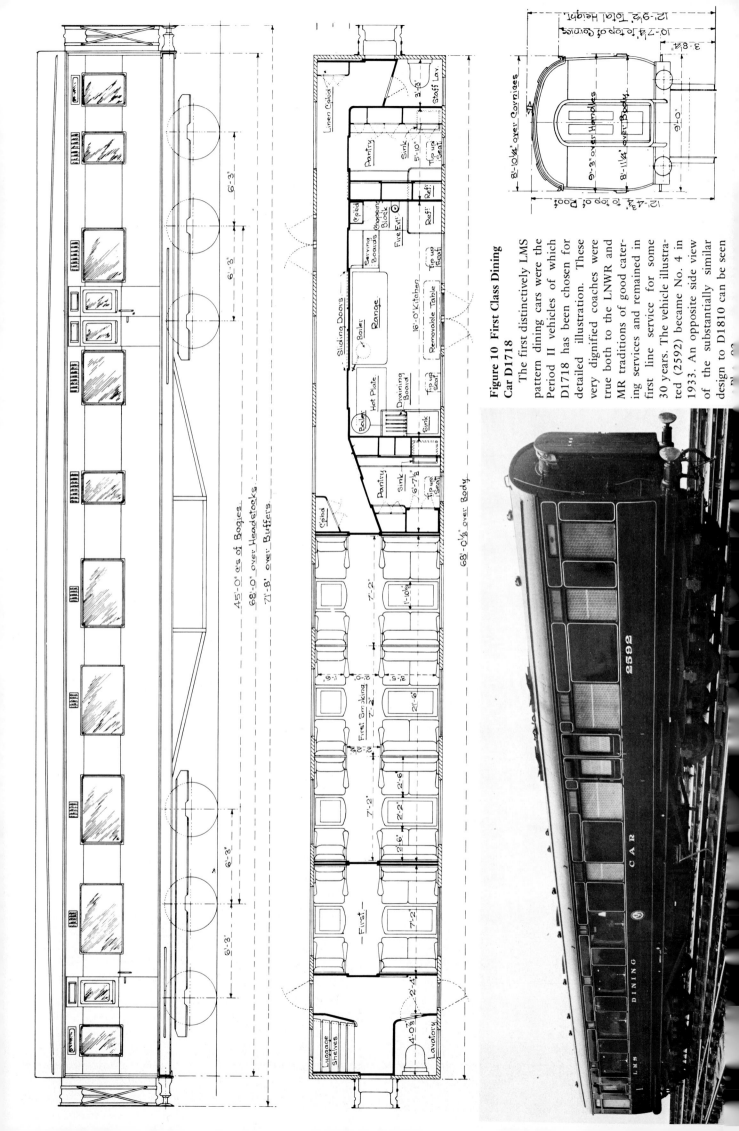

### Figure 10 First Class Dining Car D1718

The first distinctively LMS pattern dining cars were the Period II vehicles of which D1718 has been chosen for detailed illustration. These very dignified coaches were true both to the LNWR and MR traditions of good catering services and remained in first line service for some 30 years. The vehicle illustrated (2592) became No. 4 in 1933. An opposite side view of the substantially similar design to D1810 can be seen

**Plate 92** LMS Car No. 2074 of the later Period II cars to D1810 from the corridor side exhibits some subtle differences from D1718. Note the changed position of the full lining to a position between the windows and the use of six-element Stones ventilators above the seating bays, unlike the five-element Dewel ventilators of the earlier cars. The passenger door was slightly further away from the end of the coach and opposite, the toilet window was surmounted by a Stones ventilator, not the 'fall-back' type as displayed on Car 2592. Car 2074 was to Lot 616 and became No. 21 in the 1932/3 renumbering. The absence of the figure '1' on the entrance door was unusual.

accommodating 24 passengers (D1718, D1810).* The other 12 were composites with five seating bays but otherwise very similar in style (D1811). All the cars were steel panelled Period II designs. The two diagrams for the first class cars differed only in minor aspects like the precise size of the toilet and pantry areas and such detail matters as shelf design and linen cupboards. The most noticeable external difference between them when new was the livery. Both types were given full livery but the D1810 cars had lining between the windows whereas the D1718 vehicles had the lining at the edge of the windows. There were also slight variations in the ventilator design above the windows.

This 1930-32 period was the time when the LMS was actively experimenting with a variety of matters connected with the improvement of coach design and, as will be noted for some of the other Period II designs (e.g. the TOs to D1807 page 123), slight variations in detail were by no means uncommon within batches of coaches.

The Period II composite diners were, like their LNWR styled predecessors, neutral vehicles and did not carry class figures on the outside doors. They had detachable class indicator boards fitted in the window which could be changed, if need be, by the dining car staff.

In addition to the exterior innovations already mentioned, the LMS Period II diners seem to have been some of the few pre-Stanier coaches to depart from the traditional early LMS seat designs. The interior of the first class cars was quite different from the typical pattern as depicted in Figure 3 (page 31). The Pullman-like decor was probably quite deliberate and in these elegant cars, the LMS certainly achieved a most harmonious design, fit to compare with any of their pre-group ancestors from either Derby or Wolverton. The Period II Semi-RFOs (page 123) were furnished in similar style.

The bulk of LMS standard dining cars were Period III coaches. Between 1933 and 1937 no fewer than 77 new cars were introduced divided into 20 first class, 13 composite and 44 third class vehicles. The firsts and composites were, fundamentally, Stanier versions of the aforementioned Period II coaches but the thirds were new designs.

*There is a large scale model of one of these cars in the South Kensington Science Museum.

**Plate 93** LMS Car No. 10440, the Period II car to D1811, contemporary with the RFs to D1718/D1810. The detachable class boards in the windows enabled the seating to be altered to suit the dining car staff. Note also the lack of class figures on the door. This coach was renumbered 238 in 1932/3.

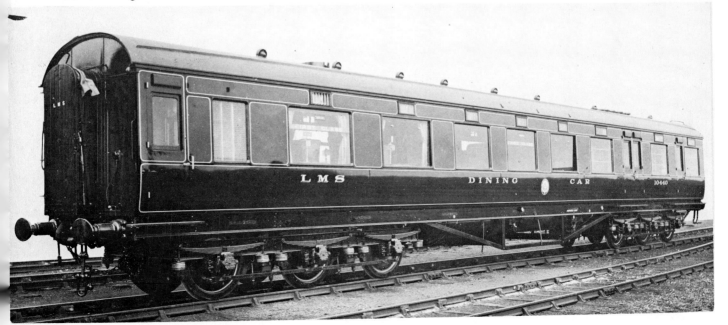

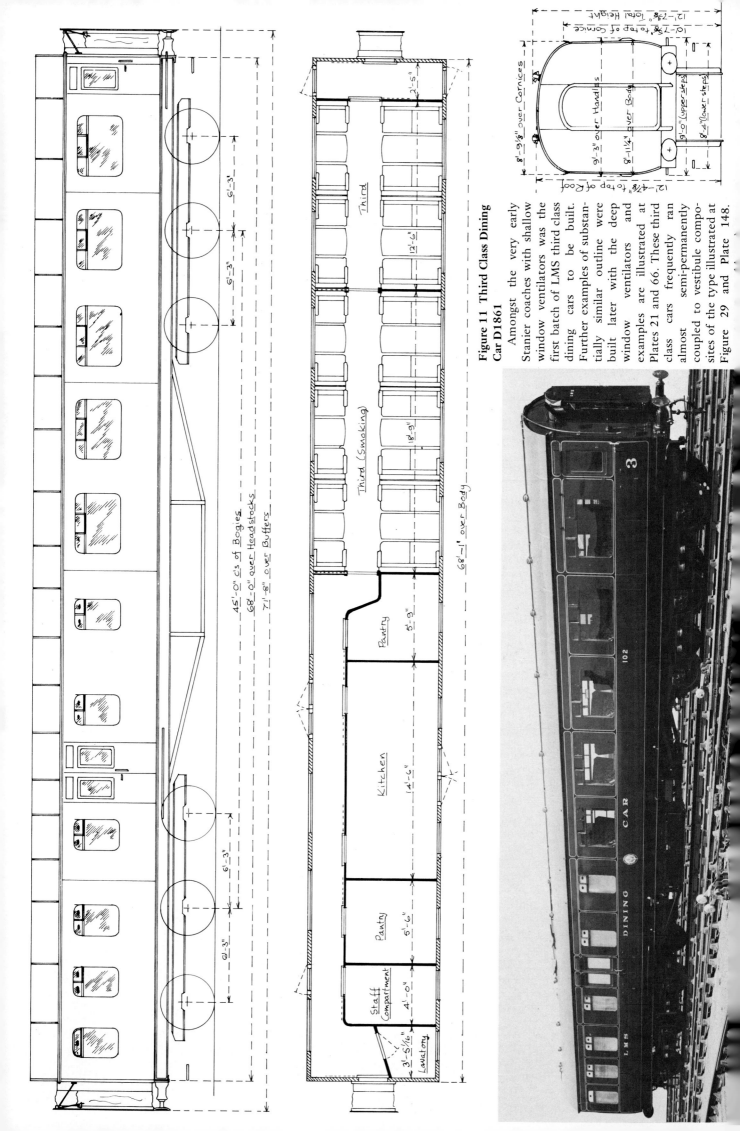

**Figure 11 Third Class Dining Car D1861**

Amongst the very early Stanier coaches with shallow window ventilators was the first batch of LMS third class dining cars to be built. Further examples of substantially similar outline were built later with the deep window ventilators and examples are illustrated at Plates 21 and 66. These third class cars frequently ran almost semi-permanently coupled to vestibule composites of the type illustrated at Figure 29 and Plate 148.

**Plates 94-95-96** These three pictures show the evolution of the first class dining car during the Stanier period. Car No. 27 was one of four built in 1933 to D1857 with shallow depth window ventilators and full livery. There can be little doubt that from the exterior point of view, the adoption of the simpler livery produced a less elegant looking vehicle (Car 33 of the 1935 batch to D1900). After the war, one of these was refurbished with loose chairs and other interior changes and given the full 1946 livery, now branded 'Restaurant Car' (Car No. 43—see also Plate 97).

Chronologically, the first Stanier dining cars to appear were the four RFs to D1857 and 10 RTs to D1861. They were built at Wolverton and Derby respectively and probably entered service simultaneously. All 14 were early Period III cars with shallow window ventilators and full livery. The remaining Stanier diners were all of orthodox Period III style with deep ventilators and simple livery (16 RFs to D1900; 13 RCs to D1938; 34 RTs to D1901/D1923). The firsts, as before, seated 24 passengers in four bays but, unlike the Period II cars had no luggage or lavatory accommodation. The thirds had five bays and 30 seats, again without luggage or lavatory accommodation. Some 13 of the latter were used as wartime ambulances and some may never have returned to the dining car service, being withdrawn as early as 1953.

The five bay, 30 seat composites, differed from the Period III first and third class diners in having luggage and lavatory areas, compensated by a somewhat shorter kitchen portion. This was because the composites most commonly ran as single unit cars whereas the firsts and thirds usually ran with at least one extra vestibule dining coach, generally being paired RF + TO or RT + CO. This need to provide more meals than in a single car necessitated a larger kitchen area than in the composites.

After the war, one of the first class cars (No. 43) was the subject of an interesting conversion to D2120. This took the form of stripping the interior and refurbishing it with double glazed windows, individual chairs and tables. The car was one of the relatively few LMS coaches to be given the full 1946 livery utilising sans-serif characters throughout and being branded 'Restaurant Car' rather than 'Dining Car'. An open first (No. 7555) was similarly treated—see page 125—but no

**Plate 97** Interior view of the post-war conversion of RF No. 43. This conversion exhibited a mixture of fixed and loose seating. The fixed seats on the right of the gangways were angled to the wall for ease of access.

other like conversions of LMS dining cars took place although some of the Buffet and Cafeteria conversions (page 86) were given loose seats. Whether the idea was a great success is not known but the loose seating concept may have had some influence on the design of some of the BR standard diners.

Two of the Period III third class cars (105 and 117) were converted to kitchen/buffet cars after Nationalisation—these are considered on pages 85/6.

## BUFFET CARS

The LMS did not seem enamoured of the Buffet Car idea (unlike the LNER) and built but five cars of the type. The prototype vehicle was a Period II coach to D1848 on a standard 57ft underframe (Car No. 100). It was followed some four years later by four similar Stanier pattern cars to D1948. There was nothing particularly remarkable about these coaches except to remark that their decor seemed to reflect all that was most hideous in the fashions of the 1930s! Both varieties seated 24 passengers in four bays.

Why the buffet car was not popular on the LMS is not clear. There may not have been enough medium distance services to necessitate large scale use of the type and, of course, the vogue for buffet type facilities was nothing like as strong in the pre-war years as it is today.

**Plate 98** LMS Period III Composite dining car to D1938 No. 250. These cars were very similar in layout to their Period II predecessors (Plate 93), even to the extent of having courtesy table lamps at the first class end only.

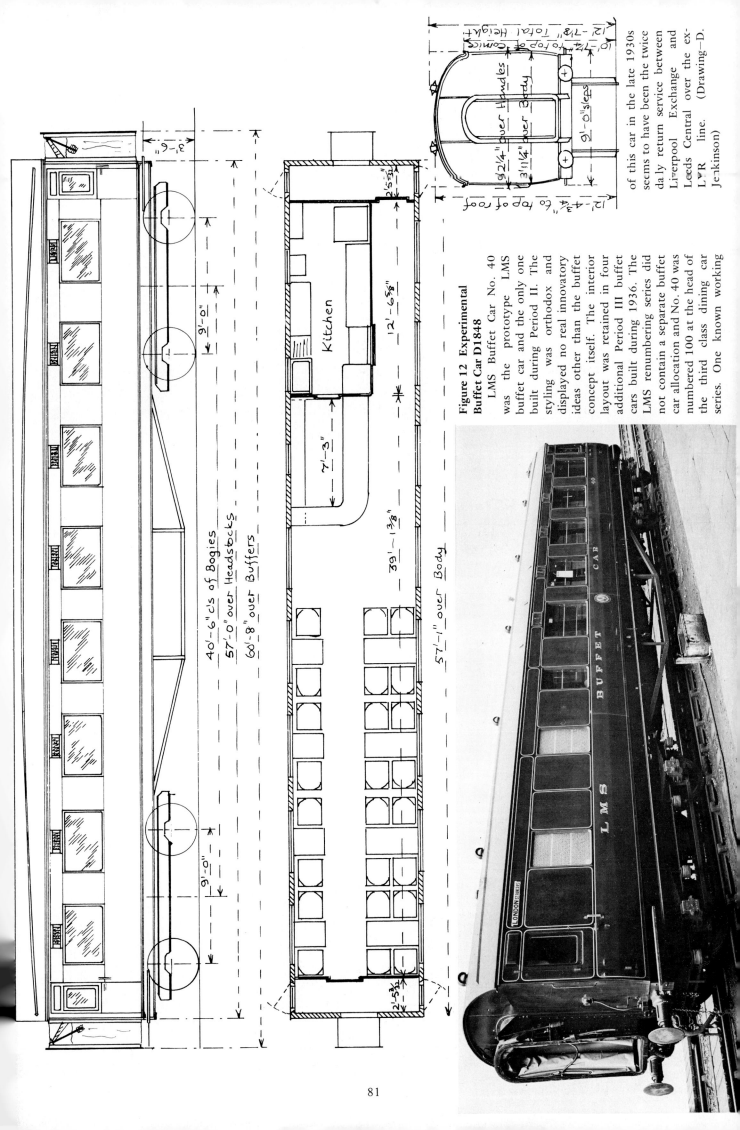

**Figure 12 Experimental Buffet Car D1848**

LMS Buffet Car No. 40 was the prototype LMS buffet car and the only one built during Period II. The styling was orthodox and displayed no real innovatory ideas other than the buffet concept itself. The interior layout was retained in four additional Period III buffet cars built during 1936. The LMS renumbering series did not contain a separate buffet car allocation and No. 40 was numbered 100 at the head of the third class dining car series. One known working of this car in the late 1930s seems to have been the twice daily return service between Liverpool Exchange and Leeds Central over the ex-L*R line. (Drawing—D. Jenkinson)

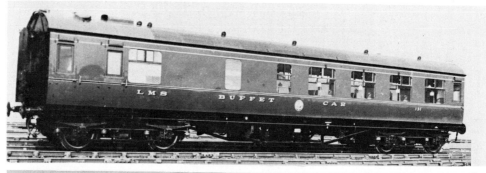

**Plates 99-100** Exterior and interior views of the proto-type Stanier buffet car to D1948 No. 131. Like the Period II example, the four Period III cars were numbered in the third class series. As far as can be deduced, these cars operated in paired circuits (i.e. one travelling in each direction daily). Known services in the late 1930s include a complex Manchester - York - Sheffield - Birmingham roster (extended to Worcester on Friday nights) and the afternoon Euston-Manchester service.

## KITCHEN ONLY CARS

By contrast with dining cars, the LMS acquired but a handful of kitchen only cars from the pre-group constituents. Indeed this type of vehicle does not seem to have found favour amongst the LMS constituent companies except the LNWR—even in the latter case it was confined to the Euston-Liverpool (Riverside) services. However, the situation was to change radically during the 1924-28 period when some 73 kitchen cars were built to D1697.

They were all high-waisted Period I style cars but they had steel-panelled exteriors after the Period II style—possibly to reduce fire risk since they employed gas cooking and lighting. The full livery adopted for them included a painted waist 'panel' and from the outside, they matched the fully-beaded Period I coaches with which they at first ran. An odd single car of the same type (30072) was built in 1932 to replace an accident victim while another car (30034) was nominally 'rebuilt' with a Stanier body in 1938. Some of the Period I kitchen cars were converted to buffet cars in the early 1950s—see page 84.

**Plate 101** Corridor side view of RK No. 312 (later 30002) to D1697. The kitchen side elevation of this particular car is at Plate 60.

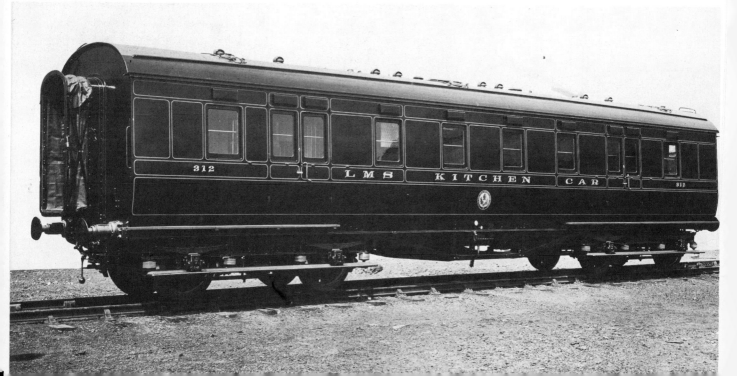

## Figure 13 Kitchen Only Car D1697

The LMS built a very large number of Kitchen only cars and this design was by far the most numerous type. It shared a 50ft length with the LMS standard full brake and along with its Period III equivalent, was the only LMS design coach with gas lighting as a standard feature. All were given the fully lined Period I livery (except possibly 30072, built in 1932) to match the fully beaded passenger carrying coaches of the day. The example illustrated (262) became 30023 in 1933. A corridor side view is given at Plate 101.

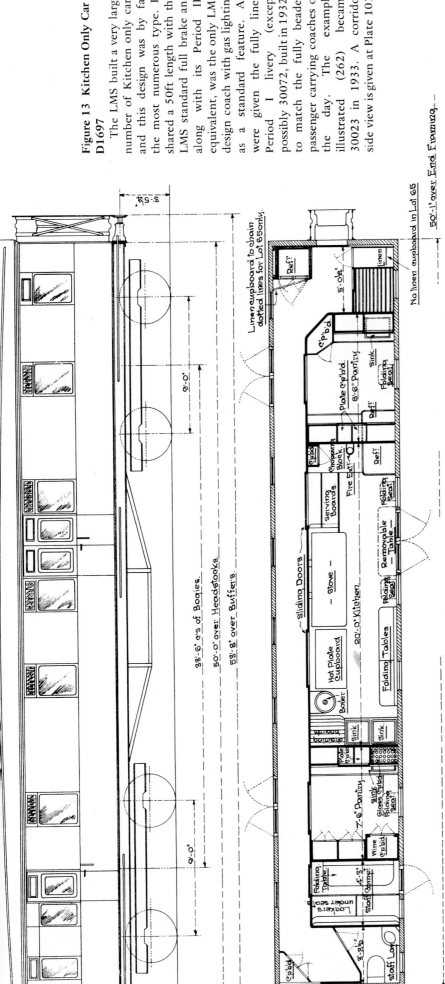

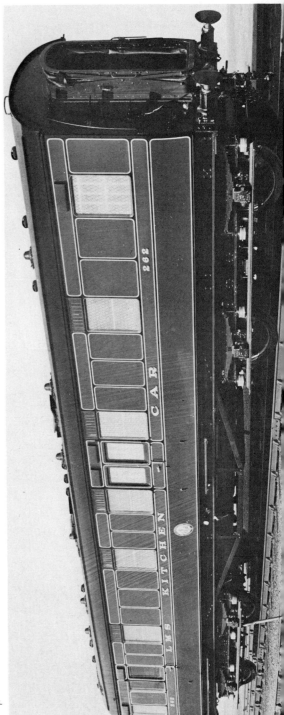

83

The large number of Period I kitchen cars may well have been a contributory reason for the relative paucity of newly constructed kitchen/diners during the first few years of the LMS. Together with the emphasis placed by the LMS on open coaches during the same period it would seem reasonable to conclude that there was a real need on many services for more dining space than could be achieved in an orthodox dining car. The wheel seemed to turn full circle after the war when many of the Period I kitchen cars were stored out of use for long periods.

In 1933, two 60ft, all-electric kitchen cars were introduced, the first one having early Period III styling. The extra length was to accommodate the diesel generating equipment and there is some evidence that the cars were introduced in connection with the 'Royal Scot' tour of America. The first of the pair (30073) did indeed go to America but the second coach was not completed until 1934 and the design was not multiplied. The all-electric idea did not find favour and the cars were not a great success, being stored out of use from 1942 until their withdrawal, still in LMS livery, in 1956. The LMS, unlike the LNER, reverted to gas cooking and lighting with the Stanier standard 50ft kitchen car to D1912.

These cars were, in all essentials, the Stanier equivalent of the Period I kitchen cars and 32 were built between 1934 and 1938 plus the nominal 'rebuild' of 30034 (page 82). In 1937, six Stanier cars were adapted for use with the blue/silver 'Coronation Scot' sets.

## POST NATIONALISATION CONVERSIONS

After Nationalisation, the buffet-cum-cafeteria car concept received a great deal of attention and many vehicles of this kind were produced by suitable conversion of older coaches; 31 LMS standard coaches were involved in this exercise and this caused the insertion of no fewer than seven new diagrams into the refreshment section of the old LMS diagram book. Although these new diagrams were dignified by a number of different names (Party Car, Cafeteria Car &c), they basically fell into two types of coach. First were a group of kitchen/buffet cars (BR code RKB) all of which had started life as LMS 12 wheel dining cars. These cars retained sufficient kitchen facility to be able to serve meals to an adjacent open coach as well as to provide snacks at the buffet counter. The other conversions were true buffet cars (BR code RB) with a kitchen portion sufficient only to provide a service of light refreshments within the confines of the vehicle itself.

**Plate 102** After the second world war, many LMS kitchen cars were redundant and a number were converted to Cafeterias—see Plate 108. Another interesting conversion was to a track recording coach. No. DM 395223 is seen in this guise at Wolverton in 1968, branded for dual heating and 100mph running. (D. Jenkinson)

**Plate 103** The experimental Period III diesel-electric car to D1855 No. 30073. Note the full livery, shallow depth sliding window ventilators and 'stretched' type running numbers of this 60ft car. Car 30074 was similar but had deep window ventilators and simple livery.

**Plate 104** The standard Period III 50ft Kitchen car to D1912 No. 30084 as altered for the 1937 Coronation Scot train. Five others were similarly treated. The general service version showed no significant external differences except for livery.

## Kitchen/Buffet Conversions

Seven LMS standard dining cars were converted to RKBs during the 1952-5 period. Six were to D2180 and these involved the pioneer LMS standard diners, the RCs to D1743. The conversion took the form of removing all but the extreme end seating bay and utilising the space previously occupied by the other four bays for an open buffet area served by a counter which connected with the kitchen. The kitchen itself remained substantially unchanged from its original form. The new buffet saloon had narrow shelves against the walls and a sort of island shelf in the centre of the open area. The one residual seating bay of the original five bay layout seems to have been left substantially unaltered.

The other 12 wheel coach to be converted to RKB form was Period III RT No 105. It had all the seating removed and a buffet counter installed adjacent to the kitchen which remained unchanged. At the end of the car away from the kitchen in the space occupied by two of the old seating bays, four sets of tables and chairs were installed giving eight seats. It was at first rostered to run with open first No. 7555 (see page 125).

**Plate 105** The saloon and bar counter of RKB No. M105M, photographed in late 1952. As can be seen, little remained of the original third class dining car interior, save for roof vents and light fittings. This was really quite a tasteful conversion compared with some contemporary efforts.

**Plate 106** Car No. M105M, rebuilt from dining car No. 105 to RKB form (D2182). The large blank panel between the kitchen and the seating area was where the buffet counter was located.

**Plate 107** Car No. M253M was ex-third class diner No. 117 as rebuilt to D2197. This rebuilt was a true Cafeteria car and the far end contained the three seating bays. (J. Alsop)

## Buffet Conversions

Between 1953 and 1955, 24 buffet cars were produced from three types of LMS standard coach. One was from a 12 wheel RT, six were from Period I kitchen cars and the remainder from Period I 60ft third class sleepers of D1709 which had been in ambulance train service during the war. They probably never ran again as sleepers, being surplus to requirements. The kitchen cars were not renumbered but all the remainder were given numbers in the LMS composite dining car list (253-270). A feature of the utilisation of these cars after conversion was the considerable number which were initially allocated to other regions than the LMR. All the conversion work was done at Eastleigh in the Southern Region.

The first conversion was of the six kitchen cars which were turned into what were called 'party cars'. They were given a small central kitchen/pantry area and each end of the car was made into a buffet saloon with a longitudinal centre table. Each saloon had eleven bar stools grouped round this table, six on one side and five on the other. Some at least were allocated to the Western Region. The conversion was to D2184.

**Plate 108** Car No. W30017M, a conversion of a Period I kitchen car to D2184 called a 'Party Car' although branded Cafeteria. (J. E. Cull)

**Plate 109** Car No. W256M was the D2195 conversion of the 60ft sleeping cars. This one was originally third class sleeper No. 512 and the conversion was classified 'Party Car'. As seen, little, if any, of the original bodywork remained on these conversions. (J. E. Cull)

All the remaining conversions took place at about the same time and carried consecutive diagram numbers (D2195—8). The running numbers were mixed up amongst the diagrams. After 253 (ex-117) the numbers reflected the order of numbering as sleeping cars. Two basic kinds of coach were produced which were called either Party Cars or Cafeteria Cars. However, to confuse matters, all were branded 'Cafeteria' on the outside.

The party cars were all to D2195 and were all ex-Period I sleeping cars. They were basically a stretched version of the converted kitchen cars with larger kitchen/pantry area but no increase in seating capacity in the end saloons. The exterior window arrangement of these cars—indeed of all the former sleeping cars—differed considerably and with doors at the extreme ends in every case, it is difficult to see how any of the bodywork of the sleeping cars (except the ends) can have been retained.

All three cafeteria diagrams shared certain features in common: all had centre kitchens and all had one end of the coach given to a conventional three-bay 18 seat dining saloon with individual chairs. The opposite end of the car was similar to the saloons in the Party Cars with a centre table and bar stools. D2197 was the ex-12 wheel RT No. 117 and had a 12 stool saloon while D2196/D2198 were ex-sleeping cars with nine-stool and seven-stool saloons respectively.

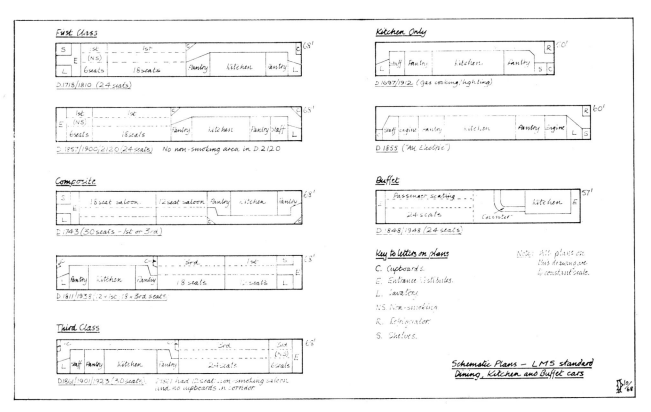

*FIGURE 14 LMS standard dining, kitchen and buffet cars—sketch plans* (Drawn by D. Jenkinson)

## TABLE 7a. SUMMARY TABLE OF LMS STANDARD DINING, KITCHEN AND BUFFET CARS

*Note:* This table should be read in conjunction with the list of standard dimensions and details on page 62.

| Type | Diag | Lot | Qty | Date | Built | Dimensions (L×W×H) | Weight | Period | Running Numbers | Withdrawal First | Withdrawal Last | Remarks |
|---|---|---|---|---|---|---|---|---|---|---|---|---|
| RF | 1718 | 478 | 12 | 1930 | Derby | | 43T | II(Flush) | 4-7, 11-18 | 11/60 | 9/62 | Lot 525 were originally marked on Diagram 1718 and certainly showed identical external features. The main changes seem to have been on lot 616 only. These had slightly longer glass vane ventilators over the windows, Stones ventilators rather than the 'fall back' type over the toilet and 'squared off' interior partition corners. The ex-works livery and toilet/pantry areas also showed differences. |
| RF | 1810 | 525 | 6 | 1930 | Derby | 68'×9'3"×12'4¾" | 45T | II(Flush) | 1-3, 8-10 | 7/59 | 7/62 | |
| | | 616 | 6 | 1932 | Wolverton | | 45T | | 19-24 | 10/60 | 9/62 | |
| RF | 1857 | 689 | 4 | 1933 | Wolverton | 68'×9'3"×12'4⅞" | 45T | III(Shallow ventilator) | 25-28 | 4/62 | 12/62 | Full livery when new. |
| RF | 1900 | 732 | 4 | 1933 | Wolverton | | 46T | III | 29-32 | 3/62 | 12/62 | Lot 732 came out with simple livery and were some of the earliest coaches to do so. They were plated 1934. Car 41 had a coal fired stove. Lots 914/1046 may have had pressure heating/ventilation equipment in common with the contemporary RCs and RTs. |
| | | 865 | 4 | 1935 | Wolverton | | 46T | | 33-36 | 11/62 | 12/64 | |
| | | 914 | 4 | 1936 | Wolverton | 68'×9'3"×12'4⅞" | 47T | | 37-40 | 12/62 | 3/66 | |
| | | 1046 | 4 | 1937 | Wolverton | | 47T | | 41-44 | 7/63 | 4/64 | |
| RF | 2120 | Ex-1046 | 1 | 1947 | Derby | 68'×9'3"×12'4⅞" | 47T | III | 43 | — | 3/62 | The post-war rebuild with loose seating and one single seating area. |
| RT | 1861 | 685 | 10 | 1933 | Derby | 68'×9'3"×12'4⅞" | 45T | III(Shallow ventilator) | 101-110 | 4/53 | 13/62 | The prototype LMS standard RT. Full livery when new. |
| RT | 1901 | 733 | 10 | 1933 | Derby | | 45T | III | 111-120 | 4/58 | 13/63 | The only real difference was that D1923 had rounded interior partition corners. All were 24 smoking plus 6 non-smoking whereas D1861 was 18+12. Lot 903 and possibly Lot 1034 had pressure heating/ventilation. |
| RT | 1923 | 852 | 10 | 1935 | Derby | | 45T | III | 121-130 | 13/62 | 13/62 | |
| | | 903 | 4 | 1936 | Derby | 68'×9'3"×12'4⅞" | 45T | | 135-138 | 13/62 | 13/62 | |
| | | 1034 | 10 | 1937 | Derby | | 45T | | 139-148 | 7/63 | 7/64 | |
| RC | 1743 | 28 | 6 | 1925 | Wolverton | 68'×9'1½"×12'4¾" | 43T | see remarks | 222-227 | All to D2180-RKB (see Table 7b below) | | The LNWR styled cars and 'neutral' in use (1st *or* 3rd). The width of 9'1½" (Plated 9'2") was the same as the contemporary SLFs to D1739—see Table 6. Plated 1924. |
| RC | 1811 | 617 | 12 | 1932 | Derby | 68'×9'3"×12'4¾" | 44T | II(Flush) | 228-239 | 8/59 | 12/62 | 'Neutral' cars. |
| RC | 1938 | 905 | 10 | 1936 | Wolverton | | 46T | III | 240-249 | 12/56 | 13/63 | All cars fitted pressure heating and ventilation equipment. |
| | | 1045 | 3 | 1937 | Wolverton | 68'×9'3"×12'4⅞" | 46T | | 250-252 | 13/63 | 13/63 | |
| RB | 1848 | 646 | 1 | 1932 | Derby | 57'×9'2¼"×12'4¾" | 29T | II(Flush) | 100 | | 2/61 | Prototype car, plated 31T by 1942. |
| RB | 1948 | 902 | 4 | 1936 | Derby | 57'×9'3"×12'4¾" | 32T | III | 131-134 | 13/62 | 2/63 | |
| RK | 1697 | 65 | 8 | 1924 | Derby | | 29T | I(Flush sided) | 30000-30007 | 6/55 | 11/59 | Lot 153: Only 19 renumbered in 1932/3, Lot 627 being the replacement for the vehicle lost in the Leighton Buzzard crash. 30034 later 'rebuilt' to D1912. Several converted to Cafeterias in 1953—see Table 7b (below). |
| | | 100 | 10 | 1925 | Derby | | 30T | | 30008-30017 | 7/56 | 2/61 | |
| | | 153 | 20 | 1925 | Derby | | 30T | | 30018-30036 | 1/56 | 7/61 | |
| | | 234 | 20 | 1926 | Derby | 50'×9'3"×12'4¾" | 30T | | 30037-30056 | 1/56 | 12/62 | |
| | | 382 | 15 | 1928 | Derby | | 29T | | 30057-30071 | 9/59 | 12/62 | |
| | | 627 | 1 | 1932 | Derby | | 30T | | 30072 | | 13/62 | |
| RK | 1855 | 670 | 2 | 1933 | Derby | 60'×9'3"×12'4⅞" | 45T III(but see remarks) | | 30073-30074 | 1/56 | 2/56 | The diesel electric cars. 30073 had shallow ventilators and full livery while 30074 had deep ventilators and simple livery not being finished until 1934. 30073 to America in 1933 and cars were probably built for this purpose. Stored out of use 1942-56 and never repainted by BR. |
| RK | 1912 | 779 | 1 | 1934 | Wolverton | | 33T | III | 30075 | — | 13/62 | Lot 956: Later examples plated 1937. Six of these cars modified for the 1937 'Coronation Scot' train (30084-30089) and on conversion tared 34T. Lot 1128: 'Rebuild' of accident victim. |
| | | 956 | 20 | 1936 | Glos. C&W | | 33T | | 30076-30095 | 7/56 | 13/65 | |
| | | 1039 | 5 | 1937 | Derby | 50'×9'3"×12'4⅝" | 35T | | 30096-30100 | 13/62 | 13/65 | |
| | | 1081 | 6 | 1938 | Derby | | 35T | | 30101-30106 | 7/56 | 12/63 | |
| | | 1128 | 1 | 1938 | Derby | | 32T | | 30034 | — | 1/56 | |

## TABLE 7b. SUMMARY OF LMS STANDARD COACHES SUBSEQUENTLY CONVERTED TO CAFETERIA/BUFFET CARS

| Type | Diag | Original Veh. Type | Qty | Date/Place Converted | Original Running Numbers | Running Numbers on Conversion | Withdrawals First | Withdrawals Last | Remarks |
|---|---|---|---|---|---|---|---|---|---|
| RKB | 2180 | RC-D1743 | 6 | 1954 Wolverton | 222-227 | 222-227 | 12/61 | 13/62 | Rebuilds of the pioneer LMS built RCs. |
| RKB | 2182 | RT-D1861 | 1 | 1954 Wolverton | 105 | 105 | — | 13/62 | Rebuild of early Period III RT. Designed to run with RFO No. 7555—see Table 9. |
| RB | 2197 | RT-D1901 | 1 | 1955 Eastleigh | 117 | 253 | not known | | Rebuild of standard Period III RT retaining kitchen and 18 seats. Unlike D2182, this conversion involved a re-numbering and was designated 'Cafeteria Car'. |
| RB | 2184 | RK-D1697 | 6 | 1953 Eastleigh | 30001/3/6/7/17/8 | 30001/3/6/7/17/8 | 13/62 | 4/65 | Rebuilds of Period I RKs. Designated 'Party Cars'. |
| RB | 2195 | SLT-D1709 | 7 | 1955 Eastleigh | 503/4/12/26/59/70/4 | 254-7/65/8/9 | 12/64 | 11/65 | Rebuilds of ex-ambulance train coaches which had originally been third class sleeping cars. D2195 designated 'Party Car' and D2196/8 designated 'Cafeteria Cars'. |
| RB | 2196 | SLT-D1709 | 6 | 1955 Eastleigh | 539/45/58/61/71/75 | 259/60/4/6/7/70 | 3/62 | 11/65 | |
| RB | 2198 | SLT-D1709 | 4 | 1955 Eastleigh | 536/48/50/3 | 258/61-3 | 3/62 | 7/63 | |

# Chapter 8 - Corridor Coaches

*Period I designs; Period II designs; Period III designs; Summary Table*

WHEN one considers the grand total of coaches built to LMS designs, it is a little surprising to find that only in the side corridor type of vehicle were all possible design and style phases represented, from the early all-door versions of the 1923-30 period to the post-nationalisation composites.

## PERIOD I DESIGNS

For the first four years or so after grouping, the Period I LMS side corridor coach was characterised by a full complement of outside doors to the compartments and most vehicles were mounted on the 57ft standard underframe. However, during the first year or two, a few small batches of non-standard coaches emerged from Wolverton some of which might almost be considered as the last of the LNWR coach designs, with, of course, the notable exception of the 12 wheel sleepers and diners.

The first of these non-standard batches was a strange little group of three FKs to D1698. These were six-compartment coaches and plated 54ft x 9ft 4in, although not really exhibiting any marked external differences from an orthodox Period I coach; if anything, they were more MR than LNWR in appearance, in spite of the 9ft 4in overall width. Of more characteristic LNWR style were five TKs to D1710 and eight BTKs to D1712. The former were 52ft 6in x 9ft 4in and converted from ambulance coaches while the latter were 57ft x 9ft 4in and converted from ambulance train Kitchen/ Mess cars. All had toplights over the corridor windows and LNWR style end panelling. The original vehicles dated from the pre-1914 period and the brakes were opposite handed to the LMS standard style. Several other similar conversions of LNWR stock also took place but were not included in the LMS Diagram Book.

Apart from these three diagrams, the remainder of the Period I coaches were to LMS standard design and will be considered by classes.

### First Class Coaches

The all-first was never a common LMS corridor coach and only 48 were built during Period I, including the above mentioned vehicles to D1698. Of the 48 coaches, no fewer than 25 were brake ended.

Chronologically, the earliest standard design was D1747 which was an all-door full first with six compartments and a centre coupé with three seats. It was a little behind the times and, with D1698, represented the only Period I full firsts with a full set of outside compartment doors.

The remaining coaches were ten full firsts to D1748 and 25 matching brake firsts to D1654. These were more spacious vehicles than their predecessors, having larger compartments. They had no outside compartment doors but the end entrance vestibules necessitated by the lack of outside doors, together with the extra compartment size, led to a reduction in passenger seating accommodation. The coaches had 5½ and 4½ compartments respectively and the 5½ compartment layout in the full firsts set the pattern until after the second world war.

Externally, the coaches were typical Period I designs but the compartments now had the Midland style twin-window arrangement which had, hitherto, been confined to open stock. The windows differed from those of the contemporary open stock in that both were surmounted by Stones pattern ventilators in the eaves panel. The left hand window was now a frameless droplight and not a heavy wood framed version. The double doors on the brake compartment of D1654 had one door opening inwards (for the guard and one opening outwards.)

**Plate 110** Period I FK No. Sc1017M in BR crimson/cream livery, August 1956. This coach was to D1748 and on the compartment side, the vehicle exhibited the 'twin window' style—see Plate 7. Note that by the time this picture was taken, much of the wood panelling had been replaced by steel and the lower waist beading removed. (J. E. Cull)

## Figure 15 Corridor First Class Brake D1654

These carriages were of far-reaching consequence. Along with their matching full firsts, they introduced the 'twin-window' style to side-corridor stock and, more importantly, removed the draughty side door from the individual compartments. Note the Stones ventilators over both compartment windows and the frameless droplight in the left hand opening. The interior compartment arrangement is given at Plate 44 and a close-up of some of the panelling detail on the opposite side can be found at Plate 58. The coach illustrated here (18503) later became 5015.

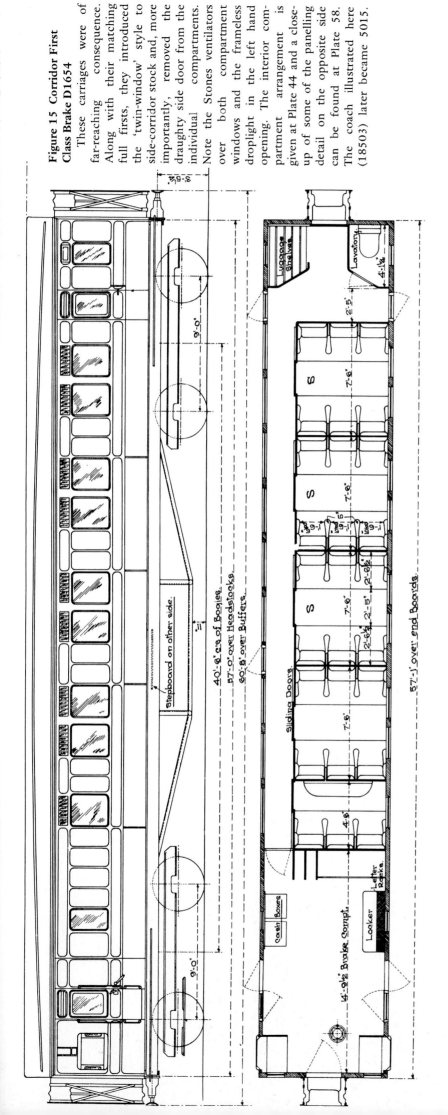

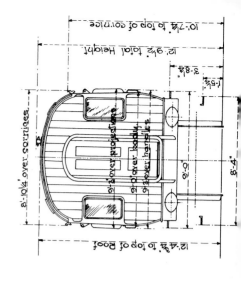

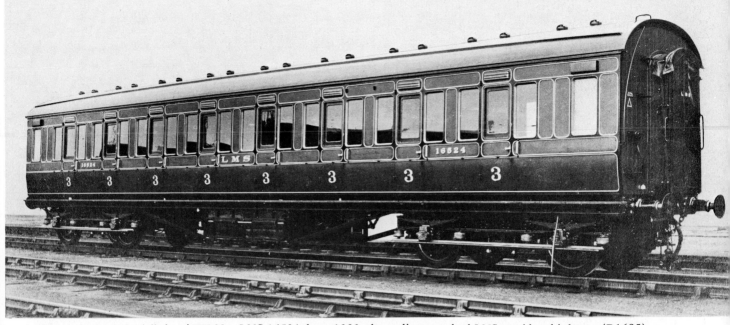

**Plate 111** Period I 'all door' TK No. LMS 16524, later 1323, the earliest standard LMS corridor third type (D1695) whose ancestry is only too obvious—see Plates 1-2. This example still retained hooded ventilators over the toilets rather than the hinged 'fall-back' type of later batches. Note also the different position of the running numbers and the alternative style of roof ventilators compared with Plate 1.

## Third Class Coaches

Apart from the odd LNWR coaches already mentioned, the all-door Period I corridor third did not vary from grouping until 1928. It was built to two diagrams (D1756, D1695); the only difference between them being the slightly greater height and the MR pattern locks and handles on the 50 coaches to D1756 which gave them a width of 9ft 1½in. Almost 300 coaches of the style were built and, unlike the firsts and composites, the twin-window style was never adopted. D1695 is also shown as 9ft 1½in wide but most seem to have been standard 9ft 3in coaches.

The brake thirds were almost equally consistent in styling apart from the eight LNWR coaches to D1712. There were again two diagrams (D1758, D1696), both all-door types, of which D1758 seems to have been slightly experimental. Although built with standard LMS fittings and 9ft 3in wide, it was a four-compartment coach, intermediate between the MR three-compartment and the later LMS standard five-compartment layout. Only 14 were built before the five compartment D1696 version came into being. This design continued building until as late as 1930, long after the Period II single window styles had appeared in other coaches. It seems that the improvement of corridor thirds was probably accorded a low priority in early LMS days.

## Composite Coaches

The corridor composite and brake composite type of coach received considerable attention by the LMS in early years and several attempts were made to achieve an ideal combination within the coach. Many of the type were built, the coaches obviously being in great demand for through working as well as for normal services and designs changes were continuous throughout the whole LMS period.

**Plate 112** Ambulance train kitchen and mess car No. 5414, photographed in September 1939. This vehicle was converted from a Period I corridor composite to D1694. Very little alteration to the original panelling was caused by this conversion. The red cross on the side is painted on the side panelling which, in the original form, marked the corridor door between the first class (far end) and third class (near end) of the vehicle. The full thirds (e.g. Plate 111) had an almost identical corridor side arrangement with a window in place of the blank panel.

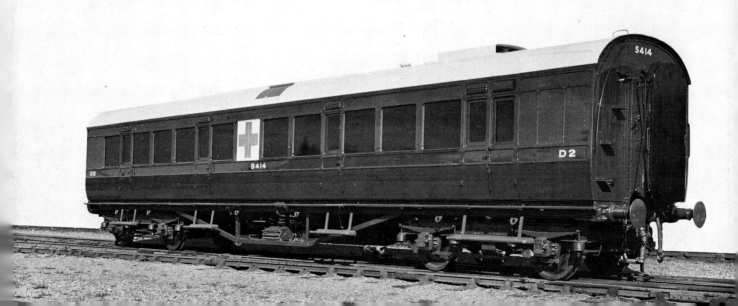

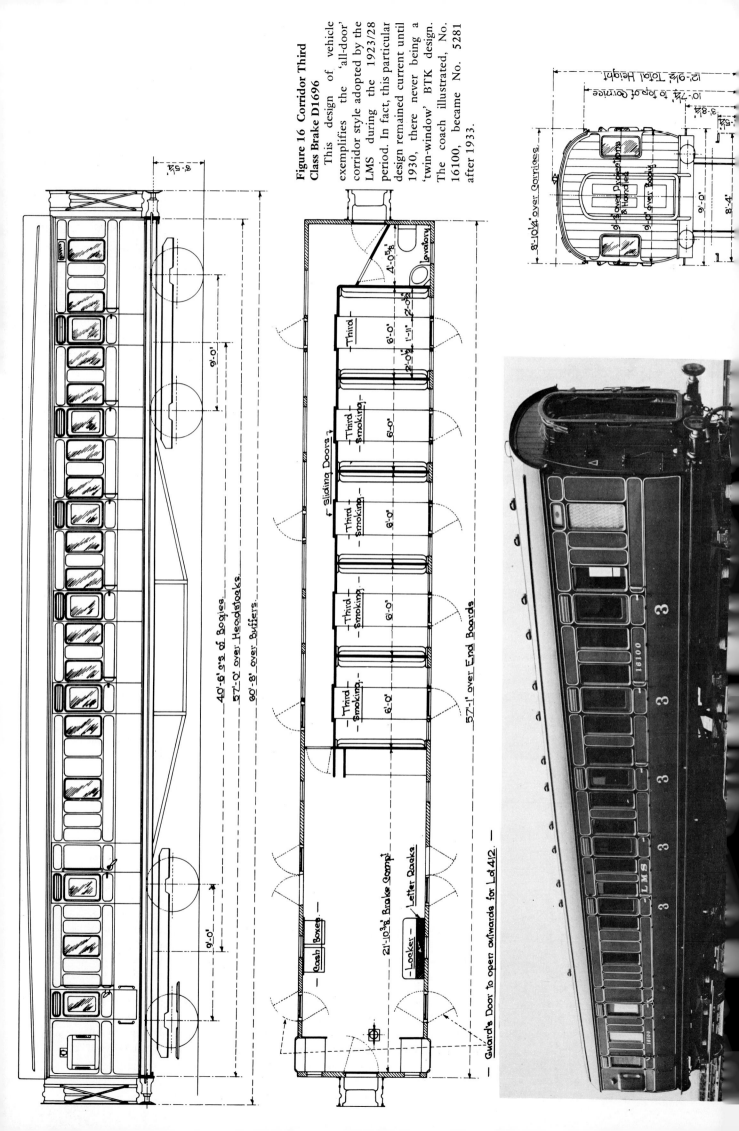

**Figure 16 Corridor Third Class Brake D1696**

This design of vehicle exemplifies the 'all-door' corridor style adopted by the LMS during the 1923/28 period. In fact, this particular design remained current until 1930, there never being a 'twin-window' BTK design. The coach illustrated, No. 16100, became No. 5281 after 1933.

**Plate 113** Period I (two-window) 60ft CK to D1716 No. 9383, later 3748. These coaches were very similar to the FKs and BFKs of a year or two earlier, but had only one Stones ventilator over the window pairs. The corridor side of these coaches had seven large (4ft 6in) windows opposite the compartments arranged in very similar fashion to the 60ft third class sleeping cars—see Plate 11.

The first design was to D1694, an orthodox, seven compartment all-door coach built in quantity. It had four third and three first class compartments. During 1925, two variants were tried. D1751 had three third and four first class compartments while in D1752 the first were split first coupé/first/first/first coupé at the expense of some lavatory space. This latter scheme was identical to the final MR design (see Frontispiece) but neither it nor the D1751 version seemed to find favour and the original D1694 coaches continued to be built until 1929.

The brake composites saw similar variations to the full composites. The first standard design was D1754 which was an all-door six compartment coach (two firsts plus four thirds), D1755 had an identical layout but with the firsts moved to the guard's end of the coach; while D1755A was a later rebuild of some of D1755 with three a side seating in the thirds, which improvement took place along with the general modernisation of many older brake composites in the 1930s—see below.

During 1928/9, the LMS must have received adverse comments about the standard of accommodation provided in its composite coaches and there were introduced some far reaching changes. From the point of view of the passenger, the first class compartments in the composites did not compare favourably with the larger compartments of the twin-window style adopted in 1927 in the corridor firsts and brake firsts. The external compartment door was probably another objection. Thus, at the end of 1929, D1716 and D1704 were introduced which brought the two-window style to the composites and brake composites.

The coaches emerged after a whole series of projected designs had been studied and rejected. These exhibited varying interior arrangements and lengths. The problem seems to have stemmed from the desire to get larger sized first class compartments, together with the necessary thirds (and luggage space, too, in the case of the brake ends) onto a standard 57ft underframe. At first layouts involving half compartments were suggested but this did not meet with approval. The LMS chiefs were not keen on reducing the size of compartment to the old value either so the final solution was to build the coaches on the 60ft underframe first introduced on the third class sleepers in 1928.

Both composite designs were late Period I vehicles and, in consequence, were transitional to the single window style. The corridor sides had single 4ft 6in windows (like the contemporary SLTs) rather than the older 3ft 0in wide corridor side windows of the twin-window firsts and brake firsts. Another point of difference was that the composites had a single nine-element Stones pattern ventilator centrally over the window pairs rather than two separate ventilators as on the first class coaches of 1927.

The perpetuation of the twin-window feature was interesting as by this time, large single windows and even Period II styling were beginning to be established in other vehicles. However, amongst the rejected designs for composite coaches were some schemes which were drawn out with single windows on the compartment side too. These would have been high waisted and very similar in appearance to the 1928 'Royal Scot' stock (see page 9). The LMS had, therefore, clearly opted for the single-window style at this time and the only reason which can be offered for the appearance of the composites with the by-now obsolete twin-window arrangement was that they were urgently needed. As it had taken some time to settle the design of the coaches it may well have been that the quickest way to get them in service was to use existing patterns and jigs. There must have been some urgency about it because barely a year was to pass before the Period II versions appeared to D1791 and D1720. On the other hand, it may have been nothing more than a convenient excuse to use up spare parts in view of the forthcoming general change in styling.

An amusing sidelight to D1704 (brake composites) was the provision of a corridor door between the first and third class sections. Apparently, and probably again because of the urgency to get them in service, the first batch of coaches was built without a connecting door. The vehicles must have gone on to the North Wales route for the Marquess of Anglesey complained about the third class passengers being able to gain easy access to the first class end of the coach and this,

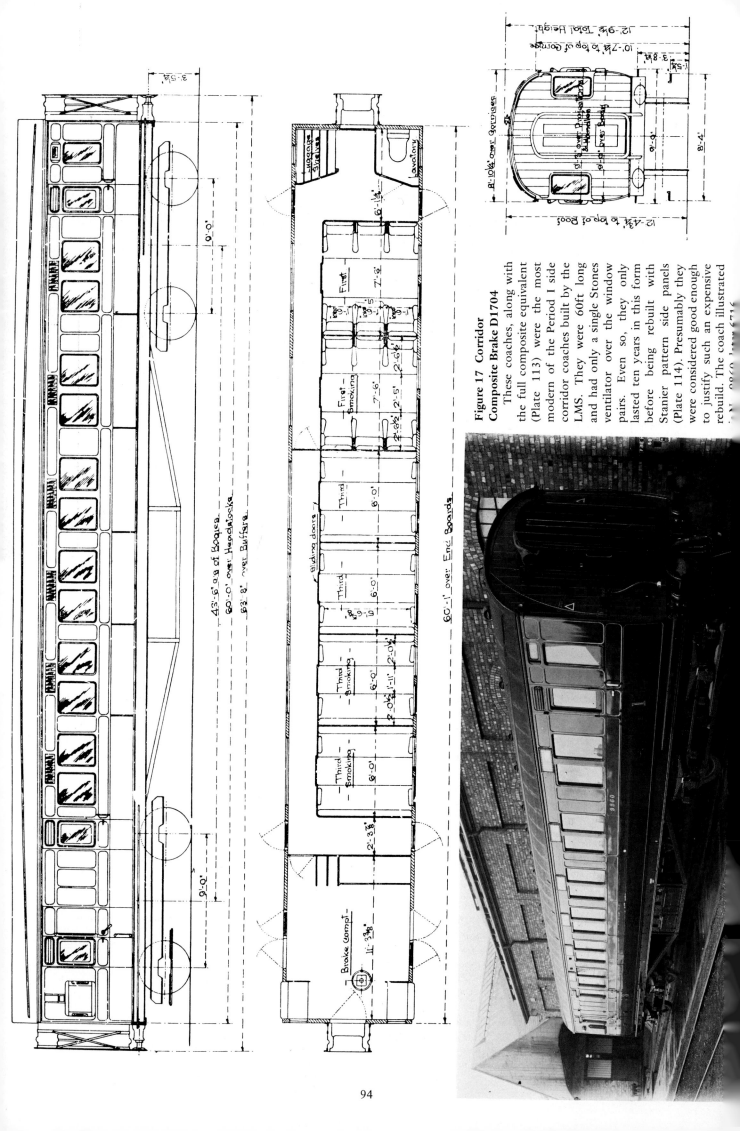

### Figure 17 Corridor Composite Brake D1704

These coaches, along with the full composite equivalent (Plate 113) were the most modern of the Period 1 side corridor coaches built by the LMS. They were 60ft long and had only a single Stones ventilator over the window pairs. Even so, they only lasted ten years in this form before being rebuilt with Stanier pattern side panels (Plate 114). Presumably they were considered good enough to justify such an expensive rebuild. The coach illustrated

**Plate 114** Rebuilt Period I BCK No. Sc6691M to D1704A seen at Colwyn Bay in BR livery. This picture clearly shows the retention by the rebuilt vehicle of the original roof.

apparently, was frowned upon. The LMS quickly rectified matters! The complaint stemmed from the fact that the D1704 coaches were originally built without a lavatory at the third class end. This was later rectified by using a portion of the, already small, brake compartment when coaches were rebuilt to D1704A (see below).

The brake composites were later given three-a-side third class seating and, still later, given Stanier style external body side panels. They retained the wood/canvas roof and the matchboard ends. This conversion coincided with the outbreak of the second world war and was held in abeyance for some time with only some of the coaches modified until policy had been settled. The decision was made to complete the rebuilding and all were eventually converted. Although the LMS was doing its best to improve coaches, two major refurbishments in about 10 years is distinctly unusual and the same sort of thing was to happen to the succeeding Period II design to D1720.

Several Period I corridor coaches were converted for ambulance use during the second world war and subsequently to full brakes. Their history in the latter guise is in Chapter 14.

## PERIOD II DESIGNS

As has been seen above, Period I style coaches continued building well after the introduction of the low waisted body styling. In consequence, only a relatively small quantity of Period II corridor vehicles were built but they represented major improvements in design and amenity.

### First Class Coaches

Unlike the thirds and composites, Period II styling was immediately adopted for first class coaches and the vehicles to D1717 were, in fact, in November 1929, the first of all the Period II designs to make an appearance. They were four compartment luxury style brake coaches with only four seats in each compartment. Everybody thus had corner seats! All compartments were differently finished and the coaches had very palatial toilets—almost miniature powder rooms. They were used on the prestige trains of the day and there is some reason to believe that they were the Period II equivalent of the Period I lounge brakes (see page 119) which were not too popular. The coaches were wood-panelled and beaded but one of them was written off in the Leighton Buzzard smash and replaced by a steel panelled version (Lot 625) in 1932.

The only other first class side corridor coaches built during this phase were again brake firsts and built to D1845. These were 4½ compartment coaches of all steel construction without conventional underframe trussing. They were built partially by outside contractors and had no raised beading. Three were rebuilt to D1962 with two-a-side seating for the 'Royal Scot'. (Text continues on page 100)

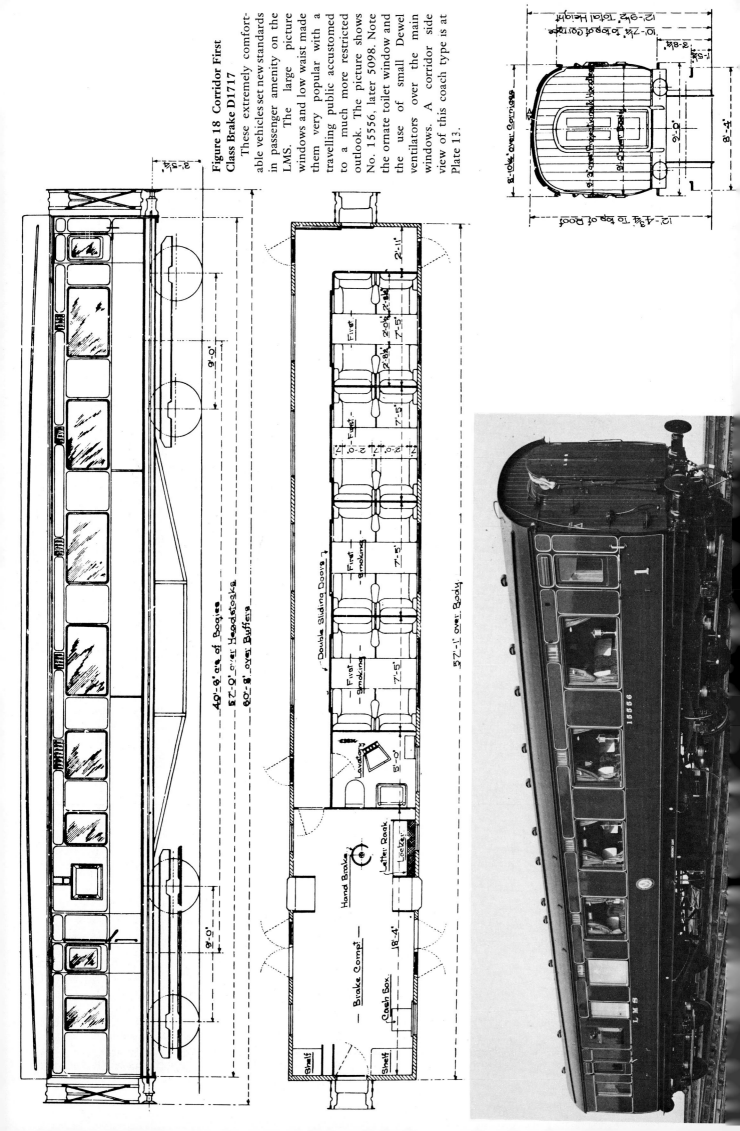

**Figure 18 Corridor First Class Brake D1717**

These extremely comfortable vehicles set new standards in passenger amenity on the LMS. The large picture windows and low waist made them very popular with a travelling public accustomed to a much more restricted outlook. The picture shows No. 15556, later 5098. Note the ornate toilet window and the use of small Dewel ventilators over the main windows. A corridor side view of this coach type is at Plate 13.

8'-10¼" over Cornices

12'-9½" Total Height
10'-7¾" to top of Cornice
3'-8¾"
1'-5¼"
2'-0"
8'-4"

12'-4¾" To Top of Roof

9'-0"

9'-0"

49'-0" c'rs of Bogies
57'-0" over Headstocks
60'-8" over Buffers

2'-1¼"

2'-11"

First

2'-8¼" 2'-0" 2'-8¼"
7'-5"

First

1'-2" 1'-2"
2'-0"
7'-5"

First
Smoking

First
Smoking
7'-5"

First
Smoking
7'-5"

Double Sliding Doors

Lavatory
5'-0"

Hand Brake

Letter Rack

Locker

Shelf

Brake Comp't

Cash Box
Shelf
18'-4"

57'-1" over Body

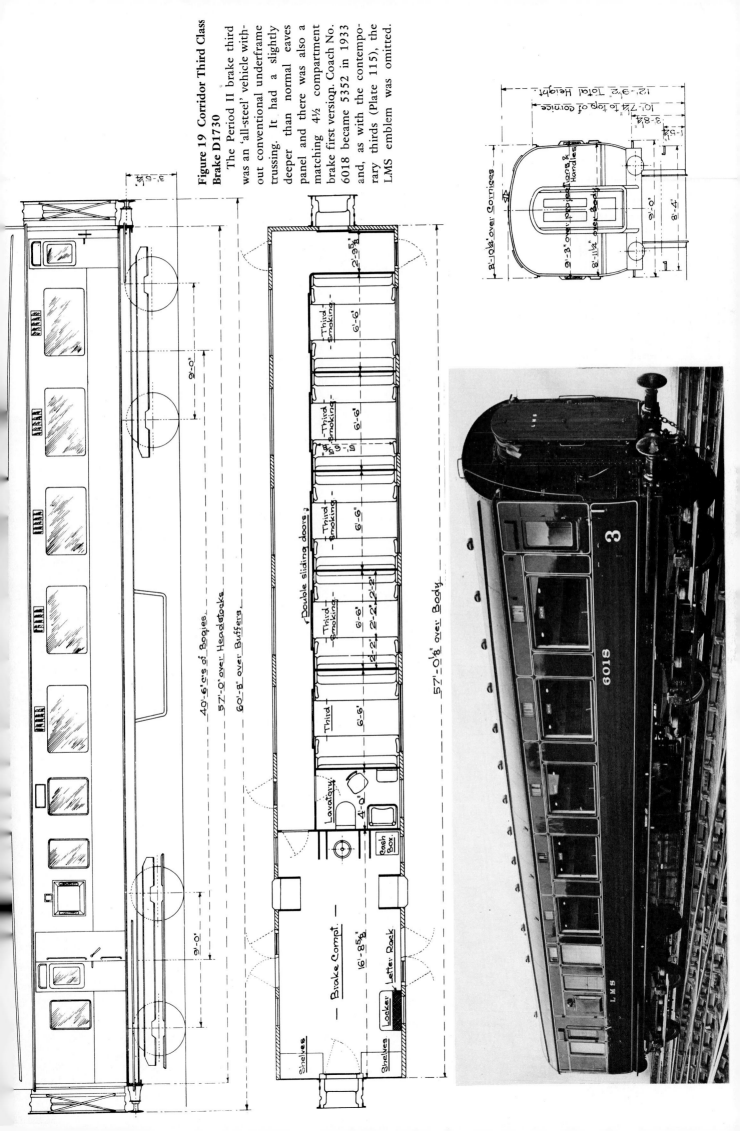

**Figure 19 Corridor Third Class Brake D1730**

The Period II brake third was an 'all-steel' vehicle without conventional underframe trussing. It had a slightly deeper than normal eaves panel and there was also a matching 4½ compartment brake first version. Coach No. 6018 became 5352 in 1933 and, as with the contemporary thirds (Plate 115), the LMS emblem was omitted.

**Plate 115** Period II 60ft TK (D1782) No. 3031 later 1502. Only ten were built, the only corridor thirds between the 'all-door' type and the Stanier designs and the only 60ft TKs. Note the absence of the LMS emblem—a not uncommon feature of LMS thirds and brake thirds even with end entrances. The handgrips for lowering the compartment droplights are clear, high on the window.

**Plate 116** Period II BCK No. 3530, later 6742 to D1720. This handsome vehicle was transitional to the steel-sided Period II designs and although it had wood panelled sides, the end panelling was steel.

**Plate 117** Rebuilt Period II BCK No. 6767 to D1720A. An interesting point about this particular batch of rebuilds was that the first class compartments were given 4ft 6in Period III windows and the thirds, 4ft 0in windows. Originally, all compartments had 4ft 6in windows.

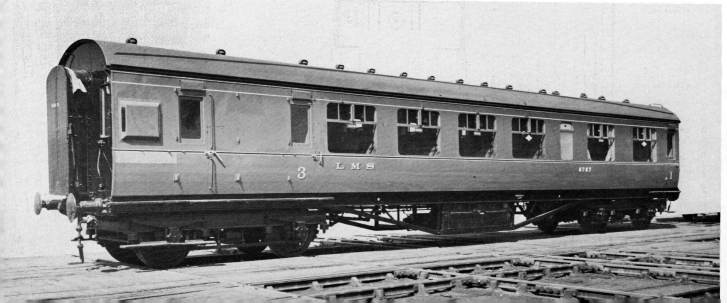

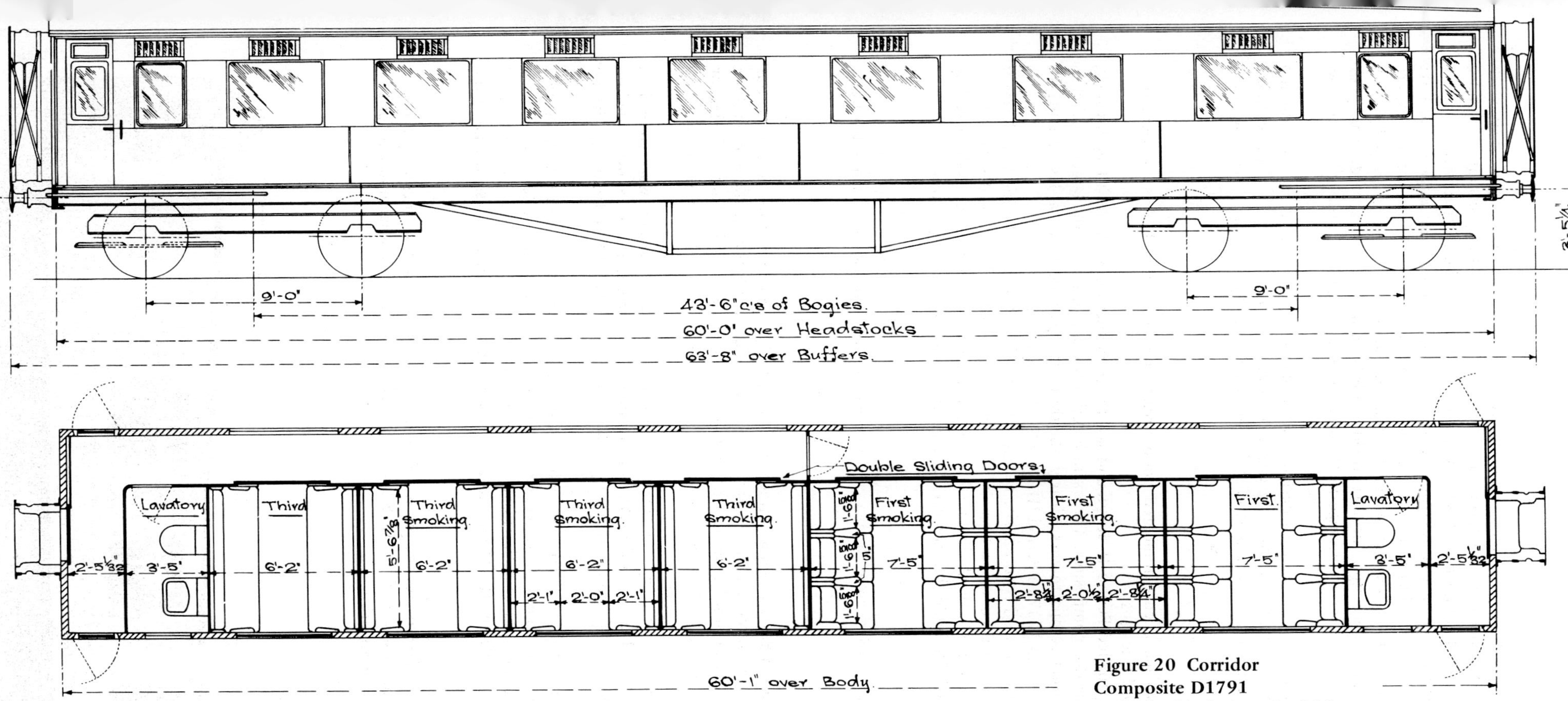
43'-6" c's of Bogies.
60'-0' over Headstocks
63'-8" over Buffers.
9'-0'
9'-0"
3'-5¼"
Double Sliding Doors
Lavatory
Third
Third Smoking.
First Smoking.
First.
60'-1" over Body.

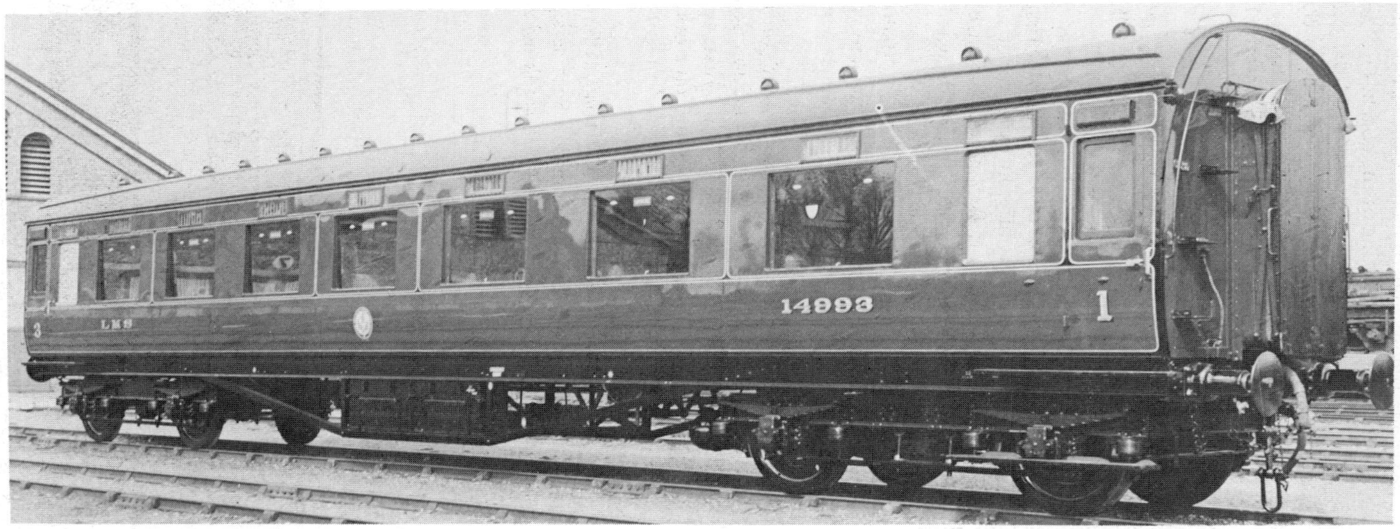
14993
1
LMS

**Figure 20 Corridor Composite D1791**

With this design of vehicle, the LMS introduced a layout for its corridor composites which was never to change again during the life of the company, all Period III examples also being built to the same essential plan. The main difference from preceding examples was the move of the entrance doors to the extreme end of the vehicle. Coach 14993 became 3810 in 1933. An interesting livery detail is the positioning of the LMS emblem under the centre window and not in the centre of the coach side. A corridor side view of this vehicle is at Plate 15.

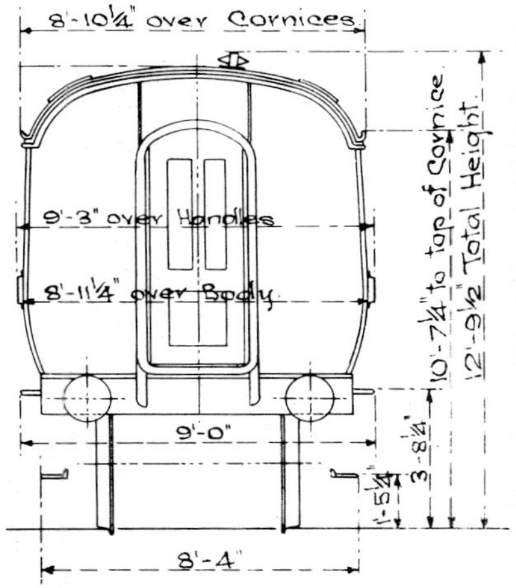
8'-10¼" over Cornices
9'-3" over Handles
8'-11¼" over Body
9'-0"
8'-4"
10'-7¼" to top of Cornice
12'-9½" Total Height

## Third Class Coaches

The late building of the all-door Period I coaches meant that Period II styling was later to appear in corridor third class coaches and, in the event, only two designs were built.

The corridor third to D1872 was a very handsome design and set completely new standards. On a 60ft underframe it had but seven compartments which were 6ft 6in between partitions—an increase of 6in over the previous size and a dimension hitherto only used in the late Period I 60ft composites. It seated four on each side of the compartment but only 10 coaches were built—possibly because it was rather an extravagant design. No reason can be adduced why the LMS departed from the 57ft length for this batch of coaches but as it was the period when the company was actively experimenting with new ideas, the coaches were probably something of an experimental design. They were, allegedly, very comfortable vehicles to ride in and remained the sole examples of 60ft corridor thirds until the end of LMS designs. They may have been built to 60ft length to match the 60ft opens (see page 123). In fact the LMS almost became a '60ft line' at this period.

The brake third version to D1730 was a much more numerous design. Externally it was of all-steel construction and matched the D1845 BFKs—page 95. Although it perpetuated the 57ft length and five compartment layout of the Period I brake third, it had the 6ft 6in compartment dimension of the 60ft corridor thirds. This made the guard's compartment rather small.

## Composite Coaches

The evolution of the Period I composite coach has been commented upon already and the Period II versions were very similar in layout to the final twin-window Period I designs.

The full composite to D1791, was a steel-panelled Period II design and saw the perpetuation of the 60ft length which, henceforward, remained standard for LMS corridor composites. The extra length provided space for the larger third class compartments and to increase the size of the toilet compartments. Clearly, the third class passenger was, at last, getting his share of new ideas. One of the coaches was rebuilt in 1937 to Period III D1969 following a fire.

The brake ended version to D1720 was the first Period II composite to appear and differed from its Period I predecessor in having the lavatory separating the two classes of accommodation. It was a wood-panelled and beaded design and, like D1704, the coaches were later modified to three-a-side third class seating and, ultimately, Stanier pattern side panelling and windows. They were very similar to the D1704 rebuilds but the centre lavatory was a distinguishing feature.

# PERIOD III DESIGNS

Period III corridor coaches went through all the variations of Stanier coach design but, considering the vast number built, the variations of layout were surprisingly few.

### First Class Coaches

The standard LMS Period III corridor first was a 56ft, 5½ compartment vehicle with 7ft 6in compartments. The various diagrams denote such differences as four or six seats in each compartment and the alteration in position of the non-smoking areas but there was, in fact, no basic change in layout until after nationalisation. These coaches included three vehicles for the 1937 'Coronation Scot' train for which a separate diagram was raised. The coaches were built new for this service and had luxury two-a-side seating.

After nationalisation, there was a slight change of design in D2121. The compartment dimension was reduced to 7ft 2in and this enabled six compartments to be achieved on the 57ft underframe. Two extra doors were also added on the corridor side of the coach (D2121). Finally, the 'porthole' type of window appeared in D2162 of 1950 but with no other significant changes.

Brake firsts were equally consistent. Until the war, a 4½ compartment layout was standardised—again with a separate diagram raised for the 1937 'Coronation Scot' stock. These latter coaches were, in fact, apart from an odd coach built in 1934, the first Stanier pattern brake firsts to be built. After nationalisation, a five-compartment brake first was introduced with 'Porthole' toilet windows and on a 60ft underframe (D2168). This represented the only change in basic design of the Period III brake first.

**Plate 118** Period III FK No. 1047 as built to D1909. All the pre-war FKs were of this general style, including those built for the 1937 Coronation Scot sets. The absence of the LMS crest on this coach was somewhat unusual for a *first* class coach, as was the 'all smoking' accommodation.

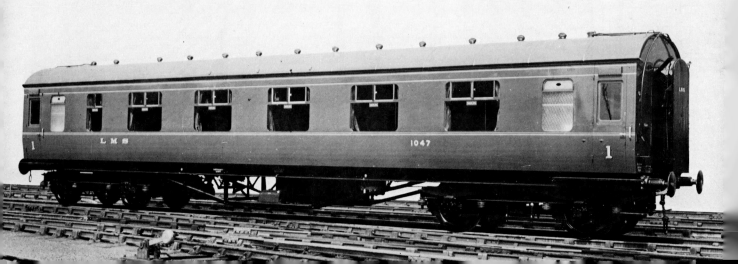

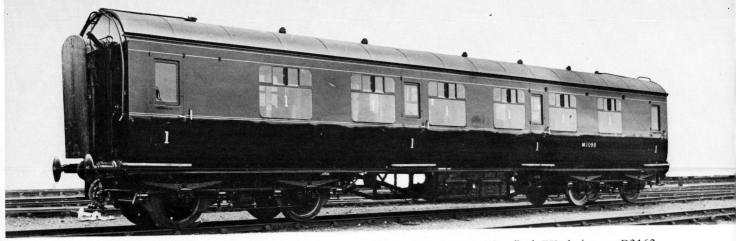

**Plate 119** *(above)* The initial post-war FK design, No. M1098 to D2121, still on a 57ft underframe but now with six compartments and two extra corridor side doors. Like the pre-war Period III FKs, these coaches had no windows opposite the toilets on the corridor side. Note the figure '1s' on the windows and the LMS livery still in use after 1947.

**Plate 120** *(below)* The final FK design to D2162 illustrated by No. M1122 as built in BR crimson/cream livery. These were 'porthole' coaches and had six compartments. However, on the corridor side, there were matching circular windows opposite the toilets. Note the shorter sliding window ventilators.

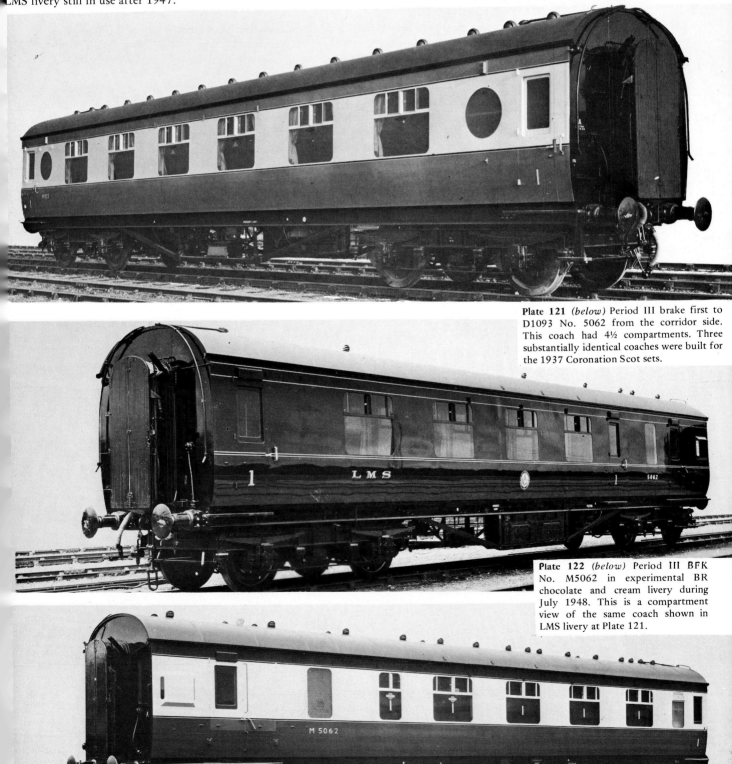

**Plate 121** *(below)* Period III brake first to D1093 No. 5062 from the corridor side. This coach had 4½ compartments. Three substantially identical coaches were built for the 1937 Coronation Scot sets.

**Plate 122** *(below)* Period III BFK No. M5062 in experimental BR chocolate and cream livery during July 1948. This is a compartment view of the same coach shown in LMS livery at Plate 121.

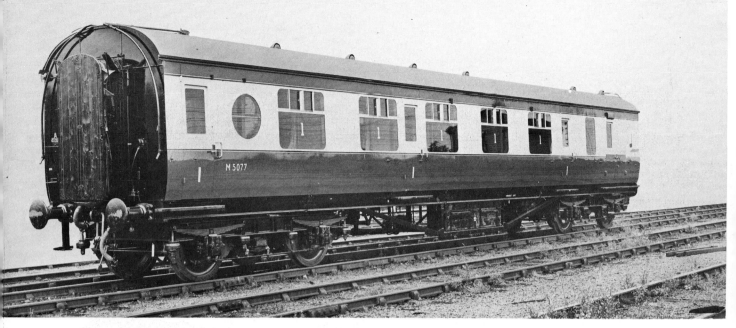

**Plate 123** 'Porthole' brake first to D2168 No. M5077 in BR crimson/cream livery as built. These were 60ft coaches the only LMS pattern BFKs to be built to this length. Note the extra corridor door, the window opposite the toilet and five main windows. They were five-compartment coaches.

## Third Class Coaches

Over 1400 Period III corridor thirds were built between 1933 and 1950 yet to only two basic layouts. The pre-war version had two doors on the corridor side while the post-war variety had four corridor doors. All were seven compartment, 57ft coaches. Of the two major types, the post-war variant was, ultimately, the more numerous—although not until after nationalisation. As late as 1968, many of the post-nationalisation coaches still survived. A reduction in compartment size from 6ft 6in to 6ft 3in was made in the first Stanier corridor thirds and this remained standard, although not adopted in the brake thirds until after the war.

Turning now to detail variations, the pre-war coaches were built to two diagrams, the earlier one being the shallow-window ventilator version. The post-war coaches were also built to two diagrams of which the later version was the porthole variety.

There was also a little batch of three luxury corridor thirds built after the war at Derby. These were the 1939 'Coronation Scot' style coaches, considered in detail in Chapter 13.

Period III brake thirds were even more numerous and showed slightly more design changes than did the full thirds. All of them exhibited one basic change from most previous LMS coaches of the type in having a standardised four-compartment layout. Mention was made on page 100 of the rather small guard's compartment in the five compartment Period II brake thirds and this may have been one reason for the dropping of one compartment from the layout.

Unusually, there were two shallow ventilator BTK diagrams issued in 1933. The earlier coaches (D1851), had one single and one double door to the guard's van while the later version (D1852) had two pairs of double doors. They were amongst the few Stanier coaches to be built before the 1932/3 renumbering. A few were converted to push-pull operation by BR (Table 8). D1905 was the standard deep-window ventilator version and was multiplied extensively until 1936 when lighter versions (D1963/D1971) made their appearance.

In 1937, a change was made by moving the toilet to the end of the coach rather than adjacent to the guard's van. This placed the compartments more between the bogies than hitherto and this design straddled the war years. It was superseded after nationalisation by D2123 and D2161 both of which had the reduced size of compartment (6ft 3in instead of 6ft 6in) and an extra corridor side door. D2161 was the porthole version and none were built until after the LMS ceased to exist. Several of the latter survived long enough to see overhauled service in the BR blue/grey livery.

**Plate 124** Pioneer Period III TK to D1860 No. 1536. This set the style for all subsequent LMS corridor thirds—a seven compartment layout with extreme end doors on a 57ft chassis. This view is from the corridor side, the compartment side being identical (except for sliding window ventilator style) to the standard Period III version at Plate 125.

**Plate 125** *(above)* A typical pre-war Stanier corridor third, this particular example being No. 1579 from the batch with full livery (D1899). Note the absence of the LMS crest. The running number was rendered in unshaded block style characters—typical of the early Stanier period.

**Plate 126** *(below)* LMS No. 2151—the post-war development to D2119. It had two extra doors on the corridor side. This picture shows the later LMS simple livery with flat topped '3s' and a reversion to scroll pattern running numbers. This time the coach *has* received a crest! Note the changed design of toilet window omitting the hinged 'fall-back' top section, compared with earlier Period III coaches.

**Plate 127** *(above)* Period III BTK No. 5461 of the pioneer Stanier design with full livery and shallow window ventilators (D1851). Note the torpedo roof vents, absence of LMS crest, unshaded block numbers and the lamp over the guard's lookout, soon discontinued on Stanier coaches and also removed from earlier vehicles. Minor changes took place between this version and the final style. The van end was soon changed to have two pairs of double doors and this was followed by the introduction of deep window ventilators. The next change was to re-position the toilet at the end of the vehicle and finally came the post-war versions with extra corridor doors.

**Plate 128** *(below)* Period III BTK No. 6006 to D1968. This was an example of the first batch of Stanier corridor brake thirds with lavatories at the end of the coach. For the intermediate design between this and Plate 127, refer to Plate 19.

**Plate 129** The final Period III design of BTK No. M27001M (D2161), the variation with extra corridor side door and 'porthole' windows. None was built until after 1947. The coach is shown in BR blue/grey livery and, as far as is known, these BTKs were the only variety of LMS pattern *day* coach to be thus treated. Note the BR type of roof vents and shorter sliding window ventilators. A compartment side view of this design is at Plate 26.

## Composite Coaches

It was again the composite coach which underwent most changes in Period III and it is not without significance that the first ever Stanier gangwayed coaches to be built were brake composites to D1850, some of which appeared in December 1932. For the most part, the significant developments were confined to the brake ended designs and the full composites retained the 60ft, seven compartment layout to the end. They only witnessed detail modifications, principally the reduction of third class compartment size from 6ft 6in to 6ft 3in with D1925 of 1935.

At the same time, Period III brake composites, although built to several designs, were not very numerous mainly because of the large scale rebuilding to Period III styling of the D1704 and D1720 coaches.

The genuine Stanier pattern brake composites still indicated that the LMS could not make up its mind what to do. Clearly the four third plus two first class arrangement of the Period I/II coaches must have given too small a brake compartment and the first Stanier examples had 3½ thirds plus 1½ firsts, still on a 60ft underframe.

This development was rather wasteful of space and seems to have flown in the face of the views current at the time the final Period I coaches were being designed—it was thus only multiplied to the tune of 22 coaches— mostly shallow ventilator types. The standard Period III version evolved from this design and saw yet another increase in length, this time to 62ft (D1932). This with a reduction to 6ft 3in third class compartments gave room for two first plus 3½ thirds and was built in some numbers, eventually becoming the numerically largest type of LMS brake composite. There were two diagrams for the coaches of almost identical style but the later one (D2010) had slightly different toilets and removable compartment tables. They were the longest side corridor LMS design coaches and the only 62ft coaches built by the company. No examples were built after the war.

**Plate 130** LMS No. 3868 from the compartment side. This coach to D1898 was typical of the pre-war Stanier CKs and was in all essentials a Period III version of Figure 20. It is one of the earlier examples in full livery but after the change to deep window ventilators.

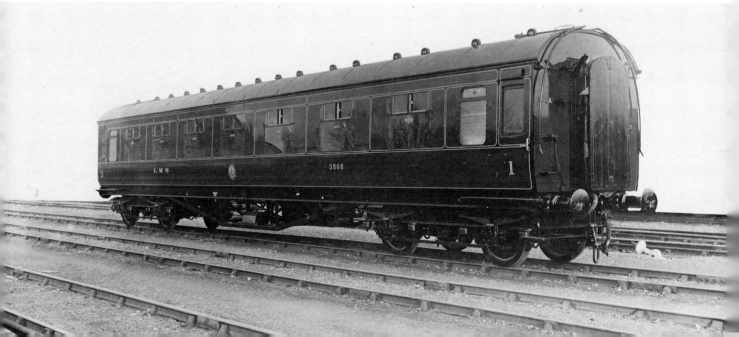

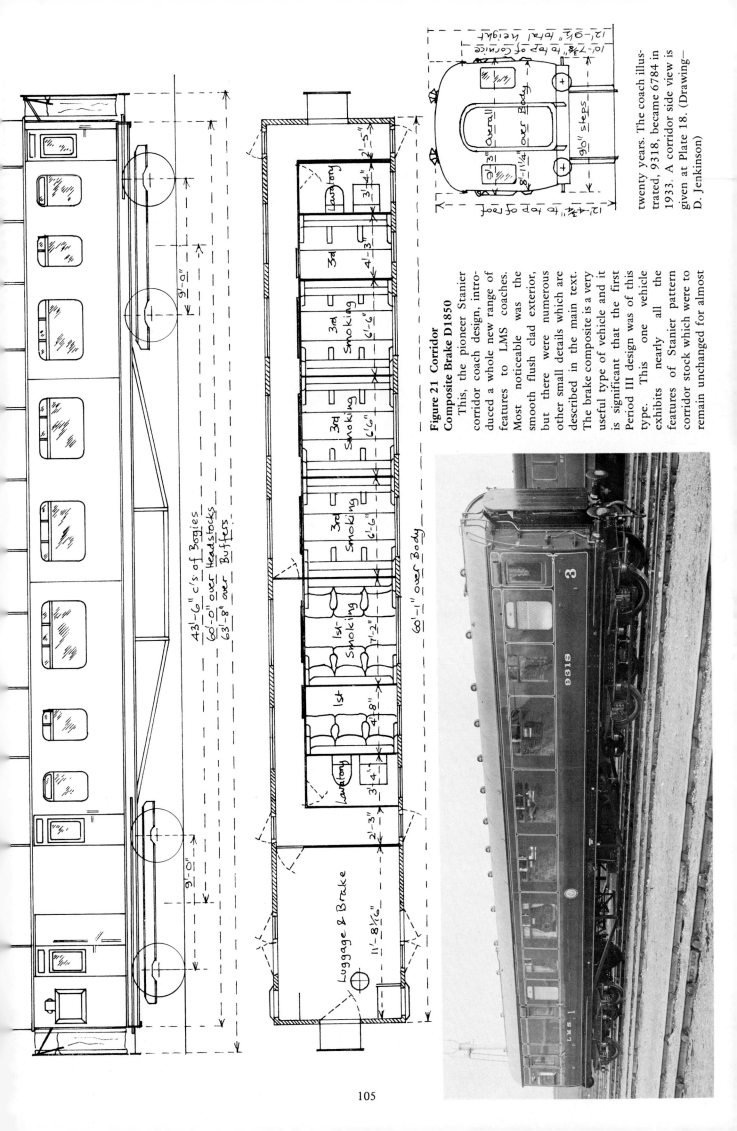

### Figure 21 Corridor Composite Brake D1850

This, the pioneer Stanier corridor coach design, introduced a whole new range of features to LMS coaches. Most noticeable was the smooth flush clad exterior, but there were numerous other small details which are described in the main text. The brake composite is a very useful type of vehicle and it is significant that the first Period III design was of this type. This one vehicle exhibits nearly all the features of Stanier pattern corridor stock which were to remain unchanged for almost twenty years. The coach illustrated, 9318, became 6784 in 1933. A corridor side view is given at Plate 18. (Drawing—D. Jenkinson)

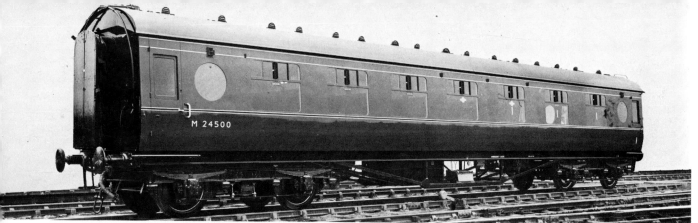

Plate 131 (above) M24500 as built to D2159 with LMS livery but BR letter prefix. This was the final style of CK with 'porthole' windows and revised end profile. These were 'all-steel' coaches with lighter section truss rods and solebars. The four truss rods are just visible between the bogies.

Plate 132 (below) M24659 of D2159 as built with BR crimson/cream livery. The tartan backed headboard is interesting. The rounded side-end junction of the exterior body panelling is perceptible. Note, by comparison with Plate 131 (the opposite side of the same type of carriage), the change to BR-type roof vents and the use of welded bogies.

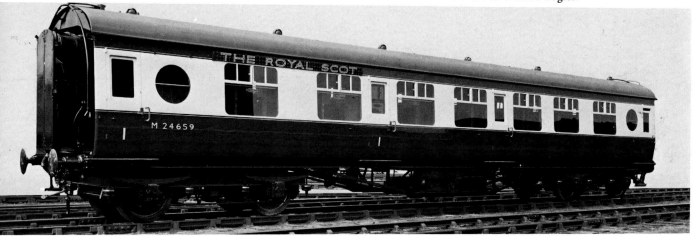

Plate 133 (above) Period III BCK to D1911, No. 6805. Apart from livery, window and roof ventilators, this design was identical to the pioneer D1850 (Figure 21).

Plate 134 (below) The final Period III BCK designs to D1932 and D2010 were 62ft coaches. The example illustrated here is a D1932 version, No. 6823, ex-shops in 1935. Note the prominent slate painted panel at the brake end.

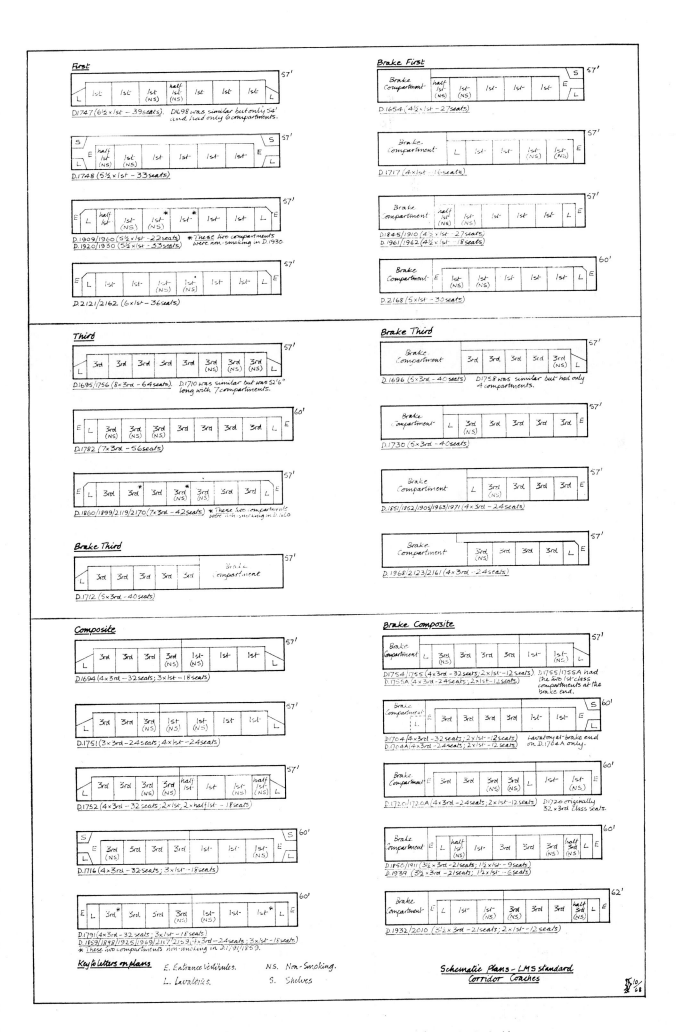

**FIGURE 22** *LMS standard corridor stock—sketch plans* (Drawn by D. Jenkinson)

## TABLE 8: SUMMARY TABLE OF LMS SIDE CORRIDOR GENERAL SERVICE COACHING STOCK

*Note:* This table should be read in conjunction with the list of standard dimensions and details on page 62.

| Type | Diag | Lot | Qty | Date | Built | Dimensions (L×W×H) | Weight | Period | Running Numbers | Withdrawals First | Last | Remarks |
|------|------|-----|-----|------|-------|-------------------|--------|--------|-----------------|-------|------|---------|
| FK | 1698 | 29 | 3 | 1924 | Wolverton | 54'×9'1½"×12'4¾" | 28T | I (All door) | 1000-1002 | 7/56 | 1/61 | Diagram shows 9'1½" width but coaches were plated 9'4" and 29T. Probably Derby issued the drawings assuming MR pattern fittings but Wolverton used up LNWR style handles &c. |
| FK | 1747 | 246 | 10 | 1926 | Wolverton | 57'×9'3"×12'4¾" | 29T | I (All door) | 1003-1012 | 5/59 | 10/61 | |
| FK | 1748 | 325 | 10 | 1927 | Wolverton | 57'×9'3"×12'4¾" | 29T | I (Two window style) | 1013-1022 | 2/59 | 10/61 | Compartment size increased from 7'3" to 7'6". |
| FK | 1920 | 775 | 1 | 1934 | Derby | 57'×9'3"×12'4⅝" | 31T | III | 1038 | — | 10/63 | The prototype Period III FK. |
| FK | 1909 | 793 | 12 | 1934 | Derby | 57'×9'3"×12'4⅝" | 31T | III | 1039-1050 | 9/62 | 1/65 | As for D1920 but with two a side seating. |
| FK | 1930 | 904 | 11 | 1936 | Wolverton | 57'×9'3"×12'4⅝" | 32T | III | 1051-1061 | 7/64 | 3/65 | Luxury finish but three a side seating. Identical to D1920 except for the arrangement of non-smoking compartments. |
| | | 1041 | 7 | 1937 | Wolverton | | 32T | | 1062-1068 | 7/64 | 11/65 | |
| | | 1092 | 7 | 1938 | Wolverton | | 31T | | 1072-1083 | 1/64 | 1/65 | |
| FK | 1960 | 1062 | 3 | 1937 | Wolverton | 57'×9'3"×12'4⅝" | 33T | III | 1069-1071 | 12/63 | 12/64 | The 1937 'Coronation Scot' coaches with two a side seating and heavier than the D1930 equivalent. Probably diverted from Lot 1041. |
| FK | 2121 | 1439 | 30 | 1948 | Wolverton | 57'×9'3"×12'4⅝" | 31T | III | 1084-1113 | 10/64 | 9/65 | The post-war version with compartments reduced from 7'6" to 7'2". All given post war LMS livery but with 'M' prefix and no 'LMS' on coach side. Fitted with final style of sliding ventilators. |
| FK | 2162 | 1585 | 15 | 1950 | Wolverton | 57'×9'3"×12'4⅝" | 30T | III (Porthole) | 1114-1128 | 12/64 | 12/65 | As for D2121 but with post-war torpedo ventilators. Finished in BR crimson/cream when new and somewhat accident prone: 1123/5 (Weedon 21/9/51); 1124 (Harrow 8/10/52). |
| BFK | 1654 | 326 | 25 | 1927 | Derby | 57'×9'3"×12'4¾" | 27T | I (Two window style) | 5011-5035 | 6/59 | 11/64 | Brake version of D1748. 5034 to Royal train (11/35). 5035 had LNER type bogies supplied in 1931 ! |
| BFK | 1717 | 477 | 6 | 1929 | Derby | 57'×9'3"×12'4¾" | 29T | II (beaded) | 5005-5009 | 13/59 | 12/62 | The pioneer Period II coaches. Only five of Lot 477 were renumbered and Lot 625 was a replacement for the missing one (old 15458) written off after the Leighton Buzzard accident. 5006 was fitted with very long wheelbase bogies. When new, the coaches had small scroll type figures. |
| | | 625 | 1 | 1932 | Derby | | 29T | II (flush) | 5010 | — | 11/61 | |
| BFK | 1845 | 582 | 15 | 1931 | see remarks | 57'×9'3"×12'4¾" | 32T | II (Flush) | 5036-5050 | 6/61 | 10/63 | Bogies and interiors built at Wolverton, the remainder by Birmingham C&W. They were 'all steel' coaches with deeper than normal eaves panelling and no conventional underframe. D1962 was a later conversion to two a side seating. |
| BFK | 1962 | Part 582 | 3 | | see remarks | 57'×9'3"×12'4¾" | 32T | II (Flush) | 5036-5038 | 11/61 | 12/61 | |
| BFK | 1910 | 776 | 1 | 1934 | Derby | 57'×9'3"×12'4⅝" | 31T | III | 5051 | — | 10/64 | The standard Period III BFK. |
| | | 1093 | 8 | 1938 | Wolverton | | 31T | | 5055-5062 | 6/64 | 3/65 | |
| BFK | 1961 | 1063 | 3 | 1937 | Wolverton | 57'×9'3"×12'4⅝" | 32T | III | 5052-5054 | 4/64 | 12/64 | The 'Coronation Scot' version of D1910 with two a side seating and heavier tare weight. |
| BFK | 2168 | 1504 | 15 | 1949 | Wolverton | 60'×9'3"×12'4⅝" | 30T | III (Porthole) | 5063-5077 | 11/64 | 5/65 | The post-war version with five 7'2" compartments on a longer underframe. All finished in BR crimson/cream livery when new and fitted with the final style of sliding ventilators. |
| TK | 1756 | 7 | 25 | 1924 | Derby | 57'×9'1½"×12'5½" | 27T | I (All door) | 1212-1236 | 6/53 | 2/61 | Coaches with MR style fittings. Lot 7 plated 1923 and both lots carried MR type works plates. |
| | | 8 | 25 | 1924 | Derby | | 27T | | 1237-1261 | 11/51 | 4/60 | |
| TK | 1710 | 87 | 5 | 1924 | Wolverton | 52'6"×9'4"×12'5½" | 28T | see remarks | 1207-1211 | 4/51 | 12/56 | The LNWR type coaches with corridor toplights and LNWR panelled ends. Converted from WWI ambulance vehicles. |
| TK | 1695 | 9 | 18 | 1924 | Derby | 57'×9'1½"×12'4¾" | 28T | I (all door) | 1262-1279 | 11/58 | 8/62 | Although shown as 9'1½" wide, this was the 9'3" wide standard Period I TK, otherwise identical to D1756. Only Lots 9/71 had MR pattern commode handles. Over 60 coaches (mostly Lot 388) saw active service in the war and only about half returned to traffic, the others being lost in France. 1301/17/33/62 had gangways removed (1948) for CLC service. Lots 147/158 plated 1925, Lot 388 plated 29T. |
| | | 71 | 17 | 1924 | Derby | | 28T | | 1280-1296 | 5/58 | 9/61 | |
| | | 95 | 45 | 1925 | Derby | | 28T | | 1297-1341 | 7/58 | 13/62 | |
| | | 147 | 40 | 1926 | Derby | | 28T | | 1342-1381 | 11/58 | 10/63 | |
| | | 158 | 40 | 1926 | Derby | | 28T | | 1382-1421 | 3/59 | 13/62 | |
| | | 388 | 75 | 1928 | Wolverton | | 28T | | 1422-1496 | 3/59 | 2/64 | |
| TK | 1782 | 551 | 10 | 1930 | Derby | 60'×9'3"×12'4¾" | 30T | II (beaded) | 1497-1506 | 5/59 | 5/62 | The palatial 60' coaches with compartments increased in size from 6'0" to 6'6". |
| TK | 1860 | 695 | 30 | 1933 | Wolverton | 57'×9'3"×12'4¾" | 31T | III (Shallow ventilator) | 1507-1536 | 8/62 | 12/64 | The first Period III TK and had full livery when new. Also the first LMS TKs with three a side seating from new. The compartment size was reduced to 6'3" on these and subsequent coaches. |
| TK | 1899 | 730 | 35 | 1933 | Derby | | 31T | III | 1537-1571 | 3/62 | 3/65 | The standard Period III TK and the most numerous single type of coach built by the LMS although eventually outnumbered by D2119 (below). Lots 730/731 were outshopped in fully lined livery. |
| | | 731 | 34 | 1934 | Derby | | 31T | | 1572-1605 | 13/61 | 4/66 | |
| | | 795 | 35 | 1934 | Derby | | 31T | | 1606-1640 | 10/62 | 6/65 | |
| | | 796 | 25 | 1934 | Derby | | 31T | | 1641-1665 | 2/62 | 12/65 | |
| | | 797 | 20 | 1934 | Derby | | 31T | | 1666-1685 | 12/62 | 11/65 | |
| | | 798 | 25 | 1934 | Derby | | 31T | | 1686-1710 | 11/61 | 3/66 | |
| | | 799 | 30 | 1934 | Derby | 57'×9'3"×12'4¾" | 31T | | 1711-1740 | 7/62 | 6/65 | |
| | | 800 | 20 | 1934 | Wolverton | | 32T | | 1741-1760 | 8/62 | 9/65 | |
| | | 801 | 35 | 1934 | Wolverton | | 32T | | 1761-1795 | 1/62 | 6/65 | |
| | | 802 | 35 | 1934 | Wolverton | | 32T | | 1796-1830 | 12/61 | 10/64 | |
| | | 803 | 30 | 1934 | Wolverton | | 32T | | 1831-1860 | 5/62 | 11/64 | |

# TABLE 8: LMS SIDE CORRIDOR STOCK (continued)

| Type | Diag | Lot | Qty | Date | Built | Dimensions (L×W×H) | Weight | Period | Running Numbers | Withdrawals First | Last | Remarks |
|---|---|---|---|---|---|---|---|---|---|---|---|---|
| TK | 1899 | 846 | 65 | 1935 | Derby | | 31T | | 1861-1925 | 5/62 | 10/65 | |
| | | 896 | 25 | 1936/7 | Derby | | 31T | | 1926-1950 | 6/63 | 4/65 | |
| | | 897 | 50 | 1936 | Derby | | 31T | | 1951-2000 | 9/62 | 11/65 | |
| | | 998 | 40 | 1937 | Wolverton | 57'×9'3"×12'4¾" | 32T | | 2001-2040 | 5/63 | 12/65 | |
| | | 1089 | 44 | 1938 | Wolverton | | 32T | | 2041-2084 | 9/62 | 8/65 | |
| | | 1090 | 45 | 1938 | Wolverton | | 32T | | 2085-2129 | 2/61 | 8/65 | |
| | | 1191 | 18 | 1939 | Wolverton | | 31T | | 2130-2147 | 13/63 | 7/65 | |
| TK | 2119 | 1405 | 50 | 1946 | Derby | | 31T | III | 2151-2200 | 13/63 | 3/67 | The post-war version with two extra doors on the corridor side. Some date discrepancies on works plates: Lot 1407 plated 1946. Lot 1447 plated 1947. Lot 1483 plated variously 1948/1949 and possibly some 1950. The change to the final style of sliding ventilator probably came somewhere in Lot 1436. Ex-works livery: Lots 1405-1436: LMS post war livery. Lots 1436-1483: LMS livery but no LMS markings. Lot 1484: BR Crimson/Cream. 2221/35/50 were converted to Tea Cars (Jan. 1950) for the Irish Mail service, three compartments being used as a serving area. 2235 was destroyed at Penmaenmawr on 27/8/50 so in April 1953, 2211 was altered to a Tea Car as a replacement. |
| | | 1406 | 50 | 1946 | Derby | | 31T | | 2201-2250 | 13/63 | 5/68 | |
| | | 1407 | 100 | 1946-7 | Derby | | 31T | | 2251-2350 | 3/64 | Many still extant (1968) | |
| | | 1436 | 116 | 1946-7 | Met-Cammell | 57'×9'3"×12'4⅝" | 31T | | 2351-2466 | 13/63 | | |
| | | 1447 | 50 | 1947-8 | Derby | | 31T | | 2467-2516 | 11/65 | | |
| | | 1483 | 200 | 1948-50 | Met-Cammell | | 31T | | 12750-12949 | 13/63 | | |
| | | 1484 | 135 | 1949-50 | B'ham C&W | | 30T | | 12950-13084 | 7/64 | | |
| TK | 2170 | 1621 | 100 | 1950 | Met-Cammell | 57'×9'2½"×12'4⅝" | 30T | III (Porthole) | 13085-13184 | 5/64 | Many still extant (1968) | All given Crimson/Cream livery and believed to have had torpedo ventilators (post-war type). |

**Note:** One further TK diagram issued (D2019) for the 1939 'Coronation Scot' coaches. These are included in Chapter 13 Table 13b.

| Type | Diag | Lot | Qty | Date | Built | Dimensions (L×W×H) | Weight | Period | Running Numbers | Withdrawals First | Last | Remarks |
|---|---|---|---|---|---|---|---|---|---|---|---|---|
| BTK | 1712 | 91 | 8 | 1924 | Wolverton | 57'×9'4"×12'5½" | 28T | see remarks | 5200-5201 / 5216-5221 | 1/51 / 3/52 | 6/51 / 4/56 | The LNWR style coaches converted from Kitchen/Mess cars. Some seem to have been plated 27T. 5200/1 had only three compartments and it is odd that they should be on the same diagram. These brakes were opposite handed to the MR and LMS standard layout. |
| BTK | 1758 | 11 | 14 | 1925 | Derby | 57'×9'3"×12'4¾" | 27T | I (All door) | 5202-5215 | 11/58 | 13/62 | These were the four compartment brakes and the building date is confirmed despite the early lot number. |
| BTK | 1696 | 125 | 40 | 1926 | Derby | | 27T | I (All door) | 5222-5261 | 5/59 | 7/62 | The standard five compartment version. Lot 412 were the last LMS corridor coaches with compartment doors. Over 80 saw active service during the war and many were lost overseas. The majority that returned were converted to full brakes to D2129/D2130—see Chapter 14. |
| | | 148 | 60 | 1926 | Derby | 57'×9'3"×12'4¾" | 27T | | 5262-5321 | 8/57 | 13/62 | |
| | | 412 | 25 | 1929-30 | Derby | | 28T | | 5322-5346 | 5/59 | 12/62 | |
| BTK | 1730 | 507 | 5 | 1930 | Met-Cammell | | 32T | II (Flush) | 5347-5351 | 11/61 | 7/63 | Lots 508/542 had Metro-Cammell bodies and underframes, the rest being built at Derby. Lot 578 were built at Wolverton, again on Metro-Cammell frames. The diagram shows all to have been 32T but apparently most were 30T. The coaches had a slightly deeper than normal eaves panel because of the 'all steel' construction and had no conventional underframe. There were slight livery variations when new viz: Lot 508: Lined edge of windows, no crest and small scroll figures. Lot 542: Lined edge of windows, rather more 'panelling' at brake end, no crest and stretched scroll figures. Lot 578: Lined between the windows and no vertical dividers in the eaves panel. Stretched scroll figures and crest carried on side. These coaches had larger Stones ventilators over the windows than the previous lots. Lot 507 was probably like Lot 508. All lots had 6'6" compartments. |
| | | 508 | 5 | 1930 | Met-Cammell | | 32T | | 5352-5356 | 5/59 | 11/62 | |
| | | 542 | 40 | 1930-1 | see remarks | 57'×9'3"×12'4⅝" | 32T | | 5357-5396 | 6/59 | 2/64 | |
| | | 578 | 50 | 1931-2 | | | 32T | | 5397-5446 | 13/58 | 5/64 | |
| BTK | 1851 | 659 | 20 | 1933 | Derby | | 30T | III (Shallow ventilator) | 5447-5466 | 11/61 | 9/65 | The first Period III design and a change to four compartments and three a side seating. Lot 659 plated 1932. Full livery from new. Torpedo vents. 5476/91/96 converted to Push-Pull (1954-5) and renumbered 3497-9 in order |
| | | Part 692 | 34 | 1933 | Derby | 57'×9'3"×12'4⅝" | 30T | | 5467-5500 | 11/61 | 13/64 | |
| BTK | 1852 | Part 692 | 16 | 1933 | Derby | 57'×9'3"×12'4¾' | 30T | III (Shallow ventilator) | 5501-5516 | 3/61 | 5/64 | As for D1851 but two pairs of double doors at brake end. Again Torpedo vents and full livery. Both D1851/2 had pre'33 numbers in stretched scroll figures for a short time. |
| BTK | 1905 | 737 | 25 | 1934 | Derby | | 30T | III | 5517-5541 | 6/62 | 3/66 | * Also 5617-5618. The standard Period III coach of which Lot 737 had full livery. Later Modifications: 5517-24 had Guard's lookout and top commode handles removed for working on the 'Sunny South Express'. 5792/5812/5814 were modernised with air conditioning in 1937 for the 'Coronation Scot' train—all tared 32T after conversion. |
| | | 738 | 27 | 1934 | Derby | | 30T | | 5542-5566* | 5/62 | 5/65 | |
| | | 739 | 25 | 1934 | Wolverton | | 30T | | 5567-5591 | 9/62 | 11/65 | |
| | | 740 | 25 | 1934 | Wolverton | | 30T | | 5592-5616 | 1/62 | 4/66 | |
| | | 794 | 25 | 1934 | Wolverton | | 30T | | 5619-5643 | 10/62 | 12/64 | |
| | | 858 | 65 | 1935 | Wolverton | 57'×9'3"×12'4⅝" | 31T | | 5644-5708 | 8/62 | 1/66 | |
| | | 859 | 60 | 1935 | Wolverton | | 31T | | 5709-5768 | 6/63 | 9/66 | |
| | | 898 | 50 | 1936 | Derby | | 30T | | 5769-5818 | 7/63 | 7/65 | |
| | | 899 | 25 | 1936 | Derby | | 30T | | 5819-5843 | 11/63 | 11/65 | |
| | | 910 | 44 | 1936 | Wolverton | | 31T | | 5869-5912 | 4/63 | 12/65 | |
| | | 911 | 44 | 1936 | Wolverton | | 31T | | 5913-5956 | 5/63 | 7/65 | |

## TABLE 8: LMS SIDE CORRIDOR STOCK *(continued)*

| Type | Diag | Lot | Qty | Date | Built | Dimensions (L×W×H) | Weight | Period | Running Numbers | Withdrawals First | Withdrawals Last | Remarks |
|---|---|---|---|---|---|---|---|---|---|---|---|---|
| BTK | 1963 | 950 | 24 | 1936-7 | Derby | 57'×9'3"×12'4¼" | 29T | III | 5845-5868 | 6/63 | 1/65 | From the numbers these may have been cancelled from Lot 899. All 25 were a little lower than D1905 but only D1971 was classified 'lightweight'. The frame of 5844 was probably a 'try-out' for the centrally trussed frame used on the articulated stock and by BR at a later date-see also p.152 although the articulated stock was first into service. |
| BTK | 1971 | 976 | 1 | 1937 | Derby | 57'×9'3"×12'2 9/16" | 26T | III | 5844 | — | 6/62 | |
| BTK | 1968 | 1035 | 64 | 1937 | Derby | 57'×9'3"×12'4¼ | 30T | III | 5957-6020 | 12/63 | 3/66 | * 20 were 'fully fabricated' and 36 were 'non-fabricated'; 26298 upwards plated 31T. Number 26190 was never used on these coaches. These were the later standard coaches with lavatories at the end of the vehicle. Lots 1408 upwards came out with post-war maroon livery, small scroll numbers and flat topped '3's'. |
| | | 1082 | 45 | 1938 | Derby | | 30T | | 26100-26144 | 12/63 | 11/65 | |
| | | 1083 | 45 | 1938 | Derby | | 30T | | 26145-26189 | 12/63 | 6/65 | |
| | | 1175 | 74 | 1939 | Derby | | 30T | | 26191-26264 | 12/63 | 10/67 | |
| | | 1192 | 56* | 1939 | Wolverton | | 30T | | 26265-26320 | 12/63 | 10/67 | |
| | | 1408 | 50 | 1945 | Derby | | 30T | | 26321-26370 | 7/64 | 11/67 | |
| | | 1409 | 75 | 1945-6 | Derby | | 30T | | 26371-26445 | 2/64 | | |
| | | 1410 | 100 | 1946 | Derby | | 30T | | 26446-26545 | 11/65 | 12/67 | |
| BTK | 2123 | 1448 | 120 | 1948-9 | Derby | 57'×9'3"×12'4¼' | 31T | III | 26546-26665 | 13/63 | many extant (1968) | Extra door on corridor side, compartments reduced from 6'6" to 6'3" and probably with last style of window ventilator. All had LMS post-war livery but no LMS marks. |
| BTK | 2161 | 1501 | 90 | 1950 | Derby | 57'×9'3"×12'4⅝" | 30T | III (P'hole) | 26666-26755 | 3/64 | 1/68 | The final variety and all built after nationalisation. Believed all BR Crimson/cream when new and with post-war (BR type) torpedo ventilators. |
| | | 1505 | 125 | 1949-50 | W'ton | | 30T | | 26756-26880 | 13/63 | many extant (1968) | |
| | | 1506 | 125 | 1950 | Wolverton | | 30T | | 26881-27005 | 11/65 | many extant (1968) | |
| | | 1575 | 40 | 1950-1 | Derby | | 30T | | 27006-27045 | 12/65 | many extant (1968) | |
| | | 1587 | 9 | 1950 | Wolverton | | 30T | | 6030-6038 | 12/64 | 10/67 | |
| | | 1597 | 50 | 1950 | Wolverton | | 30T | | 27046-27095 | 11/65 | still extant (1968) | |
| CK | 1694 | 30 | 41 | 1924 | Wolverton | 57'×9'3"×12'4¾" | 29T | I (All door) | 3505-3545 | 4/57 | 11/61 | The standard Period I CK, perpetuated after other versions had been tried out. 3531 recorded on LNWR bogies at some time. Several modified to 9'1½" for use in M&CR section narrow set of coaches, including 3535/3659/60/85/8/94/3701. 39 coaches to wartime ambulances. Survivors rebuilt as full brakes (see Chapter 14). |
| | | 72 | 15 | 1925 | Wolverton | | 29T | | 3546-3560 | 3/57 | 10/61 | |
| | | 120 | 25 | 1925 | Wolverton | | 28T | | 3561-3585 | 3/57 | 4/61 | |
| | | 157 | 35 | 1925 | Derby | | 28T | | 3586-3620 | 5/57 | 3/62 | |
| | | 207 | 35 | 1926 | Wolverton | | 28T | | 3621-3655 | 1/58 | 13/62 | |
| | | 319 | 50 | 1927-8 | W'ton | | 28T | | 3656-3705 | 5/59 | 10/62 | |
| CK | 1751 | 101 | 5 | 1925 | Wolverton | 57'×9 3"×12'4¾" | 29T | I (All door) | 3500-3504 | 1/58 | 3/62 | The 4×1st + 3×3rd version with slightly smaller toilets to compensate. |
| CK | 1752 | 139 | 25 | 1925 | Wolverton | 57'×9'3"×12 5½" | 28T | I (All door) | 3706-3730 | 4/57 | 7/62 | The version with 2×1st + 2×½1st + 4×3rd. Even smaller toilets than D1751. |
| CK | 1716 | 450 | 50 | 1930 | Wolverton | 60'×9'3"×12'4¾" | 30T | I (2-window) | 3731-3780 | 5/59 | 10/63 | Early coaches plated 1929, but all built 1930. |
| CK | 1791 | 531 | 48 | 1931 | Wolverton | 60'×9'3' ×12'4¾" | 32T | II (Flush) | 3781-3828 | 8/59 | 7/64 | Early coaches plated 1930. 3818 later rebuilt to D1969 after a fire—see below. |
| CK | 1859 | 694 | 35 | 1933 | Wolverton | 60'×9'3"×12'4¾" | 33T | III (Shallow ventilator) | 3829-3863 | 2/62 | 4/65 | Full livery when new, torpedo ventilators. |
| CK | 1898 | 728 | 35 | 1934 | Wolverton | 60'×9'3"×12'4⅝" | 32T | III | 3864-3898 | 6/62 | 11/64 | Lot 728 had full livery and were mostly plated 1933 but Lot 729 may have had simple style since most coaches carried 1934 works plates. Lot 728 had torpedo vents. |
| | | 729 | 35 | 1934 | Wolverton | | 32T | | 3899-3933 | 5/62 | 2/66 | |
| CK | 1925 | 856 | 20 | 1935-6 | Derby | 60'×9'3"×12'4⅝" | 32T | III | 3934-3953 | 4/63 | 2/65 | The standard version and almost identical in layout to D1859/D1898. Lot 856 all plated 1935. The thirds were reduced from 6'6" to 6'3" and the extra space given to the lavatories. * Official date—coach (4027) was actually broken up in 1965! |
| | | 862 | 70 | 1935 | Wolverton | | 33T | | 3954-4023 | 10/62 | 7/65 | |
| | | 912 | 45 | 1936 | Wolverton | | 32T | | 4024-4068 | 11/63 | 8/67* | |
| | | 913 | 45 | 1936 | Wolverton | | 32T | | 4069-4113 | 4/63 | 1/65 | |
| CK | 1969 | 1042 | 69 | 1937 | Wolverton | 60'×9'3"×12'4⅝" | 32T | III | 4114-4182 | 9/62 | 12/65 | This version was identical to D1925 except that the interior layout of the toilet was changed to have the WC adjacent to the vestibule wall of the toilet rather than on the wall adjacent to the passenger compartments. Lot 1100 plated 1938. Coaches 4327-9 were the only locomotive hauled passenger carrying coaches built in 1940 and the last until 1945. |
| | | Part 531 | 1 | 1937 | Wolverton | | 32T | | 3818 | — | 4/64 | |
| | | 1099 | 33 | 1938-9 | W'ton | | 33T | | 4183-4215 | 13/63 | 9/65 | |
| | | 1100 | 40 | 1939 | Wolverton | | 33T | | 4216-4255 | 5/63 | 11/65 | |
| | | 1189 | 44 | 1939 | Wolverton | | 32T | | 4256-4299 | 12/63 | 12/66 | |
| | | 1190 | 30 | 1939-40 | W'ton | | 32T | | 4300-4329 | 13/63 | 11/65 | |
| CK | 2117 | 1403 | 50 | 1946-7 | W'ton | 60'×9 3"×12'4⅝" | 31T | III | 4330-4379 | 9/61 | 4/67 | The post-war version with two extra doors on the corridor side. All given post-war LMS livery style, Lot 1446 with 1946 insignia. Lots 1440/6 probably had last style of window ventilator. |
| | | 1404 | 75 | 1946-7 | W'ton | | 31T | | 4380-4454 | 3/64 | some extant (1968) | |
| | | 1440 | 100 | 1947-8 | W'ton | | 31T | | 4800-4899 | 13/63 | 12/67 | |
| | | 1446 | 60 | 1947 | Derby | | 31T | | 4455-4514 | 7/64 | 11/67 | |
| CK | 2159 | 1499 | 75 | 1949 | Derby | 60'0¾"×9'3"×12'4½" | 30T | III (P'hole) | 24500-24574 | 12/63 | many still extant (1968) | The 'all steel' design with the modified profile. Most had post-war (BR style) torpedo vents but there were exceptions. LMS livery on Lot 1499, BR on remainder. |
| | | 1500 | 75 | 1949-50 | Derby | | 30T | | 24575-24649 | 13/63 | many still extant (1968) | |
| | | 1586 | 90 | 1950 | Derby | | 30T | | 24650-24739 | 13/63 | many still extant (1968) | |

| Type | Diag | Lot | Qty | Date | Built | Dimensions (L×W×H) | Weight | Period | Running Numbers | Withdrawals First | Last | Remarks |
|------|------|-----|-----|------|-------|--------------------|--------|--------|-----------------|------------------|------|---------|
| BCK | 1754 | 31 | 29 | 1924 | Wolverton | 57'×9'3″ 12'4¾″ | 29T | I (All door) | 6600-6628 | 8/56 | 8/63 | Brake version of D1694. |
| BCK | 1755 | 208 | 30 | 1926 | Wolverton | 57'×9'3″×12'4¾″ | 29T | I (All door) | 6629-6658 | 3/59 | 6/62 | As for D1754 but firsts at brake end adjacent to guard's van. Lot 320 later rebuilt to D1755A with three a side in the thirds. |
| | | 320 | 25 | 1927 | Wolverton | | 29T | | 6659-6683 | 5/59 | 5/63 | |
| BCK | 1704 | 454 | 50 | 1929-30 | W'ton | 60'×9'3″×12'4¾″ | 30T | I (2-window) | 6684-6733 | 2/59 | 5/64 | Later to D1704A—three a side 3rds with Period III side panels (c. 1940). An extra toilet was fitted at brake end between guard's compartment and entrance. |
| BCK | 1720 | 490 | 25 | 1930 | Wolverton | 60'×9'3″×12'4¾″ | 30T | II (Beaded) | 6734-6758 | 5/59 | 7/64 | Later to D1720A with three a side thirds and later still (c. 1940) given Period III side panels as per D1704. Before rebuilding, 6741/5/51/65/7/71/7/9 had lookouts and top commode handles removed for working on the 'Sunny South Express'. |
| | | 550 | 25 | 1930 | Wolverton | | 30T | | 6759-6783 | 5/59 | 2/64 | |
| BCK | 1850 | 658 | 20 | 1932-3 | W'ton | 60'×9'3'×12'4¾″ | 33T | III (Shallow ventilator) | 6784-6803 | 6/60 | 9/64 | The first Period III gangwayed design, many being plated 1932. Coaches had full livery when new, stretched scroll pre-'33 numbers and torpedo ventilators. |
| BCK | 1939 | Part 658 | 2 | 1933 | Wolverton | 60'×9'3″×12'4¾″ | 33T | III (Shallow ventilator) | 6784-6785 | — | 11/63 | Converted to have luxury first class with two a side seating. |
| BCK | 1911 | 777 | 2 | 1934 | Wolverton | 60'×9'3″×12'4¾″ | 32T | III | 6804-6805 | 8/62 | 6/64 | Deep ventilator version of D1850 and with rounded interior partition corners. |
| BCK | 1932 | 861 | 35 | 1935 | Wolverton | 62'×9'3″×12'4⅝″ | 35T | III | 6806-6840 | 11/63 | 10/65 | The standard version with 62' underframe and two first class compartments. |
| | | 908 | 16 | 1936 | Wolverton | | 35T | | 6841-6856 | 12/63 | 4/65 | |
| BCK | 2010 | 1098 | 20 | 1938 | Wolverton | 62'×9'3″×12'4⅝″ | 35T | III | 6857-6876 | 13/63 | 8/65 | As for D1932 but layout of toilet was changed and the vehicles had removable tables. 6876 was altered to a secretary vehicle in 1957, reverting to normal in 1958. Many of the 62' underframes were converted to car flats. |

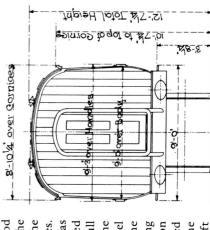

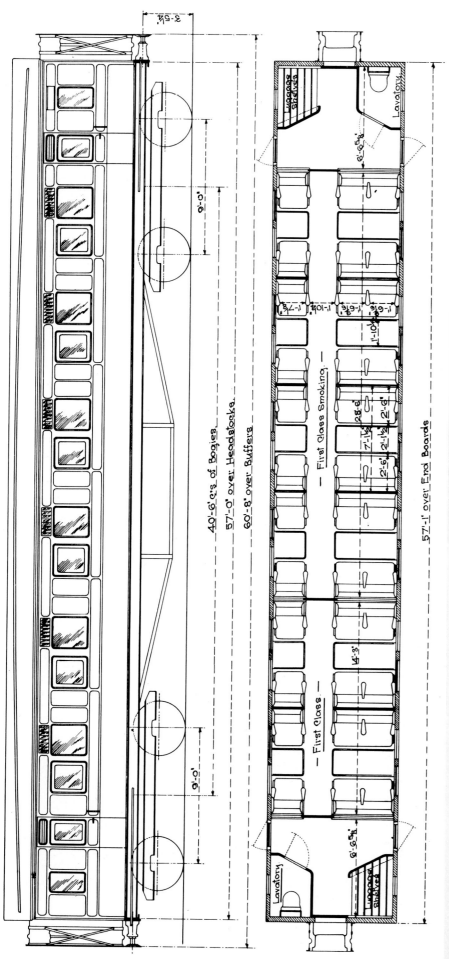

### Figure 23 First Class Vestibule Coach D1742

This highly typical Period I open coach design was the most numerous of all the various LMS open first types. They were often used as dining cars, being marshalled for the purpose next to a full kitchen car. Note that the positioning of the waist panel vertical dividers prevented the 'LMS' and emblem being placed centrally, a situation which was probably rectified for the emblem when the LMS was moved to the left hand end. This coach, 15665

# Chapter 9 - Vestibule Coaches

*Introduction; Period I designs; Period II designs; Period III designs; Summary Table*

THE gangwayed open coach, or 'vestibule' carriage as the company preferred to call it, was an exceedingly common LMS design and for the first 10 years or more after grouping, this type of vehicle was built in considerably larger numbers than the contemporary side corridor designs. The fashion began to change during the 1930s when the first of the eventual 4000-odd Stanier style side corridor vehicles began to enter service. Even so, Period III open coaches were built to the extent of over 1000 vehicles and, all told, there were put into service over 2750 open coaches to LMS design, mostly before the war. To these must be added the 55 articulated open pairs built for excursion work and considered in Chapter 12.

This large scale perpetuation of the open coach by the LMS tempts speculation as to why it was such a favoured design since none of the pre-group constituents had favoured the open layout to the extent which the LMS was to do. There was obviously a need for some open stock for dining purposes but this would only account for a small proportion of the total built. No official view has been traced but one possible idea is that the well established Midland Railway tradition of allowing the passengers to travel all the way in the dining cars was beginning, at the time of grouping, to lead to a preference for travelling in open coaches. Certainly, the first LMS standard open coaches were unmodified MR designs. However, according to other sources, the general public were not too enamoured of open coaches on express trains—for example the GWR discontinued building them—so one can hardly really credit that the LMS attracted a different type of passenger than did the other companies! It therefore seems that there may well have been other contributory reasons and the authors are inclined to think that train weight might have been the decisive factor.

There is no doubt that the weight of coach per passenger carried is far less in the case of the open type than in the side corridor coach and, in the light of the MR and early LMS small engine policy, the building of open coaches was probably the easiest way to increase passenger accommodation at minimum cost in extra train weight. Much of the open stock was, of course, used on excursions too where weight is a consideration, but it seems not entirely irrelevant that by 1939/40, when the LMS at last had a reasonable stock of modern express passenger motive power, the building of vestibule coaches all but ceased. There were but a few hundred open coaches built after the war compared with over 2500 side corridor coaches and this imbalance between the two types had never before been witnessed on the LMS. In fact, it was not until this vast post-war building of side corridor coaches took place that the total of all LMS design corridor coaches became appreciably greater than that of LMS designed vestibule vehicles. Since most of this post-war building took place after nationalisation it can safely be stated that as far as the LMS itself was concerned, the vestibule coach was almost as important as the side corridor vehicle. It is interesting to reflect that in the last few years, British Railways have built only open vehicles for second class passengers and most of the important inter-city expresses are now without side-corridor second class accommodation. It must be remembered too that open coaches give slightly more room to seat four-a-side (two-plus-two) than a four-a-side corridor coach. Since latter-day LMS corridor coaches and BR side corridor vehicles allocated to the LMR had three-a-side seating, open vehicles are clearly more economic—whatever the views of passengers.

In the analysis which follows, vestibule dining vehicles will be considered along with their general service equivalents since, for the most part, they were little different in style. The main difference was in the seating arrangements. All dining coaches, first or third, had pairs of seats at one side of the gangway and single seats at the other. The general service open firsts were of similar layout but the third class vehicles had two-and-two seating giving a 33 per cent increase in passenger carrying capacity over the two and one arrangement. They also often tended to be a little more cramped in terms of knee room than did the dining coaches.

## PERIOD I DESIGNS

With the exception of a few specialised designs which appeared in 1928, all Period I vestibule stock was derived from the MR twin-window style (see Plate 4). In fact, some of the first LMS coaches were actually built to MR diagrams, albeit in 1923. These were the composites Nos 9700—4 and the thirds Nos 7600—29. Even the first LMS diagrams proper still exhibited MR pattern countersunk locks and handles. There can be no real doubt that whatever the precise reason for the proliferation of open stock after grouping, it was Midland in origin!

Externally, all three classes of coach were very much alike. The firsts had six bays seating 36, the thirds had seven bays seating 56, together with a 42 seat dining version, while the composites had two first class plus 4½ third class bays seating 12 and 35 respectively. The third class end of this version had one seat missing to allow for the offset connecting door between the saloons. All varieties were wood panelled and beaded in orthodox Period I style and all had 57ft underframes.

The first class coaches were all to D1742 (Figure 23) and some, at least, must initially have been utilised for dining purposes. There is little to note about them except to remark that one was converted into a club saloon (later numbered 818) before the 1932/3 renumbering.

The thirds were a little more variable, there being four LMS diagrams plus the aforementioned coaches (7600—29) which are listed on page 175 of the MR Diagram Book. The initial LMS diagram (D1353) was basically the same as the MR version and had the 9ft 1½in width. It was followed by the standard D1692 version with 9ft 3in width while D1699 was the 42 seat dining version. Finally there was a matching five-bay brake ended version to D1693.

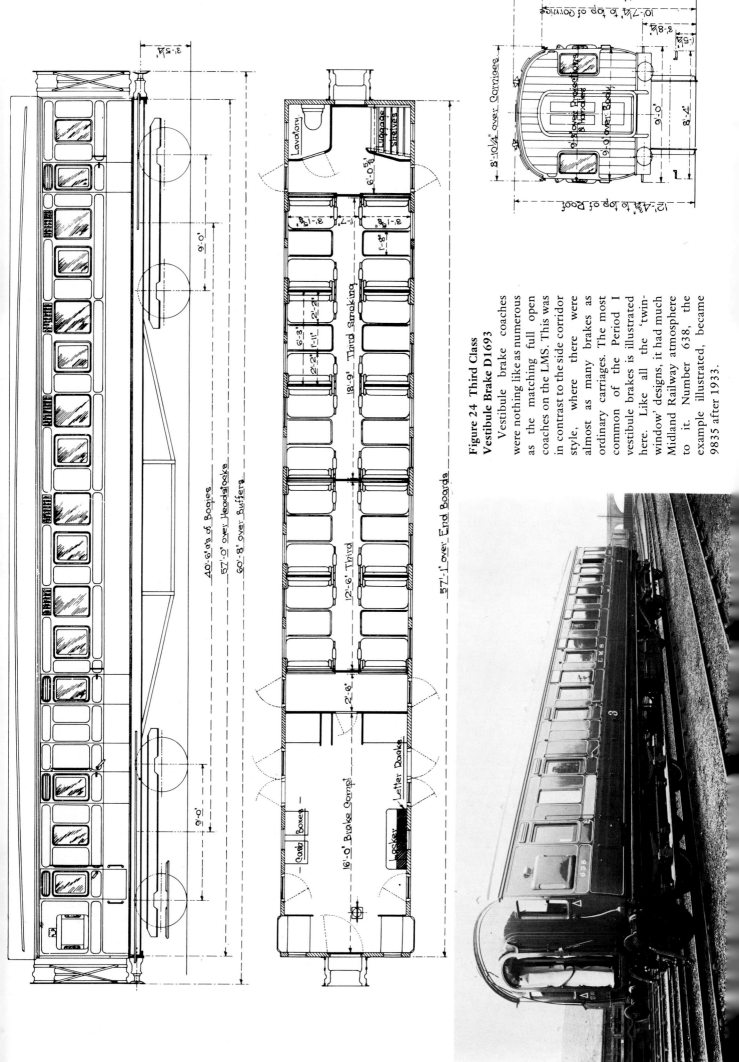

**Figure 24  Third Class
Vestibule Brake D1693**

Vestibule brake coaches were nothing like as numerous as the matching full open coaches on the LMS. This was in contrast to the side corridor style, where there were almost as many brakes as ordinary carriages. The most common of the Period I vestibule brakes is illustrated here. Like all the 'twin-window' designs, it had much Midland Railway atmosphere to it. Number 638, the example illustrated, became 9835 after 1933.

**Plate 135** Period I coach No. 3465, later 9701. This was one of the five COs actually listed in the MR diagram book. Note the MR style locks and handles. The LMS standard version to D1744 was identical except for the door handles and odd minor details.

The composites, of which there were only 20, were built to D1744 except for the first five (9700–4) which were built in 1923 and appear on page 174 of the MR Diagram book. Apart from the door handles and locks there was no external difference.

During the building of these coaches at Wolverton and Derby, an all-steel version of the full third and brake third designs was built by outside contractors. It is generally understood that these batches were ordered partly to assist the steel industry at the time. The full thirds to D1745 were the steel equivalents of D1692 and the brake ends to D1746 were the equivalents of D1693 which they actually preceded into service. All the steel coaches had flush exteriors but were given fully lined out livery with an imitation waist panel. The batches originating from the different makers exhibited detail variations and livery modifications and these are itemised in the summary tables. Internally they were arranged in identical manner to the LMS built wooden bodied versions.

Towards the end of Period I, in 1928, three designs of coach were introduced which were of more than usual interest in that they paved the way for the single window styles of Period II. There were but 35 coaches all told but they had a pleasing appearance and have been much described and illustrated in other works than this. The most numerous and the most conventional of the three was D1706 which was a seven bay, 42 seat dining coach with high waist and single windows; 25 were built and they were classified as neutral—i.e. for first and/or third class use. In many ways the style was a more up to date version of the D1699 two-window diners and in 1932/3 the coaches were renumbered with the vestibule third diners. It is somewhat doubtful if they were much used as first class dining coaches since shortly after they were built, the more spacious Period II open first made its appearance. (Text continues on page 119)

**Plate 136** 56-seat 'all-steel' open third No. 6206, later 7971 of the batch built by Cammell-Laird to Lot 184. Note the 'squared-off' window corners, simplified full livery and outward facing solebar channel.

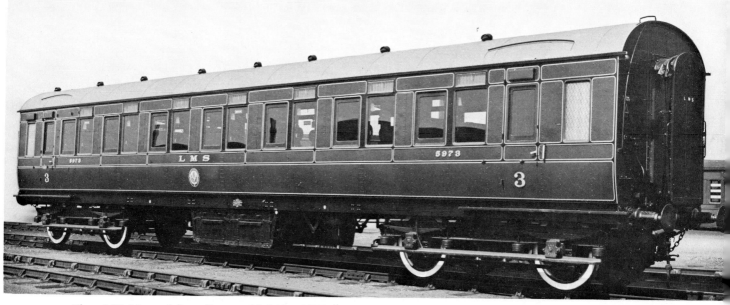

**Plate 137** 56-seat 'all-steel' open third No. 5973, later 7916 of the batch built by Birmingham C & W to Lot 183. Note that on this batch, the pseudo, full 'panelling' was much more elaborate, the roof did not have a full rainstrip, and the style was more heavily riveted. The solebar was of plain section.

**Plate 138** 40-seat 'all-steel' open third brake No. 7670, later 9816 of the batch built by Leeds Forge to Lot 181. This time the full livery was combined with full roof rainstrip, more prominently riveted roof, louvre type door vents and even shallower than normal plain section solebar.

**Plate 139** BR heating van No. M44420M converted from an 'all steel' vestibule third of 1925/6 vintage.

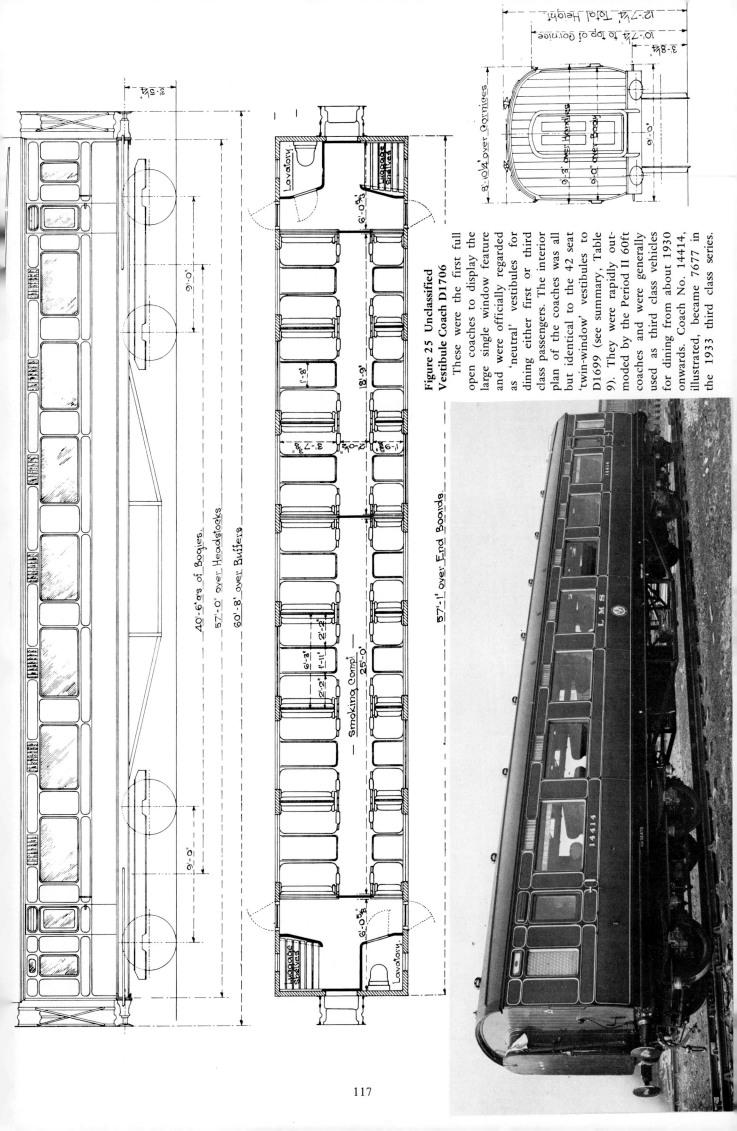

**Figure 25 Unclassified Vestibule Coach D1706**

These were the first full open coaches to display the large single window feature and were officially regarded as 'neutral' vestibules for dining either first or third class passengers. The interior plan of the coaches was all but identical to the 42 seat 'twin-window' vestibules to D1699 (see summary, Table 9). They were rapidly out-moded by the Period II 60ft coaches and were generally used as third class vehicles for dining from about 1930 onwards. Coach No. 14414, illustrated, became 7677 in the 1933 third class series.

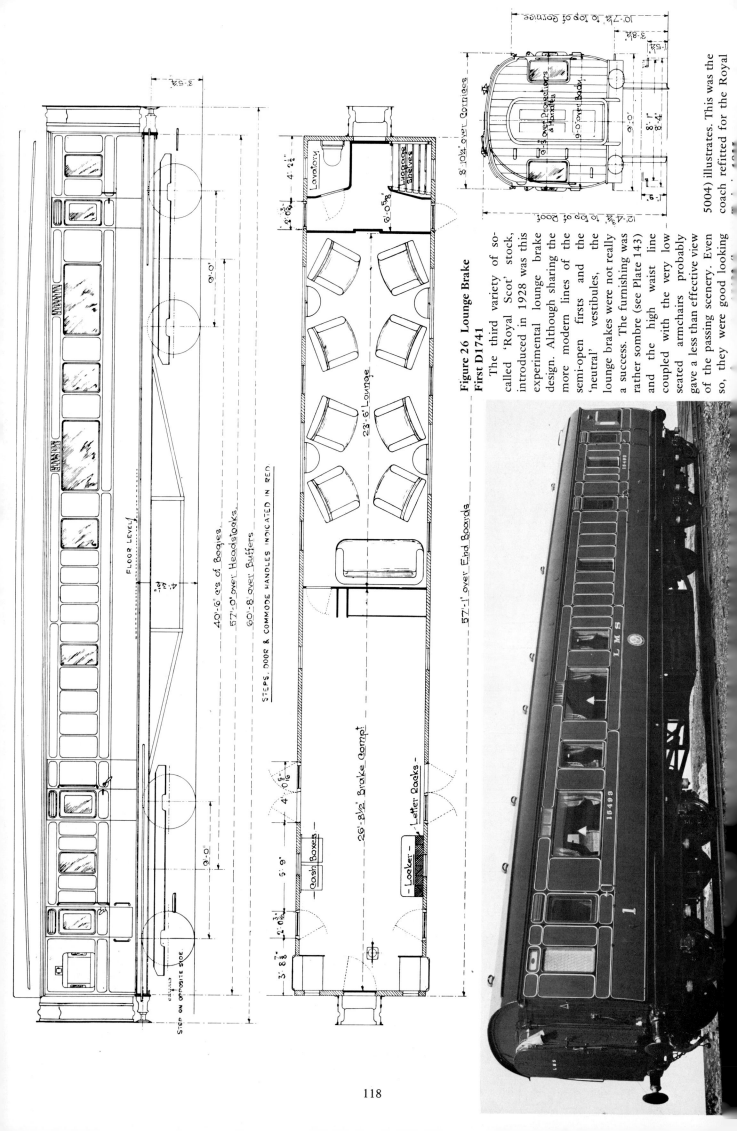

Lovatory

Luggage Shelves

4'-2½"

2'-0½"

6'-0⅝"

23'-6' Lounge

3'-5¼"

9'-0"

FLOOR LEVEL

9'-0"

4'-3½"

40'-0' c's of Bogies.

57'-0' over Headstocks.

60'-8' over Buffers.

STEPS, DOOR & COMMODE HANDLES INDICATED IN RED.

STEP ON OPPOSITE SIDE.

57'-1' over End Boards.

26'-8½" Brake Compt.

Cash Boxes -

Letter Racks -

Locker -

4'-0½"

5'-9'

3'-7'

2'-0½"

8'-8'

10'-7¼' to top of Cornice.

8'-8¾'

1'-5¾'

9'-0"

8'-1'

8'-4'

9'-3' over Projectors & Handrails.

9'-0' over Body.

8'-10¼' over Cornices.

12'-4¾' to top of Roof.

### Figure 26 Lounge Brake First D1741

The third variety of so-called 'Royal Scot' stock, introduced in 1928 was this experimental lounge brake design. Although sharing the more modern lines of the semi-open firsts and the 'neutral' vestibules, the lounge brakes were not really a success. The furnishing was rather sombre (see Plate 143) and the high waist line coupled with the very low seated armchairs probably gave a less than effective view of the passing scenery. Even so, they were good looking

5004) illustrates. This was the coach refitted for the Royal

**Plates 140-141** The first class corridor/vestibule coaches (or semi-open firsts) to D1707 were one of the three varieties of coach to introduce the large single window style to the passenger seating areas of LMS coaches. These views show the compartment side of No. 15933 (later 1027) and the corridor side of 15412 (later 1023). The centrally positioned door on the corridor side rather spoiled the symmetry of the insignia layout.

The other two 1928 designs were more experimental and do not readily fit into the general classification of LMS coaching stock adopted in this survey. Only five of each kind were built. One was a semi-open first, or corridor/vestibule car to quote the diagram book. It had three compartments which seated a total of 12 passengers only, so each passenger had a corner seat. All compartments were finished differently in high quality Empire timber and the corridor led to a central toilet-cum-powder room containing a separate chair and fitted with a most ornate patterned, full width glass window! Beyond the toilet was a conventional, three-bay, 18 seat dining saloon. Although numbered with the corridor firsts, these coaches are listed in the dining car section of the LMS diagram book and almost always ran next to a kitchen car or kitchen/diner. It therefore seems more logical to consider them with other Period I dining coaches.

The other experimental 1928 design was a first class lounge brake to D1741. These were renumbered in 1932/3 at the head of the corridor brake first list but this may have been because there were no other LMS open first brakes to justify a separate number series. They were, in fact, fully open coaches and had accommodation for 10 passengers in deep leather armchairs and settees. They were lavishly equipped with occasional tables, carefully decorated with selected wood veneers and fully carpeted and the single window styling was again adopted. Unfortunately, although very luxurious, they do not seem to have been very popular and saw little more than 10 years in active passenger service, being out of use during the war. The high waist coupled with the low armchairs may have somewhat impeded the view from the window. At all events, unlike the semi-opens, they were not repeated in Period II and seem to have been replaced by the luxury brake first of D1717—page 95.

It seems odd in some ways that the lounge idea was not repeated a year or two later since its concept would appear to have been more suited to the low-waisted coach style and in this form it might have been more successful.

These two experimental designs, together with the matching open dining coach, have often been referred to as 'Royal Scot' stock and indeed, they were first used on that train. However, at no time did the LMS ever build a special set of coaches for the Royal Scot train and these 1928 designs were also included in some of the other prestige trains of the day. They were extremely good coaches and although few in number, were indicative of the way the LMS design teams were moving.

Lounge brake No 5004 was refitted for the Royal Train in November 1935 and seems to have lost its lower waist panel beading at about the same time. No 5003 became the Preston District inspection saloon during 1947-9 but all five lounges were converted to full brakes during 1949-50 and ran for some 16 more years as 31872—6 in the same order of numbering. The semi-opens lasted until the mid 1950s and four of these were later converted for departmental use as riding/tool vans, the fifth becoming a cycle van for attaching to excursion trains. How were the mighty fallen!

Many Period I open coaches were converted to wartime ambulances, returning in many cases as full brakes. Their history in the latter guise is given in Chapter 14. (Text continues on page 123)

**Plate 142** The dining saloon of semi-RFO No. 15933 (Plate 140). The seat design was very similar to the standard Period I/II pattern but the Period II semi-RFOs (Figure 27) had seat designs very similar to those of the Period II dining cars (Plate 91).

**Plate 143** Interior of Brake First Lounge No. 15493.

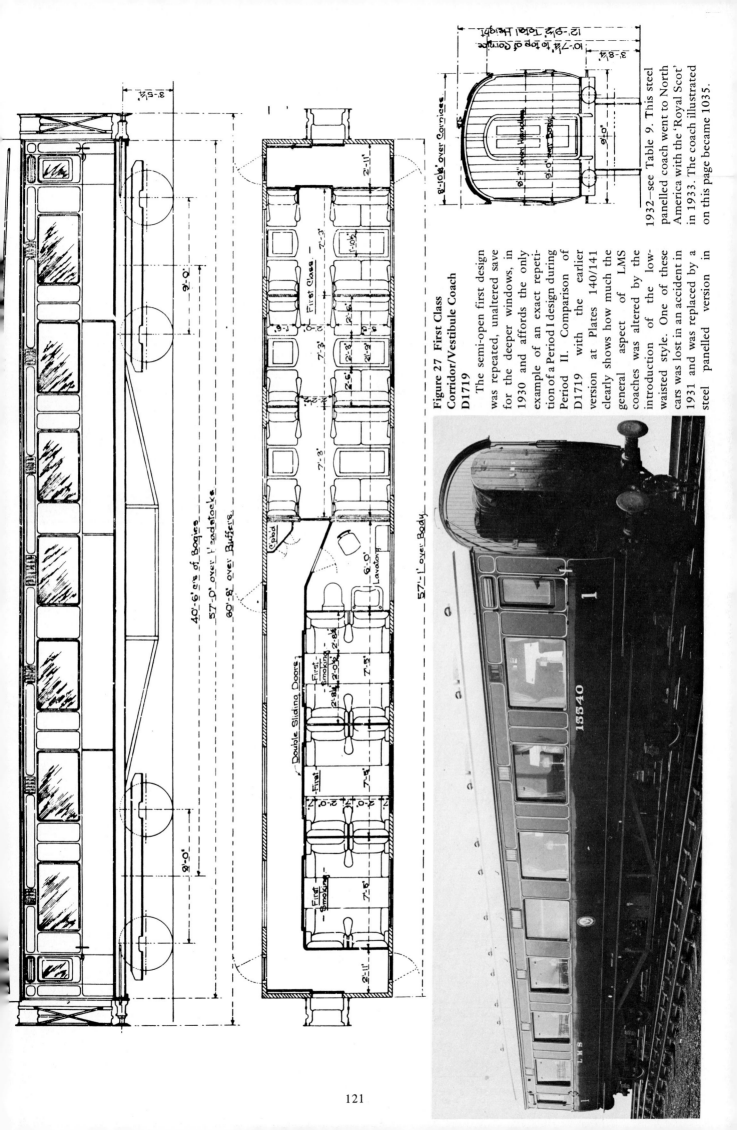

### Figure 27 First Class Corridor/Vestibule Coach D1719

The semi-open first design was repeated, unaltered save for the deeper windows, in 1930 and affords the only example of an exact repetition of a Period I design during Period II. Comparison of D1719 with the earlier version at Plates 140/141 clearly shows how much the general aspect of LMS coaches was altered by the introduction of the low-waisted style. One of these cars was lost in an accident in 1931 and was replaced by a steel panelled version in 1932—see Table 9. This steel panelled coach went to North America with the 'Royal Scot' in 1933. The coach illustrated on this page became 1035.

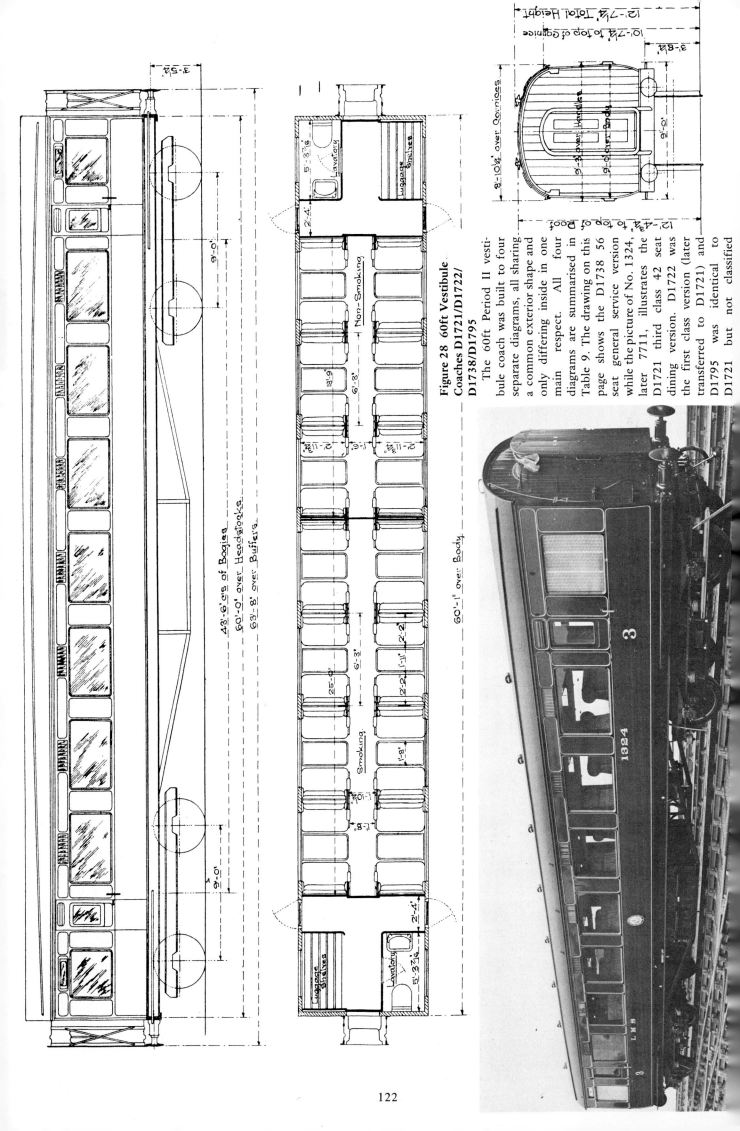

**Figure 28 60ft Vestibule Coaches D1721/D1722/ D1738/D1795**

The 60ft Period II vestibule coach was built to four separate diagrams, all sharing a common exterior shape and only differing inside in one main respect. All four diagrams are summarised in Table 9. The drawing on this page shows the D1738 56 seat general service version while the picture of No. 1324, later 7711, illustrates the D1721 third class 42 seat dining version. D1722 was the first class version (later transferred to D1721) and D1795 was identical to D1721 but not classified

Plate 144 Period II 56-seat 57ft third class coach No. 8867 (D1897), one of the last pre-Stanier gangwayed coaches to be built and introducing suspended gangways. The coach displays its new (1933) number in unshaded block figures. The original number was 12031 but it is not certain if the vehicle ever carried it—the picture is clearly of an ex-works new coach. Earlier examples from this diagram had Stones ventilators over all passenger windows—see Plate 14.

## PERIOD II DESIGNS

The first Period II open coach was the low-waisted version of the semi-open first just considered. Ten were built of which one was wrecked at Leighton Buzzard in 1931. It was replaced by a steel panelled version (Lot 626). Other than these coaches, which were not really new designs as such, there were only two designs of Period II open coach. One was a 60ft variety with wood panelling and full beading while the other was a 57ft steel panelled design. Together they totalled 426 coaches.

The 60ft design was the first to appear (in 1930) and was built to no fewer than four separate diagrams depending on the seating arrangement and designed utilisation. Externally, all four diagrams were identical.

The first to appear were 25 coaches to D1722. These were 42 seat, seven bay first class coaches, designated dining vehicles. They were immediately followed by 25 third class diners to D1721. There is no difference shown on the diagrams but the firsts may have had softer seating. However, when the firsts were downgraded to third class in 1934 on the advent of the 65ft Stanier open first, the coaches were inserted on D1721 and are shown as such in the diagram book. This is sufficient evidence that there was no real difference between the two versions.

Later in 1930, 75 more coaches of the type were built, all to the same lot number but to two more diagrams. The first 25 were 56 seaters to D1738 and the last 50 reverted to 42 seaters but were given a new diagram D1795. As far as can be seen, the only justification for a new Diagram number for the 42 seat version was the fact that, originally, they were classed as general service rather than dining vestibules and appear in a different place in the Diagram book. They were, however, identical to D1721/2 and on the renumbering in 1932/3 they were placed in the vestibule third dining coach block. One of these 50 was written off at Leighton Buzzard in 1931 and was replaced by a steel panelled version (Lot 628). This was the only coach of the 126 built not to have raised beading. One of the downgraded firsts was later rebuilt with a Stanier body—see page 129.

The 57ft coaches were all to one diagram (D1807) and appeared in 1931/2. They were all 56 seat general service third class coaches and were all steel panelled. In a sense it was this group of coaches which really established steel panelling as an LMS standard practice. The coaches were building when Sir William Stanier took over as CME and the final 100 coaches had suspended type gangways rather than the scissors type. They also exhibited other slight differences to the first 200 and this may have been the first sign of the Stanier influence. One was lost before 1933, so only 299 received 1932/3 numbers.

Internally, the length saved in the 57ft coaches was all taken from the toilet/luggage accommodation and the passenger saloon was the same size as on the 60ft coaches. The 57ft vehicles had 4ft 0in windows whereas the 60ft coaches had 4ft 6in windows.

## PERIOD III DESIGNS

Stanier pattern open coaches were not, relatively speaking, as numerous as their matching side corridor designs. As has been explained on page 113, this reversal of the 1923–32 trend only really became marked after the second world war when corridor coach construction far outstripped that of vestibule designs. Nevertheless, well over 1000 Period III open coaches were built, all except for a few first class coaches being completed before the LMS ceased to exist.

The Period III open first was introduced in 1934 on the same type of 65ft underframe as the pioneer fixed berth third class sleepers (page 69). They thus share the distinction of being the longest locomotive hauled LMS eight-wheeled coaches.

**Plate 145** The 65ft Period III RFO to D1902 No. 7495. This coach, from the 1934 batch, was finished in full livery. Note the table lamps in the windows. Three similar coaches were refurbished for the 1937 Coronation Scot sets.

**Plate 146** The orthodox Period III FO was a 60ft vehicle. Compared with the 65ft coach, luggage shelves were omitted and both toilets moved to one end. No. 7555 is illustrated as converted in 1947 to an experimental dining car with loose seats (D2118), and in the full 1946 livery with sans serif letters and numbers and straw lining.

**Plate 147** 60ft FO No. M7481 (D2160) as turned out in 1948 with 'porthole' windows, shorter sliding window vents, LMS pattern '1' on the windows and torpedo ventilators. These were the post-war versions of the Period III FOs, the only 'porthole' vestibule coaches of any class and the only LMS-pattern vestibules to be built after 1947

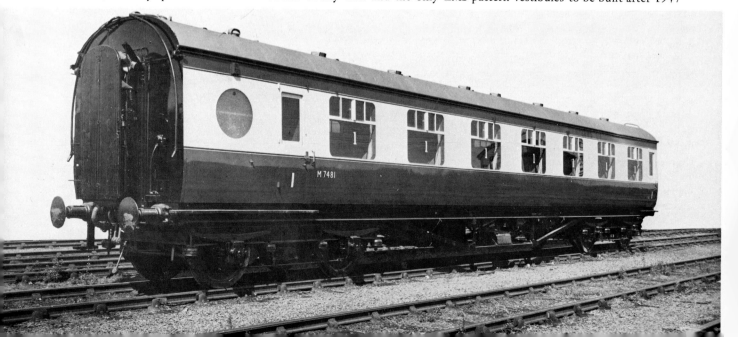

Plate 148 Experimental 'lightweight' CO No. 9729 in full livery (D1984). This 'one-off' diagram was the only Period III composite vestibule with deep window ventilators and full livery. The remaining open composites were of identical appearance but with simple livery.

Plate 149 All but one of the LMS vestibule composites had perfectly standard interior fittings and features (either Period I or Period III). This picture shows the exception—No. 9729—which had new design seats, carpets, upholstery pattern and roof lining. The picture it taken from the first class end. As far as is known, no other coaches were thus finished. The general decor is even more typical of the mid-1930s than most LMS coaches of the period.

The cars themselves were spacious and luxurious seven bay 42 seaters and were classified as dining cars. They had table lamps and generally Pullman-like interiors and were the cause of the Period II open first being downgraded to third class. Three were refurbished in 1937 for the 'Coronation Scot' train.

Two batches of these 65ft cars were built (in 1934 and 1939) and they were separated by a general service 60ft design with the same passenger accommodation but no luggage space at the ends. It seems clear that, although not classified as diners, these 60ft cars were frequently used for dining purposes and after the war, one of them (7555), was rebuilt with double glazing and loose seating to match the converted first class kitchen/diner No. 43 (page 79) although they did not run together in service.

A porthole window version of the 60ft type was built in 1949 and these coaches were the only LMS pattern open coaches to be built after nationalisation. They were given some of the numbers vacated by the downgraded Period II open firsts.

The Period III vestibule composites were even less variable. All were six bay, 36 seat coaches on 57ft underframes seating 18 first and 18 third in a two-and-one arrangement. There was both a shallow and a deep window ventilator version and the first coach of the latter type was a special lightweight one-off to D1984. It employed welded construction and had a non-standard interior decor.

These composites were not classified as dining coaches although they seem to have been mainly used for this purpose. Many were semi-permanently paired with their contemporary matching third class kitchen/diners. This RT + CO arrangement seems to have been more favoured on the LMS than the RF + TO pairing although the latter was common enough.

By far the most common Period III vestibule coaches were general service third class vehicles. In fact, there were no Stanier pattern vestibule thirds built as dining coaches although some were later converted—see below. No doubt the already existing Period I and II coaches were more than enough to cover dining needs, there being 165 of the 42 seat variety already in existence.

There were several subtle changes in the interior layout of the Stanier pattern open third and all varieties were built in some numbers. The earliest to D1904 was basically a Period III version of the 57ft Period II design with lavatory and luggage space at both ends of the coach. Nine of these were converted to 42 seaters in 1937 for the 'Coronation Scot' train and were the only 42 seat Stanier pattern open thirds.

D1904 was followed by a 7½ bay, 60 seat variety to D1915. These were very numerous coaches and the extra half bay was achieved by eliminating the luggage space and placing both lavatories at one end. The lack of luggage space indicates that they were probably designed as excursion vehicles although many doubtless, went into general service use.

In 1938 a reversion to 56 seats was made (D1999) but not to the D1904 layout. The luggage shelves at the end were still omitted and the extra space shared equally between the seven seating bays giving more leg room. These were the last general service open coaches and went on building after the war—the only variety of open coach to do so in any quantity. (Text continues on page 129)

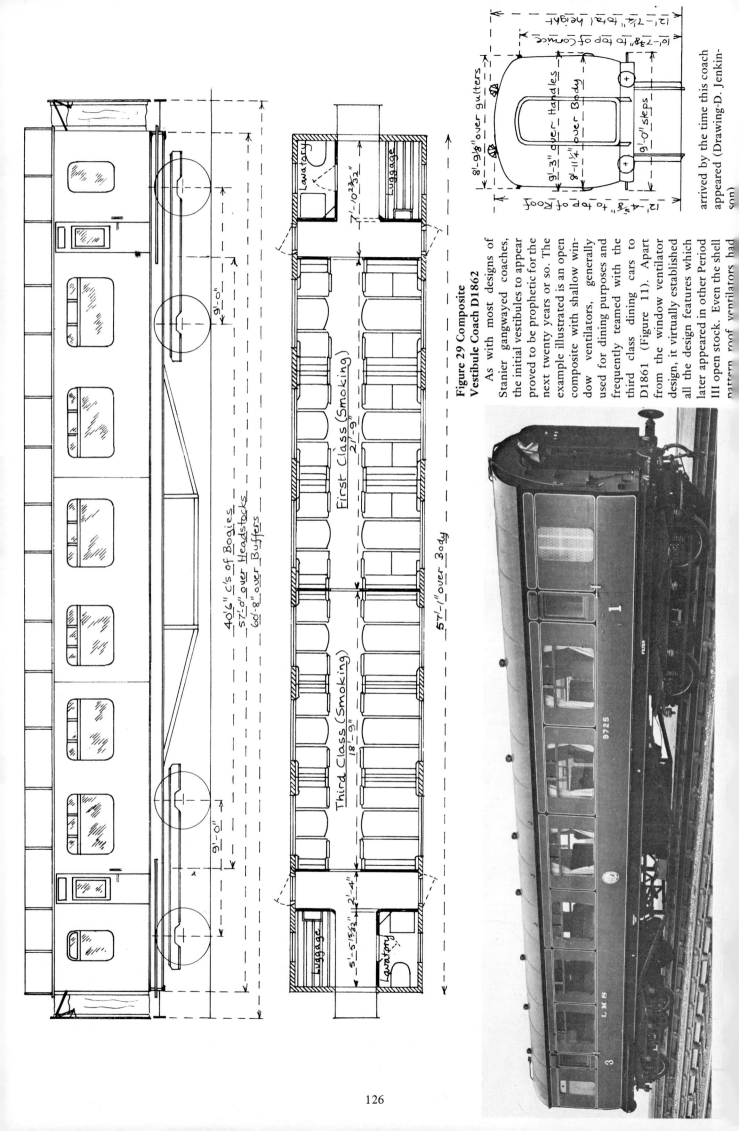

**Figure 29 Composite Vestibule Coach D1862**

As with most designs of Stanier gangwayed coaches, the initial vestibules to appear proved to be prophetic for the next twenty years or so. The example illustrated is an open composite with shallow window ventilators, generally used for dining purposes and frequently teamed with the third class dining cars to D1861 (Figure 11). Apart from the window ventilator design, it virtually established all the design features which later appeared in other Period III open stock. Even the shell pattern roof ventilators had arrived by the time this coach appeared (Drawing-D. Jenkinson)

*Drawing dimensions:*

9'-0"
40'6" c's of Bogies
57'-0" over Headstocks
60'-8" over Buffers
9'-0"

Lavatory
7'-10 23/32"
Luggage
First Class (Smoking) 27'-9"
Third Class (Smoking) 18'-9"
2'-4"
5'-5 15/32"
Luggage
Lavatory
57'-1" over Body

8'-9⅛" over gutters
9'-3" over Handles
8'-11¼" over Body
10'-7⅝" to top of cornice
12'-1-7½" total height
12'-4⅝" to top of Roof
9'-0" steps

126

**Plate 150** *(above)*. Seven bay open third No 9004 (D1981). This was one of nine coaches altered to 42 seats from 56 seats (D1904) for use in the 1937 Coronation Scot sets. The D1904 version is shown at Plate 62.

**Plate 151** *(below)*. 7½-bay open third No 9088 (D1915). Note that the toilets are now located at one end only. For the opposite side of this type, see Plate 20.

**Plate 152** *(above)*. Period III open third No. M27309 to D1999. This was the final style of LMS open third reverting to seven bays but retaining lavatories at one end only. It is shown painted in experimental chocolate and cream livery in 1948.

**Plate 153** *(below)*. Six-bay open third brake No 9933 (D1916). This was the second style of Stanier BTO and followed a five bay version with longer brake portion.

**Plate 154** The final Period III BTO to D2008, No 27948. This 5½-bay design has an even smaller brake compartment than the earlier six bay design.

### First Class

| L | 12 seat saloon | 24 seat saloon | S | 57' |
|---|---|---|---|---|
| E | | | E | |
| S | non-smoking | | L | |

D.1742 (36 seats)

| S | 24 seat dining saloon | 18 seat dining saloon | L | 60' |
|---|---|---|---|---|
| E | | | E | |
| L | | non-smoking | S | |

D.1722 (42 seats) — *Third class coaches D1721/1795 were identical. Third class D1788 was 36 seat version (centre gangway). D1722 downgraded to 3rd class later.*

| S | 12 seat dining saloon | 30 seat dining saloon | L | 65' |
|---|---|---|---|---|
| E | | | E | |
| | non-smoking | | S | |

D.1902 (42 seats)

| L | 12 seat saloon | 30 seat saloon | L | 60' |
|---|---|---|---|---|
| E | | | E | |
| L | non-smoking | | | |

D.1917/2160/2118 (42 seats) — *bar saloon + 42 seat saloon with loose chairs on D.2118*

### Third Class — see also D.1722 above)

| S | 24 seat dining saloon | 18 seat dining saloon | L | 57' |
|---|---|---|---|---|
| E | | | E | |
| L | | non-smoking | | |

D.1699/1706/1981 (42 seats) — *gangway on opposite side — D.1981*

| S | 32 seat saloon | 24 seat saloon | L | 57' |
|---|---|---|---|---|
| E | | | E | |
| L | | non-smoking | S | |

D.1353/1692/1895/1904 (56 seats)

| | 36 seat saloon | 24 seat saloon | L | 57' |
|---|---|---|---|---|
| E | | | E | |
| | | non-smoking | L | |

D.1915/1915A (60 seats)

| | 32 seat saloon | 24 seat saloon | L | 57' |
|---|---|---|---|---|
| E | | | E | |
| | | non-smoking | L | |

D.1999 (56 seats)

| S | 32 seat saloon | 24 seat saloon | L | 60' |
|---|---|---|---|---|
| E | | | E | |
| S | | non-smoking | L | |

D.2021 (56 seats)

### First Class Corridor/Vestibule

| E | 1st | 1st | 1st | L | 1st dining saloon 18 seats | E | 57' |
|---|---|---|---|---|---|---|---|

D.1707/1719 (3 x 1st comps. — 12 seats; 1 x 1st saloon — 18 seats)

### First Class Lounge Brake

| | Brake Compartment | 1st Class Lounge 10 seats | L | 57' |
|---|---|---|---|---|
| | | | E | |
| | | | S | |

D.1741 (10 seats)

### Composite

| S | 3rd non-smoking 12 seats | 3rd 23 seats | 1st 12 seats | L | 57' |
|---|---|---|---|---|---|
| E | | | | E | |
| L | | | | S | |

D.1744 (12 x 1st; 35 x 3rd seats)

| S | 3rd 18 seats | 1st 18 seats | L | 57' |
|---|---|---|---|---|
| E | | | E | |
| L | | | S | |

D.1862/1984/1903 (18 x 1st; 18 x 3rd seats)

### Third Class Brake

| | Brake Compartment | 16 seat saloon non-smoking | 24 seat saloon | L | 57' |
|---|---|---|---|---|---|
| | | E | | E | |

D.1740/1693/1913 (40 seats)

| | Brake Compartment | 16 seat saloon non-smoking | 32 seat saloon | L | 57' |
|---|---|---|---|---|---|
| | | E | | L | |

D.1916/1946 (48 seats)

| | Brake Compartment | 12 seat saloon | 32 seat saloon non-smoking | L | 57' |
|---|---|---|---|---|---|
| | | E | | E | |

D.2008 (44 seats)

### Key to letters on plans

E . Entrance Vestibules

L . Lavatories

S . Shelves.

*Note: All plans on this drawing are to a constant scale*

*Schematic Plans — LMS standard Vestibule (Open) Coaches*

*FIGURE 30 LMS standard vestibule stock—sketch plans* (Drawn by D. Jenkinson)

In addition to the full thirds, there were several types of Period III vestibule third brake coaches. None were built in any great quantity. The first design to D1913 was the Period III version of D1693 with five bays and 40 seats. This was followed by a rather more numerous six bay design for excursion use. This latter type was built to two diagrams (D1916/D1946), although there was no apparent difference. Finally, in 1938 there was introduced a 5½ bay, 44 seat design to D2008 which matched the full open 56 seaters of the same year. This last design had an even smaller brake compartment than the preceding six bay type and the extra space caused by the elimination of the half bay was, like its D1999 equivalent given to the passengers in the form of extra leg room.

Finally, there were diagrams issued for an odd 60ft Period III open third and two 1939 pattern 'Coronation Scot' open thirds. The latter are considered in Chapter 13 while the former was a rebuild on the original frames of 60ft Period II coach No. 9034 which had been involved in the Irish Mail accident at Crewe on April 14, 1937. The original 9034 was one of the downgraded open firsts with 42 seats but the Stanier rebuild was a 56 seater. All in all this was quite a lot of fuss to make about one coach when there were so many hundreds of the other types in service. This, and others like it, were probably accountancy rebuilds.

A few LMS open coaches were converted for push-pull use by BR. Details are given in Table 9 and the conversion involved D1692 D1807.

### TABLE 9: SUMMARY TABLE OF LMS STANDARD GANGWAYED VESTIBULE COACHES, INCLUDING VESTIBULE DINING COACHES

*Note:* This table should be read in conjunction with the list of standard dimensions and details on page 62. However, before tabulating the vestibule stock, some notes on the 1932/3 renumbering as it applied to vestibule coaches are necessary. Vestibule firsts were numbered between 7400-7599, thirds between 7600-9699, composites between 9700-9799 and third brakes from 9800 upwards. In the first and composite blocks, the numbers ran consecutively through the diagrams—oldest coaches coming first—but in the third class block there were complications. The coaches built to MR diagrams came first followed by the vestibule third diners (i.e. those with 2 + 1 seating). Finally came the general service open thirds starting at 7765. However, the downgrading of D1722 (see p.123) came after this renumbering so there was no space for the coaches in the third dining series without a great deal of fresh renumbering. These 42 seaters were, therefore, given the lowest available numbers in the general service series and do not run consecutively with the other coaches of the type. Finally, the all-steel coaches were numbered 'inside' D1692 in date order thus:

7826-7875—D1692 built in 1925
7876-8075—'All steel' built 1925/6
8076-8580—D1692 built 1927 and later

There was no need to split up the first class and composite coaches in this way since all the firsts and most of the composites could have been used for dining if need be.

| Type | Diag | Lot | Qty | Date | Built | Dimensions (L×W×H) | Weight | Period | Running Numbers | Withdrawals First | Last | Remarks |
|------|------|-----|-----|------|-------|--------------------|--------|--------|-----------------|-------------------|------|---------|
| FO | 1742 | 80 | 6 | 1925 | Derby | | 28T | I (2- | 7400-7405 | 3/59 | 12/61 | Many of these were probably used for |
| | | 138 | 10 | 1925 | Derby | 57'×9'3"×12'4¾" | 28T | 28T window) | 7406-7414 | 4/59 | 11/62 | dining although not classified RFO. One |
| | | 155 | 20 | 1925 | Derby | | 28T | | 7415-7434 | 3/59 | 13/62 | coach from Lot 138 was rebuilt into saloon |
| | | 293 | 30 | 1926/7 | Derby | | 28T | | 7435-7464 | 8/57 | 12/62 | and renumbered 818 in 1932-3 (Scrap: 6/62). |
| RFO | 1722 | 519 | 25 | 1930 | Derby | 60'×9'3"×12'4¾" | 30T | II (Beaded) | 7465-7489 Became 9030-54 see remarks | | | Downgraded to RTO on advent of D1902. |
| RFO | 1902 | 734 | 25 | 1934 | Wolverton | 65'×9'3"×12'4⅝" | 35T | III | 7490-7514 | 10/62 | 10/64 | Lot 734 had full livery when new. 7507-9 modified for use with the 1937 'Coronation |
| | | 1187 | 10 | 1939 | Wolverton | | 35T | | 7566-7575 | 13/64 | 6/65 | Scot' sets and tared 36T on conversion. |
| FO | 1917 | 845 | 10 | 1935 | Derby | | 32T | III | 7515-7524 | 8/63 | 12/64 | The 60' general service version numbered |
| | | 909 | 14 | 1936 | Wolverton | 60'×9'3"×12'4⅝" | 32T | | 7525-7538 | 5/63 | 2/63 | in the middle of D1902. Many were |
| | | 995 | 27 | 1937 | Wolverton | | 32T | | 7539-7565 | 12/63 | 4/65 | used for dining purposes, although not classed as such. 7555 rebuilt to D2118. |
| RFO | 2118 ex-995 | | 1 | 1947 | Derby | 60'×9'3"×12'4⅝" | 32T | III | 7555 | — | 1/65 | Altered to have individual chairs for dining purposes. LMS post war livery and 1946 style insignia on conversion. It later ran with RB No. 105—see Table 7b. |
| FO | 2160 | 1503 | 20 | 1949 | Wolverton | 60'×9'3"×12'4⅝" | 31T | III (P'hole) | 7465-7484 | 11/64 | 6/65 | Post-nationalisation version of D1917. All BR crimson/cream when new with last style of sliding ventilators and torpedo ventilators (post-war pattern). The last vestibule coaches of LMS style to be built. |
| Semi-RFO | 1707 | 379 | 5 | 1928 | Derby | 57'×9'3"×12'4¾" | 29T | I (Single-window) | 1023-1027 | 10/56 | 4/57 | The pioneer single window designs with four seats per compartment, all differently furnished. Four went to departmental use and one to a cycle van on withdrawal. Sometimes referred to as 'Royal Scot' stock. |
| Semi-RFO | 1719 | 488 | 10 | 1930 | Derby | 57'×9'3"×12'4¾" | 29T | II (Beaded) | 1028-1036 | 7/55 | 10/60 | The Period II version of D1707. Only nine of Lot 488 were renumbered, one having |
| | | 626 | 1 | 1932 | Derby | | 29T | II (Flush) | 1037 | | 8/56 | been lost in the Leighton Buzzard smash of 1931 (old 15318). Lot 626 was the replacement for this car and is thought possible that it was, in fact, a rebuild of the victim using a new body on the old frames. |

129

## TABLE 9: LMS VESTIBULE COACHES *(continued)*

| Type | Diag | Lot | Qty | Date | Built | Dimensions (LxWxH) | Weight | Period | Running Numbers | Withdrawals First | Withdrawals Last | Remarks |
|---|---|---|---|---|---|---|---|---|---|---|---|---|
| BFO Lounge | 1741 | 378 | 5 | 1928 | Derby | 57'x9'3"x12'4¾" | 27T | I (Single-window) | 5000-5004 | 12/49 | 13/50 | 'Royal Scot' stock again and not very popular designs. 5003 to America in 1933 with the Royal Scot train, later becoming Preston District inspection saloon (1947-49). 5004 refitted for Royal Train (11/35) losing the waist panel beading at the time. On withdrawal all were converted to BG and numbered 31872-6 in same order. |
| TO | — | — | 30 | 1923 | Derby | 57'x9'1½"x12'5½" | 27T | I (2-window) | 7600-7629 | 6/56 | 1/61 | Although built in 1923 and given LMS series numbers in the 1932/3 renumbering, these coaches were listed on p. 175 of the MR Diagram Book. |
| TO | 1353 | 1 | 25 | 1924 | Derby | 57'x9'1½"x12'5½" | 26T | I (2-window) | 7765-7789 | 2/58 | 8/62 | The LMS version of the MR design but still with MR pattern locks/handles. Lot 1 plated 1923. |
| | | 16 | 6 | 1924 | Derby | | 27T | | 7790-7795 | 11/55 | 7/60 | |
| | | 94 | 30 | 1924 | Derby | | 27T | | 7796-7825 | 6/57 | 11/61 | |
| TO | 1692 | 154 | 50 | 1925 | Derby | 57'x9'3"x12'4¾" | 27T | I (2-window) | 7826-7875 | 7/53 | 3/62 | The official 9'3" wide version of D1353. Many of Lot 154 were 28T. Several later Push Pull conversions (c.1938): 8477—3464; 8509—3463; 8520—3462; 8539—3465. This was the most common LMS TO design and 8207 is preserved in the National collection. |
| | | 302 | 100 | 1927 | Derby | | 27T | | 8076-8175 | 5/59 | 12/63 | |
| | | 343 | 80 | 1927/8 | Derby | | 27T | | 8176-8255 | 5/59 | 9/63 | |
| | | 355 | 100 | 1928 | Derby | | 27T | | 8256-8355 | 5/59 | 13/63 | |
| | | 375 | 100 | 1928 | Derby | | 27T | | 8356-8455 | 5/59 | 1/64 | |
| | | 431 | 125 | 1929 | Derby | | 27T | | 8456-8580 | 5/59 | 12/62 | |
| TO | 1745 | 183 | 50 | 1925/6 | B'ham C&W | | 30T | I (2-window 'all steel') | 7876-7925 | 5/59 | 13/62 | Numbered 'inside' D1692 and the 'all steel' version of D1692. Lot 184 had 'square' cornered panelled lining without vertical waist and eaves panel dividers and had a roof rainstrip. Other lots had rainstrip over doors only. All had rivetted steel roofs. Lot 185 had slightly more rounded window corners with radiussed corner between coach sides and coach ends. All versions given full livery with waist 'Panel'. 21 of Lot 185 were converted by BR to Heater Vans during 1958-63. |
| | | 184 | 50 | 1925/6 | Camm/Laird | | 30T | | 7926-7975 | 5/57 | 13/62 | |
| | | 185 | 100 | 1926 | Met. C&W | | 30T | | 7976-8075 | 9/58 | 9/64 | |
| RTO | 1699 | 156 | 35 | 1925 | Derby | 57'x9'3"x12'4¾" | 27T | I (2-window) | 7630-7664 | 5/59 | 13/61 | The 42 seat dining version of D1692. |
| RTO | 1706 | 411 | 25 | 1929 | Derby | 57'x9'3"x12'4¾" | 27T | I (Single-window) | 7665-7689 | 5/59 | 13/62 | Originally classified RUO but probably rarely used for first class passengers. These were the matching coaches to the 1928 Semi-FOs and Lounge brakes. As diners they were rapidly outmoded by the 60' Period II styles and hence, presumably, renumbered in the RTO series. |
| RTO | 1721 | 491 | 25 | 1930 | Derby | 60'x9'3"x12'4¾" | 29T | II (Beaded) | 7690-7714 | 5/59 | 13/63 | Lot 519 downgraded ex-D1722 (RFO). 9034 was later rebuilt to D2021. Lot 519 plated 29T. |
| | | 519 | 25 | 1930 | Derby | | 30T | | 9030-9054 | 5/59 | 10/63 | |
| TO | 1738 | part 522 | 25 | 1930 | Derby | 60'x9'3"x12'4¾" | 30T | II (Beaded) | 8880-8904 | 6/58 | 5/63 | The 56 seat version of D1721. For some reason they were renumbered after D1807 in 1932/3. |
| TO | 1795 | part 522 | 50 | 1930 | Derby | 60'x9'3"x12'4¾" | 30T | II (Beaded) | 7715-7763 | 5/59 | 8/64 | The official 'non-dining' 42 seat version of D1721 although numbered in the dining series. There was no difference between the two. Only 49 of Lot 522 were renumbered in 1932/3 and Lot 628 was a replacement of the 50th coach (old 14733) which was involved in the Leighton Buzzard smash of 1931. It went to the USA in 1933 with the 'Royal Scot'. |
| | | 628 | 1 | 1932 | Derby | | 30T | II (Flush) | 7764 | — | 12/61 | |
| TO | 1807 | 575 | 140 | 1931 | Derby | 57'x9'3"x12'4¾" | 29T | II (Flush) | 8581-8720 | 5/60 | 7/64 | Seating area the same as D1721/38/95 but smaller lavatories and luggage spaces. Lots 575/597 had wide Stones ventilators over all main windows but Lots 648/654 had narrow Stones ventilators over droplights only (2nd and 5th from left) and hooded metal ventilators over the rest. Lots 648/654 had suspended type gangways. Lots 575/597 had 'panel' lining between the windows. Lots 648/654 had lining at edge of windows. *Push Pull conversions* (all in 1951): 8723—3484; 8748—3485; 8865—3486. One of Lot 654 was lost before renumbering. |
| | | 597 | 60 | 1931 | Wolverton | | 29T | | 8721-8780 | 7/59 | 2/66 | |
| | | 648 | 50 | 1932 | Wolverton | | 29T | | 8781-8830 | 12/59 | 1/64 | |
| | | 654 | 50 | 1932 | Derby | | 29T | | 8831-8879 | 13/60 | 7/64 | |
| TO | 1904 | 736 | 25 | 1933 | Derby | 57'x9'3"x12'4⅝" | 30T | III | 8905-8929 | 11/62 | 2/65 | Period III version of D1807. Lot 736 had full livery when new. Some converted in 1937 to D1981 (below). |
| | | 804 | 50 | 1934 | Met/Camm. | | 30T | | 8930-8979 | 5/62 | 2/64 | |
| | | 805 | 50 | 1934 | B'ham C&W | | 30T | | 8980-9029 | 5/62 | 12/64 | |
| RTO | 1981 | 804 | 3 | 1937 | Wolverton | 57'x9'3"x12'4⅝" | 32T | III | 8931/50/61 | 10/62 | 10/64 | Converted to 42 seat dining versions for the 1937 'Coronation Scot' sets and pressure ventilated on conversion. |
| | | 805 | 6 | 1937 | Wolverton | | 32T | | 8993/6/9003 9004/6/29 | 8/62 | 10/64 | |
| TO | 1915 | 843 | 60 | 1935 | Derby | 57'x9'3"x12'4¾" | 30T | III | 9055-9114 | 8/63 | 11/65 | The 60 seat excursion version of the Period III TO. Lot 954 plated 30T. 5 or 6 sold to Jamaica (1964) as passenger vehicles. |
| | | 857 | 60 | 1935 | Wolverton | | 31T | | 9115-9174 | 11/62 | 3/65 | |
| | | 894 | 56 | 1936 | Derby | | 30T | | 9175-9230 | 6/63 | 10/65 | |
| | | 953 | 100 | 1936 | Met/Camm. | | 31T | | 9231-9330 | 12/62 | 7/65 | |
| | | 954 | 100 | 1936 | B'ham C&W | | 31T | | 9331-9430 | 4/63 | 2/66 | |

## TABLE 9: LMS VESTIBULE COACHES *(continued)*

| Type | Diag | Lot | Qty | Date | Built | Dimensions (L×W×H) | Weight | Period | Running Numbers | Withdrawals First | Withdrawals Last | Remarks |
|---|---|---|---|---|---|---|---|---|---|---|---|---|
| TO | 1915A | 996 | 4 | 1937 | Wolverton | 57'×9'3"×12'4⅝" | 30T | III | 9431-9434 | 10/64 | 3/65 | As for D1915 but slightly lower total height (12'10¼" as against 12'11⅛") and supposedly lighter in weight. |
| TO | 1999 | 1084 | 48 | 1938 | Derby | 57'×9'3"×12'4⅝" | 28T | III | 9435-9482 | — | 9/66 | A reversion to 56 seats with more space for the passenger than the previous 56 seat version to D1904. Lot 1084 were plated 29T. Lot 1400 were the first vehicles to be built by the LMS after the 1939-45 war. All post-war batches had small scroll numbers with flat topped '3' and Lot 1438 probably had the last style of window ventilators. All post-war pre-1948 batches were probably maroon not crimson when new. Some of Lot 1438 given experimental BR liveries from new. Lot 1127 was a replacement. Some of these coaches only had sliding vents in 1st/3rd/5th/7th windows and some had second hand chassis. |
| | | 1188 | 34 | 1939 | Wolverton | | 31T | | 9483-9516 | — | 10/65 | |
| | | 1127 | 1 | 1938 | Wolverton | | 29T | | 8335 | — | 2/64 | |
| | | 1400 | 50 | 1945 | Wolverton | | 30T | | 27100-27149 | 13/63 | 12/76 | |
| | | 1401 | 100 | 1945/6 | W'ton | | 30T | | 27150-27249 | 8/64 | a few | |
| | | 1402 | 100 | 1947 | Wolverton | | 30T | | 27250-27349 | 5/64 | extant | |
| | | 1438 | 100 | 1947/8 | W'ton | | 30T | | 27350-27459 | 13/63 | (1968) | |
| TO | 2021 | 1126 | 1 | 1938 | Derby | 60'×9'3"×12'4⅝" | 30T | III | 9034 | -- | 3/65 | A 'one-off' rebuild of a D1721 accident victim. A new diagram was needed as the existing 60' underframe was used. The coach was rebuilt as a 56 seater and had removable tables. |

*Note:* One further TO diagram issued (D2153) for the 1939 'Coronation Scot' coaches. These are included in Chapter 13.

| Type | Diag | Lot | Qty | Date | Built | Dimensions (L×W×H) | Weight | Period | Running Numbers | Withdrawals First | Withdrawals Last | Remarks |
|---|---|---|---|---|---|---|---|---|---|---|---|---|
| BTO | 1746 | 181 | 20 | 1926 | Leeds Fge | 57'×9 3"×12'4¾" | 31T | I (2-window 'all steel' | 9800-9819 | 5/59 | 9/62 | The 'All steel' brake version of D1745. Coaches were fully lined with pseudo waist 'panel'. Early coaches in Lot 181 were plated 1925 and Lot 182 were plated as 30T. Lot 181 had full length rainstrips and both lots had rivetted steel roof. 9821/8 converted to DMU in 1957! |
| | | 182 | 15 | 1926 | B'ham C&W | | 31T | | 9820-9834 | 3/57 | 13/62 | |
| BTO | 1693 | 303 | 35 | 1927 | Wolverton | 57'×9'3"×12'4¾" | 28T | I (2-window) | 9835-9869 | 5/59 | 11/63 | The conventional wood panelled brake version of D1692. Identical layout to D1746. Early coaches of Lot 328 plated 1927. |
| | | 328 | 20 | 1928 | Wolverton | | 28T | | 9870-9889 | 9/60 | 3/64 | |
| BTO | 1913 | 806 | 20 | 1934 | Pickering | 57'×9'3"×12'4⅝" | 30T | III | 9890-9909 | 5/62 | 10/65 | Period III version of D1693/1746. This batch may have had serif figures when new —see note to D1946 (below). |
| BTO | 1916 | 844 | 26 | 1934 | Derby | 57'×9'3"×12'4⅝" | 30T | III | 9910-9935 | 5/63 | 3/65 | Six bay, 48 seat excursion version with shorter brake compartment. Possibly excursion stock and matches the D1915 full third version (above). |
| BTO | 1946 | 895 | 14 | 1936 | Derby | 57'×9'3"×12'4⅝" | 30T | III | 9936-9949 | 1/64 | 5/65 | Same layout as D1916. Lot 955 appear to have had scroll numbers and this may have been a feature of the coaches built by Pickering & Co. |
| | | 955 | 50 | 1936 | Pickering | | 31T | | 9950-9999 | 11/63 | 5/65 | |
| | | 997 | 6 | 1937 | Wolverton | | 31T | | 27900-27905 | 10/63 | 11/64 | |
| BTO | 2008 | 1085 | 5 | 1938 | Derby | 57'×9'3¾"×12'4⅝" | 29T | III | 27906-27910 | 12/63 | 10/64 | A 5½ bay type with even less brake van space than D1916/D1946. The extra space was given to the passenger—c.f. D1999 (TO) . Lot 1174 also plated 29T. All plated 9'3" although shown 9'3¾" on diagram. |
| | | 1174 | 46 | 1939 | Derby | | 30T | | 27911-27956 | 12/63 | 12/66 | |

| Type | Diag | Lot | Qty | Date | Built | Dimensions (L×W×H) | Weight | Period | Running Numbers | Withdrawals First | Withdrawals Last | Remarks |
|---|---|---|---|---|---|---|---|---|---|---|---|---|
| CO | — | — | 5 | 1923 | Derby | 57'×9'1½"×12'5½" | 27T | I (2-window) | 9700-9704 | 1/58 | 12/60 | Although built in 1923, these coaches were listed on page 174 of the MR Diagram Book. They were all but identical to D1744 except that there was a single panel between 1st and 3rd class ends on the outside of the coach. |
| CO | 1744 | 2 | 5 | 1924 | Derby | 57'×9'1½"×12'5½" | 27T | I (2-window) | 9705-9709 | 1/58 | 9/61 | The official LMS version. Diagram shows 9'1½" width but Lot 93 was plated 9'3" and did not have MR type fittings. |
| | | 93 | 10 | 1925 | Derby | | 28T | | 9710-9719 | 7/59 | 11/61 | |
| CO | 1862 | 697 | 9 | 1933 | Derby | 57'×9'3"×12'4⅝" | 32T | III (Shallow ventilator) | 9720-9728 | 7/62 | 1/64 | Full livery when new. These were almost always used for dining purposes having 2+1 seating at both ends of the coach. Diagram shows 10 coaches but only 9 built. |
| CO | 1984 | 725 | 1 | 1934 | Derby | 57'×9'3"×12'2⅛" | 29T | III | 9729 | — | 1/64 | Welded construction and lighter weight than D1862. Full livery from new and the coach may have been the last of Lot 697, given a new diagram and lot number because of the experimental construction. |
| CO | 1903 | 735 | 10 | 1934 | Derby | 57'×9'3"×12'4⅝" | 31T | III | 9730-9739 | 7/62 | 11/64 | The standard deep ventilator version and like all Period III COs, appear to have been used as diners. They were 'fluid' in use with detachable class boards inside the coach between the saloons. However, the coaches had '1' and '3' on the outside doors. |
| | | 853 | 10 | 1935 | Derby | | 30T | | 9740-9749 | 11/62 | 13/64 | |
| | | 1049 | 4 | 1938 | Wolverton | | 31T | | 9750-9753 | 9/64 | 6/65 | |
| | | 1101 | 5 | 1939 | Wolverton | | 31T | | 9754-9758 | 8/64 | 6/65 | |

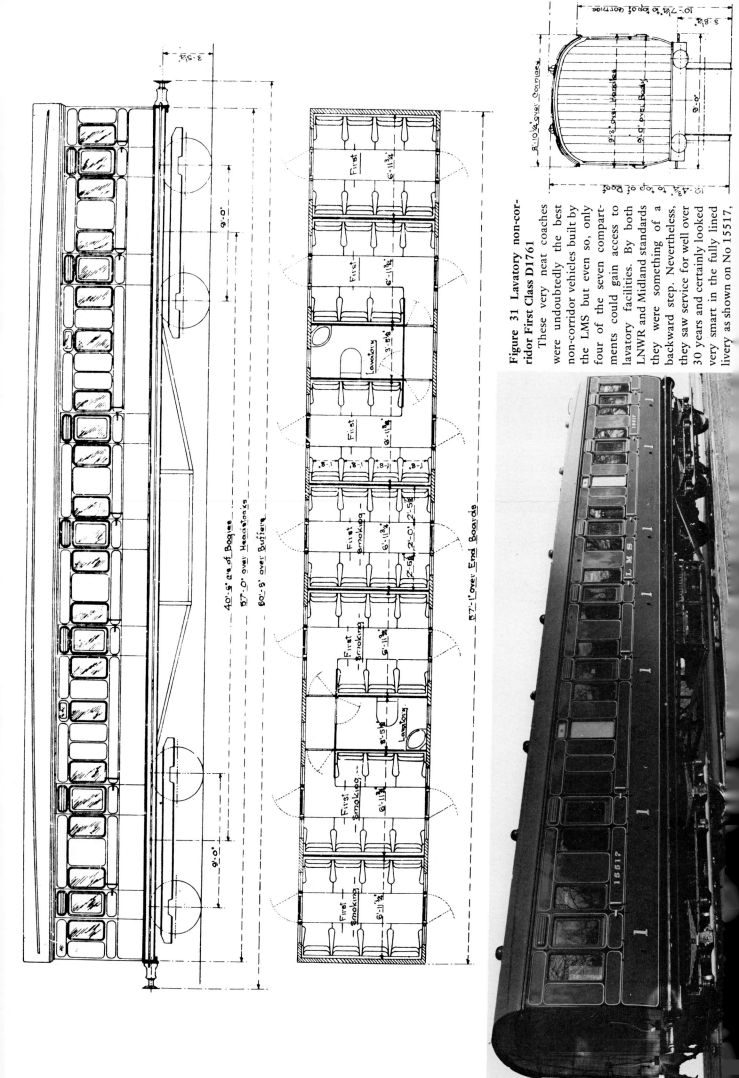

**Figure 31 Lavatory non-corridor First Class D1761**

These very neat coaches were undoubtedly the best non-corridor vehicles built by the LMS but even so, only four of the seven compartments could gain access to lavatory facilities. By both LNWR and Midland standards they were something of a backward step. Nevertheless, they saw service for well over 30 years and certainly looked very smart in the fully lined livery as shown on No 15517,

# Chapter 10 - 57ft Non-Corridor Stock

*57ft Lavatory Stock; 57ft Non-lavatory Stock; North London Sets; Push-Pull Stock; Summary Tables.*

WITH but a few exceptions (see Chapter 11), all general service non-corridor coaches built by the LMS were mounted on 57ft chassis. Apart from external style changes which followed the usual LMS sequence, the layout of non-corridor stock hardly varied at all from the early Period I standard coaches to the end of the Stanier phase. Since there was so little change, the best way to appreciate what actually did take place is to consider coaches by their generic types rather than by design periods. The bulk of 57ft stock does not seem to have been designed to run in sets and was generally supplied against a divisional requirement for 'x' seats. It is therefore not readily possible to do more than describe the types built. However there were a few small batches of 57ft coaches built for the North London services which were supplied in set formations. As these coaches also differed slightly in layout from the standard general service coaches, they have been considered and tabulated separately.

## 57′ LAVATORY STOCK

The LMS was not a great builder of non-corridor lavatory stock and produced only three basic 57ft designs. No 57ft lavatory stock was built after 1930, moreover, only 50 coaches were built after the close of Period I. It seems from a study of the coach construction minutes that by 1930 it was becoming LMS policy to use older corridor stock for its intermediate cross-country services. These would give rather better accommodation than non-corridor coaches, especially in relation to toilet facilities and the company presumably felt that this aspect of the situation was more important than the newness of any non-corridor coaches.

First class lavatory coaches were only built during Period I and totalled 30 vehicles to D1761. Built in 1927 they were seven compartment coaches with two separated lavatories to which four compartments could gain access. These compartments had only seven seats and a short corridor connecting two compartments was located alongside each lavatory.

Composite coaches were eight-compartment vehicles built to one basic design although they appeared with both Period I and Period II styling (D1686 D1736). They again had two lavatories, this time placed side by side to which access was gained from two first class and two third class compartments by intermediate short corridors.

The remaining 57ft lavatory designs were third brakes with one lavatory accessible from two of the five compartments. They were again built with both Period I and Period II styling to D1685 and D1737. Another detail difference was the offset toilet window in the Period I type but centred in the Period II version.

The lavatory full firsts were used for general service and mixed somewhat indiscriminately amongst older vehicles. However, the composites and brake thirds were, in theory, designed as two, three or four coach inter-district lavatory sets formed CL + BTL; BTL + CL + BTL or BTL + CL + CL + BTL respectively.

From contemporary observers' reports, it would seem that this tidy pattern was rarely witnessed and many of the LMS lavatory coaches were simply used as replacements for older stock. For example, local sets might be composed of an ex-LNWR BTL plus an LMS standard CL or perhaps two LMS standard BTLs flanking a Midland CL. According to one extremely reliable source, the formations were too untidy to suggest any deliberate attempt to deliver them as sets but they may have been made into sets as required. They were also mixed with non-lavatory stock.

A few more non-corridor lavatory composite coaches were built on 54ft chassis but these were all for the Tilbury section and are considered in the next chapter.

### TABLE 10a: SUMMARY TABLE OF LMS STANDARD 57′ NON-CORRIDOR LAVATORY STOCK

*Note:* This table should be read in conjunction with the list of standard dimensions and details on page 62.

| Type | Diag | Lot | Qty | Date | Built | Dimensions (L×W×H) | Weight | Period | Running Numbers | Withdrawals First | Withdrawals Last | Remarks |
|---|---|---|---|---|---|---|---|---|---|---|---|---|
| FL | 1761 | 249 | 30 | 1927 | Wolverton | 57′×9′3″×12′4¾″ | 28T | I | 18000-18029 | 4/57 | 2/64 | The only LMS design of FL. |
| CL | 1686 | 126 | 20 | 1926/7 | Derby | 57′×9′3″×12′4¾″ | 26T | I | 19026-19045* | 5/59 | 2/64 | The so-called 'Inter-District' composites. It is doubtful if many were formed up with the BTLs into strict sets. |
| | | 389 | 50 | 1929 | Wolverton | | 28T | | 19046-19095 | 5/59 | 13/64 | |
| | | 446 | 75 | 1929 | Wolverton | | 28T | | 19096-19170 | 5/59 | 9/64 | |
| CL | 1736 | 529 | 25 | 1930 | Wolverton | 57′×9′2¼″×12′4¼″ | 30T | II | 19171-19195 | 5/59 | 7/64 | The Period II version of D1686. |
| BTL | 1685 | 127 | 50 | 1926/7 | Derby | 57′×9′3″×12′4¾″ | 26T | I | 25000-25049 | 5/59 | 8/67† | Again 'Inter-District' coaches. Lot 127 was plated 27T. |
| | | 290 | 50 | 1927 | Ntn Hth | | 26T | | 25050-25099 | 5/59 | 1/65 | |
| | | 398 | 73 | 1928/9 | Ntn Hth | | 26T | | 25100-25172 | 3/58 | 8/64 | |
| | | 448 | 75 | 1928/9 | Ntn Hth | | 26T | | 25173-25247 | 5/59 | 4/65 | |
| BTL | 1737 | 530 | 25 | 1930 | Ntn Hth | 57′×9′3¼″×12′4¾″ | 27T | II | 25248-25272 | 5/59 | 8/64 | The coaches were plated 9′3″ although the diagram shows 9′3$\frac{3}{16}$″ for some reason. The Period II version of D1685. Plated 28T. |

* The numbering of the compcsites started at 19026. The numbers between 19000 and 19025 were occupied by 54′ composites built for the LT&S sets and listed in Table 11.

† One survivor only to this date (25048). Remainder scrapped before 1965.

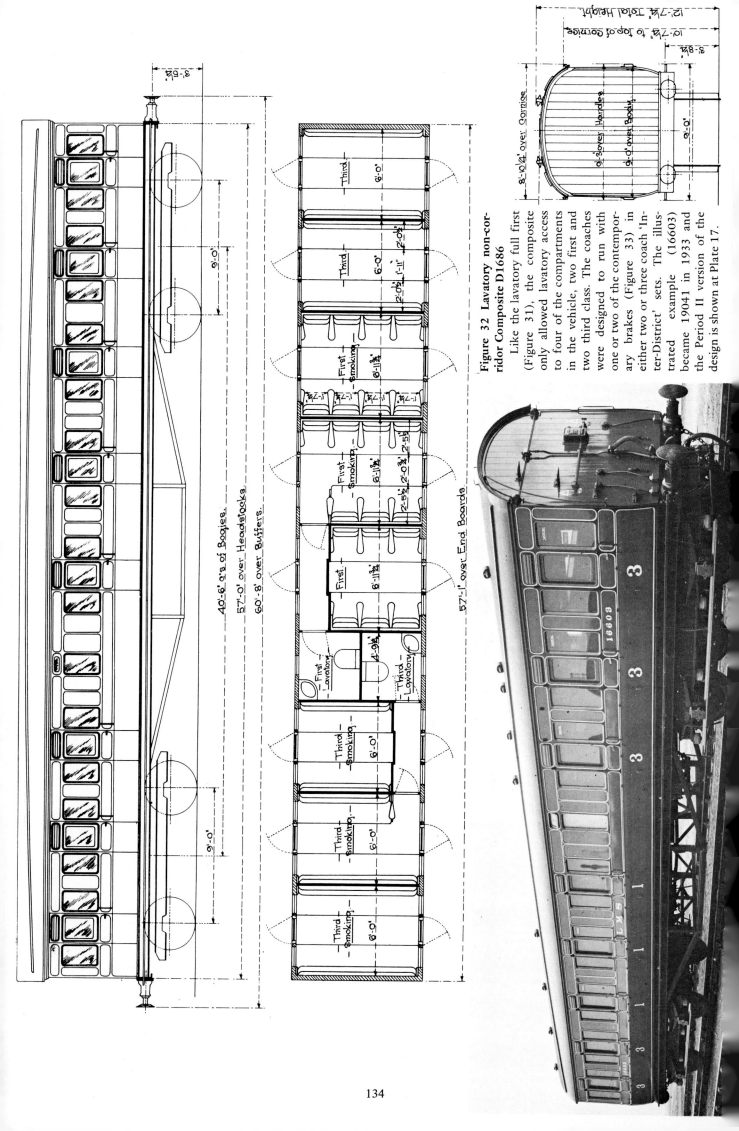

**Figure 32** Lavatory non-corridor Composite D1686

Like the lavatory full first (Figure 31), the composite only allowed lavatory access to four of the compartments in the vehicle, two first and two third class. The coaches were designed to run with one or two of the contemporary brakes (Figure 33) in either two or three coach 'Inter-District' sets. The illustrated example (16603) became 19041 in 1933 and the Period II version of the design is shown at Plate 17.

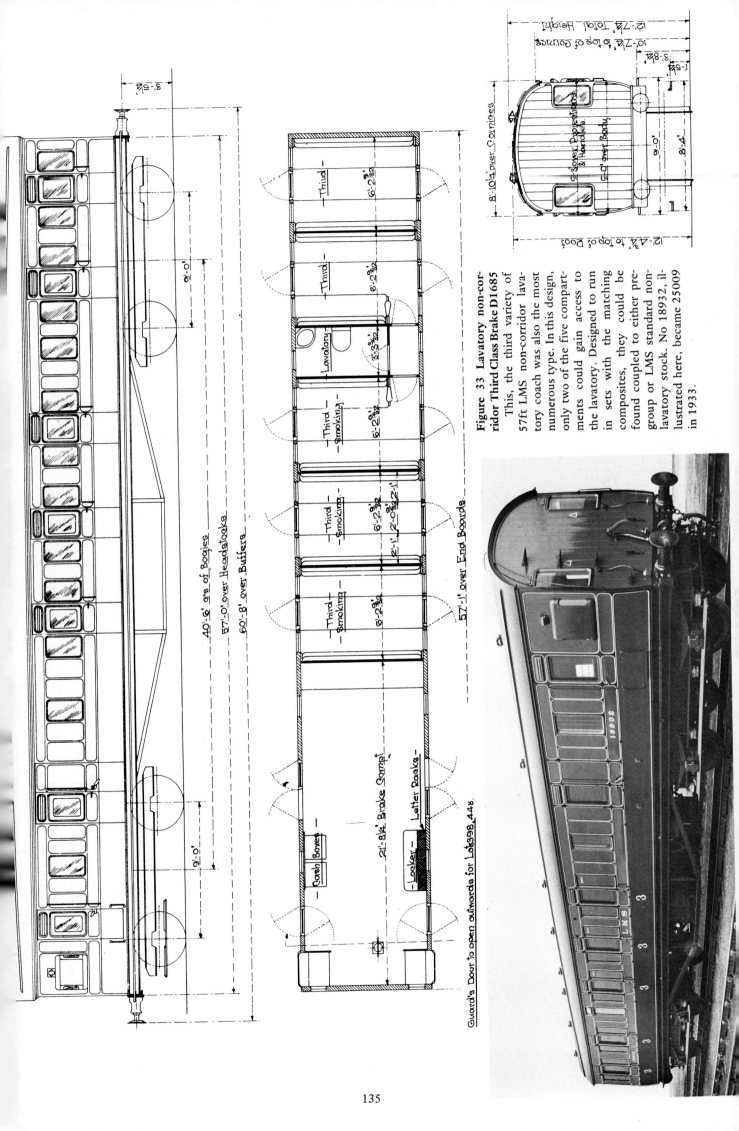

**Figure 33 Lavatory non-cor-ridor Third Class Brake D1685**
This, the third variety of 57ft LMS non-corridor lava-tory coach was also the most numerous type. In this design, only two of the five compart-ments could gain access to the lavatory. Designed to run in sets with the matching composites, they could be found coupled to either pre-group or LMS standard non-lavatory stock. No 18932, il-lustrated here, became 25009 in 1933.

Guard's Door to open outwards for Lots 398, 448.

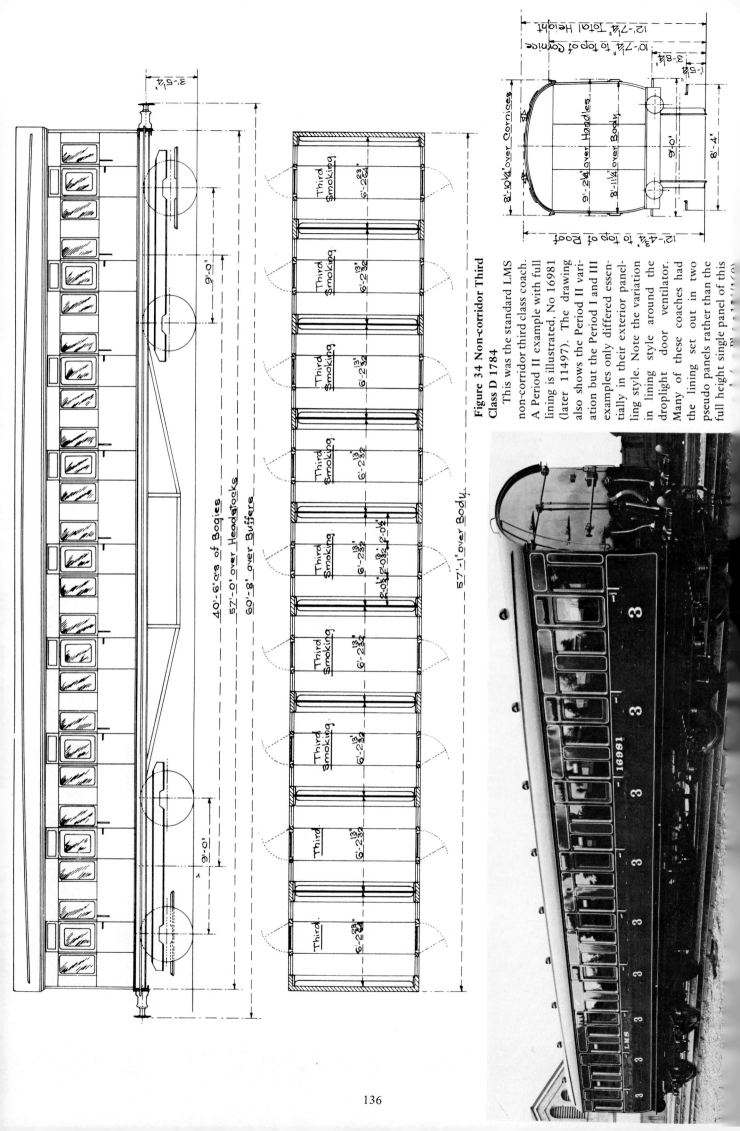

**Figure 34 Non-corridor Third Class D 1784**

This was the standard LMS non-corridor third class coach. A Period II example with full lining is illustrated, No 16981 (later 11497). The drawing also shows the Period II variation but the Period I and III examples only differed essentially in their exterior panelling style. Note the variation in lining style around the droplight door ventilator. Many of these coaches had the lining set out in two pseudo panels rather than the full height single panel of this

136

## 57′ NON-LAVATORY STOCK

### First Class

All LMS non-corridor firsts were eight-compartment coaches, mostly built during Period I (D1702). None were built during Period II but a handful of Period III versions were built in the 1930s. These were, technically, the last of the LMS non-corridor firsts, but somewhat surprisingly, a further group of 15 were built after nationalisation in 1951. These seem to have been used in Scotland on the downgrading of the five-a-side Cathcart Circle first class coaches (see page 148) and may have been a contributory factor to the non-appearance of a BR standard non-corridor full first.

### Third Class

Non-corridor thirds were built in great quantity in all three design periods and continued building until 1951. All were nine-compartment 108 seat vehicles and the only real change, apart from the exteriors, was the occasional reshuffling of the non-smoking compartments. Some of the coaches, especially the later ones, were either fitted for or converted to push-pull working.

Third brakes were almost equally consistent being six compartment coaches seating 72 passengers. They were again built in quantity during all three periods and continued in production until 1951/2. Many were fitted for push-pull use.

There were two principal exceptions to the normal LMS standard non-corridor brake third. One was a six compartment brake *second* for the North London sets (D1723/D1797) while the North London brake third was a *seven* compartment vehicle (D1733/D1783). These coaches are considered in more detail below.

### Composite

Once again, the standard layout never varied from grouping until 1950. LMS design non-corridor composites for general service were nine compartment coaches arranged, like their LNWR ancestors, with three first class compartments in the centre. Again they were built in all three periods and contained their quota of push-pull vehicles. Because of the first class compartments, the third class compartments in the composites were shorter between partitions than they were in the full thirds and brake thirds.

The only LMS designed variation was an eight-compartment coach containing six first class compartments of somewhat large dimensions between partitions. The other two compartments were either second class (D1731/D1786) or third class (D1732/D1785). They were again designed for use on the North London section and are considered below.

The final composites to be given LMS series numbers were to D2189. These were built at Swindon to GWR design after nationalisation. Apparently Derby and Wolverton were fully occupied with work and the coaches were urgently needed. They had four first class compartments with five-a-side seating and were 59ft 2in over frames. Included in this survey merely for the sake of completeness, they were built to GWR Diagram E156 (GW lots 1749/1772).

**Plate 155.** Interior view of brake compartment of a Period III non-corridor brake third believed to be No 21034 of D1964A, built 1949.

**Plate 156.** Period II BT No 16630, later 20526 (D1735). This coach was one of the last Period II vehicles to be built (1932) and the slightly simplified form of the fully lined livery between the windows probably anticipated the early Stanier style. See also Plate 160 and Figure 34.

**Plate 157.** Period III non-corridor first No M10124 built in 1951 to a 1938 diagram (D1997). Note the unlined BR red livery and BR-type torpedo ventilators.

**Plate 158.** Period III non-corridor composite to D1921A, No M16751 built in 1949. This coach, apart from the lack of company initials, was outshopped in final LMS livery, and did not carry figure 3 on any compartment doors. Slightly shorter third class compartments were provided in the composite coaches than in the full thirds.

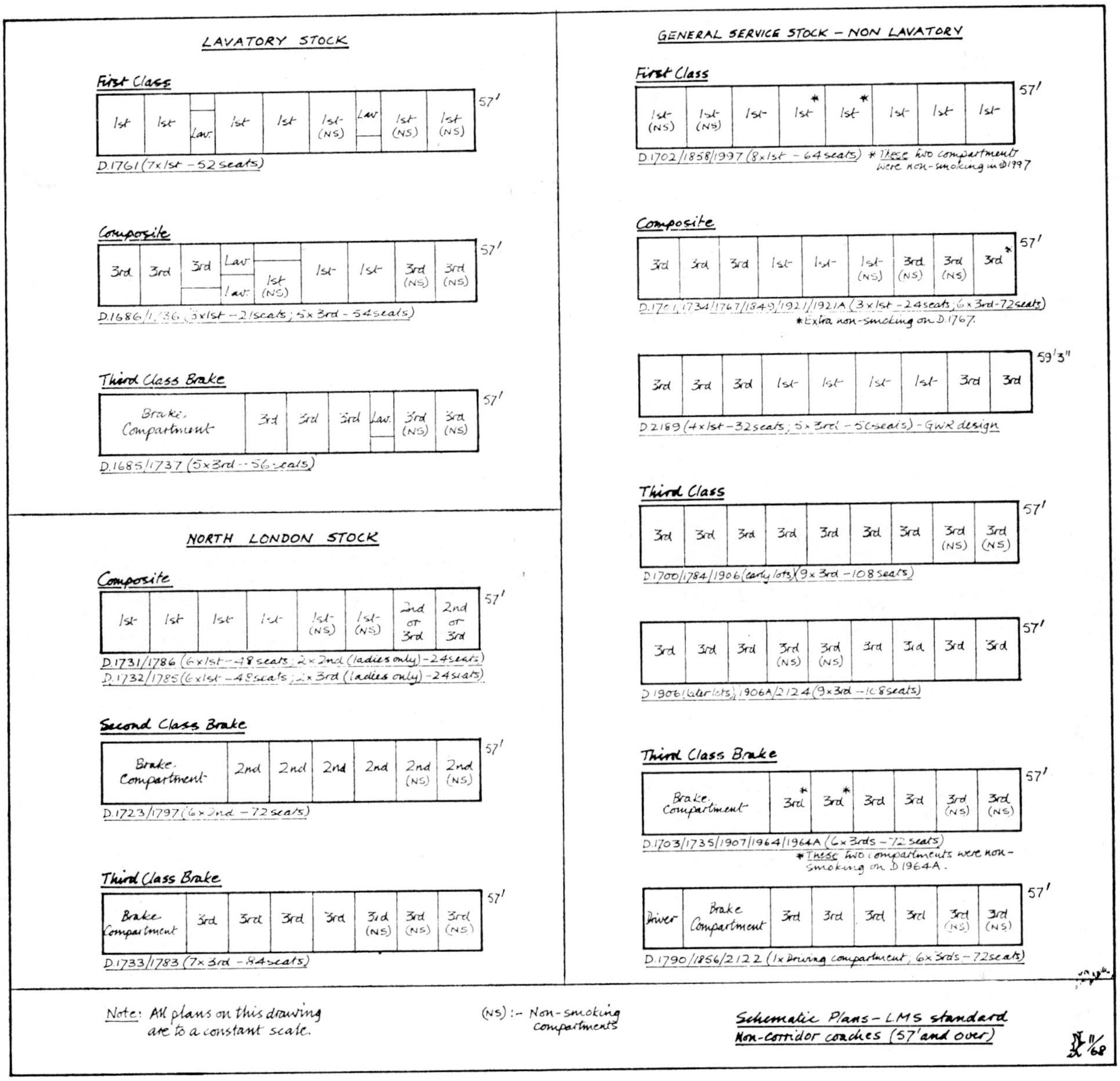
LAVATORY STOCK
First Class
1st 1st Lav. 1st 1st 1st (NS) Lav. 1st (NS) 1st (NS)
57'
D.1761 (7×1st – 52 seats)
Composite
3rd 3rd 3rd Lav. 1st (NS) Lav. 1st 1st 3rd (NS) 3rd (NS)
57'
D.1686/1736 (3×1st – 21 seats; 5×3rd – 54 seats)
Third Class Brake
Brake Compartment 3rd 3rd 3rd Lav. 3rd (NS) 3rd (NS)
57'
D.1685/1737 (5×3rd – 56 seats)
NORTH LONDON STOCK
Composite
1st 1st 1st 1st 1st (NS) 1st (NS) 2nd or 3rd 2nd or 3rd
57'
D.1731/1786 (6×1st – 48 seats; 2×2nd (ladies only) – 24 seats)
D.1732/1785 (6×1st – 48 seats; 2×3rd (ladies only) – 24 seats)
Second Class Brake
Brake Compartment 2nd 2nd 2nd 2nd 2nd (NS) 2nd (NS)
57'
D.1723/1797 (6×2nd – 72 seats)
Third Class Brake
Brake Compartment 3rd 3rd 3rd 3rd 3rd (NS) 3rd (NS) 3rd (NS)
57'
D.1733/1783 (7×3rd – 84 seats)
GENERAL SERVICE STOCK – NON LAVATORY
First Class
1st (NS) 1st (NS) 1st 1st* 1st* 1st 1st 1st
57'
D.1702/1858/1997 (8×1st – 64 seats) *These two compartments were non-smoking in D1997
Composite
3rd 3rd 3rd 1st 1st 1st (NS) 3rd (NS) 3rd (NS) 3rd*
57'
D.1701/1734/1767/1849/1921/1921A (3×1st – 24 seats; 6×3rd – 72 seats)
*Extra non-smoking on D.1767.
3rd 3rd 3rd 1st 1st 1st 1st 3rd 3rd
59'3"
D.2189 (4×1st – 32 seats; 5×3rd – 50 seats) – GWR design
Third Class
3rd 3rd 3rd 3rd 3rd 3rd 3rd 3rd (NS) 3rd (NS)
57'
D.1700/1784/1906 (early lots) (9×3rd – 108 seats)
3rd 3rd 3rd 3rd (NS) 3rd (NS) 3rd 3rd 3rd 3rd
57'
D.1906 (later lots) 1906A/2124 (9×3rd – 108 seats)
Third Class Brake
Brake Compartment 3rd* 3rd* 3rd 3rd 3rd (NS) 3rd (NS)
57'
D.1703/1735/1907/1964/1964A (6×3rds – 72 seats)
*These two compartments were non-smoking on D.1964A.
Driver Brake Compartment 3rd 3rd 3rd 3rd 3rd (NS) 3rd (NS)
57'
D.1790/1856/2122 (1× Driving compartment, 6×3rds – 72 seats)
Note: All plans on this drawing are to a constant scale.
(NS):– Non-smoking compartments
Schematic Plans – LMS standard Non-corridor coaches (57' and over)
DJ 11/68

*FIGURE 35 LMS standard 57ft non-corridor stock—sketch plans* (Drawn by D. Jenkinson)

## TABLE 10b: SUMMARY TABLE OF LMS STANDARD 57' NON-CORRIDOR (NON-LAVATORY) STOCK FOR GENERAL SERVICE

*Note:* This table should be read in conjunction with the list of standard dimensions and details on page 62.

| Type | Diag | Lot | Qty | Date | Built | Dimensions (L×W×H) | Weight | Period | Running Numbers | Withdrawals First | Withdrawals Last | Remarks |
|---|---|---|---|---|---|---|---|---|---|---|---|---|
| F | 1702 | 32 | 4 | 1924 | Wolverton | 57'×9'3"×12'4¾" | 28T | I | 10027-10030 | 5/58 | 1/60 | The most common non-corridor first class coach to LMS design. Lot 32 had MR fittings and was 9'1½" wide. No 9'1½" issued. Lots 248/321 plated 27T. 10000-26 were 54' coaches—see Table. |
| | | 121 | 25 | 1926 | Wolverton | | 27T | | 10031-10055 | 7/58 | 9/64 | |
| | | 248 | 20 | 1927 | Wolverton | | 28T | | 10056-10075 | 8/58 | 13/62 | |
| | | 321 | 30 | 1928 | Wolverton | | 28T | | 10076-10105 | 10/58 | 13/62 | |
| F | 1858 | 693 | 4 | 1933 | Derby | 57'×9'3"×12'4⅝" | 30T | III | 10106-10109 | 12/61 | 4/66 | Period III version of D1702. Lot 693 ha full livery when new. 10111-2 were 54 coaches—see Table 11. |
| | | 778 | 1 | 1934 | Derby | | 30T | | 10110 | — | 10/64 | |
| F | 1997 | 1048 | 4 | 1938 | Wolverton | 57'×9'3"×12'4⅝" | 30T | III | 10113-10116 | 2/62 | 4/65 | Identical to D1858 except for the disposition of non-smokers and the slightly increased height over ventilators. Lot 1048 plated 1937. Lot 1632 had post-war type torpedo vents and were outshopped in BR crimson livery. |
| | | 1632 | 15 | 1951 | Wolverton | | 30T | | 10117-10131 | 3/64 | 4/66 | |
| C | 1701 | 33 | 49 | 1925 | Wolverton | 57'×9'3"×12'4¾" | 28T | I | 16028-16076 | 5/59 | 1/64 | The standard Period I composite, matching D1702/D1703. Lot 81 seems to have been ordered for eight three car sets with Lot 82 (BT—D1703) and was built with short buffers. They were not marshalled with Lot 82! 16000-6 were NL stock (see Table 10c) and 16007-27 were 51' and 54' stock (Table 11). |
| | | 81 | 8 | 1927 | Derby | | 26T | | 16077-16084 | 5/59 | 3/65 | |
| | | 122 | 80 | 1926 | Wolverton | | 27T | | 16085-16164 | 10/57 | 7/64 | |
| | | 247 | 51 | 1926/7 | W'ton | | 27T | | 16165-16215 | 5/59 | 12/63 | |
| | | 322 | 80 | 1927 | Wolverton | | 27T | | 16216-16295 | 2/58 | 11/65 | |

## TABLE 10b: LMS STANDARD 57' NON-CORRIDOR GENERAL SERVICE STOCK *(continued)*

| *Type* | *Diag* | *Lot* | *Qty* | *Date* | *Built* | *Dimensions* (L×W×H) | *Weight* | *Period* | *Running Numbers* | *Withdrawals First* | *Withdrawals Last* | *Remarks* |
|---|---|---|---|---|---|---|---|---|---|---|---|---|
| C | 1767 | 229 | 30 | 1926/7 | Ntn Hth | 57'×9'3"×12'4¾" | 26T | I | 16296-16325 | 5/59 | 6/65 | An odd batch with slightly different compartment dimensions from the otherwise identical D1701. The firsts were a little larger and the thirds a little smaller. They were built without dynamos to run with BTs 20206-20235 (D1703) and the arrangement of non-smoking compartments differed from D1701. |
| C | 1734 | 526 | 43 | 1930/31 | W'ton | 57'×9'2¼"×12'4¾" | 27T | II | 16331-16368 | 5/59 | 7/64 | The Period II version of D1702. Some at least of Lot 526 were plated 29T.<br>‡ Motor fitted coaches, originally allocated 16326-30. |
| | | | | | | | | | 17900-17904‡ | 3/61 | 9/64 | |
| | | 581 | 100 | 1931/2 | W'ton | | 29T | | 16369-16468 | 8/58 | 10/65 | |
| C | 1849 | 650 | 20 | 1932 | Wolverton | 57'×9'3"×12'4⅝" | 30T | II | 16469-16488 | 6/59 | 1/65 | This was an interesting diagram. It was a Period II diagram but Lots 684/704 were actually Period III coaches. All carried full livery and Lots 684/704 were some of the few Stanier coaches to be given torpedo ventilators before the adoption of the shell type. Coach layout identical to D1734 but with slightly modified compartment dimensions. 16489-95 were NL stock (see Table 10c)<br>* Motor fitted coaches. |
| | | 684 | 55 | 1933 | Derby | | 30T | III | 16496-16535 | 2/62 | 1/66 | |
| | | | | | | | | | 17905-17919* | 4/62 | 12/65 | |
| | | 704 | 34 | 1933 | Derby | | 30T | III | 16536-16569 | 4/63 | 12/65 | |
| C | 1921 | 741 | 25 | 1933/4 | Derby | 57'×9'3"×12'4⅝" | 30T | III | 16570-16594 | 9/62 | 7/64 | The genuine Period III diagram but otherwise no difference from the Period I and II predecessors. All are believed to have had simple livery but Lot 741 is not confirmed.<br>* Motor fitted coaches |
| | | 742 | 20 | 1934 | Derby | | 30T | | 16595-16614 | 9/62 | 1/66 | |
| | | 849 | 32 | 1935 | Derby | | 30T | | 16615-16644 | 9/62 | 12/65 | |
| | | | | | | | | | 17920-17921* | 3/64 | 13/64 | |
| C | 1921A | 901 | 27 | 1936 | Derby | 57'×9'3"×12'4⅝" | 30T | III | 16645-16671 | 4/63 | 6/66 | 3" less over stepboards and $\frac{3}{16}$" higher over roof vents than D1921. Lot 1449 had simple LMS livery but no LMS markings. Lot 1450 was probably similar. Lot 1576 believed to have had BR livery from new. Lots 1450/1576 seem to have had post-war torpedo type ventilators. Lot 1102 plated 1938; Lot 1576 plated 29T.<br>* Motor fitted coaches<br>† Motor fitted coaches given vacant overflow numbers in the lavatory composite series. |
| | | 1047 | 36 | 1938 | Wolverton | | 30T | | 16672-16706 | 4/63 | 2/66 | |
| | | | | | | | | | 17922* | | | |
| | | 1102 | 40 | 1939 | Wolverton | | 30T | | 16707-16746 | 7/63 | 9/66 | |
| | | 1449 | 50 | 1949 | Derby | | 28T | | 16747-16796 | 2/64 | 12/66 | |
| | | 1450 | 20 | 1949 | Derby | | 28T | | 17923-17942* | 1/64 | 7/66 | |
| | | 1576 | 10 | 1950 | Wolverton | | 28T | | 19377-19386† | 2/64 | 11/66 | |
| C | 2189 | 1648 | 45 | 1952/3 | Swindon | 59'2"×9'3"×12'3¾" | 29T | see notes | 16797-16841 | 6/64 | 6/66 | GWR style coaches built after nationalisation to a resuscitated pre-war design. Their numbers had M prefix and W suffix with BR livery from new. GWR Diagram E156—lots 1749/1772. |
| | | | | | | | 29T | | | | | |
| | | 1661 | 35 | 1953 | Swindon | | 29T | | 16842-16816 | 1/64 | 11/67 | |
| T | 1700 | 102 | 38 | 1925 | Wolverton | 57'×9'3"×12'4¾" | 27T | I | 10850-10887 | 5/59 | 12/63 | The standard Period I full third. Lot 510 were for the North London sets—see Table 10c<br>*Conversions to motor fitted stock:*<br>11170 to 15998 c.1935<br>11284 to 15999 c.1935<br>*Plating discrepancies:*<br>Lot 231 plated 28T, Lot 305 plated 27T and all plated 1927. |
| | | 103 | 20 | 1925 | Ntn Hth | | 28T | | 10888-10907 | 2/60 | 12/63 | |
| | | 124 | 42 | 1925 | Ntn Hth | | 28T | | 10908-10949 | 8/58 | 5/63 | |
| | | 231 | 50 | 1926 | Ntn Hth | | 27T | | 10950-10999 | 2/58 | 13/64 | |
| | | 305 | 50 | 1927/8 | Ntn Hth | | 26T | | 11000-11049 | 7/58 | 13/63 | |
| | | 361 | 100 | 1928 | Wolverton | | 27T | | 11050-11149 | 11/58 | 11/64 | |
| | | 390 | 50 | 1928 | Wolverton | | 27T | | 11150-11199 | 9/58 | 12/63 | |
| | | 410 | 68 | 1928/30 | Derby | | 26T | | 11200-11267 | 11/58 | 4/65 | |
| | | 447 | 50 | 1929 | Wolverton | | 28T | | 11268-11317 | 5/59 | 9/64 | |
| | | 492 | 50 | 1930 | Ntn Hth | | 28T | | 11318-11367 | 5/59 | 11/64 | |
| | | 510 | 6 | 1930 | Derby | | 27T | | 11368-11373 | 2/62 | 7/64 | |
| T | 1784 | 523 | 50 | 1930/1 | Derby | 57'×9'2¼"×12'4¾" | 28T | II | 11374-11423 | 5/59 | 9/64 | The Period II version of D1700. Lots 554/642 were for the North London sets—see Table 10c. Lot 554 had bodies built at Newton Heath on Derby built chassis. 11606-23 were 54' coaches (Table 11)<br>*Conversions to motor fitted stock:*<br>11403 to 15997 c.1935 |
| | | 528 | 78 | 1930 | Wolverton | | 28T | | 11424-11501 | 2/59 | 11/64 | |
| | | 554 | 4 | 1931 | see notes | | 29T | | 11502-11505 | 3/61 | 3/64 | |
| | | 580 | 100 | 1932 | Derby | | 28T | | 11506-11605 | 6/59 | 12/65 | |
| | | 642 | 4 | 1932 | Derby | | 28T | | 11624-11627 | 10/60 | 1/64 | |
| T | 1906 | 682 | 50 | 1933 | Derby | 57'×9'3"×12'4⅝" | 30T | III | 15858-15859‡ | 11/62 | 2/64 | Period III version of D1700. Note the reversion to this diagram in 1939 after a number of coaches had been built to D1906A.<br>‡ Motor fitted; Lot 683 may also have been originally intended as a motor fitted batch. 11705-16 were 54' coaches (Table 11). |
| | | | | | | | | | 11628-11675 | 4/62 | 6/66 | |
| | | 683 | 4 | 1933 | Derby | | 30T | | 11676-11679 | 4/62 | 11/63 | |
| | | 743 | 25 | 1934 | Derby | | 30T | | 11680-11704 | 7/63 | 3/66 | |
| | | 847 | 25 | 1935 | Derby | | 29T | | 11717-11741 | 4/63 | 2/67 | |
| | | 1194 | 40 | 1939 | Wolverton | | 30T | | 12158-12197 | 12/63 | 12/66 | |
| | | 1195 | 30 | 1939/40 | W'ton | | 30T | | 12198-12227 | 7/60 | 8/66 | |
| T | 1906A | 906 | 55 | 1936 | Wolverton | 57'×9'3"×12'4⅝" | 30T | III | 11742-11796 | 4/62 | 12/66 | Identical to D1906 except for re-arranged smoking/non smoking and very minor dimensional differences. The frame of one of Lot 1094 was used for one vehicle of the BR XP64 demonstration train!<br>§ Motor fitted |
| | | 907 | 55 | 1936 | Wolverton | | 30T | | 11797-11851 | 11/61 | 9/67 | |
| | | 1036 | 60 | 1937 | Derby | | 29T | | 11852-11911 | 10/63 | 9/67 | |
| | | 1043 | 55 | 1937 | Wolverton | | 30T | | 11912-11966 | 3/62 | 8/67 | |
| | | 1044 | 55 | 1937 | Wolverton | | 30T | | 11967-12021 | 12/61 | 9/67 | |
| | | 1094 | 67 | 1938 | Wolverton | | 30T | | 12022-12087 | 12/63 | 9/67 | |
| | | | | | | | | | 15860§ | — | 7/64 | |
| | | 1095 | 70 | 1938 | Wolverton | | 30T | | 12088-12157 | 12/61 | 13/66 | |
| T | 2124 | 1451 | 30 | 1949 | Derby | 57'×9'3"×12'4⅝" | 28T | III | 15862-15891 | 13/63 | Not known | Generally as per D1906A but with roof vents closer together. No apparently good reason for the change in diagram but as the first two lots were built motor fitted, the diagram change may have been for this reason. Lot 1633 was plated 1950. All are thought to have had post-war torpedo ventilators and the following ex-works livery:<br>Lot 1451—LMS simple livery, no LMS markings<br>Lot 1578—BR lined out crimson<br>Lot 1633—BR unlined crimson |
| | | 1578 | 15 | 1950 | Wolverton | | 28T | | 15892-15906 | 12/63 | 9/66 | |
| | | 1633 | 40 | 1951 | Wolverton | | 28T | | 12228-12267 | 1/64 | 11/66 | |

| Type | Diag | Lot | Qty | Date | Built | Dimensions (L×W×H) | Weight | Period | Running Numbers | Withdrawals First | Withdrawals Last | Remarks |
|---|---|---|---|---|---|---|---|---|---|---|---|---|
| BT | 1703 | 82 | 16 | 1927 | Derby | 57'×9'3"×12'4¾" | 26T | I | 20140-20155 | 5/59 | 7/64 | The standard Period I coach. Lot 82 emerged very late for such a low lot number and Lot 141 was also a late arrival. Lot 82 may have been ordered with Lot 81 (C—D1701) for a particular need for three coach sets which failed to materialise and was thus held back until needed for general service. They were general service coaches when they did enter service. 20299 was later used as a Morecambe-Heysham driving trailer (1950). 20000-139 were 54' coaches (Table 11). |
| | | 141 | 50 | 1927 | Derby | | 27T | | 20156-20205 | 5/59 | 2/63 | |
| | | 230 | 30 | 1926/7 | Ntn Hth | | 27T | | 20206-20235 | 5/59 | 1/65 | |
| | | 289 | 51 | 1927 | Ntn Hth | | 27T | | 20236-20286 | 11/58 | 1/64 | |
| | | 335 | 50 | 1928 | Ntn Hth | | 27T | | 20287-20336 | 7/58 | 11/64 | |
| | | 356 | 50 | 1928 | Ntn Hth | | 27T | | 20337-20386 | 9/59 | 4/66 | |
| BT | 1735 | part 33 527 | | 1930 | Derby | 57'×9'3 3/16"×12'4¾" | 27T | II | 20540-20572 | 5/59 | 8/65 | The Period II version of D1703 but again with a change to Period III styling at Lot 681 without a change of diagram. Lots 681/687 had full livery and torpedo ventilators. *Motor fitted conversions:* 20553—24472; 20554—24467; 20557—24468; 20564—24462; 20565—24460; 20597—24470; 20602—24471; 20461—24473; 20469—24464; 20470—24465; 20471—24466. Lot 1147 was a one for one replacement of an accident victim destroyed in 1937 at Birmingham. *Plating discrepancies:* Lot 562 plated 28T. |
| | | 562 | 40 | 1930/1 | Ntn Hth | | 27T | | 20387-20426 | 3/60 | 10/65 | |
| | | 621 | 45 | 1931/2 | Derby | | 28T | | 20427-20471 | 5/60 | 5/65 | |
| | | 647 | 15 | 1932 | Derby | | 28T | | 20472-20486 | 11/59 | 13/64 | |
| | | 649 | 50 | 1932 | Derby | | 28T | | 20487-20536 | 3/60 | 4/65 | |
| | | 681 | 20 | 1933 | Wolverton | | 29T | III | 20700-20719 | 6/61 | 4/66 | |
| | | 687 | 122 | 1933 | Wolverton | | 29T | | 20577-20699 | 12/59 | 1/67 | |
| | | 1147 | 1 | 1938 | Wolverton | | 29T | | 20584 | — | 13/63 | |
| BT (Driving) | 1790 | part 7 527 | | 1930 | Derby | 57'×9'3"×12'4¾" | 27T | II | 24403-24409 | 7/59 | 1/64 | The driving trailer version of D1735. The post-1932 conversions to driving trailers of D1735 closely resembled D1790 except that they had flush glazing on the control end windows rather than the Period II windows of D1790. The D1790 coaches were built as normal BTs on D1735 and altered to motor fitted in 1930-2. It is not clear if many saw service as normal BTs between these dates (probably only 24403/4). |
| BT (Driving) | 1856 | 688 part | 17 | 1933 | Wolverton | 57'×9'3"×12'4⅝" | 30T | III | 24410-24426 | 5/63 | 12/65 | The Period III driving trailer although the Diagram is Period II. Lot 688 had full livery with torpedo ventilators. The length was quoted as 57'1" on the works plate—technically correct but it was more common to quote 57' only, omitting the odd inch. |
| | | 850 part | 2 | 1935 | Derby | | 29T | | 24427-24428 | 1/64 | 4/66 | |
| | | 1037 | 1 | 1937 | Derby | | 29T | | 24429 | — | 2/64 | |
| BT | 1907 | 744 | 30 | 1934 | Wolverton | | 29T | III | 20720-20749 | 12/61 | 7/65 | The Period III version of D1703. 20781-4 were 54' coaches (Table 11). |
| | | 745 part | 31 | 1934 | Wolverton | 57'×9'3"×12'4⅝" | 29T | | 20750-20780 | 6/61 | 6/66 | |
| | | 850 | 30 | 1935 | Derby | | 29T | | 20785-20814 | 1/62 | 9/65 | |
| BT | 1964 | 900 | 64 | 1936 | Derby | 57'×9'3 3/16"×12'4⅝" | 28T | III | 20815-20878 | Not known | 2/67 | As for D1907 but the guard's van end was altered to have two pairs of double doors. Plated 30T. |
| BT | 1964A | part 49 1037 | | 1937/8 | Derby | | 28T | III | 20879-20927 | 12/61 | 1/67 | Identical to D1964 but with roof vents closer together. The official reason for the change in diagram was the alteration in position of the non-smoking areas. This may have been the reason for D1921/D1921A and D1906/D1906A (above) but has not been confirmed. Lot 1441—simple LMS livery but no LMS marks. Lots 1485/1634—post war torpedo vents and BR livery. 20966 was used as a Morecambe-Heysham trailer in 1950. |
| | | 1086 | 44 | 1938 | Derby | | 28T | | 20928-20971 | 11/63 | 2/66 | |
| | | 1087 | 50 | 1938 | Derby | 57'×9'3 3/16"×12'4⅝" | 28T | | 20972-21021 | 4/61 | 1/67 | |
| | | 1441 | 60 | 1949 | Derby | | 28T | | 21022-21081 | 12/63 | 8/67 | |
| | | 1485 | 50 | 1951 | Glos. C&W | | 28T | | 21082-21131 | 13/63 | 6/67 | |
| | | 1634 | 120 | 1951 | Wolverton | | 28T | | 21132-21251 | 12/63 | 9/67 | |
| BT (Driving) | 2122 | 1442 | 30 | 1949 | Wolverton | 57'×9'3"×12'4⅝" | 29T | III | 24430-24459 | 1/64 | 7/66 | As for D1856 but van doors slightly altered in position. Post-war torpedo ventilators. Lot 1442—LMS livery but no LMS marks; Lot 1577—BR livery. |
| | | 1577 | 15 | 1950 | Wolverton | | 29T | | 24317-24331 | 3/64 | 13/66 | |

**Plate 159.** Period II (North London area) 1st/2nd class composite No 11149, later 16003 (D1786), one of the only two types of LMS standard coach, outside the NCC area, to be branded second class. The other was a six-compartment brake second identical in exterior style to the general service brake third. The two types were built to both Period I and II diagrams. The coach illustrated was downgraded to 1st/3rd about 1938 but was not renumbered.

# NORTH LONDON SETS

As already stated, the vast majority of 57ft stock built by the LMS was for general service and not formed into strict sets of coaches. However, the North London passenger stock inherited at grouping was a pretty gruesome collection of semi-museum pieces and it was not too long before the LMS put into service some new sets of standard 57ft coaches for the Broad Street-Alexandra Park services. Externally they matched the general service stock of the day but because of the different nature of the services, they were formed into sets. Five types of coaches were provided of which the full thirds were to standard LMS diagrams although built as separate North London lots. The other four types differed slightly as outlined above and thus necessitated new diagrams. The provision of second class accommodation was unique on the LMS except for the NCC, but the coaches themselves seem to have been little different from their third class contemporaries. Three classes survived on these and the related LNER suburban services until 1938. There is evidence that the seating might have been a little softer than in the thirds but the seating capacity was the same and the amount of knee room was also identical to that in the thirds.

Sufficient coaches were provided to make up seven six-coach sets. Three sets were Period I in styling and delivered in 1930 while there were four Period II sets delivered two each in 1931 and 1932. The coaches were formed up as follows: BT/T/T/C(3rd-1st)/C(1st-2nd)/BS. Of the seven sets, the coaches delivered to Lots 55x in 1931 have been confirmed in this formation and from this, the likely composition of the remainder has been deduced (Table 10c). At a later date, the second class branding was abolished (c. 1938) and the brake seconds were renumbered in the brake third series. The first/second composites were downgraded but retained their numbers as no separate series had been allocated to them.

## TABLE 10c  SUMMARY TABLE OF SEPARATE DIAGRAMS RAISED FOR NORTH LONDON 57' STOCK TOGETHER WITH TRAIN SET FORMATIONS

*Note:* This table should be read in conjunction with the list of standard dimensions and details on page 62.

| Type | Diag | Lot | Qty | Date | Built | Dimensions (L×W×H) | Weight | Period | Running Numbers | Withdrawals First · Last | | Remarks |
|------|------|-----|-----|------|-------|--------------------|--------|--------|-----------------|-------|-------|---------|
| C(1/2) | 1731 | 512 | 3 | 1930 | Derby | 57'×9'3"×12'4¾" | 27T | I | 16000-16002 | 8/60 | 6/63 | The eight compartment composite with 6 first and two second class compartments. |
| C(1/2) | 1786 | 556 | 2 | 1931 | see notes ⎱ Derby ⎰ | 57'×9'2¼"×12'4¾" | 28T | II | 16003-16004 | 11/62 | 2/64 | Lot 556 had bodies built at Newton Heath with bogies/underframe at Derby. The Period II version of D1731. |
|        |      | 644 | 2 | 1932 |  |  | 28T |  | 16005-16006 | 12/62 | 5/63 |  |
| C(1/3) | 1732 | 511 | 3 | 1930 | Derby | 57'×9'3"×12'4¾" | 27T | I | 16489-16491 | 5/59 | 10/62 | The first/third version of D1731. |
| C(1/3) | 1785 | 555 | 2 | 1931 | see notes ⎱ Derby ⎰ | 57'×9'2¼"×12'4¾" | 29T | II | 16492-16493 | 7/61 | 6/64 | The Period II version of D1732. Lot 555 built as for Lot 556—see above. |
|        |      | 643 | 2 | 1932 |  |  | 28T |  | 16494-16495 | 10/41 | 1/62 |  |
| BS | 1723 | 513 | 3 | 1930 | Derby | 57'×9'3"×12'4¾" | 27T | I | 24900-24902 | 13/62 | 4/64 | Six compartment brake seconds but otherwise identical to the general service D1703 brake third. Downgraded to BT and renumbered 22196-8 c.1938. |
| BS | 1797 | 557 | 2 | 1931 | see notes ⎱ Derby ⎰ | 57'×9'3³⁄₁₆"×12'4¾" | 28T | II | 24903-24904 | 3/63 | 8/63 | The Period II version of D1723. Lot 557 plated 27T and built as for Lot 556—see above. Downgraded to BT and renumbered 22199-202 c.1938. |
|    |      | 645 | 2 | 1932 |  |  | 28T |  | 24905-24906 | 9/61 | 2/64 |  |
| BT | 1733 | 509 | 3 | 1930 | Derby | 57'×9'3"×12'4¾" | 27T | I | 20537-20539 | 7/63 | 10/63 | The seven compartment brake third—otherwise identically styled to the general service D1703. |
| BT | 1783 | 553 | 2 | 1931 | see notes ⎱ Derby ⎰ | 57'×9'3³⁄₁₆"×12'4¾" | 27T | II | 20573-20574 | 7/59 | 6/61 | The Period II version of D1733. Lot 553 built as for Lot 556—see above. |
|    |      | 641 | 2 | 1932 |  |  | 27T |  | 20575-20576 | 12/62 | 7/64 |  |

*Note:* Fourteen all thirds were also built for these services but these coaches were identical to the general service all thirds and are listed under these diagrams on Table 10b. Their running numbers were as follows:

Period I coaches (Lot 510) : 11368-11373 (D1700)
Period II coaches (Lot 554) : 11502-11505 (D1784)
    ,,    ,,  (Lot 642) : 11624-11627(D1784)
Lot 554 was built as for Lot 556—see note to D1786 (above).

*North London six coach sets* (confirmed individual coaches shown in italic numerals)

| Set Number | Brake Third | Third | Third | Compo (1/3) | Compo (1/2) | Brake Second | Remarks |
|------------|-------------|-------|-------|-------------|-------------|--------------|---------|
|            | 20537 | 11368 | 11369 | 16490 | 16000 | 24900 (later 22196) | The three Period I sets of coaches |
|            | 20538 | 11372 | 11371 | 16491 | 16002 | 24902 (later 22198) |  |
| *N.18*     | *20539* | *11373* | *11370* | *16489* | *16001* | *24901 (later 22197)* |  |
| *N.16*     | *20573* | *11502* | *11503* | *16492* | *16003* | *24903 (later 22199)* | The four Period II sets of coaches |
| *N.17*     | *20574* | *11504* | *11505* | *16493* | *16004* | *24904 (later 22200)* |  |
|            | 20575 | 11624 | 11625 | 16494 | 16005 | 24905 (later 22201) |  |
|            | 20576 | 11626 | 11627 | 16495 | 16006 | 24906 (later 22202) |  |

## PUSH-PULL STOCK

As explained on page 17, the LMS never designed any separate motor fitted vehicles and all the LMS standard push-pull stock was identical in styling to the contemporary non-corridor stock. Push-pull vehicles were usually listed on the same diagrams as the normal coaches while in many cases, normal non-corridor LMS coaches were later converted to motor fitted style with little if any change in appearance except for the windows in the driving end. Although these conversions etc are listed in the summary tables, it has been thought desirable to give a separate list of all motor fitted coaches either built or rebuilt to LMS standard designs and this information is appended below.

There were also push-pull conversions of LMS design gangway stock but these were relatively few in number and no diagrams have been located for them. The conversions took place in the 1950s and involved coaches from the following diagrams:

BTK   D1851 (originally built 1932)        TO   D1692 (originally built 1929)        TO   D1807 (originally built 1932)

Such details as are known are given in the 'Remarks' columns of Tables 8 and 9.

---

### TABLE 10d: SUMMARY OF LMS STANDARD MOTOR FITTED STOCK

*Note:* This table only includes details of motor fitted stock which was of standard LMS pattern non-corridor design. It does, however, include all vehicles which were converted to motor fitted form although built as standard non-corridor coaches. Undated conversions are all believed to have been c. 1934.

*Driving Trailers*

| Running Numbers | Date built/ converted | Lot | Type/Remarks |
|---|---|---|---|
| 24400-24402 | 1927 | part 79 | 54' Period I coaches converted 1927—the only 54' LMS Standard motor fitted vehicles. |
| 24403-24409 | 1930-2 | part 527 | 57' Period II coaches converted 1930-32 but 24405-9 probably entered service motor fitted. |
| 24410-24429 | 1932-38 | 688, 750, 1087 | Period III coaches built as driving trailers to D1856 |
| 24430-24459 | 1949 | 1442 | 57' Post-war Period III driving trailers to D2122 |
| 24317-24331 | 1950 | 1577 | 57' As per 24430-24459 |
| 24460 | | 527 | 57' Period II coach converted from 20565 |
| 24462 | | 527 | 57' Period II coach converted from 20564 |
| 24464 | c.1934 | 621 | 57' Period II coach converted from 20469 |
| 24465 | c.1934 | 621 | 57' Period II coach converted from 20470 |
| 24466 | c.1934 | 621 | 57' Period II coach converted from 20471 |
| 24467 | | 527 | 57' Period II coach converted from 20554 |
| 24468 | | 527 | 57' Period II coach converted from 20557 |
| 24470 | c.1935 | 687 | 57' Period III coach converted from 20597 |
| 24471 | c.1935 | 687 | 57' Period III coach converted from 20602 |
| 24472 | c.1935 | 527 | 57' Period II coach converted from 20553 |
| 24473 | 1934 | 621 | 57' Period II coach converted from 20461 |

*Note:* The missing 244xx series numbers were carried by pre-group vehicles.

*All thirds*

| Running Numbers | Date built/ converted | Lot | Type/Remarks |
|---|---|---|---|
| 15858-15859 | 1933 | 682 | 57' Period III built new |
| 15860 | 1938 | 1094 | 57' Period III built new |
| 15861 | c.1938 | 1044 | 57' Period III ex-12010 |
| 15862-15891 | 1949 | 1451 | 57' Period III built new |
| 15892-15906 | 1950 | 1578 | 57' Period III built new |
| 15997 | c.1935 | 523 | 57' Period II ex-11403 |
| 15998 | | 390 | 57' Period I ex-11162 |
| 15999 | | 447 | 57' Period I ex-11284 |

*Composites*

| Running Numbers | Date built/ converted | Lot | Type/Remarks |
|---|---|---|---|
| 17900-17904 | 1931 | 526 | Originally allocated 16326-30 in compo list but converted to push-pull before getting these numbers. 57' Period II coaches. |
| 17905-17919 | 1933 | 684 | 57' Period III coaches built new.  Full livery and torpedo ventilators. |
| 17920-17921 | 1935 | 849 | 57' Period III coaches built new |
| 17922 | 1938 | 1047 | 57' Period III coach built new |
| 17923-17942 | 1949 | 1450 | 57' Period III coaches built new |
| 17944 | | 650 | 57' Period II coach ex-16478 |
| 17946 | | 33 | 57' Period I coach ex-16066 |
| 17947 | | 526 | 57' Period II coach ex-16343 |
| 17948 | | 581 | 57' Period II coach ex-16432 |
| 17949 | | 581 | 57' Period II coach ex-16434 |
| 17950 | | 581 | 57' Period II coach ex-16435 |
| 17951 | | 526 | 57' Period II coach ex-16356 |
| 17952 | | 122 | 57' Period I coach ex-16101 |
| 17954 | c.1935 | 684 | 57' Period III coach ex-16523 |
| 17955 | c.1935 | 684 | 57' Period III coach ex-16522 |
| 17956 | c.1935 | 684 | 57' Period III coach ex-16521 |
| 17957 | 1934 | 526 | 57' Period II coach ex-16347 |
| 19377-19386 | 1950 | 1576 | 57' Period III coaches built new |

*Note:* Except for 17943, which was never used, the missing 179xx numbers were carried by pre-group vehicles.

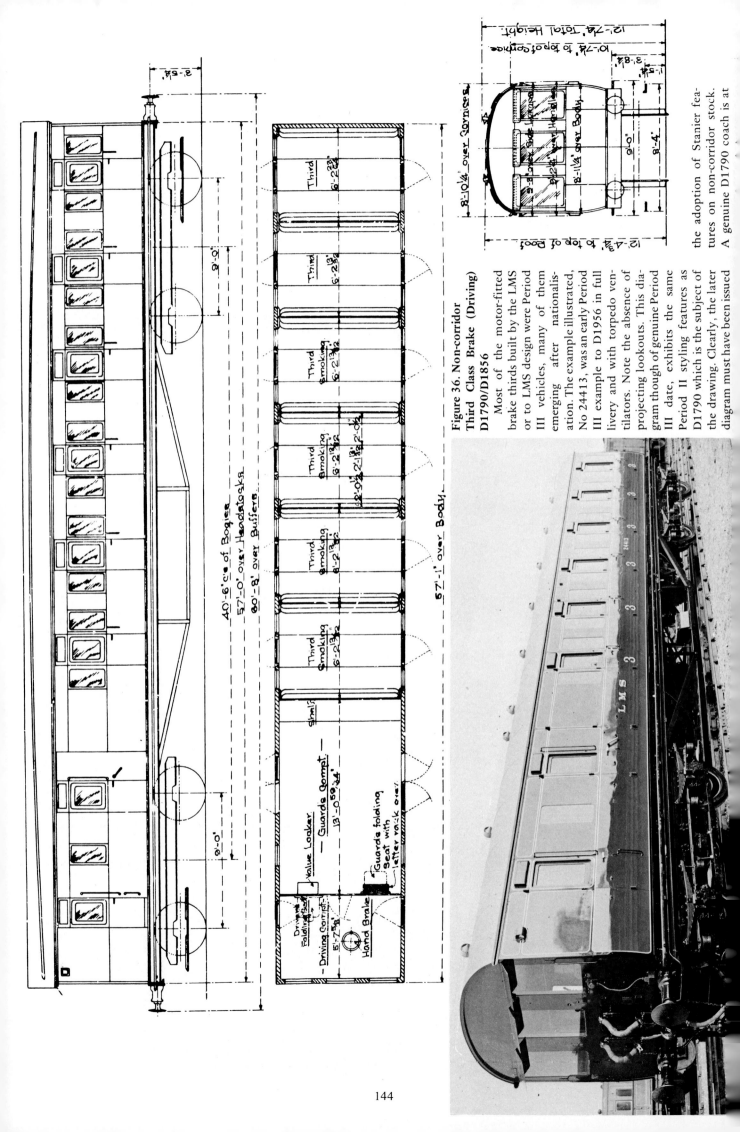

**Figure 36. Non-corridor Third Class Brake (Driving) D1790/D1856**

Most of the motor-fitted brake thirds built by the LMS or to LMS design were Period III vehicles, many of them emerging after nationalisation. The example illustrated, No 24413, was an early Period III example to D1956 in full livery and with torpedo ventilators. Note the absence of projecting lookouts. This diagram though of genuine Period III date, exhibits the same Period II styling features as D1790 which is the subject of the drawing. Clearly, the later diagram must have been issued the adoption of Stanier features on non-corridor stock. A genuine D1790 coach is at

**Plate 160** *(above)*. Motor-fitted Period II BT (driving) No 24404 (D1790), built as a conventional BT to D1735 but altered very soon to a motor driving brake. Its original number (pre-1933) was 17195. The repaired panel above the guard's lookout clearly indicates the position of the side lamp before conversion to motor-fitted form. The year of the picture taken at Ambergate, is probably 1934.

**Plate 161** *(right)*. Period III non-corridor end elevation of a coach fitted for push-pull working. The coach was non-corridor third No M15893 of D2124, built 1950.

145

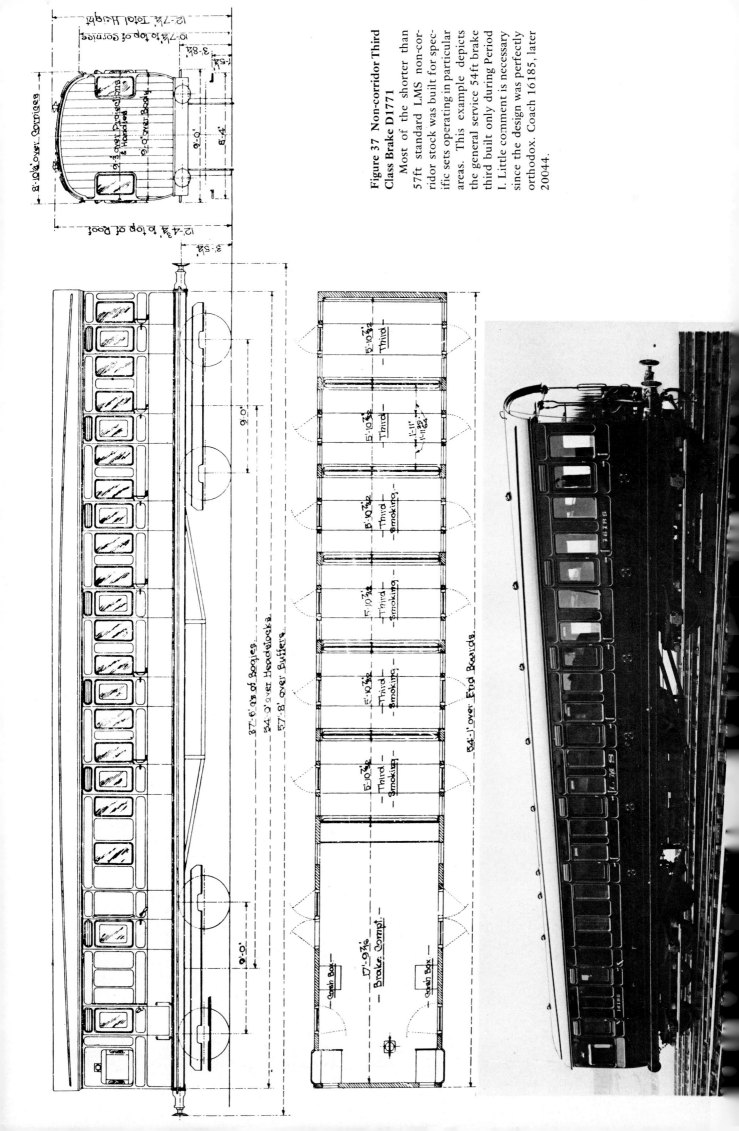

**Figure 37 Non-corridor Third Class Brake D1771**

Most of the shorter than 57ft standard LMS non-corridor stock was built for specific sets operating in particular areas. This example depicts the general service 54ft brake third built only during Period I. Little comment is necessary since the design was perfectly orthodox. Coach 16185, later 20044.

# Chapter 11 - 51ft and 54ft Non-Corridor Stock

*Introduction; Period I designs; Period II and III designs; The London, Tilbury & Southend Sets; Cathcart Circle Stock; General Service Stock; Summary Table.*

IT is often assumed that the LMS built two lengths of non-corridor stock (57ft and 54ft) more or less indiscriminately but this was not quite true. The general policy was to build only 57ft coaches and with but a few exceptions, shorter stock was only built for specific services in specific areas. Thus, the analysis of the shorter stock is closely linked to the services for which they were designed. Therefore, in addition to describing the vehicles, this chapter will also concern itself with the services for which they were built.

Virtually all the short non-corridor coaches were on a 54ft underframe, this length being traceable back to the Midland Railway. The only exception to this length was a batch of 51ft composite coaches built for the Cathcart Circle suburban services in Glasgow during 1926. These were the only 51ft passenger carrying vehicles ever built by the LMS. Although most of the short stock was built for these services in Glasgow or for the Tilbury section, there was in addition a small number of general service 54ft coaches; but these represent an insignificant total when compared with the 57ft general service non-corridor stock. They may, however, have been built to satisfy a preference in parts of the system for a 54ft as opposed to a 57ft length. Three of these 54ft coaches were used for motor train working.

Like their 57ft contemporaries, the shorter coaches were only built to four basic types: firsts, composites, thirds and brake thirds. The LMS never designed a standard non-corridor brake first or brake composite.

## PERIOD I DESIGNS

By far the largest number of short coaches were built during Period I and they included the only general service representatives of the length.

Full firsts were eight compartment coaches, most for the LT&S services and the wood panelled coaches were built to two diagrams (D1759/D1762). The earlier diagram had the MR 9ft 1½in width while D1762 was the 9ft 3in LMS version. Two more identical coaches to D1759 were also built with some of the compartment walls thickened to provide a composite version. This was to D1764 and the reasons for this rather odd and quite unique conversion are explained later, when the formation of the LT&S sets is discussed.

There was, of course, an orthodox Period I wood panelled, 54ft composite and these coaches were also confined to the Tilbury section. They contained lavatories and there were two diagrams. D1763 was a seven compartment coach and had the MR style fittings with the two lavatories separated, one towards each end of the vehicle. The later version to D1765 with the LMS 9ft 3in width and eight compartments had both lavatories placed side-by-side in the centre of the coach and this layout of lavatory composite remained standard on the LT&S lines until the end of the LMS responsibility for providing coaches.

The thirds and brake thirds were, like the firsts 54ft coaches, the main difference being the reduced compartment size necessitated by the 54ft underframe. The full thirds still retained nine compartments while the brake ends had either six or seven compartments. The six compartment version was for general service while the wood panelled seven compartment design was for use on the LT&S section. There were again diagrams covering both 9ft 1½in widths in both thirds and brake thirds (Thirds—D1768/D1769; Brake thirds—D1770/D1771/D1772).

It was during Period I that the Cathcart Circle stock was introduced. This differed from the normal Period I short stock in having steel panelling. Thus, the coaches were exactly similar in appearance to the orthodox Period II coaches and may, perhaps, be regarded as the prototype Period II non-corridor vehicles. However, the Cathcart Circle coaches were given full Period I livery with painted waist panel and this, initially distinguished them from the true Period II coaches.

The Cathcart Circle stock was provided in three types (first, brake third and composite), all built by outside manufacturers. The full firsts to D1760 were identical to the fully beaded D1762 (above), but had five-a-side seating and no armrests. The brake thirds were built to the same seven compartment diagram as the LT&S stock (D1772) but did not, of course, have the raised beading and wood panelling of the Tilbury coaches.

Plate 162. Period III 54ft seven-compartment brake third No 20781 (D1914) built for the LT&S services.

The composites were the only 51ft coaches built to an LMS diagram (D1766). They were eight compartment vehicles identical in layout to the second design of LT&S centre lavatory composite (D1765) except for the omission of the lavatories which was the reason for the reduced length. The first class compartments were again devoid of armrests and seated five-a-side. Like their matching five-a-side full firsts, the coaches were later written down to third class and re-numbered. They were the shortest LMS standard locomotive hauled single unit passenger-carrying coaches.

## PERIOD II AND III DESIGNS

All Period II and III designs of short non-corridor coaches were 54ft vehicles and all were for the LT&S services. The only really curious feature about them was the fact that the Period III coaches were actually built to Period II diagrams with the exception of the brake thirds. Why this was so is not known but it may be compared with the 57ft stock where in some cases there was a change from Period II to Period III on the same diagram—see Table 10b, pages 139-41. By 1930, the make-up of the LT&S sets had been standardised and the 54ft coaches of Periods II and III were only built to four specific types: full firsts, full third, lavatory composite and seven compartment brake third. In terms of compartment layout they were identical to the final Period I designs.

## THE LONDON, TILBURY & SOUTHEND SETS

The 54ft vehicles for this section of the LMS were built to form 17 semi-close coupled sets of 11 coaches. The sets were generally branded 'F&S 2xx' (the F&S standing for Fenchurch Street and Southend) and the make-up for one set was generally as follows: BT/T/T/T/CL/F/CL/T/T/T/BT. The 54ft length was probably adopted because of platform or loop lengths on the Tilbury line.

The first two sets (F&S 241/2) were not quite of this standard layout as they each contained two full firsts and only one composite, the latter being of the 'separated' lavatory type. It seems that the Operating Department must have felt that this formation gave too much first class space and requested a reduction in future sets. However, the next two sets (F&S 243/4) were already building at the time and the only way to reduce the first class space would be to turn one of the firsts into a composite. This seems the most likely explanation for the curious conversion of only two coaches to D1764 mentioned above. If the coaches had not been built there would have been no good reason why two more of the lavatory composites could not have been substituted for the two unwanted firsts. Moreover, if the conversion of these two firsts to composite took place *after* the coaches entered service one would have logically expected two coaches from sets F&S 241/2 to be likewise altered and this was never done.

By the time subsequent sets were in production, the new centre lavatory composite had been designed and two of these replaced one of the firsts and the older staggered lavatory composite. It seemed hardly worthwhile having lavatories at all, for only two compartments—one first and one third—were served, a total of four out of the entire set.

The diagrams show that some of the 54ft LT&S coaches were built with four short buffers and some with short buffers at one end and long buffers at the other. In general, the short buffered ends were semi-permanently coupled together while the long buffers were provided where the sets were divided into shorter units at off-peak hours. Although in later years the splitting of sets and the reversal of sections caused the pattern to be somewhat confused (too much so to analyse here), the general principles seem to be as outlined below.

The basic 11 coach set was divided as follows: BT+T/T+T+CL+F/CL+T/T+T/BT, the long buffers being at the outer ends of these sections. The most general off-peak reduction was to remove the three-coach CL+T+T portion, leaving an eight coach unit. Frequently, the detached three coach sections would be coupled in pairs with two loose brakes to form further sets. One can only presume that this splitting was to reduce the average daily mileage of any specific vehicle of these intensively-used coaches so as to lengthen the period between overhauls. Table 11 lists the LT&S sets as they were when originally built and as running until at least 1939. After the war, they became a little split up but sufficient coaches have been verified in the original sets by eye witnesses to establish that the overall pattern changed hardly at all.

## CATHCART CIRCLE STOCK

The Cathcart Circle coaches were built to form eight five-coach sets with spare vehicles. The formation of a set was as follows: BT/C/F/C/BT with a total of 160 first class seats and 264 thirds. Unfortunately, it has not been possible to confirm the running numbers of the coaches in each individual set but published information at the time shows that seven sets came from Hurst Nelson and one set and eight spare coaches from Pickering and Company. There could have been a further set made from the spares but whether this was done is not known. Table 11 includes an attempt to reconstruct the probable formation of the Cathcart Circle sets but has not been confirmed. In about 1938, nine composites were marked down to thirds and renumbered, followed in about 1941 by the ten firsts and in 1953 by the remaining composites. Details are given with Table 11.

## GENERAL SERVICE STOCK

The 54ft coaches not accounted for by the LT&S/Cathcart Circle sets were 78 thirds to D1768 and 94 brake thirds to D1770/D1771. These seemed to be fairly widespread in use and, no doubt, were more acceptable than the 57ft coaches in many parts of the Midland Division because of their 54ft length. Nevertheless, they seem to have been indiscriminately mixed with 57ft stock when in service and some fairly typical observed formations on the Midland Division using the 54ft coaches would include 54ft BT/57ft CL/57ft BT or 54ft BT/57ft CL/57ft BTL as local sets and 54ft BT/54ft T/54ft T/57ft T/54ft BT as an excursion set.

There were a few motor fitted 54ft coaches and these are covered on page 143 although details are also included in the summary table to this chapter.

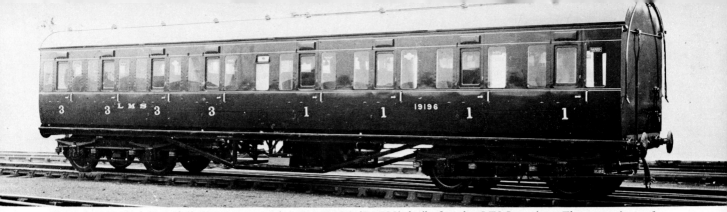

**Plate 163.** Period II 54ft lavatory composite No 19196 (D1788) built for the LT&S services. These coaches, of which four only were built were the only Period III non-corridor lavatory vehicles.

### TABLE 11: SUMMARY TABLE OF LMS STANDARD 51' AND 54' NON-CORRIDOR STOCK

| Type Diag | Lot | Qty | Date | Built | Dimensions (L×W×H) | Weight | Period | Running Numbers | Withdrawals First | Last | Remarks |
|---|---|---|---|---|---|---|---|---|---|---|---|
| F 1759 | 12 part | 4 | 1924 | Derby | 54'×9'1½"×12'5½" | 26T | I | 10000-10003 | 6/61 | 12/63 | LT&S stock with MR fittings and with alternate long/short buffers. Lot 12 for sets F&S 241/2; Lot 96 for F&S 243/4. |
| | 96 | 2 | 1924 | Derby | | 26T | I | 10004-10005 | 11/60 | 13/62 | |
| F 1760 | 212 | 7 | 1926 | Hurst Nelson | 54'×9'3"×12'4¾" | 27T | I (Steel panelled) | 10017-10023 | 7/59 | 6/61 | The Cathcart Circle coaches with five a side seating. Downgraded to 3rd class (c.1941). |
| | 213 | 3 | 1926 | Pickering | | 27T | | 10024-10026 | 11/60 | 2/62 | |
| F 1762 | 129 | 2 | 1926 | Derby | 54'×9'3"×12'4¾" | 26T | I | 10006-10007 | 1/45 | 2/62 | LT&S stock with LMS standard fittings. Otherwise identical to D1759 and fitted with alternate long/short buffers. One each in sets F&S 245-252. |
| | 331 | 2 | 1927 | Derby | | 26T | | 10008-10009 | 5/61 | 3/62 | |
| | 394 | 2 | 1928 | Derby | | 26T | | 10010-10011 | — | 2/62 | |
| | 432 | 2 | 1929 | Derby | | 26T | | 10012-10013 | 2/62 | 3/62 | |
| F 1787 | 558 | 3 | 1931 | see notes | 54'×9'2¼"×12'4¾" | 28T | II | 10014-10016 | 2/62 | 5/62 | LT&S stock with alternate long/short buffers. Lot 558 was built at Newton Heath on Derby chassis. Note change to Period III on same diagram. Lot 558 was for sets F&S 253-5; Lot 819 for F&S 264/5. |
| | 819 | 2 | 1934 | Derby | | 29T | III | 10111-10112 | 9/61 | 3/62 | |
| CL 1763 | 13 | 2 | 1924 | Derby | 54'×9'1½"×12'5½" | 25T | I | 19022-19023 | 9/61 | 12/61 | The first LT&S style CL with separated lavatories. All with short buffers and one each in sets F&S 241-4. Diagram shows 9'1½" width but some coaches may not have had MR pattern locks/handles. No reason can be given why they were numbered after D1765/D1788. |
| | 97 | 2 | 1924 | Derby | | 25T | | 19024-19025 | 11/61 | 12/61 | |
| C 1764 | part 96 | 2 | 1924 | Derby | 54'×9'1½"×12'5½" | 26T | I | 16026-16027 | — | 2/62 | These were the coaches modified from D1759 to have thicker compartment walls and hence smaller third class compartments. Although built to 9'1½" diagram they did not have MR pattern handles &c. One each in sets F&S 243-4. |
| C 1766 | 216 | 14 | 1926 | Hurst Nelson | 51'×9'3"×12'4¾" | 27T | I (Steel panelled) | 16007-16020 | 2/60 | 13/61 | Cathcart Circle coaches with five a side firsts. Downgraded to third class. (c.1938/1953). |
| | 217 | 5 | 1926 | Pickering | | 27T | | 16021-16025 | 6/60 | 6/64 | |
| CL 1765 | 130 | 4 | 1926 | Derby | 54'×9'3"×12'4¾" | 26T | I | 19000-19003 | 6/61 | 3/62 | LT&S stock with the centre lavatory and LMS fittings. Replaced D1763 and had one more first class compartment. Two from each lot had long/short buffers, two all short. Two coaches per set in F&S 245-252. |
| | 332 | 4 | 1927 | Derby | | 26T | | 19004-19007 | 5/59 | 4/62 | |
| | 395 | 4 | 1928 | Derby | | 26T | | 19008-19011 | 6/61 | 12/61 | |
| | 433 | 4 | 1929 | Derby | | 26T | | 19012-19015 | 3/62 | 6/62 | |
| CL 1788 | 559 | 6 | 1930 | see notes | 54'×9'2¼"×12'4¾" | 28T | II | 19016-19021 | 6/61 | 6/62 | The Period II and III versions of D1765. Lot 559 built as for Lot 558 (above). Buffers as per D1765. Lot 559 was for sets F&S 253-5; Lot 820 for F&S 264/5. |
| | 820 | 4 | 1935 | Derby | | 29T | III | 19196-19199 | 7/61 | 4/62 | |
| T 1768 | 14 | 12 | 1924 | Derby | 54'×9'1½"×12'5½" | 26T | I | 10700-10711 | 5/61 | 6/62 | The official 9'1½" version but Lot 78 did not have MR handles and was 9'3" wide. Lots 14/98 may have been similar and were the LT&S coaches. These had four of each lot with long/short buffers and eight with all short buffers. Six coaches into each of sets F&S 241-244. Lots 60/78 were the general service lots and Lot 60 *was* 9'1½". |
| | 98 | 12 | 1924 | Derby | | 26T | | 10712-10723 | 8/60 | 4/62 | |
| | 60 | 40 | 1924/5 | Ntn Hth | | 27T | | 10772-10811 | 5/59 | 1/64 | |
| | 78 | 38 | 1924 | Derby | | 26T | | 10812-10849 | 5/59 | 13/62 | |
| T 1769 | 131 | 12 | 1926 | Derby | 54'×9'3"×12'4¾" | 26T | I | 10724-10735 | 5/58 | 4/62 | These were the *official* 9'3" coaches and all for LT&S sets (six each to F&S 245-252) Eight of each lot had long/short buffers and four all short—a reversal of D1768. |
| | 333 | 12 | 1927 | Derby | | 26T | | 10736-10747 | 9/59 | 4/62 | |
| | 396 | 12 | 1928 | Derby | | 26T | | 10748-10759 | 6/61 | 4/62 | |
| | 434 | 12 | 1929 | Derby | | 26T | | 10760-10771 | 6/61 | 4/62 | |
| T 1789 | 560 | 18 | 1931/2 | see notes | 54'×9'2¼"×12'4¾" | 29T | II | 11606-11623 | 7/60 | 4/62 | The Period II/III LT&S coaches. Buffers as per D1769. Lot 560 plated 27T and built as for Lots 558/559 (above). F&S sets 253-5/264/5. |
| | 821 | 12 | 1935 | Derby | | 29T | III | 11705-11716 | 4/61 | 2/62 | |
| BT 1770 | 15 | 4 | 1924 | Derby | 54'×9'1½"×12'5½" | 26T | I | 20091-20094 | 7/61 | 12/61 | The 9'1½" diagram but Lot 61 (at least) plated 9'3" and the others may have been similar. Lots 15/99 were LT&S (F&S sets 241-4) with alternate long/short buffers & 7 comps. Lot 61 had six compartments and was probably plated 27T. |
| | 61 | 20 | 1925 | Ntn Hth | | 24T | | 20000-20019 | 7/58 | 7/62 | |
| | 99 | 4 | 1924 | Derby | | 26T | | 20095-20098 | 4/61 | 2/62 | |
| BT 1771 | 79 | 24 | 1925 | Derby | 54'×9'3"×12'4¾" | 26T | I | 20020-20040 | 5/59 | 1/64 | The official 9'3" six compartment general service coaches, plated 1924. * Driving Trailers, converted 1927. |
| | | | | | | | | 24400-24402* | 9/60 | 2/65 | |
| | 128 | 50 | 1925 | Derby | | 26T | | 20041-20090 | 10/58 | 3/64 | |
| BT 1772 | 132 | 4 | 1926 | Derby | 54'×9'3"×12'4¾" | 26T | I | 20099-20102 | 2/62 | 2/62 | The 9'3" seven compartment coaches for LT&S and Cathcart Circle sets. Note that in this case a separate diagram was raised for the seven compartment version. Lots 214/5 were Cathcart Circle, remainder LT&S. LT&S coaches had long buffers at brake end, short at opposite end and were for sets F&S 245-252. |
| | 214 | 14 | 1926 | Hurst Nelson | | 26T | I (Flush) | 20103-20116 | 6/59 | 13/62 | |
| | 215 | 5 | 1926 | Pickering | | 26T | I (Flush) | 20117-20121 | 1/60 | 6/60 | |
| | 334 | 4 | 1927 | Derby | | 26T | | 20122-20125 | 3/60 | 4/62 | |
| | 397 | 4 | 1928 | Derby | | 26T | | 20126-20129 | 6/61 | 4/62 | |
| | 435 | 4 | 1929 | Derby | | 26T | | 20130-20133 | 11/61 | 3/62 | |
| BT 1841 | 561 | 6 | 1932 | see notes | 54'×9'2¼"×12'4¾" | 27T | II | 20134-20139 | 4/61 | 6/62 | This time, two diagrams were raised for the Period II/III stock, the van of D1914 being slightly shorter. Lot 561 was built as for Lots 558-560 (above). Coaches for F&S sets 253-5; 264/5. |
| BT 1914 | 822 | 4 | 1934 | Derby | 54'×9'3"×12'4⅝" | 29T | III | 20781-20784 | 7/60 | 2/62 | |

## TABLE 11: SUMMARY TABLE OF LMS STANDARD 51′ AND 54′ NON-CORRIDOR STOCK *(continued)*

| Type | Diag | Lot | Qty | Date | Built | Dimensions (L×H×W) | Weight | Period | Running Numbers | Withdrawals First | Withdrawals Last | Remarks |
|---|---|---|---|---|---|---|---|---|---|---|---|---|

*London Tilbury and Southend set formations*

| Date in service | Set No | Third Brake | Third | Third | Third | Lavatory Compo | First | Lavatory Compo | Third | Third | Third | Third Brake | Remarks |
|---|---|---|---|---|---|---|---|---|---|---|---|---|---|
| 1924 | F&S 241 | 20091 | 10700 | 10701 | 10702 | 19022* | 10000 | 10001† | 10703 | 10704 | 10705 | 20092 | These were the non-standard Period I sets. * 'separated' CLs † full firsts no lavatories ‡ converted composites, no lavatories |
| 1924 | F&S 242 | 20093 | 10706 | 10707 | 10708 | 19023* | 10002 | 10003† | 10709 | 10710 | 10711 | 20094 | |
| 1924 | F&S 243 | 20095 | 10712 | 10713 | 10714 | 19024* | 10004 | 16026‡ | 10715 | 10716 | 10717 | 20096 | |
| 1924 | F&S 244 | 20097 | 10718 | 10719 | 10720 | 19025* | 10005 | 16027‡ | 10721 | 10722 | 10723 | 20098 | |
| 1926 | F&S 245 | 20101 | 10730 | 10731 | 10732 | 19002 | 10007 | 19003 | 10733 | 10734 | 10735 | 20102 | The standard Period I sets. Set 246 emerged before set 245 and had the lower numbered coaches. |
| 1926 | F&S 246 | 20099 | 10724 | 10725 | 10726 | 19000 | 10006 | 19001 | 10727 | 10728 | 10729 | 20100 | |
| 1927 | F&S 247 | 20122 | 10736 | 10737 | 10738 | 19004 | 10008 | 19005 | 10739 | 10740 | 10741 | 20123 | |
| 1927 | F&S 248 | 20124 | 10742 | 10743 | 10744 | 19006 | 10009 | 19007 | 10745 | 10746 | 10747 | 20125 | |
| 1928 | F&S 249 | 20126 | 10748 | 10749 | 10750 | 19008 | 10010 | 19009 | 10751 | 10752 | 10753 | 20127 | |
| 1928 | F&S 250 | 20128 | 10754 | 10755 | 10756 | 19010 | 10011 | 19011 | 10757 | 10758 | 10759 | 20129 | |
| 1929 | F&S 251 | 20130 | 10760 | 10761 | 10762 | 19012 | 10012 | 19013 | 10763 | 10764 | 10765 | 20131 | |
| 1929 | F&S 252 | 20132 | 10766 | 10767 | 10768 | 19014 | 10013 | 19015 | 10769 | 10770 | 10771 | 20133 | |
| 1931 | F&S 253 | 20134 | 11606 | 11607 | 11608 | 19016 | 10014 | 19017 | 11609 | 11610 | 11611 | 20135 | The Period II sets |
| 1931 | F&S 254 | 20136 | 11612 | 11613 | 11614 | 19018 | 10015 | 19019 | 11615 | 11616 | 11619 | 20137 | |
| 1931 | F&S 255 | 20138 | 11618 | 11617 | 11620 | 19020 | 10016 | 19021 | 11621 | 11622 | 11623 | 20139 | |
| 1934 | F&S 264 | 20781 | 11705 | 11706 | 11707 | 19196 | 10111 | 19197 | 11708 | 11709 | 11710 | 20782 | The Period III sets |
| 1934 | F&S 265 | 20783 | 11711 | 11712 | 11713 | 19198 | 10112 | 19199 | 11714 | 11715 | 11716 | 20784 | |

*Note:* For some reason, coaches 11617/9 were placed in the wrong sets and appeared to stay there.

*Cathcart Circle sets*

The following table gives the probable composition of the sets as first built

| Third Brake | Compo | First | Compo | Third Brake | Remarks |
|---|---|---|---|---|---|
| 20103 | 16007 | 10017 | 16008 | 20104 | The Hurst Nelson sets |
| 20105 | 16009 | 10018 | 16010 | 20106 | |
| 20107 | 16011 | 10019 | 16012 | 20108 | |
| 20109 | 16013 | 10020 | 16014 | 20110 | |
| 20111 | 16015 | 10021 | 16016 | 20112 | |
| 20113 | 16017 | 10022 | 16018 | 20114 | |
| 20115 | 16019 | 10023 | 16020 | 20116 | |
| 20117 | 16021 | 16024 | 10022 | 20118 | The Pickering set |

*Spare Coaches and Renumbering*

1 The following Pickering coaches were probably the initial spare vehicles:

Firsts: 10025/6
Compos: 16023-5
Brakes: 20119-21

2 On downgrading, the firsts and composites received the following numbers:

16007-25 Became 13468-70; 12268-70; 13471-3; 12271-2; 13474-5; 12273; 13476; 12274-7 in the same order. The 134xx series was the 1938 batch and the 122xx series the 1953 batch.

10017-26 Became 13426-35 in the same order. The downgrading was c.1941 but some of the renumbering was as late as 1950.

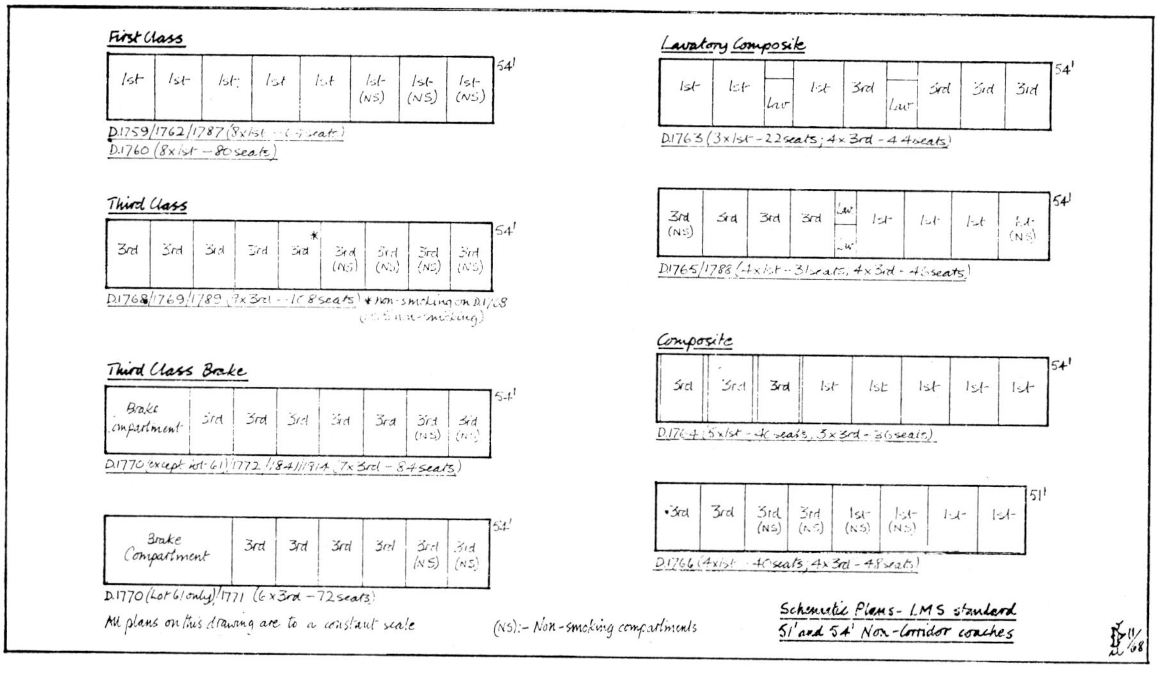


*FIGURE 38 LMS standard 51ft and 54ft non-corridor stock—sketch plans* (Drawn by D. Jenkinson)

# Chapter 12 - Articulated General Service Stock

*Introduction; Historical Background; The Inter-District sets; The 10 coach vestibule sets;*
*Conclusions; Summary of coaches built.*

UNLIKE the LNER, where articulation of passenger stock was commonplace, the LMS did not make great use of the articulated principle. However, this was not for want of trying and the vehicles of the type which were built during 1937 shed interesting light into the operating and other problems which faced the LMS during the mid-1930s. Thanks to the existence of much contemporary correspondence which has been made available to the authors, a good deal of the background to the LMS articulated stock is known and can be recorded.

LMS articulated coaches fell into two categories; namely the general service coaches of 1937 and the special vehicles built for the second 'Coronation Scot' train of 1939/40. The story of this latter train is sufficiently complex to merit special treatment so this chapter merely concerns itself with the general service articulated stock.

## HISTORICAL BACKGROUND

The first relevant references to articulation come in correspondence between various departments in 1935. On 9th April of that year a letter was sent from the commercial side to Stanier, relevant extracts from which are quoted:

'It appears...that if we are to advance in effecting material economies in coal consumption with our passenger trains...and keep the size of locomotives within reasonable limits... it is necessary that serious consideration should be given to reducing the weight per seat of our vehicles. I know that you have given considerable thought to this question and...that it has been under the consideration of the research department for some time. It is a matter of complex nature because it is essential that the amenities and comfort to the travelling public should not be reduced.

I detail below the weight, seating and weight per seat of the vestibule, corridor and non-corridor stock it is proposed to build in 1936...

| Type | Weight Tons | No. of seats | Weight per seat T. | Cwt. | Qrs. |
|------|-------------|--------------|---------------------|------|------|
| *Vestibules* | | | | | |
| First | 30 | 42 | 14 | 1 | |
| Third | 31 | 60 | 10 | 1 | |
| *Corridor* | | | | | |
| First | 30 | 33 | 18 | 1 | |
| Composite | 33 | 42 | 15 | 3 | |
| Third | 31 | 42 | 14 | 3 | |
| *Non-Corridor* | | | | | |
| Composite | 27 | 96 | 5 | 3 | |
| Third | 27 | 108 | 5 | 0 | |

The fact that a corridor third vehicle weighs 14cwt 3qrs per seat is...a very serious matter, and I may say that in a conversation the Vice-President had with me the other day he mentioned a figure of 5cwts per seat as being the ideal to be aimed at.

So far as the 1936 building programme is concerned...there is insufficient time to make any radical change in the design..., and I shall feel much obliged if you will kindly see what steps can be taken in the 1937 Carriage Building Programme on the lines set out in this letter...

This enquiry partially coincided with Stanier's own views and, in fact, he had already asked Vice-President Sir Harold Hartley the previous week for permission to conduct experiments in articulation using pre-group stock:

'The question of providing articulated train sets has arisen from time to time, and the more recently in connection with vestibule excursion sets and sleeping cars, and in order that some experience may be obtained with this type of stock it is recommended that a three-coach set be prepared for experimental purposes by converting three existing vehicles, and providing the same with two articulated bogies and two heavy bogies for the leading and trailing ends.'

This letter was forwarded to the commercial department and the two separated lines of thought were fused in a letter to Vice-President E. J. H. Lemon which, inter alia, contained the following paragraph:

'Articulation may be the means of reducing the weight per seat and on this account I think it would probably be sound to carry out the experiment suggested by Mr. Stanier to Sir Harold Hartley in his letter of April 2nd.'

The up-shot of all this was that the experimental work was given the go-ahead by Sir Harold Hartley while Vice-President Lemon expressed his own views to the commercial side as follows:

'I am obliged to you for your letter of the 9th and note your views regarding the articulation of sleeping cars and excursion sets. I do not think we need trouble too much regarding the former, as in view of the number of sleeping cars compared with our total carriage stock the benefits from articulation would not be material.

As regards the excursion sets, I can see the difficulty which would arise from a loading and unloading point of view*. I think, however, a more profitable line of attack would be our three-coach sets and combinations of such for suburban and local train working. We have a considerable number of three coach sets and articulation might mean a reduction of 10 tons per set, which is appreciable.'

*The original design scheme for the vestibule ten coach set was for 'loose' brake ends and twin open third articulated pairs. The latter would have but one centre door on each side compared with two per side on the standard stock. This was thought to be a disadvantage on a frequently stopping excursion type train.

151

The experimental three coach set involved using normal pre-group stock and in view of the trial nature of the project, the design showed only a one ton saving over the separated vehicles and not the envisaged 10 ton saving. This caused a little heart searching until Stanier pointed out that the experiment was to try out the articulation principle and that new vehicles of the type would show the desired savings in coach weight. The approval for the conversion was given on May 23, 1935, and on the same day, diagrams were also requested of the CME for the following production types of articulated stock:

a. *Inter-District three-coach set comprising:*

| | Seating | | |
|---|---|---|---|
| | First | Third | |
| Non-corridor Third Brake | | 72 | (6 compartments) |
| Non-corridor Composite | 24 | 72 | (3+6 compartments) |
| Non-corridor Third Brake | | 72 | (6 compartments) |
| Total | 24 | 216 | |

b. *10 coach articulated vestibule train made up as follows:*

Vestibule Third Brake ⎤
Vestibule Third ⎬ 3-coach set, articulated
Vestibule Third ⎦

Vestibule Third ⎤
Vestibule Third ⎦ 2-coach set, articulated

Vestibule Third ⎤
Vestibule Third ⎦ 2-coach set, articulated

Vestibule Third ⎤
Vestibule Third ⎬ 3-coach set, articulated
Vestibule Third Brake ⎦

Meanwhile, the experimental set chosen for conversion was the MR four coach St. Pancras and Bedford set No. 37, built in 1910. The new articulated bogies were provided on three coaches while the fourth vehicle was unaltered. The set went into Derby works in June 1935 and the formation was thus:

Brake Third No. 23198 ⎤
Third No. 14234 ⎬ articulated
First No. 10529 ⎦
Brake Third No. 23217 left unaltered

There was some delay in providing the diagrams for the new sets and in November 1935 a reminder was sent by the commercial staff to the CME who replied that 'we are not now working on the lines of the memorandum of the meeting held on 23rd May'. Diagrams were submitted by Stanier but he pointed out that precise weights could not be determined until the 'proposed experimental vestibule coach has been designed and built'.

It would appear that the commercial side was not aware of the proposal to build an experimental coach and it went to some pains to inform the CME that too much delay was undesirable:

'It is very desirable that the question of building of 10 coach articulated vestibule trains should be sufficiently advanced to enable a definite conclusion to be arrived at when consideration is given to the 1937 Carriage Renewal Programme early next year.'

Stanier was, however, in a position to re-assure the commercial department that the design work would be finished in time. The experimental 'one-off' vestibule coach cannot be traced in the diagram book but there was an experimental Corridor brake third built to D1971 (Coach No. 5844) which employed the centrally trussed frame used on the articulated stock and tared some 3—4 tons less than a conventional coach. Although not in service until December 1937, this may have been the vehicle referred to in the correspondence since it carried a lower lot number than the articulated stock.

There were certain minor aspects of the layout of the proposed three-coach unit for inter-district services which were not liked by HQ at first. These were mainly in the nature of compartment sizes and whether or not to have identically

**Plate 164.** The centrally trussed experimental brake third to D1971, No 5844, which was almost certainly the experimental vehicle built to evaluate the underframe for the articulated stock.

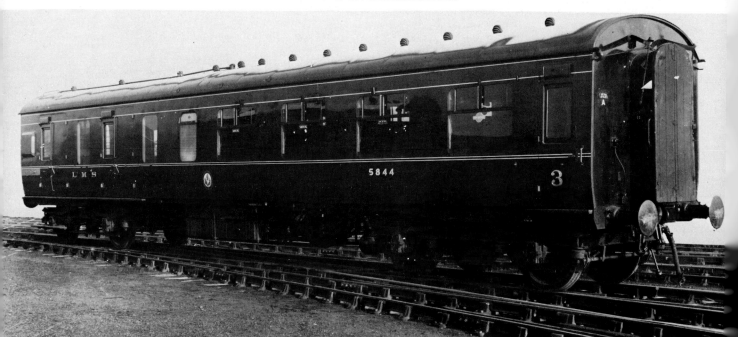

**Plate 165** Non-corridor articulated triple BT+C+BT No 60003/4/5 (D1995). Note the conventional trussing of these coaches compared with the vestibule stock, also the oval buffers.

sized brake compartments at each end. However, it is clear that by the end of 1935, the decision had been made to build articulated stock during 1937 and the proposed layouts were therefore submitted to the Operating Divisions for their comments on the proposed layout of the sets and their general suitability. The 10-coach excursion set diagrams were sent in December 1935 and the three-coach inter district sets were submitted to the Divisions in January 1936. From this point it is simpler to consider the two designs separately.

## THE INTER-DISTRICT SETS

The original proposal for the divisions to scrutinise was not quite the same as the original design study requested on May 23, 1935. The final proposal was for a reduction of the composite from nine to eight compartments thus enabling the commercial department's wish for larger third class compartments to be provided for in the composite coach. Thus the envisaged three-coach unit was to be in the form BT+C+BT seating 72 thirds; 24 firsts plus 60 thirds, and 72 thirds respectively. There was an alternative suggestion for a version with five thirds in one brake end and seven thirds at the opposite end. The replies from the Divisional Managers were somewhat revealing and the relevant extracts are worth quoting:

*Midland Division*
'As you know, most of the local services of this Division are scheduled to consist of two coach sets, supplemented by extras where required. The occupation of coaches has been analysed, and it is found that the introduction of the proposed three coach unit would definitely involve more coaches. ...I suggest that for this Division a suitable two coach unit could be provided i.e. composite seating 24 first, 60 thirds and a third brake seating 72 thirds and giving a brake compartment 16ft 9in long.'

*Western Division*
'So far as the Western Division is concerned I consider that a three-car Inter-District articulated set is what is required and not a 2-car set, which I understand is suggested would be the right formation for the Midland Division.'

*Central Division*
'I cannot recommend the building of any 3-coach articulated sets for use on this Division for the reason that none of the 3-coach sets which are in general traffic on the Division remain at that formation but are made up to as many as nine or ten vehicles during some part of their workings.
I should, however, be prepared to accept 15 four-coach articulated sets for use on the Manchester and Oldham Branch, these sets could be formed as follows:

Third Brake ⎤
Third ⎥
Composite ⎬ To seat 24 firsts and 312 third class passengers
Third Brake ⎦

...two-coach units of the type suggested by the Midland Division would offer too much First Class accommodation for general use on this Division.'

*Northern Division*
'It is suggested that the brake compartment at each end be reduced in size sufficient to admit an additional third class compartment in each coach and that the centre coach instead of having three first and five third class compartments should have four firsts and four third class compartments.
The effect of these proposals would increase the seating capacity of the train to 32 first class and 216 third class seats, and there would be ample brake van accommodation for luggage, etc.'

In the event, the design was still further modified and was built with only seven compartments in the centre coach (4F+ 3T), although the Scottish suggestion of seven compartments in the brake ends was adopted. As far as is known, the coaches were mostly employed in Scotland. Photographs show some sets in use on Euston—Northampton services, although these workings are not thought to have lasted long. More information would be welcomed by the authors on workings by the three-coach non-corridor articulated sets.

The wide measure of divisional disagreement, and in some cases, scarcely veiled antipathy towards these articulated sets must almost certainly have been a major factor behind the building of only one batch to D1995, details of which are appended at the end of the chapter.

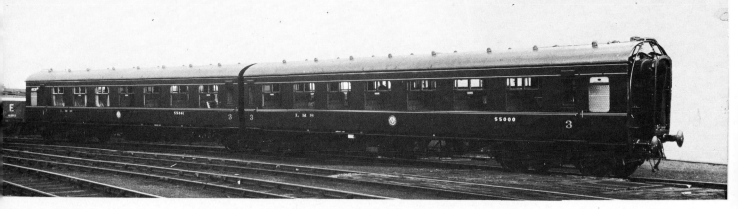

Plate 166. Articulated twin TO+CO No 55000/1 (D1967) as built. Note the somewhat deeper than usual eaves panel for a Period III design.

Plate 167. Close-up of the reinforced centre bogie of twin TO+CO No 55000/1.

Plate 168. A constructional view of the centrally trussed underframe of one of the vestibule sets, viewed from the articulated end.

# THE 10 COACH VESTIBULE SETS

The original proposal submitted for divisional comment envisaged an all-third train formed BTO+TO+TO/ /TO+TO/ / TO+TO/ /TO+TO/BTO. All would be 57ft coaches except for the centre vehicles of the triplets which were designed as 48ft 3in sections. The lengths were determined partially by the length of point locking bars (45ft) which affected the bogie centre dimensions and secondly by the overhang which might cause running restrictions. In general they were designed to run on lines cleared for the 60ft stock. Unlike the case of the non-corridor sets, the comments from the Divisions were more in unison:

| | |
|---|---|
| *Midland Division* | The Midland Division stated that the train was too big. The division in the proposed trains for including kitchen cars was regarded as 'useless from a Dining Car Department point of view, as they will not serve meals more than two vehicles away from the Kitchen'. The Division also felt that there should be first class accommodation and that each coach should have a sliding door to enable separate parties of up to about 30 to be accommodated in one vehicle. Finally, the Midland Division felt that the proposed lavatories at one end only of the vehicles were not suitable where two parties were accommodated in the same vehicle. |
| *Western Division* | This division also recommended eight car trains with an extra composite or first class coach to provide first class seating. This division also felt that the lavatories should be re-arranged. |
| *Central Division* | The Central Division did not feel the train was the wrong length but like the Midland and Western Divisions recommended re-positioned lavatories and suggested 18 first class seats in one of the 10 coaches. Like the Midland Division, the absence of internal partitions was not favoured. |
| *Northern Division* | 'So far as the Northern Division is concerned, I think the unit will be suitable and if one train is included in the building programme for Scotland it will be kept continuously employed, at any rate during the summer months'. The Division felt that it would be unnecessary to provide first class seating in the train. |

As a result of these suggestions, the proposed scheme was altered to a 10 coach configuration of articulated pairs to the following scheme: BTO+TO/ /TO+TO/ /TO+CO/ /TO+TO/ /TO+BTO. The dropping of the short centre vehicle of the triplet scheme enabled all coaches to be the same 54ft length (actually 54ft 3in) and thus enabled the design staff to incorporate the suggested modifications to toilet layout. Interior partitions and first class seating were also provided and in this form the coaches were built to D1965/D1966/D1967. Bogie centres were 46ft 6¾in.

This might have been the end of the matter but in March 1937, a fresh list of running restrictions was stipulated over and above those applicable to the 60ft stock, which restrictions had hitherto, been the only ones envisaged. This caused mild panic at Euston House when Stanier informed the commercial staff of the Chief Engineer's decision. The comments from the Commercial Manager were curt and to the point: ·

'...I would point out, however, that the restrictions at and near Preston and at Blackpool and Morecambe will practically mean that the sets, although built for the heavy excursion traffic at those points, will not be capable of running thereto, and the restriction at Chester will also considerably hamper us in the manipulation of the heavy excursion traffic at the peak periods.
The list of restrictions generally is a formidable one for vehicles engaged in excursion traffic and is one which we certainly did not anticipate when the diagrams were signed...
I shall be glad if you will kindly again approach the Engineer and see whether...it is possible to give us more latitude in the working of the sets.'

This plea seems to have had some effect and the Chief Engineer relented a little although not at Chester. He did, however, point out that the tendency to enlarge coaching stock and thus diminish clearances did make more urgent the necessity for improving the matter of clearances on the line as a whole.

When the divisions were finally advised of the restrictions, some amusing side effects followed. At Shilton, between Nuneaton and Rugby, it was stated that the signalman would not be aware which trains were conveying the new stock and it was therefore suggested that the articulated coaches be totally banned from the Rugby-Nuneaton line. This was not thought desirable and the upshot was that a decrepit and unused milk loading stage at Shilton, which was the feature fouling the loading gauge of the articulated sets, was removed. This enabled other restrictions on out of gauge loads on the up slow line between Nuneaton No.1 and Rugby No.7 boxes to be removed as well.

The restrictions on working into Blackpool and Morecambe were waived because the vehicles were fitted with windows of a type which 'prevented the passenger from putting his head through' and as the stations were termini, the speed of the coaches would be slow.

The Chester restriction was more serious and the Western Division Superintendent of Operations commented:

'So far as the restriction on the new articulated sets is concerned, I am afraid this will entirely preclude the use of these sets in working to or from North Wales, the Wirral or Birkenhead. Although there are two other up roads and down roads, and an up and down platform line over which such trains could be worked it would be exceedingly difficult to identify the trains which were conveying these articulated sets in order to ensure that they were run through Chester station over one of the other roads and not over the restricted roads.
You will appreciate the restricted roads are the two roads through the 'yard' over which we normally work a large number of excursion trains on which the articulated stock would be expected to run.'

As if to pile Ossa upon Pelion, the other three companies also put forward a fearsome list of restrictions for the LMS articulated sets. The LNER excluded them from all its lines in Scotland, England north of Northallerton, large parts of the West Riding and many areas of East Anglia. The Southern would not have them at all (!) and many GWR branches were excluded. Not surprisingly, the original batches were not repeated and all the 11 sets were allocated to the Central Division, virtually confined to LMS lines.

## CONCLUSIONS

The LMS articulated experiment cannot really be considered a success. It was not that the coaches were no good in themselves but the widely differing requirements of the Divisions, coupled with the widespread running restrictions— which applied equally to both vestibule and non-corridor sets although probably affecting the vestibule sets more often— militated against the general service aspect of their design. They were lighter than comparable general service vehicles and gave identical standards of accommodation but the LMS in general never really took to them.

Nevertheless, the special circumstances of the 'Coronation Scot' train caused the LMS to look again at articulation as a means to save weight, this time on high speed services over its principal main line. These 1939/40 trains had as complex a history as their general service precursors and are considered in the next chapter.

Plans were in hand for the construction of further general service articulated stock from 1940 onwards which, presumably, would have been based on the constructional principles of the Coronation Scot sets. These were to have included three, four, five and six car sets of non-corridor type made up from twin and triplet units. These plans were shelved because of the war and were never revived afterwards.

### TABLE 12: SUMMARY OF ARTICULATED GENERAL SERVICE COACHES BUILT DURING 1937

*Note:* All coaches were built at Derby, all were Period III style with simple livery.

| Type | Diag | Lot | No of sets | Wt | Dimensions (L×W×H) | Running Numbers | Withdrawals First | Last | Remarks |
|------|------|-----|-----------|-----|------|------|------|------|---------|
| Triple BT+C+BT | 1995 | 1038 | 11 | 76T | 162'4½"×9'3"×12'4⅝" | 60000-60032 | 5/63 | 10/64 | The non-corridor sets. The brake ends were 56'4¼" long and the centre vehicle was 47'6" long. The numbers of the individual coaches ran consecutively in threes thus 60000+60001+60002 and the composites always had the middle number of the three. Bogie centres were 48'7½", underframes conventionally trussed. |
| Twin BTO+TO | 1965 | 1000 | 22 | 49T | 109'7½"×9'3"×12'2⁹⁄₁₆" | 52500-52543 | 1/64 | 4/65 | Both elements were 54'3" long and the even numbers of each pair were the open third end, odd numbers the brake end. |
| Twin TO+TO | 1966 | 1001 | 22 | 49T | 109'7½"×9'3"×12'2⁹⁄₁₆" | 50000-50043 | 11/63 | 2/65 | Only one end had a non-smoking compartment and this was the even numbered end of the pair. |
| Twin TO+CO | 1967 | 1002 | 11 | 49T | 109'7½"×9'3"×12'2⁹⁄₁₆" | 55000-55021 | 11/63 | 3/65 | The first class section had two and one seating and there was, initially, no non-smoking area in the set. The even numbers of the pairs were the third class ends. The third class saloon next to the first class section had one seat less adjacent to the partition because of the offset gangway to the first class area. |

*Footnotes:*

1. Initially, the vestibule sets were formed into 11 ten-coach excursion sets classified as Central Division Extra Trains and branded on the ends CEN DIV ET. They were numbered 250-260 but only set 256 has been confirmed in full formation. Some were incorrectly plated.

2. There were no real innovations in the coaches themselves except for the centrally trussed underframes of the vestibule sets which effected a slight reduction in height. Bodies and interiors of both varieties of coach were conventionally arranged and the first class bays in the vestibule sets differed from the thirds solely in having 2 and 1 seating. Leg room and bay length was identical to the thirds.

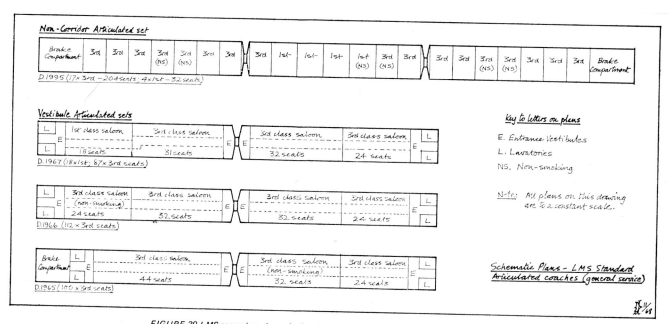

FIGURE 39 LMS general service articulated stock—sketch plans (Drawn by D. Jenkinson)

# Chapter 13 - The 'Coronation Scot' sets

*Introduction; The 1937 sets; The 1939-40 sets; The Post-War story;*
*The 1939-40 stock described; Conclusions; Summary Tables.*

IT is, perhaps, not inappropriate that the method of treatment adopted in this survey should result in the 'Coronation Scot' stock being allotted the thirteenth chapter; for, indeed, the 'Coronation Scot' was an unlucky train.

The inter-company rivalry in the matter of speed in the 1930s is too well known to need any amplification here and, of course, it led principally to the ultra high speed services and trains on the East Coast Route which, with their matching Class A4 4—6—2 locomotives, tended to steal much of the limelight.

It was not to be expected that the LMS would remain entirely unmoved in the face of all this activity from Kings Cross and after the announcement by the LMS of its forthcoming 1937 high speed service, the train and its engine were awaited with more than the usual interest. It duly appeared in the famous blue and silver livery and achieved immediate fame by the hair raising speed trial down Madeley bank when the LMS temporarily wrested the steam locomotive speed record from the LNER at the cost of a new set of crockery for the dining cars and more than a few red faces in high places! The only commendable thing about this escapade seems to have been the leading bogie on the locomotive which literally saved the day for the LMS. When the 'Coronation Scot' service as such was seen to be on a 6½ hour Euston-Glasgow timing it appeared to some as though the LMS had conceded defeat to its rivals. Add to this the fact that the coaches themselves were mostly reconditioned existing vehicles albeit of the latest style, and it is not surprising that the story gained currency that the LMS had provided an answer to the LNER very much on the cheap.

This may, in some respects, have been true. Not everyone on the LMS was anxious to promote this gimmick approach to travel and any form of ultra special service such as the 'Coronation Scot' must inevitably demand a greater proportion of the Company's time and energy than a more normal service would do. Although the authors have not been able to trace the 'Coronation Scot' train right back to its source, the evidence which has been scrutinised does suggest that permission to build trains may have been granted only if it could be achieved at low cost. Even the streamlining of the locomotives seems to have been a rather half-hearted last minute affair and although much has been made of the 'true aerodynamic form' of the streamline casing and the wind tunnel testing of the shape, this may well have been no more than an accidental by-product of cloaking Stanier's masterpiece to satisfy the publicity department. Apart from the sloping smoke-box top, there was precious little difference between the de-streamlined and non-streamlined 'Coronation' Class 4—6—2s as we were all able to see from 1945 onwards.

Something better than the 1937 trains would have emerged in 1940 had not the world been at war. Thus the 'Coronation Scot' ceased to run and, like its LNER contemporaries, was never to be seen as such again. However, this book is about LMS coaches and although the train itself may have had an unhappy history, the coaches built for it were some of the finest vehicles ever made for the LMS and thus deserve special consideration.

## THE 1937 SETS

The 1937-9 'Coronation Scot' service was operated by nine-coach sets of the latest Stanier pattern coaches which had been specially converted for the task. Three complete sets were provided (two working and one spare) and the train ran to the following formation:

BFK / FK / RFO / RK / RTO / RTO / RK / RTO / BTK

Although all the third class open coaches were 42 seaters, thus qualifying for the RTO classification, they were used for all the way travelling. They were, moreover, the only 42 seat open third class coaches of Period III styling.

Most of the coaches selected for the sets were taken from the latest batches of new stock and were completely refitted inside and, except for the kitchen cars, were equipped with a pressure heating and ventilation system. There were no spare corridor firsts or first brakes available so these coaches were built new for the service. The total cost of providing the coaches was quoted as £27,000 which must be considered very low in relation to the average cost of £2,000—£2,500 per coach had new vehicles been built. If one allows some half of this figure of £27,000 for the six new vehicles, the conversion of the remaining 21 averaged out at some £700 per coach.

This aspect of the 1937 coaches has tended to foster the impression that, apart from the blue and silver livery, the coaches were little different from ordinary LMS vehicles. As far as appearance and body styling was concerned this was so but by no stretch of the imagination could the interiors be so glibly dismissed. The perpetuation in the kitchen cars of gas cooking and gas lighting was also logical since the LMS had had unhappy experience of electric cooking in its experimental 1933 kitchen cars and doubtless the experience with those vehicles caused the company to prefer its traditional and well proved system. As the largest provider of dining car facilities in the country it presumably had sufficient experience to draw upon.

Within the train, the first class compartments seated but two-a-side and were most tastefully and comfortably finished, while the open saloons were equally spacious. The coaches were trimmed with matched wood veneers and facing of selected Empire timber, this being true to LMS tradition, while upholstery was in soft and restful shades of blue, brown and green. Lighting in the vestibule cars was by tubular strip supplemented by table lamps and in the compartments, bell pushes were provided for calling the attendant. In some respects, although less modern and radical than their LNER counterparts, they probably did not date so quickly as did the East Coast coaches.

The fact is that in the middle 1930s, the average LMS long distance stock was so far ahead of that of most of the country that there probably seemed no real need to build special vehicles for the 'Coronation Scot' service. After all, the LMS had long abandoned outside compartment doors on its corridor coaches which idea was still being perpetuated elsewhere and moreover, had been giving armrests to the third class passenger for years.

Admirers of the LNER trains will, doubtless, feel that the above remarks are tainted with prejudice but it does seem to the authors that contemporary writers, in giving rightful praise to Gresley's magnificent coaches, gave less than their due share of credit to the 1937 'Coronation Scot' trains. The LNER sets were superb trains and certainly unsurpassed for comfort but it cannot be denied that the normal wood panelled LNER stock was not really suitable for conversion to the streamline image whereas the LMS flush sided stock could more readily be thus treated. Moreover, it is a matter of personal taste whether the stainless steel and chromium trimmings of the LNER trains were preferable to the wood veneers of the LMS coaches. Even so, the fact that all the first class passengers in the LNER trains had individual single seats probably gave them the edge in passenger appeal. Moreover, they were a complete breakaway from anything the LNER had hitherto built whereas the LMS sets were merely luxury developments of an already well-established trend and therefore probably seemed less progressive.

The coaches themselves are listed in the appropriate chapters dealing with the individual coach types but the formation of the sets themselves is tabulated at the end of this chapter. The coaches were laid up for the duration of the war, two sets at Horwich and one at Lostock Hall. They re-entered general service in 1947 but not as set trains.

## THE 1939—40 SETS

Some sources have claimed that dissatisfaction with the 1937 coaches was the main reason behind the building of the ill-fated 1939—40 'Coronation Scot' stock but perusal of contemporary records does not bear this out. The authors have found no recorded evidence that they were built because the 1937 stock was considered inferior or inadequate, although this may have been a contributory factor.

In October 1937, the LMS decided to exhibit a complete 'Coronation Scot' train and locomotive in 1939 at the proposed New York World Fair. In early November 1937, the Chief Operating Manager stated that in this case a new corridor first and brake first would be needed if a new set of coaches was contemplated 'as there are no suitable vehicles of these types which can be withdrawn from our existing stock without detriment to our ordinary business'. The implication behind this statement can only be that the original intention was to exhibit a 1937 type train.

At the end of November, the LMS Executive Committee resolved to build a complete new 'Coronation Scot' type train with a sleeping car to replace one of the kitchens. The cost of the train was to be charged to the 'Coronation Scot' Suspense Account and brought into the renewal programme for the year it was due to enter service in Great Britain, namely 1940. Stanier was invited to proceed with the design on the lines agreed and no mention was ever made of the necessity to build a better train to compete with those of the LNER.

By the beginning of December, the first proposed designs for the new train had been sketched out. It was to be a 10-coach set made up of three articulated triplets and a single coach arranged as follows:

BFK+FO+FO/ /RFO (with cocktail lounge and bar) +RK+RTO (with buffet)/ /TO+TO+TO/ /BTK

The articulated triplets would have two 65ft sections and 51ft 6in centre portion, while the loose brake was to be the normal 57ft length. Several objections were raised to some of the design features and these can be summarised as follows:

a. The first FO should be an FK, first class passengers not liking to travel in open coaches!
b. The second FO should be a semi-RFO thus balancing the number of first class compartments and dining seats.
c. The buffet should be in the leading TO, not the RTO and this would give more third class dining seats.

The second proposal followed shortly afterwards and the layout was as follows:

BFK+FK+Semi-FK and cocktail lounge/ /RFO+RK+RTO/ /Semi-RTO+TK+TK/ /BTK

This all-corridor formation (except for the dining areas) was to remain a feature of all future schemes considered and differed basically from the 1937 trains in having separate third class dining seats. Thus, more seat units would have to be provided for the same number of passengers and hence the desire to save weight by articulation. The main objection to the planned interior layout seemed to be that the walk to the toilets, which features were to be segregated 'Ladies' and 'Gentlemen', could be excessive under certain circumstances! At the same time as this proposal was submitted, Stanier also proposed an identical train made up of 10 separate coaches and this idea seemed to be his own preferred choice:

'If the train is made up as an articulated train..., the total weight of the train would be 309 tons, but we have no experience of articulated trains in this high speed work. Further, the articulation must be the LMS type otherwise you will not get the seating arrangement, and this is an entirely new type which has not been tried out yet, and is only being used on the three car light unit, which will be out early in January, and until this arrangement is thoroughly tested, I would not recommend our using it on a special train of this kind'.

This is the first mention in the files of the 'LMS type' of articulation and, indeed, the earlier general service articulated stock had been built on the Gresley principle. Stanier obviously preferred the idea of separate coaches and therefore asked the commercial side which of the 10 cars they were prepared to omit to keep the weight around the 300 ton mark. However, the operating staff were not keen on losing space so Stanier tried again. This time he produced the first twin articulated scheme which would have been formed as follows:

BFK+FK/ Semi-FK and cocktail lounge +RFO/ /RK+RTO/ /Semi-RTO+TK/ /TK+BTK

This had the same layout as the preceding suggestion and provision was also made for an optional twin pair (presumably TK+TK) which could be added to make a 12 coach set at peak loading periods. The designed length was 59ft 5¼in per coach.

This was still not quite what was wanted although Stanier had agreed to improve the distribution of the toilets and dispense with separate Ladies' and Gentlemen's toilets. He was, therefore, asked to prepare a set 11 coach train (five pairs plus a loose third) with a further loose third for strengthening and this was done. At the same time it was resolved that for the American tour, the Semi-RTO+TK would be omitted and a sleeping car would be marshalled between the corridor first and the cocktail lounge.

**Plate 169.** The American train photographed from the first class end with twin BFK+FK leading. Note the distinctive shape of the guard's lookout and the absence of droplights in the double door of the brake portion. All the cars in the train were branded on the outside "Lounge Car", "Dining Car", etc. with the sole exception of the leading BFK+FK.

When this 11 coach set plus extra corridor third was sketched out, the main objection seemed to be that the loose thirds were to be 57ft long and the operating side felt that this might not be as roomy as the 59ft 5¼in dimension of the articulated halves. Stanier therefore produced a 59ft 5¼in loose third design. At the same time, the extra 12th coach was, after all, deemed unnecessary and the 11 coach formation was finally settled.

Incredible though it may seem, all these design studies took place during December 1937, and 1938 was ushered in with the train formation more or less decided. Stanier had suggested a complete open third instead of the semi-open third but the Board preferred the original settled.

It was not until February 1938 that the obvious anomaly that would exist in 1940 (when the new set was to be introduced to run with the 1937 sets) seemed to receive any attention. The Chief Commercial Manager and the Chief Operating Manager therefore wrote a joint letter to Vice-President Lemon from which, the following extract is relevant:

'...it would be undesirable for the following reasons to utilise the new train in conjunction with two of the existing design and layout:
1) It would be inconsistent to have trains of different type in a service of this kind. Were two trains of different type in use at one time we should have the new train leaving Euston Monday, Wednesday and Friday and the old type train on Tuesday and Thursday in one week, and the reverse in the following week,...

2) Whereas in one train every third class seat is reserved, in the other the dining seats are fluid.

3) To enable reservation to be effected for the different types of train on different days, there would require to be assurance some weeks ahead which train would be in service on any particular day...any attempt at reservation in such circumstances would be fraught with danger from errors by the reservation clerks.

In the circumstances will you kindly say that you agree to the building of two further trains as now proposed in the 1939 Carriage Renewal Programme for the Coronation Scot Service, in which case the existing Coronation Scot vehicles could be painted the standard colour and be remarshalled and used in the Royal Scot services.'

It will be noted that no mention was made of the superior nature of the 1939/40 coaches nor were comparisons drawn with the LNER sets. One must, therefore, conclude that the design of the trains was occasioned solely by the New York Fair and the decision to build three sets was mainly for operating convenience. Doubtless, however, the LMS publicity men were happy enough at the prospect of a new train for them to advertise when it did enter revenue service.

During early 1938 the design of seating was discussed, the Company not liking the idea of proposed loose chairs in the diners, while Stanier asked whether, for appearance sake, the double doors to the brake ends might be built without droplights. This was agreed subject to there being windows at the coach ends.

By May 1938, preparations for the American tour were well under way and a diagram of the proposed train was submitted. This showed that only seven of the new style coaches together with a sleeping car were intended for the USA viz: BFK+FK/ /Semi-FK (with cocktail lounge) +RFO/ /RK+RTO/ /SLF/ /BTK. The reason for the reduction in number of vehicles from the American formation originally envisaged (see above) has not been ascertained—possibly it may have had something to do with the time available for building the coaches. However, the proposed loose brake third was a new development and as this had played no part in any of the original design studies, it was queried. No reason can be discovered why it was proposed unless it was because the articulated TK+BTK could not be built in time. The train had to have a brake end and possibly a loose brake third of the new type seemed the quickest solution.

Stanier was, accordingly, asked if, on return from America, the loose brake end was to be articulated with its corridor third partner but he replied that it was not and would go into general service on return. The remaining coaches of the American train (Semi-RTO+TK/ /TK/ /TK+BTK) would be built during 1939 and added to the other six vehicles when they came back from the USA.

The idea of a non-standard 'one-off' brake third was not particularly welcome and by July 1938 the proposal had been changed to that of a 'Club Car' brake coach which was the form in which it was finally built. Presumably this would give the opportunity for further displaying LMS coach building techniques and after the American tour it could be used in the Manchester-Blackpool Club Car trains.

There was a certain amount of trouble in getting the first class sleeping car away from the traffic people during the summer of 1938 because it was needed in service. However, after the summer services were concluded, car 377 was sent to Derby Works for the necessary modifications to provide staff sleeping accommodation.

Thus, by the Autumn of 1938, the American train was all but ready for its transatlantic venture. Nowhere has been found mention of the reasons for the decision to change the livery from the blue/silver of the 1937 sets to the red and gold scheme of the USA tour train but this was done and in this guise, after display at Euston, the train was safely shipped to America in January 1939.

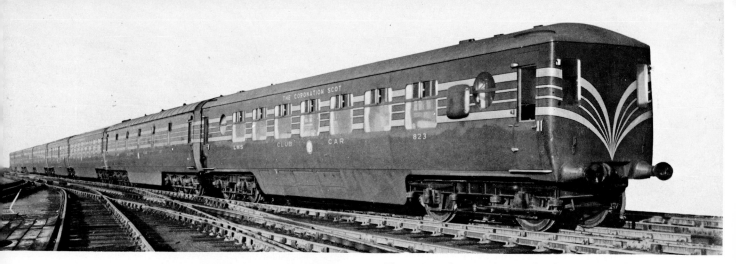

Plate 170. The American train photographed from the Club Car end. This picture clearly shows the difference in profile between the 1939/40 stock and the traditional LMS stock as exemplified by the sleeping car which is the second vehicle in the train. On return from America the panels between the bogies were removed below footboard level.

Plate 171. The luxury two per side compartments of the 1939 articulated Coronation Scot set. The coach is not identified but is probably 56000/1.

Plate 172. Interior view of the vestibule first class dining coach of the American train.

With the American train safely away, the CME then turned to the question of the remaining coaches to be built for the 1940 sets and to complete the American train. He suggested that for the two new 1940 sets, the articulated kitchen car and vestibule third diner should be made as separate vehicles and he also suggested that the Commercial Department might examine closely the general desirability of perpetuating the cocktail lounge in the British trains. The Commercial Manager's letter to acting Vice-President Davies on this issue makes amusing reading:

'...the question arises as to whether the Cocktail Bar should be perpetuated in the three new Coronation Scot trains which will eventually be put into service between Euston and Glasgow Central.

The vehicle with the Cocktail Bar is marshalled in the first class portion of the train and we do not consider it would be sound to allow third class passengers to make use of the Cocktail Bar as to do so they would have to pass through the Vestibule First diner.

We understand that the L.N.E. Company have experimented with a Cocktail Bar on their Scotch services but the bar had to be taken away and the vehicles concerned altered, owing to the third class passengers making use of it for beer drinking and disturbing the convenience of first class and other passengers...'

In February 1939, Vice-President Hartley agreed to the conversion of the cocktail lounge of the American train to a semi-open first on its return to Britain and also instructed that the matching vehicles for the new 1940 sets should be built from the outset as semi-open firsts. Thus the final formations of the envisaged 1940 Coronation Scot trains were as follows:

a. American Train     BFK+FK/ /Semi-RFO+RFO/ /RK+RTO/ /Semi-RTO+TK/ /TK/ /TK+BTK

b. Two new sets     BFK+FK/ /Semi-RFO+RFO/ /RK/ /RTO/ /Semi-RTO+TK/ /TK/ /TK+BTK

By this time, international affairs were overruling all other matters and the building of the 1940 coaches, then under construction, was suspended. In April 1941, the authority for the building of the Coronation Scot stock was cancelled.

## THE POST-WAR STORY

For three years the LMS was concerned with larger issues than prestige trains but by April 1944, the situation was such that the CME, now Mr. C. E. Fairburn, could write to the Chief Operating Manager as follows:

'...I have now got some details available for the Coronation Scot coaches which were held up when war broke out. The situation is as follows:

The number of coaches is 25 and we have got all the underframes complete with bogies for these and a certain amount of bodywork had been done on 11 of the vehicles. 14 are corridor but only two are loose vehicles, the other 12 being matched with other vehicles as articulated twins.

Underframes with bodies erected  – 8
Underframes with floor only     – 2

So far as the material side is concerned, we have material as follows:'

There then follows a long list of supplies which were in hand for the coaches. The CME's letter concludes:

'You will see that there is a number of these cars that we could finish reasonably quickly; the limiting item seems to be key sheeting, of which we have got a supply for five only. We have not been able to get this for other vehicles but just recently we have reason to believe that the position may have eased somewhat on that...

I should be glad to have your views on the matter as to whether you think we should open up this lot number again or not. Under existing circumstances where material is tight it seems unfortunate to leave this material lying and it would be better converted into vehicles as far as possible.'

It should be noted that the 25 vehicles referred to did not include either of the kitchen cars for the 1940 trains but referred to all the other coaches designated for the new trains. The initial response to Mr. Fairburn's proposal was not particularly hopeful:

'...Under the circumstances, I consider it would not be sound to proceed with the construction of these 'Coronation Scot' trains during the war, because if they were to be turned out it would be necessary for them to be put on one side and stabled under cover until the 'Coronation Scot' trains, with all they entail in regard to limiting travel to the seats provided are reintroduced after the war...

It is my view that immediately after the war and not till then, consideration should be given to the completion of the 25 vehicles to which you refer...'

The CME seems to have anticipated something like this sort of reply for in his next submission he introduced further facts in support of his desire to re-commence building the coaches:

'...the real difficulty I see in adopting the policy proposed by you is that no account has been taken of the time that these Coronation Coaches will probably be required to be constructed...if they are required in any period, say, from one to four years after the war and perhaps even longer, they will just be required at the time when our shops are really doing all they can to provide standard coaches.

All these coaches are special in every way. ...and to introduce them into the Works at a time when we are trying as near as possible to mass produce, would I am afraid have a very serious effect on our rate of production of standard coaches.

If we could commence almost immediately and proceed as far as labour and materials permit, we would expect to get the bulk of the work done before we started on standard coaches...'

The operating manager was still not over keen on the idea but appreciated Fairburn's point and he replied that he had no objection to the work proceeding provided that suitable covered storage space could be found for the completed coaches until they were needed in service. The resumption of work was, of course, subject to approval from the LMS Board since authority for building had been cancelled. Thus, in a memorandum to the Board on April 21, 1944, the President of the Executive (W. V. Wood) wrote as follows:

'During the interval between the expiry of certain aircraft contracts and the date at which materials will be available to begin the construction of the 800 coaching vehicles for which authority is asked at this Board, it would be convenient if the CME could proceed as far as possible with the completion of the 'Coronation Scot' coaches. This would enable him to employ any carriage building staff previously engaged on aircraft work and it would be a useful way of re-training them on actual carriage building of which they have done practically none for five years...the work on the 'Coronation Scot' coaches would cease immediately material for the 800 vehicles began to be available.

The approval of the Board is asked for the resumption of work on the 'Coronation Scot' coaches on the above conditions.'

Authority for resumption on these terms was granted on April 27, 1944 and in the autumn of the same year, the partially completed coaches were returned from store at Abergavenny and Spondon to Derby works. Construction

**Plate 173.** Post-war Coronation Scot type corridor third to D2019, No 2148.

recommenced almost at once but progress was slow. The aim was to have them finished before the anticipated large scale post-war building started but in the event, several more years were to pass before the coaches finally took to the rails. Post-war replacement of general service coaches was obviously given top priority and from the leisurely rate of progress on the 'Coronation Scot' coaches one must conclude that work was suspended on them many times during the 1945—49 period.

By mid-1945, the first of the vehicles were approaching partial completion and were scheduled to be placed again in store—destined once more for Abergavenny. By 1946, only 11 coaches had been part completed—they were without seats, some fittings and external paint and the first nine consisted of the following vehicles:

| Type | Running Numbers |
|---|---|
| Artic BTK+TK | 56500—56501 |
| Artic Semi-TO+TK | 56300—56301 |
| Artic BFK+FK | 56002—56003 |
| Loose TK | 2148 |
| Loose RTO | 9517—9518 |

These coaches completed the American train and provided certain vehicles of the later sets. They were shortly joined by the last of the BFK+FK twins (56004-56005). On May 29, 1946, a recommendation was made which helped to seal the fate of the new vehicles. The Chief Operating Manager wrote to Vice-President G. L. Darbyshire in some detail explaining his views on the matter of high speed trains and the paragraphs relating to the 'Coronation Scot' sets ran as follows:

'...My considered view is that it will be some considerable time before we shall be in a position on the LMS to contemplate the introduction of such high speeds as existed pre-war because of the effect of the war-time years on the maintenance of our rolling stock and track.

...to introduce ultra high speed working with permanent way slacks of a more severe nature than existed pre-war would mean bad time-keeping and result in an outcry from the public on the score of unpunctuality...

In view of the facts brought out in this memorandum I recommend that the three 'Coronation Scot' sets painted blue with silver lining which have been stored since September 1939, should be repainted in the standard colours and the vehicles forming these trains should be utilised in our best passenger trains in the same way as any other stock...

If this is agreed, consideration can then be given to what is to be done with the red and gold 'Coronation Scot' vehicles which are now being returned to us from America and the other vehicles...which were authorised to be built for forming three new 'Coronation Scot' trains'.

This suggestion was agreed and the 1937 sets were brought into use for general service. The new CME, Mr. H. G. Ivatt, was asked about the possibility of converting the first class coaches of the 1937 sets to three-a-side seating but stated that this could not be done in the stipulated time available as it would need new seats to be made. However, he also stated that some of the American coaches could likewise be made quickly available for general service if required. With regard to the incomplete coaches, Ivatt stated:

'...The whole of these coaches...can be taken in hand this autumn, when it is anticipated that the work in connection with Ambulance Train Vehicles (conversion and restoration) will be dropping off. But this means the whole of the 25 vehicles could be completed in time for the summer timetable—1947—without interference with the planned production of other new coaches.'

Ivatt also stated that the incomplete first class coaches could be altered to seat three-a-side without much additional expense.

The partly completed coaches were, therefore, sent back yet again from Abergavenny during the winter of 1946-7 and consideration was now given as to how best to employ them on completion. By this time, one gets a strong impression from the documentary evidence that the LMS regarded the coaches as something of a millstone round its neck. The non-gangwayed brake ends were not really suitable for general service but the Chief Operating Manager decided, one feels somewhat resignedly, that he was prepared to accept the position '...rather than recommend that further expenditure be incurred in altering them to standard ends with gangway connection.'

Excluding the Club brake and the articulated kitchen pair, there were 29 vehicles to find services for and in February 1947, all 29 were offered to the Central Division, the Chief Operating Manager commenting:

'...it is desirable to find some suitable service in which as many as possible of them can be kept in sets which are not normally subject to change in formation, etc.

In particular, the two brake vehicles for each of the three intended 'Coronation Scot' sets form part of a twin articulated with the outside end bowed and not fitted with a gangway and if it can be avoided it is desirable that these be not used in main line services, where the necessity frequently arises for attaching other vehicles outside the brake.

...I shall be obliged if you will give early consideration to the possibility of making use of any of these coaches in any appropriate residential service between Manchester (Victoria) and Blackpool or Southport...I am particularly anxious that you should find use for the units which embody the vehicles with bowed ends if at all practicable.'

No doubt to the relief of the operating staff, the Central Division stated that it could use 23 of the coaches in set trains on the Manchester—Southport services and could absorb all the non-gangwayed brake ends. Thus, as the coaches were finished they were sent to Lostock Hall for stabling until sufficient were available for forming into sets.

The remaining six coaches not allocated to the Central Division (Semi-RFO+RFO; Semi-RTO+TK; loose TO and loose TK) were offered to the Western Division which said it could use the first class pair on one of the Liverpool—Euston turns and could place the third class coaches in the Wolverhampton—Euston services. In the event, the four third class coaches were not utilised because of their low seating capacity. One was stored at Abergavenny Junction (the open third) and the other three went to Craven Arms.

The first recorded working of the 1939/40 stock in this country was in October 1947 when the following set was formed to work a Blackpool—Liverpool residential turn: BFK+FK/ /Semi-TO+TK/ /TK+BTK. The firsts were the American pair and the thirds the coaches built to complete the American train. From this point onwards, the balance of the stock was completed during the autumn and winter of 1947/8 except for the two outstanding TK+BTK pairs which did not emerge until 1949 and 1951. Table 13c, appended after this chapter, lists the known workings to which the coaches were allocated on first entering service although they later became somewhat scattered.

The articulated RK+RTO and the Club Brake saloon were nobody's friends at first but the Club Car eventually found its way onto the North Wales Land Cruise train along with a number of other rather unusual vehicles. The Kitchen twin was placed in store at Craven Arms on return from the USA and while at Craven Arms it lost a bogie to Chairman's saloon No. 45005 in 1947. It would appear that unequal axle loading was causing distortion to the underframe and it ultimately went into Derby works for attention. No recorded working for the kitchen pair has been located and it may never have left Derby again as it was scrapped in early 1952.

**Plate 174.** Post-war semi-RTO+TK to D2017 No 56302/3. This was one of the articulated types not built for the 1939 tour train.

# THE 1939–40 STOCK DESCRIBED

All the 1939-40 stock, whether articulated or loose was built to a common 59ft 5¼in length which was occasioned by the maximum permissible distance between point locking bars on the articulated pairs; the loose coaches were built to matching dimensions. Externally the coaches were quite distinctive—even apart from the original livery of the American set. Body framing was of steel with solebar and cantrail combined in one unit, and the angle between roof and sides at the cantrail was rather sharper than the orthodox Period III coach. Views of the American train show a clear distinction between the profile of the sleeping car and the 1939-40 stock proper.

The underframes were centrally trussed on all the coaches and the whole sub-structure was of welded construction. Windows were double-glazed and on the American train, the bodyside panelling was carried down between the bogies to obscure the underframes. India rubber fairings covered the gaps between the coaches of the American set and were painted to match the train.

Another characteristic styling point was the circular pattern of toilet windows. These were, in effect, the precursors of the porthole style although not exactly similar. They had a central horizontal bar and the upper half hinged inwards. Similar matching windows but without hinged top sections were placed on the sides opposite the toilets to balance the appearance. The guard's lookout on the brake ends was also of a new shape—impossible to describe in words but clear enough from pictures. All main windows were of Period III style with shorter sliding portions rather like the post-war pattern. Brake ends were slightly bow-ended and without gangway connections.

The American train carried the crimson and gold 'Coronation Scot' livery and the gold stripes converged to a 'V' at the outer ends of the train as they also did on the front of the locomotive. Post-war coaches were built without the lower bodyside fairings and had the standard LMS livery, some of the later coaches also being outshopped without LMS markings where they post-dated Nationalisation. The American coaches were altered to match this style when they went into service in this country.

Inside, the vehicles followed traditional LMS practice; first class compartments seated four and thirds seated six, while all open saloons were designed as diners and thus seated two-and-one each side of the gangway with a one-and-one arrangement adjacent to the entrances. The familiar LMS wood veneers were extensively employed but in the dining saloons the LMS did make some concessions to the fashions of the day—whether this was a good thing or not is hard to say. Walls were faced in leather (grey in the first and green in the thirds) while seats were also leather upholstered (dull pink in the firsts and brown in the thirds). The cocktail lounge of the American train was a patriotic example of the decor of the later 1930s with blue leather wall facings, blue carpets, red and white curtains and ivory ceiling. The club saloon had brown oak facings and coral pink (!) leather armchairs. However, colour schemes apart which are, after all, a matter of personal preference, the vehicles themselves were superlatively comfortable and well-thought out designs. The corridor thirds were particularly luxurious having but six compartments, 6ft 6in between partitions.

Telephones were fitted in the compartments of the American train but were later removed and never put into the post war coaches. Although Ivatt had considered the conversion of the two-a-side seating to three-a-side, this was not carried out and the post-war firsts were built with two-a-side compartments as well. Finally, the kitchen car of the American train was not of the usual LMS gas cooking type but was fitted with a solid fuel cooking range designed to burn smokeless fuel. It is not known if the two loose kitchen cars would have been similar had they ever been built. Perhaps the LMS intended to use the 60ft all electric kitchen cars of 1933—we shall never know.

**Plate 175.** Third class compartment interior of 56302/3.

**Plate 176.** Interior view of the first class dining area of the semi-open firsts built after the war. It is believed to be the interior of 56102/3. Note the post-war reversion to traditional LMS finishes compared with Plate 172.

# CONCLUSIONS

Thus was concluded the complicated and rather sad story of the 'Coronation Scot'. It was a train conceived at the zenith of British steam railway operating and but for the war might well have attracted fresh laurels with the new coaches. However, this was not to be and, after the war, changing conditions and attitudes saw to it that not even a partial revival of the streamline age could be attempted. Nevertheless, the 1939-40 coaches were rather too good to waste—as indeed were the LNER streamline sets and one wonders why none of these vehicles were ever reformed for the Anglo-Scottish services. Although a high speed timing might not have been possible, one feels that limited accommodation luxury trains would have attracted custom and been of inestimable publicity value to the railway service during those early post-war austerity years and might have helped to offset the high construction costs of such specialised vehicles. This lack of enterprise is even more surprising when one recalls the very early post-war re-introduction of the much heavier, and even more wasteful of space, Pullman trains.

## TABLE 13a: THE 1937 'CORONATION SCOT' SETS

The 1937 sets were made of coaches to the following coach diagrams, details of which are given after the appropriate chapters:

| | | |
|---|---|---|
| Corridor Brake First | D1961 | 3 built Wolverton 1937 (Lot 1063) |
| Corridor First | D1960 | 3 built Wolverton 1937 (Lot 1062) |
| Vestibule First Diner | D1902 | 3 converted Wolverton 1937 (Lot 734) |
| Kitchen Only Car | D1912 | 6 converted Wolverton 1937 (Lot 956) |
| Vestibule Third Diner | D1981 | 9 converted Wolverton 1937 ex-D1904 (Lots 804/5) |
| Corridor Brake Third | D1905 | 3 converted Wolverton 1937 (Lot 898) |

*Set Formations* (Note: One source claims that the 'reserve' set ran on LNWR bogies. This is not confirmed nor is it known which set was the official 'reserve')

| BFK | FK | RFO | RK | RTO | RTO | RK | RTO | BTK |
|---|---|---|---|---|---|---|---|---|
| 5052 | 1069 | 7507 | 30084 | 8996 | 8993 | 30086 | 8961 | 5812 |
| 5053 | 1070 | 7508 | 30089 | 9003 | 9006 | 30085 | 9004 | 5792 |
| 5054 | 1071 | 7509 | 30087 | 8950 | 9029 | 30088 | 8931 | 5814 |

## TABLE 13b: THE 1939-40 'CORONATION SCOT' COACHES

*Note:* All coaches were built at Derby and had the following over body dimensions: $59'5\frac{1}{4}'' \times 9'2\frac{5}{8}'' \times 12'2\frac{3}{16}''$. Bogie centres were 51'9'' for the articulated pairs and $42'11\frac{1}{4}''$ for the loose coaches. Articulated pairs were 120' long over body. The loose coaches were plated 60' long and brake ends were $9'3\frac{1}{4}''$ over projections.

| Type | Diag | Lot | Qty | Date | Weight | Running Numbers | Withdrawals First | Last | Remarks |
|---|---|---|---|---|---|---|---|---|---|
| Twin BFK+FK | 2014 | 1148* | 1 set | 1939 | 57T | 56000-56001 | — | 1/65 | Plated 58T. |
| | | 1176A | 2 sets | 1947 | 57T | 56002-56005 | 4/65 | 11/65 | |
| Twin Semi-FK+RFO | 2015 | 1149* | 1 set | 1939 | 58T | 56100-56101 | — | 2/64 | Initially with a cocktail lounge. |
| Twin Semi-RFO+RFO | 2138 | 1177A | 2 sets | 1948 | 55T | 56102-56105 | 4/64 | 11/65 | The post-war version of D29015. |
| Twin RK+RTO | 2016 | 1150* | 1 set | 1939 | 66T | 56200-56201 | — | 4/52 | First coaches scrapped. |
| Twin Semi-RTO+TK | 2017 | 1151A | 1 set | 1947 | 58T | 56300-56301 | — | 3/66 | |
| | | 1179A | 2 sets | 1948 | 58T | 56302-56305 | 4/65 | 11/65 | |
| Twin BTK+TK | 2018 | 1153A | 1 set | 1947 | 58T | 56500-56501 | — | 12/66 | 56502/3 in service in 1949. |
| | | 1181A | 2 sets | 1951 | 58T | 56502-56505 | 13/63 | 6/64 | |
| TK | 2019 | 1152A | 1 | 1947 | 33T | 2148 | — | 10/67 | Oval Buffers. Lot 1180A plated 31T. |
| | | 1180A | 2 | 1949 | 33T | 2149-2150 | 13/66 | 11/67 | |
| Club Car | 2020 | 1164* | 1 | 1939 | 31T | 823 | — | 4/63 | |
| RTO | 2153 | 1178A | 2 | 1947 | 30T | 9517-9518 | 9/67 | 13/67 | Oval Buffers |

\* Coaches to USA in 1939.

## TABLE 13c: FIRST RECORDED WORKINGS OF 1939-40 'CORONATION SCOT' STOCK IN BRITAIN

| Coach Numbers | Date to traffic | Time | Details of Working From | To |
|---|---|---|---|---|
| 56000-56001 | 6th October 1947 | 0900 | Blackpool | Liverpool |
| | | 1640(SX) | Liverpool | Blackpool |
| | | 1310(SO) | | |
| 56002-56003 | 9th February 1948 | 0750(SX) | Southport | Manchester |
| | | 0805(SO) | ,, | ,, |
| | | 1610(SX) | Manchester | Southport |
| | | 1125(SO) | ,, | ,, |
| 56004-56005 | 1st December 1947 | 0855 | Southport | Manchester |
| | | 1722(SX) | Manchester | Southport |
| | | 1350(SO) | ,, | ,, |
| 56100-56101 | Not Known | Not known but believed allocated to same set as 56002/3. | | |
| 56102-56103 | 9th February 1948 | 1000(SX) | Southport | Manchester |
| | | 0830(SO) | | |
| | | 1810(SX) | Manchester | Southport |
| | | 1245(SO) | | |
| 56104-56105 | about mid-1948 | between Euston and Wolverhampton† | | |
| 9517 | 26th July 1948 | as for 56102/3 | | |
| 9518 | to store Dec. 1947 | | | |
| 56300-56301 | 6th October 1947 | as for 56000/1 | | |
| 56302-56303 | 26th July 1948 | 0743(SX) | Blackpool | Manchester |
| | | 1703(SX) | Manchester | Blackpool |
| 56304-56305 | to store May 1948 | | | |
| 2148 | 1st December 1947 | as for 56004/5 | | |
| 2149 | Not Known | allocated to Central Division | | |
| 2150 | to store, date unknown | | | |
| 56500-56501 | 6th October 1947 | as for 56000/1 | | |
| 56502-56503* | May 1949 | as for 56102/3 | | |
| 56504-56505* | Not Known | allocated to Central Division | | |

\* These coaches are shown in the LM diagram book as having entered service in 1951 and are quoted as such in Table 13b above. The 1951 date only applies to the last pair of coaches (56504/5).

† Not, apparently between Euston and Liverpool as planned—see p 163.

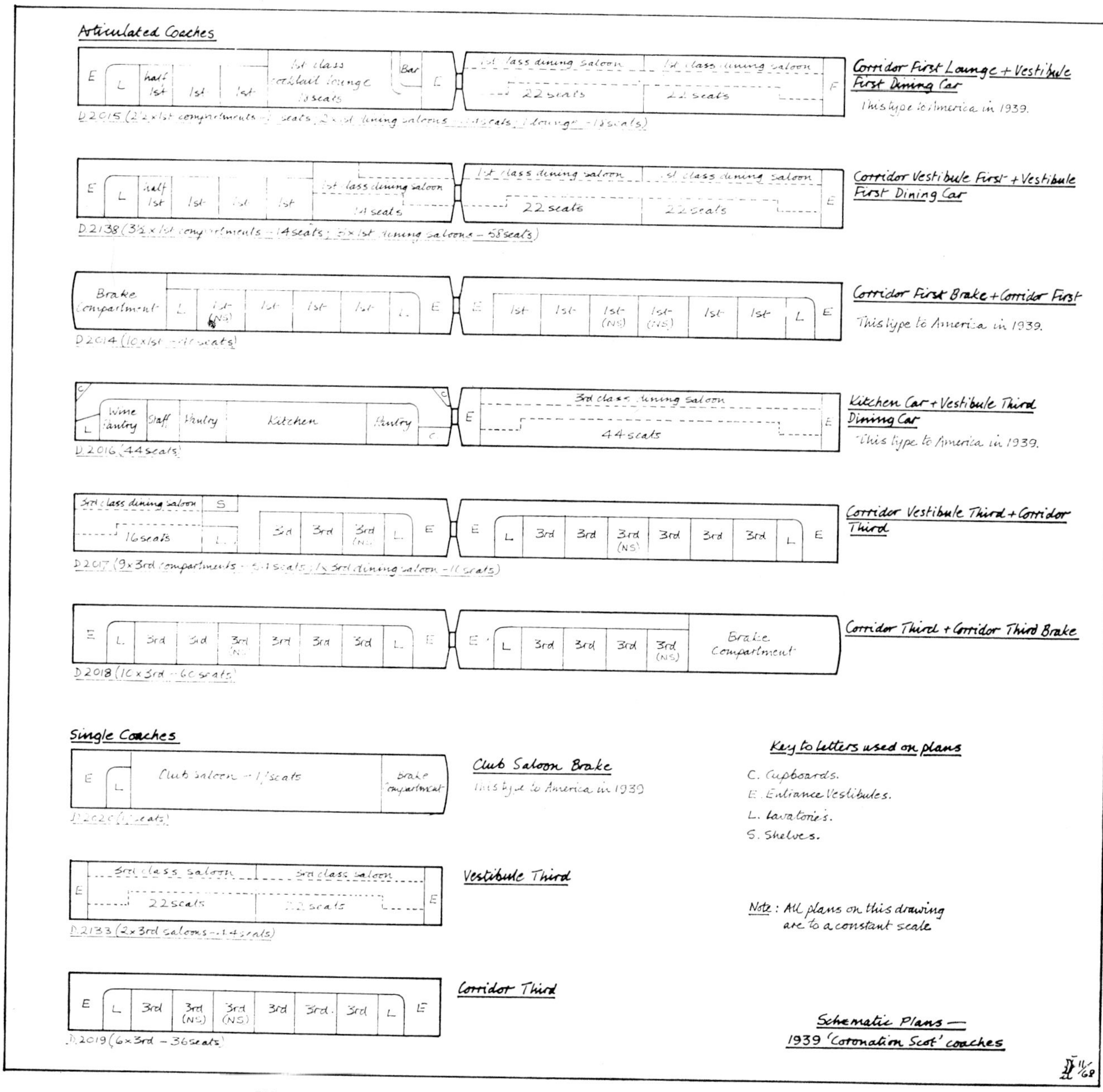

**Articulated Coaches**

D.2015 (2½ × 1st compartments – ? seats, 2 × 1st dining saloons – ?? seats, 1 lounge – 18 seats)
*Corridor First Lounge + Vestibule First Dining Car*
This type to America in 1939.

D.2138 (3½ × 1st compartments – 14 seats; 2 × 1st dining saloons – 58 seats)
*Corridor Vestibule First + Vestibule First Dining Car*

D.2014 (10 × 1st – 44 seats)
*Corridor First Brake + Corridor First*
This type to America in 1939.

D.2016 (44 seats)
*Kitchen Car + Vestibule Third Dining Car*
This type to America in 1939.

D.2017 (9 × 3rd compartments – 54 seats, 1 × 3rd dining saloon – 16 seats)
*Corridor Vestibule Third + Corridor Third*

D.2018 (10 × 3rd – 60 seats)
*Corridor Third + Corridor Third Brake*

**Single Coaches**

D.2020 (? seats)
*Club Saloon Brake*
This type to America in 1939

D.2133 (2 × 3rd saloons – 44 seats)
*Vestibule Third*

D.2019 (6 × 3rd – 36 seats)
*Corridor Third*

**Key to letters used on plans**

C. Cupboards.
E. Entrance Vestibules.
L. Lavatories.
S. Shelves.

Note: All plans on this drawing are to a constant scale

Schematic Plans —
1939 'Coronation Scot' coaches

FIGURE 40 LMS 1939 'Coronation Scot' stock—sketch plans (Drawn by D. Jenkinson)

**Plate 177.** Post-war Twin BFK+FK No 56004/5. Compare with view of the similar pre-war pair at Plate 169.

# Chapter 14 - Passenger Brake Vans and GPO vehicles

*Introduction; World War I Conversions; Period I designs; Period III designs; World War II Conversions;*
*Post Office vehicles, Summary Tables*

THE terms Periods I, II and III while suitable for most vehicles described in this work, are not quite comprehensive enough when considering the passenger full brakes built to LMS diagrams. Considerable numbers of full brakes were built as conversions from older stock which had seen a variety of previous uses. The section headings in this chapter; therefore, reflect this fact.

## WORLD WAR I CONVERSIONS

The first vehicles to be considered are not really LMS standards at all, although they were all given LMS diagrams. They consisted of a number of ex-pre group coaches which had been in Government service during the first world war as ambulance trains. Following their release, some were converted at Newton Heath and others at Wolverton, a policy which was to be repeated in large measure at the end of the second world war some 22 years later.

There were 63 vehicles concerned spread over eight LMS diagrams. The coaches largely appear to have eluded photographers and only one official photograph has come to light. From the diagrams issued it is possible to give a generalised statement about the more obvious differences between the various types and for ease of reference, these details have been incorporated into Table 14a which covers these conversions.

The only general comment which can be made is that most of the diagrams were fully beaded (except D1713/4) and all would have been given the full livery when converted.

## PERIOD I DESIGNS

The construction of LMS standard full brakes began with D1778 in 1925. This was a typical Period I design and was built to a 50ft length. This length remained standard with but few exceptions for LMS bogie brakes and appears to have been a case of the LMS adopting an LNWR standard length as it did for so many of its standard types. The vans themselves had a central guard's lookout with a single door to the right of it. Flanking this central feature were two pairs of double doors. This arrangement of doors and lookout was to remain unchanged in all subsequent designs of LMS standard bogie full brakes.

Two coaches from D1778 were converted to Bullion Vans 44597/9 in 1953. These were 30414/58 and were finally withdrawn in 1966. The conversion was to D2183.

The need for passenger full brakes must have been somewhat urgent during the middle 1920s, and 1926 saw the introduction of the first of an eventual 360 all-steel brakes built by outside contractors. These coaches were to D1715 and lacked conventional underframes. They were in all respects contemporary with and structurally similar to the open stock referred to on p.9. They were of the same length and layout as the orthodox Period I full brakes and all but one were finished in fully-lined livery when new.

The exception was old No. 7898 (later 30562), one of the batch built by the Birmingham Railway Carriage & Wagon Company to Lot 291. This coach was given a vitreous enamelled steel body. The idea was to reduce the time spent in shops—especially paint shops—and after the many difficulties were overcome, the vehicle entered traffic. The usual standard finish, including numbers and letters, was achieved but the process seems to have been incapable of producing the lining out. Thus it entered service in plain crimson hue. No paint was used above the chassis except around the door margins and gangways. All side and roof panels were enamelled. The experiment does not seem to have been a success and no evidence has been located that any other coaches were similarly treated. (Text continues on page 171)

**Plate 178.** Period I 'all-steel' BG to D1715 No 7898, later 30562. This was the experimental vehicle given an unlined enamel finish but its style (e.g. steel roof and lack of conventional under-frame) was typical of all the 1925/6 full brakes.

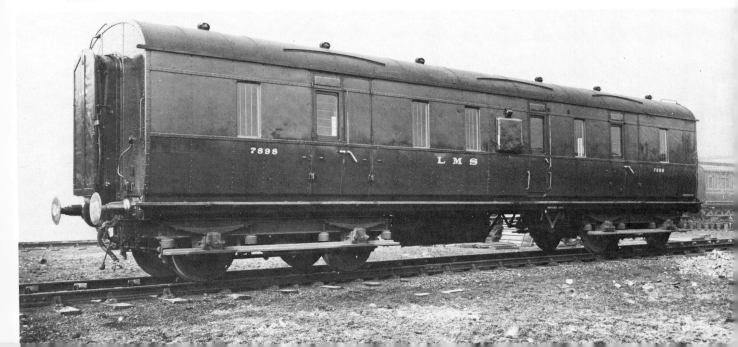

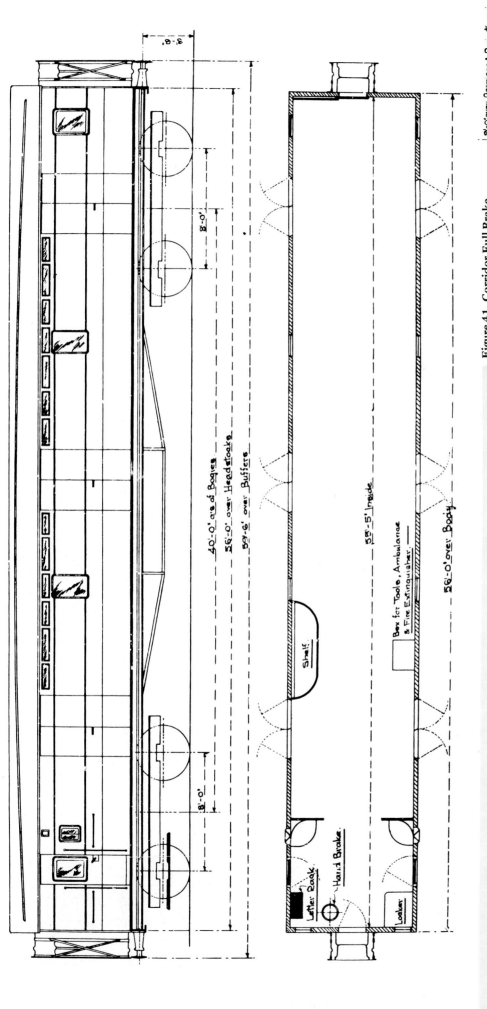

40'-0" c/s of Bogies

56'-0" over Headstocks

59'-6" over Buffers

3'-6"

8'-0"

8'-0"

55'-5" Inside

56'-0" over Body

Shelf

Box for Tools, Ambulance
& Fire Extinguisher

Letter Rack

Hand Brake

Locker

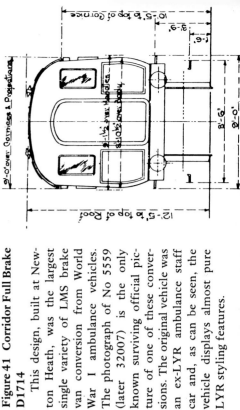

10'-5½" to top of Cornice

8'-9"

9'-6"

2'-0" over Cornices & Projections

2-1½" over Handles
shots over Body

8'-6"

2'-0"

12'-5½" to top of Roof

### Figure 41 Corridor Full Brake D1714

This design, built at Newton Heath, was the largest
single variety of LMS brake
van conversion from World
War I ambulance vehicles.
The photograph of No 5559
(later 32007) is the only
known surviving official picture of one of these conversions. The original vehicle was
an ex-LYR ambulance staff
car and, as can be seen, the
vehicle displays almost pure
LYR styling features.

**Figure 42 Corridor Full Brake D1778**

The LMS Period I 50ft full brake to D1778, though not the most numerous of the several 50ft diagrams, undoubtedly established the style for all subsequent full brakes to LMS design. As can be seen from the picture of 5509 (later 30528), these coaches were all given the fully lined livery, probably lined in gold rather than yellow in order to match the gangwayed stock with which they most often ran. Note the non-standard torpedo ventilators of this Wolverton built example.

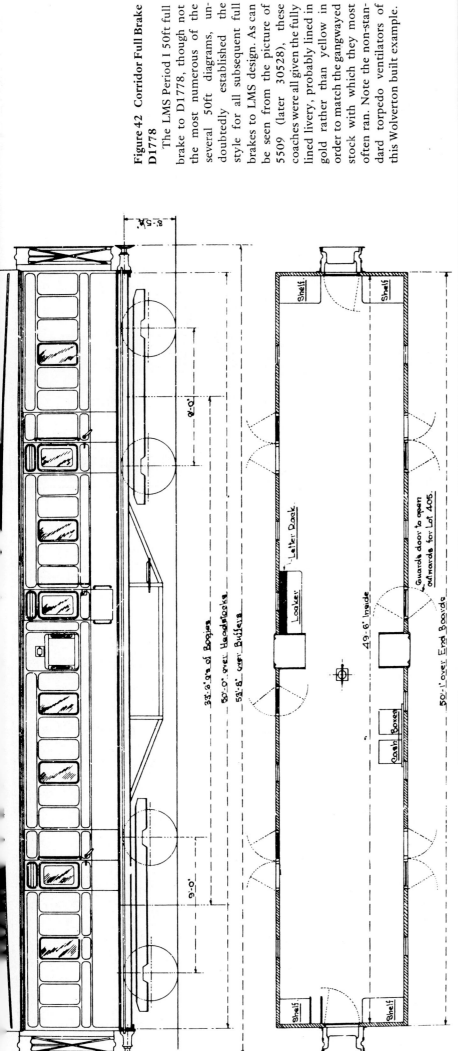

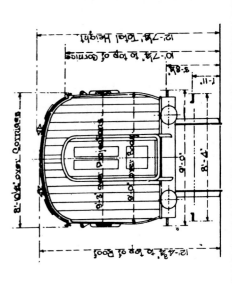

**Figure 43 Corridor Full Brake D1796**

Although six wheel full brakes were very common amongst the LMS constituent companies, the LMS itself did not build any until 1932. D1796 was one of the very first Stanier carriage diagrams and, as with all the early Stanier stock, was given the full livery. This particular design also had torpedo ventilators and side lights above the lookouts. It was also one of the few Stanier designs to emerge before the major re-numbering scheme and early examples had old series numbers such as 2860, illustrated, which later became 32907. These vehicles lasted a long time and were later fitted with stoves.

*Below:* Interior view of six-wheel brake to D1796 No. M32958. Externally, these vehicles were very similar to the later D2000 version shown at Plate 179.

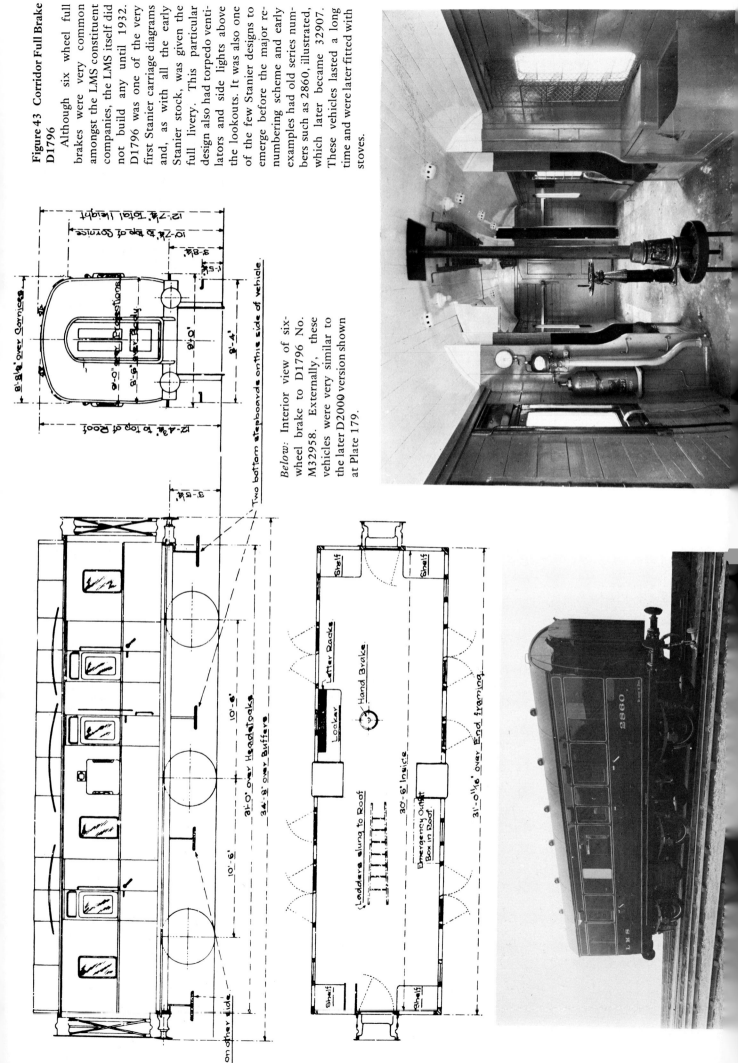

**Plate 179.**
Period III six-wheeled full brake No 32977 (D2000). Note the beading strips at the waist and above the window. These vehicles later became more familiarly known as 'Stove R'.

The all-steel brakes exhibited small but noticeable differences between batches. This took the form of presence or absence of outside rivets, horizontal reinforcement strips and so on. The differences generally related to the works where built and some are listed in Table 14b.

An accident to the 'Royal Highlander' at Dinwoodie in 1928 revealed the fact that the all-steel brake marshalled at the front of the train had absorbed a great deal of the impact and thus had minimised the damage to the passenger carrying coaches. The LMS therefore made an attempt to marshal as many trains as possible with these steel brakes at the outer ends. As may be expected, the complications of carriage rostering rendered the scheme somewhat abortive in many cases. However, this story may have had some bearing in the eventual adoption in this country of integral steel construction for passenger stock in later years. The final batch of all-steel brakes entered service in 1930 and no further full brakes were built until after Stanier had taken office.

## PERIOD III DESIGNS

The first Period III full brakes appeared almost as soon as Stanier had arrived on LMS. These were to D1796 and appeared in 1932 and 1933 and were six-wheel vehicles. In their later years they became known as 'Stove R'.

An interesting feature of these vans is that the diagram clearly shows short rainstrips on the roof over the doors which suggests that the design had been thought out before Stanier took office. The vehicles in fact were built with the characteristic Stanier ribbed roof and it seems possible that, just as in other matters, so in coaches, the CME started innovating almost as soon as he arrived.

Another externally distinguishing aspect of these coaches was the two strips of steel beading above and below the windows. These were, presumably, to cover the steel panel joints and were to become a typical feature of the pre-war Stanier full brake in all its guises. It seems odd that the passenger carrying coaches of contemporary design did not exhibit these beading strips and no reason can be offered why the brakes had this feature. Eventually, the full brakes also omitted the beading strip, the first diagram to do so being D2007.

When first built, D1796 carried lamps over the guard's lookout but these were later removed to conform with standard Stanier practice as there was no longer any need for fully braked trains of passenger-type stock to carry side lamps. During the second world war and following complaints from the guards, these vehicles were fitted with stoves.

At the same time as Wolverton was building D1796, Derby began to produce the 50ft Period III full bogie brake to D1854. These were identical in size and layout to the Period I designs but exhibited the Period III full brake styling as first seen on the six-wheel brakes—including the horizontal beading strips and side lamps.

Further six-wheelers followed to D2000 in 1938. These were 9ft 0in wide as opposed to the 8ft 9in of D1796 but the only real difference was a change in position of the guard's brake wheel to the centre of the coach. The diagram does not show any horizontal beading strip on D2000.

As with the preceding examples, the next 50ft design overlapped the construction of six-wheel brakes. This was D2007 which became numerically the largest LMS full brake diagram. It hardly differed from D1854 and it is difficult to deduce why a new diagram was issued. Some later lots of D2007 were rated as having 12T carrying capacity but not all were thus distinguished. There were also slight external detail changes such as the omission of the beading in later lots (believed Lot 1357 upwards). The building of these 50ft brakes went on well into the war years and they were some of the very few LMS coaches to be built between 1940 and 1945.

Another wartime variant was D2100. These were 57ft brakes built on second hand underframes. The general layout was identical to the 50ft vans. The building of 57ft vans seems a little odd—especially during the war—and the most likely solution seems to be that vans were needed and old underframes were available—hence the new design. These 57ft coaches were rated as 12T carrying capacity except for the two vehicles 31900-1 which were 8T. This latter pair were given the underframes of the ex-LNWR Royal Train coaches 5154-5 which had been given new underframes in 1937! The chassis for the remainder of this 57ft series came from war damaged coaches. The 57ft brakes did not have horizontal beading strips.

A pointer to the reason for the sudden building of 57ft vans is given by the consecutive Lots 1357/8 on the 50ft diagram D2007. These total 114 coaches which is an unusual figure. However, with the 57ft vans to Lot 1359, the total

**Plate 180.** Period III standard full brake No 30965 (D2007). Note the beading strips at the waist and above the windows. This distinctive feature of many Period III full brakes was absent from later lots to this diagram.

**Plate 181.** The wartime Period III full brake to D2100 built to 57ft length as opposed to the standard 50ft. The coach depicted is M31927M as running in 1965. The general arrangement of doors, windows etc was identical to the 50ft types. (R. J. Essery)

**Plate 182.** World War II LMS ambulance train No 8—converted from Period I corridor stock. The first four vehicles, in order, started life as the following types: BTK (D1696); TO(D1692); CK(D1694); CK(D1694). Vehicles of this ambulance coach type were selected for conversion to full brakes.

rises to 150 which is much more typical of the LMS. It is felt reasonable to postulate that the 57ft vans may have been ordered as 50ft vehicles on D2007 but wartime economy made it cheaper to utilise spare 57ft underframes and thus save quite a quantity of new rolled steel section.

After the war, the final 50ft diagram was issued. This was D2171 and appeared in 1948. These coaches were contemporary with the porthole stock and were rated as 12T carrying capacity. They had no raised outside beading strip and were given post-war torpedo ventilators. They were otherwise all but identical to the pre-war 50ft Period III types.

Thus, in summary, although several diagrams were issued for Period III full brakes, there were really only two types, the 50ft standard and the six-wheelers. The 57ft batch was, it is felt, no more than a wartime expedient and not, therefore, of any crucial significance in design terms.

## WORLD WAR II CONVERSIONS

As has been mentioned in Chapters 8 and 9, a considerable number of early LMS standard Period I gangwayed stock was requisitioned by the Government at the beginning of the second world war for conversion into ambulance trains. When released from this role they were further converted into full brakes to two separate diagrams (D2129 and D2130). Since there were more than two types of Period I coach involved, the exterior arrangement of these converted brakes displayed a bewildering variety of styles. As far as can be seen, both the brake van diagrams involved coaches from all the Period I types concerned.

It is only possible to give the most general description of these conversions in the space available, although full details do exist and it is possible to trace the history of most of the coaches involved.

Both diagrams had the guard located at one end of the vehicle, both diagrams were 57ft over headstocks and 9ft 0in wide over body, but D2130 is shown as 2¼in higher overall. D2130 had lookouts and two opposite inward opening doors at one end, two outward opening double doors close to the lookouts and two offset outward opening double doors about three quarters of a coach length from the guard's end. D2129 had the guard's seat on the opposite side to D2130 and the first pair of double-opening doors were offset and about one third of a coach length from the guard. The double doors furthest from the guard in this diagram were opposite each other. Finally, D2129 is shown as having the single doors near the lookout as opening outward. Many of these converted full brakes still showed signs of their original Period I types and reasonably characteristic examples of them are shown in the accompanying pictures.

As with the World War I conversions, these latter day conversions are listed separately and will be found in Table 14c.

Plate 183. Post-World War II ex-ambulance full brake No M31731M as running in 1964. This was the D2129 version and prior to becoming an ambulance the coach was Period 1 to No 8561 (D1692).

Plate 184. The D2130 ex-ambulance full brake as running in 1965. This coach, M31775M was originally Period I CK No 3672 (D1694). As can be seen, quite a substantial amount of its original panelling survived both the ambulance and the brake conversion.

## TABLE 14a: LMS PASSENGER BRAKE VANS I—WORLD WAR I CONVERSIONS

| Diag | Lot | Qty | Date | Built | Dimensions (L×W×H) | Weight | Running Numbers | Withdrawals First | Last | Remarks |
|---|---|---|---|---|---|---|---|---|---|---|
| 1713 | 64 | 16 | 1924 | N Heath | 56'×9'0"×12'5" | 26T | 31971-31986 | 2/54 | 12/60 | Ex-LYR Ward/Personnel cars |
|  | 360 | 1 | 1929 | N Heath |  | 25T | 32017 | — | 12/59 |  |
| 1714 | 69 | 30 | 1924 | N Heath | 56'×9'0"×12'5" | 26T | 31987-32016 | 10/53 | 2/63 | Ex-LYR Ambulance Staff cars. |
| 1773 | Part 70 | 2 | 1924 | Wolverton | 45'×9'3"×12'7½" | 21T | 31953-31954 | 1/37 (31954) | 12/47 (31953) | Ex-LNWR Ward Cars (with clerestory) |
| 1774 | Part 70 | 1 | 1924 | Wolverton | 57'×8'11"×12'5½" | 26T | 32018 | — | 12/51 | Ex-LNWR Brake/Infections car |
| 1776 | Part 70 | 2 | 1924 | Wolverton | 50'×8'11"×12'5½" | 24T | 31956-31957 | 1/56 (31956) | 12/56 (31957) | Ex-LNWR Pharmacy car |
| 1777 | Part 70 | 9 | 1924 | Wolverton | 54'×8'11"×12'5½" | 25T | 31958-31966 | 5/55 | 2/59 | Ex-LNWR Ward Cars |
| 1780 | 88 | 1 | 1924 | Wolverton | 49'10"×8'11"×12'3" | 24T | 31955 | — | 6/47 | Ex-LNWR Pharmacy car |
| 1711 | 90 | 1 | 1924 | Wolverton | 57'×8'11"×12'5½" | 26T | 32019 | — | 12/57 | Ex-LNWR Brake/Infections car |

## TABLE 14b: LMS PASSENGER BRAKE VANS II—STANDARD DESIGNS

*Note:* This table should be read in conjunction with the list of standard dimensions and details on page 62.

| Diag | Lot | Qty | Date | Built | Dimensions (L×W×H) | Period | Running Number | Withdrawals First | Last | Remarks |
|---|---|---|---|---|---|---|---|---|---|---|
| 1778 | 218 | 75 | 1925/6 | Wolverton | 50'×9'3"×12'4¾" | I | 30400-30474 | 5/61 | 4/67 | Lot 405 Plated 9'0" wide. 30414 and 30458 to Bullion Vans 1953. Lot 405 may, originally, have contained 50 coaches. |
|  | 219 | 25 | 1926 | N Heath |  |  | 30475-30499 | 10/59 | 9/67 |  |
|  | 405 | 49 | 1928 | Wolverton |  |  | 30500-30548 | 4/63 | 12/67 |  |
| 1715 | 291 | 50 | 1926/7 | B'ham C&W | 50'×9'0"×12'4¾" (All steel) | I (All steel) | 30549-30598 | 3/60 | 10/67 | * plus 31948 Layout identical to D1778 but no conventional underframe—merely a battery support bracket at one side. Lot 292 was heavily rivetted, remainder had less rivets but a prominent waist strip. The Birmingham C&W vehicles also had a top strip above the windows. All varieties had short rainstrips over the doors rather than a single end-to-end rainstrip. |
|  | 292 | 50 | 1927 | Met C&W |  |  | 30599-30648 | 11/58 | 12/66 |  |
|  | 344 | 50 | 1928 | Camm/Laird |  |  | 30649-30698 | 3/57 | one (30654) extant 1968 |  |
|  | 345 | 50 | 1927/8 | B'ham C&W |  |  | 30699-30747* | 12/58 | 9/67 |  |
|  | 460 | 50 | 1929 | B'ham C&W |  |  | 30748-30797 | 8/58 | 4/68 |  |
|  | 461 | 50 | 1929 | Camm/Laird |  |  | 30798-30847 | 2/60 | a few extant in 1968 |  |
|  | 536 | 30 | 1930 | Metro Cammell |  |  | 30848-30877 | 3/65 | a few extant in 1968 |  |
|  | 537 | 30 | 1930 | B'ham C&W |  |  | 30878-30907 | 7/63 | 1/68 |  |
| 1796 | 664 | 25 | 1932 | Wolverton | 31'×8'9"×12'4¾" (six-wheel) | III | 32900-32924 | 3/65 | Majority extant 1968 | Very early Stanier vehicles. Outshopped in full livery with torpedo vents. Beading strips at waist and above windows. |
|  | 669 | 50 | 1933 | Wolverton |  |  | 32925-32974 | 9/63 |  |  |
| 1854 | 665 | 25 | 1932/3 | Derby | 50'×9'0"×12'4⅝" | III | 30908-30932 | 8/64 | a few still extant | First Stanier version of the standard 50' van. Lots 665/686 had full livery and torpedo vents. Lot 780 had torpedo vents but probably simple livery. Beading strips as with D1796. |
|  | 686 | 25 | 1933 | Derby |  |  | 30933-30957 | 4/66 |  |  |
|  | 780 | 6 | 1934 | Wolverton |  |  | 30958-30963 | 2/66 | 6/67 |  |
| 2000 | 1091 | 25 | 1938 | Wolverton | 31'×9'0"×12'4⅝" (six wheel) | III | 32975-32999 | 13/66 | Majority extant 1968 | Officially 3" wider than D1796 but both types had standard 8'6" wide body. Hand-brake re-positioned compared with D1796. Most had standard Period III shell vents but some had torpedo type. |
|  | 1262 | 20 | 1940 | Wolverton |  |  | 33000-33019 | 8/64 |  |  |
| 2007 | 1096 | 25 | 1938 | Wolverton | 50'×9'0"×12'4⅝" | III | 30964-30988 | 3/65 | virtually all extant 1968 | No apparent difference to D1854. From Lot 1260 upwards many were rated at 12T carrying capacity (Standard value 8T). Lots 1260/1 all plated 1939. Beading strips on bodyside seem to have finished with Lot 1305. Lot 1358 had second hand underframes. |
|  | 1097 | 25 | 1938/9 | Wolverton |  |  | 30989-31013 | 3/65 |  |  |
|  | 1198 | 25 | 1939 | Wolverton |  |  | 31014-31038 | 11/67 |  |  |
|  | 1260 | 20 | 1940 | Derby |  |  | 31039-31058 | 5/66 |  |  |
|  | 1261 | 50 | 1939/40 | Wolverton |  |  | 31059-31108 | 8/66 |  |  |
|  | 1304 | 50 | 1940/41 | Derby |  |  | 31109-31158 | 5/66 |  |  |
|  | 1305 | 50 | 1941 | Wolverton |  |  | 31159-31208 | 6/67 |  |  |
|  | 1357 | 110 | 1941 | Wolverton |  |  | 31210-31319 | 10/65 |  |  |
|  | 1358 | 4 | 1944 | Wolverton |  |  | 31320-31323 | all extant 1968 |  |  |
|  | 1444 | 25 | 1947 | Wolverton |  |  | 31324-31348 | all extant 1968 |  |  |
| 2100 | Part 1359 | 2 | 1944 | Wolverton | 57'×9'0"×12'4⅝" | III | 31900-31901 | 9/66(31901) | 31900 extant 1968 | The 57' wartime version on second hand underframes. All rated 12T capacity except 31900/1 which were 8T. This pair were given the underframes of ex-LNWR Royal coaches 5154/5. No beading on body side of this design. |
|  | Part 1359 | 34 | 1944 | Wolverton |  |  | 31902-31935 | All extant 1968 |  |  |
| 2171 | 1508 | 25 | 1949/50 | Wolverton | 50'×9'0"×12'4⅝ | III | 31349-31373 | all extant (except for accident withdrawals) in 1968 |  | The post-war 50' design. All rated 12T capacity but no fundamental difference from D1854/D2007. Exteriors had no raised beading strip. The vans had BR type torpedo vents and all out shopped without LMS markings (many probably in BR livery from new). |
|  | 1563 | 25 | 1949 | Derby |  |  | 31374-31398 |  |  |  |
|  | 1579 | 15 | 1950 | Derby |  |  | 31399-31413 | 5/68 | Most extant 1968 |  |
|  | 1588 | 15 | 1950 | Wolverton |  |  | 31414-31428 | 3/65 |  |  |

### Addenda

Not surprisingly, the passenger full brakes were generally the longest lived by far of LMS pattern gangwayed coaches, many receiving either a full BR blue or BR blue/grey repaint. Many are still in service (1977) but a large number have been converted to non-gangway form.

# TABLE 14c: LMS PASSENGER BRAKE VANS—III— WORLD WAR II CONVERSIONS

Two diagrams were involved (D2129/D2130), both being 57'×9'3'' but D2129 was 12'7¼'' high and D2130 was 12'9½'' high (both measured over roof vents). There were no standard details to the designs as such except that all had originated from Period I wood panelled gangwayed stock. The coaches were numbered in the 31700-31871 series with the following gaps: 31794-6; 31828; 31839; 31845; 31859; 31863; 31867. This gave 163 actual vehicles, 81 of which were converted to D2129, the remainder to D2130. The numbers did not run consecutively through the diagrams so the following table is listed in number order **not** diagram order. The conversions took place at Derby and Wolverton between 1946 and 1949. All were scrapped by the end of 1967.

| Running Number | Original Coach | Type of ambulance vehicle from which converted | Brake van Diagram |
|---|---|---|---|
| 31700 | TO No. 7827 | Ward Car | D2129 |
| 31701 | TO No. 8150 | Ward Car | D2130 |
| 31702 | TO No. 7875 | Not known | D2129 |
| 31703 | TO No. 8139 | Ward Car | D2130 |
| 31704 | TO No. 8154 | Ward Car | '' |
| 31705 | TO No. 8090 | Ward Car | '' |
| 31706 | TO No. 8076 | Ward Car | '' |
| 31707 | TO No. 7838 | Ward Car | D2129 |
| 31708 | TO No. 7852 | Not known | '' |
| 31709 | TO No. 7848 | Ward Car | '' |
| 31710 | TO No. 7856 | Not known | '' |
| 31711 | TO No. 8089 | Ward Car | D2130 |
| 31712 | TO No. 8131 | Ward Car | '' |
| 31713 | TO No. 8101 | Ward Car | '' |
| 31714 | BTK No. 5261 | Ward and Brake Car | D2129 |
| 31715 | BTK No. 5254 | Ward and Brake Car | '' |
| 31716 | CK No. 3623 | Spare Car | '' |
| 31717 | TO No. 8525 | Spare Car | '' |
| 31718 | BTK No. 5294 | Spare Car | '' |
| 31719 | BTK No. 5328 | Spare Car | D2130 |
| 31720 | TO No. 8557 | Ward Car | D2129 |
| 31721 | TO No. 8574 | Ward Car | '' |
| 31722 | TO No. 8489 | Ward Car | '' |
| 31723 | TO No. 8486 | Ward Car | '' |
| 31724 | TO No. 8457 | Ward Car | '' |
| 31725 | TO No. 8492 | Ward Car | '' |
| 31726 | TO No. 8471 | Ward Car | '' |
| 31727 | TO No. 8549 | Ward Car | '' |
| 31728 | TO No. 8483 | Ward Car | '' |
| 31729 | TO No. 8576 | Ward Car | '' |
| 31730 | TO No. 8513 | Ward Car | '' |
| 31731 | TO No. 8561 | Ward Car | '' |
| 31732 | TO No. 8522 | Ward Car | '' |
| 31733 | TO No. 8551 | Ward Car | '' |
| 31734 | TO No. 8460 | Ward Car | '' |
| 31735 | TO No. 8510 | Ward Car | '' |
| 31736 | TO No. 8474 | Ward Car | '' |
| 31737 | TO No. 8535 | Ward Car | '' |
| 31738 | TO No. 8534 | Ward Car | '' |
| 31739 | TO No. 8533 | Ward Car | '' |
| 31740 | TO No. 8506 | Ward Car | '' |
| 31741 | TO No. 8502 | Ward Car | '' |
| 31742 | TO No. 8536 | Ward Car | '' |
| 31743 | TO No. 8580 | Not known | '' |
| 31744 | TO No. 8381 | Ward Car | D2130 |
| 31745 | TO No. 8411 | Ward Car | '' |
| 31746 | TO No. 8364 | Ward Car | '' |
| 31747 | TO No. 8470 | Ward Car | D2129 |
| 31748 | TO No. 8503 | Ward Car | D2129 |
| 31749 | TO No. 8365 | Ward Car | D2130 |
| 31750 | TO No. 8573 | Ward Car | D2129 |
| 31751 | TO No. 8369 | Ward Car | D2130 |
| 31752 | TO No. 8370 | Ward Car | '' |
| 31753 | TO No. 8575 | Ward Car | D2129 |
| 31754 | TO No. 8367 | Ward Car | D2130 |
| 31755 | TO No. 8421 | Ward Car | '' |
| 31756 | BTO No. 9879 | Ward and Brake Car | '' |
| 31757 | BTO No. 9882 | Ward and Brake Car | '' |
| 31758 | BTO No. 9870 | Ward and Brake Car | '' |
| 31759 | BTO No. 9872 | Ward and Brake Car | '' |
| 31760 | BTO No. 9878 | Ward and Brake Car | '' |
| 31761 | BTO No. 9871 | Ward and Brake Car | '' |
| 31762 | BTO No. 9880 | Ward and Brake Car | '' |
| 31763 | BTO No. 9886 | Ward and Brake Car | '' |
| 31764 | BTO No. 9863 | Ward and Brake Car | '' |
| 31765 | BTO No. 9865 | Ward and Brake Car | '' |
| 31766 | BTO No. 9888 | Ward and Brake Car | '' |
| 31767 | BTO No. 9835 | Ward and Brake Car | D2129 |
| 31768 | CK No. 3640 | Personnel Car | '' |
| 31769 | CK No. 3647 | Personnel Car | '' |
| 31770 | CK No. 3699 | Personnel Car | '' |
| 31771 | CK No. 3696 | Personnel Car | '' |
| 31772 | CK No. 3666 | Personnel Car | '' |
| 31773 | CK No. 3687 | Personnel Car | '' |
| 31774 | CK No. 3686 | Personnel Car | '' |
| 31775 | CK No. 3672 | Personnel Car | '' |
| 31776 | CK No. 3662 | Personnel Car | '' |
| 31777 | CK No. 3591 | Personnel Car | '' |
| 31778 | CK No. 3676 | Personnel Car | D2130 |
| 31779 | CK No. 3682 | Personnel Car | D2129 |
| 31780 | CK No. 3681 | Ambulance Kitchen Car | '' |
| 31781 | CK No. 3700 | Ambulance Kitchen Car | '' |
| 31782 | CK No. 3661 | Ambulance Kitchen Car | '' |
| 31783 | CK No. 3665 | Ambulance Kitchen Car | '' |
| 31784 | CK No. 3680 | Ambulance Kitchen Car | '' |
| 31785 | CK No. 3698 | Ambulance Kitchen Car | '' |
| 31786 | CK No. 3669 | Ambulance Kitchen Car | '' |
| 31787 | CK No. 3692 | Ambulance Kitchen Car | '' |
| 31788 | CK No. 3695 | Ambulance Kitchen Car | D2130 |
| 31789 | CK No. 3689 | Ambulance Kitchen Car | D2129 |
| 31790 | CK No. 3683 | Ambulance Kitchen Car | '' |
| 31791 | CK No. 3668 | Probably Ambulance Kitchen Car | '' |
| 31792 | TO No. 8390 | Spare Car | D2130 |
| 31793 | TO No. 8454 | Spare Car | '' |
| 31794-6 | Number series vacant | | |
| 31797 | TO No. 8458 | *Note:* From this point onwards | D2129 |
| 31798 | TO No. 8484 | it is not possible to state the | '' |
| 31799 | TO (No. 8498?) | type of ambulance vehicle | '' |
| 31800 | TO No. 8413 | from which each full brake | D2130 |
| 31801 | TO No. 8436 | was converted. However, the | '' |
| 31802 | TO No. 8455 | two diagrams for the full | '' |
| 31803 | TO No. 8339 | brakes indicate that the fol- | '' |
| 31804 | TO No. 8269 | lowing additional types of | '' |
| 31805 | TO No. 8389 | ambulance coach were also | '' |
| 31806 | TO No. 8493 | involved: kitchen and mess | D2129 |
| 31807 | TO No. 8518 | cars; brake infection and boil- | '' |
| 31808 | TO (No. 8393?) | er cars; pharmacy cars; brake | D2130 |
| 31809 | TO No. 8336 | and stores cars; brake, stores | '' |
| 31810 | TO No. 8374 | and boiler cars; dressing and | '' |
| 31811 | TO No. 8468 | baggage cars. | D2129 |
| 31812 | TO No. 8358 | | D2130 |
| 31813 | TO No. 8529 | | D2129 |
| 31814 | TO No. 8577 | | '' |
| 31815 | TO No. 8563 | | '' |
| 31816 | TO No. 8542 | | '' |
| 31817 | TO No. 8447 | | D2130 |
| 31818 | TO No. 8299 | | |
| 31819 | TO No. 8482 | | D2129 |
| 31820 | TO No. 8378 | | D2130 |
| 31821 | TO No. 8379 | | |
| 31822 | TO No. 8579 | | D2129 |
| 31823 | TO No. 8388 | | D2130 |
| 31824 | TO No. 8516 | | D2129 |
| 31825 | TO (No. 8435?) | | D2130 |
| 31826 | TO No. 8463 | | D2129 |
| 31827 | BTO No. 9869 | | '' |
| 31828 | Number vacant | | |
| 31829 | BTO (No. 9860?) | | '' |
| 31830 | BTO No. 9883 | | D2130 |
| 31831 | BTK No. 5316 | | '' |
| 31832 | BTK No. 5242 | | '' |
| 31833 | BTK No. 5237 | | '' |
| 31834 | BTK No. 5231 | | '' |
| 31835 | BTK No. 5257 | | '' |
| 31836 | BTK No. 5337 | | '' |
| 31837 | BTK (No. 5230?) | | '' |
| 31838 | BTK No. 5250 | | '' |
| 31839 | Number vacant but allocated to BTK No. 5235 lost overseas | | |
| 31840 | BTK No. 5311 | | '' |
| 31841 | BTK No. 5262 | | '' |
| 31842 | BTK No. 5282 | | '' |
| 31843 | BTK No. 5259 | | '' |
| 31844 | BTK No. 5275 | | '' |
| 31845 | Number vacant but allocated to BTK No. 5310 lost overseas | | |
| 31846 | BTK No. 5241 | | '' |
| 31847 | BTK No. 5304 | | '' |
| 31848 | BTK No. 5255 | | '' |
| 31849 | BTK No. 5260 | | '' |
| 31850 | BTK No. 5301 | | '' |
| 31851 | BTK No. 5273 | | '' |
| 31852 | BTK No. 5253 | | '' |
| 31853 | BTK No. 5265 | | '' |
| 31854 | BTK No. 5281 | | '' |
| 31855 | BTK No. 5228 | | '' |
| 31856 | BTK No. 5271 | | '' |
| 31857 | BTK No. 5333 | | '' |
| 31858 | BTK No. 5315 | | '' |
| 31859 | Number vacant | | |
| 31860 | BTK No. 5324 | | D2129 |
| 31861 | BTK No. 5341 | | D2130 |
| 31862 | BTK No. 5302 | | '' |
| 31863 | Number vacant | | |
| 31864 | BTK No. 5297 | | '' |
| 31865 | BTK No. 5278 | | '' |
| 31866 | BTK No. 5267 | | '' |
| 31867 | Number vacant | | |
| 31868 | CK No. 3648 | | D2129 |
| 31869 | CK (No. 3678?) | | D2130 |
| 31870 | CK No. 3634 | | D2129 |
| 31871 | CK No. 3705 | | |

# POST OFFICE VEHICLES

In the LMS/LMR carriage diagram book there are listed 68 GPO vehicles built to no less than 20 separate diagrams. Of these 20 diagrams, two account for some 36 of the 68 coaches involved so it will readily be appreciated that unlike most other LMS design coaches, it is not really possible to make any form of valid generalisation about Post Office coaches, other than to say they were of two basic types; stowage and sorting vans.

As far as the authors can deduce the reasons for this variety probably stem from the operation of the vehicles themselves. Firstly, Post Office vehicles generally seem to have been built as planned replacements on a one-for-one basis for vehicles scheduled to be withdrawn. Thus the replacement coach often had to satisfy the requirements of the service being operated by the coach/coaches scheduled for withdrawal. This probably meant, in turn, that many vehicles were tailor-made for specific services. This would undoubtedly give one possible reason for the number of one-off diagrams and the often quite trivial but bewildering differences in such matters as interior fittings and so forth which these vehicles displayed.

Unfortunately, however, it has not been possible to find any evidence of the utilisation of Post Office coaches which sheds much light on the situation and the only information which has survived is that pertaining to the coaches themselves which is summarised, as far as it is known, in Table 14d.

Turning now to the vehicles themselves, it is possible to make a few comments which are generally applicable to most LMS Post Office coaches. The division into Periods I, II and III was only immediately noticeable in the method of roof construction adopted—there being no fully beaded LMS Post Office coaches. Full livery was adopted for the pre-1934 built examples when new but this was only a transitory difference.

As far as there was a typical design it is represented by D1792 (Fig. 44). These were 60ft coaches and the diagram was current from 1930 to 1939 so it contains both Period II and Period III coaches. Internally, the layout was typical of all LMS *sorting* coaches. The corridor connection was offset and the sorting racks were on the non-corridor side. From the outside the racks could be distinguished by 'bulges' in the exterior panelling. The corridor side of the coach carried the pick-up net which was located at the right hand end of the coach. Most LMS sorting coaches had a lavatory on the shelf side at the same end as the pick-up nets. However, a few individual coaches did not have this lavatory—even though it was shown on the diagram.

Deviations from this style in such diagrams as D1908 and D1970 were mainly in the nature of variations in length from the normal 60ft or slight alterations to the interior. One presumes that the length deviations which justified fresh diagrams were probably made to enable the coaches to run on lines with a more limited loading gauge than would clear the standard 60ft coach.

Some sorting carriages were not fitted with pick-up apparatus although carrying the recessed body side panelling where it would have been fitted. Some of these coaches may have originally had the nets but this is not known with certainty. Detail differences where known are given in the summary table but there are gaps in the available information.

There were rather fewer stowage vans built to LMS design than sorting vans; in general they were shorter in length although there were some 60ft examples. In so far as there was an interior design for these vehicles it took the form of the occasional provision of such features as wardrobes (for the GPO staff?), lavatories, folding tables, ovens and so forth. In general, however, these vehicles usually possessed a completely unfurnished interior and such fittings as were provided, if any at all, occupied but a small proportion of the floor space. Most vehicles in the stowage category were of standard LMS lengths (e.g. D1793), but there were two noteworthy exceptions.

**Plate 185.** Post Office sorting van 3242, later 30232, was the first LMS TPO vehicle to be built (D1794) and was a 'one-off' coach. Apart from the LMS standard underframe, it was very much in the LNWR/WCJS tradition as regards body styling. Even the LMS gave its pseudo panelling an LNWR look by the semi-circular ends to the waist lining panels.

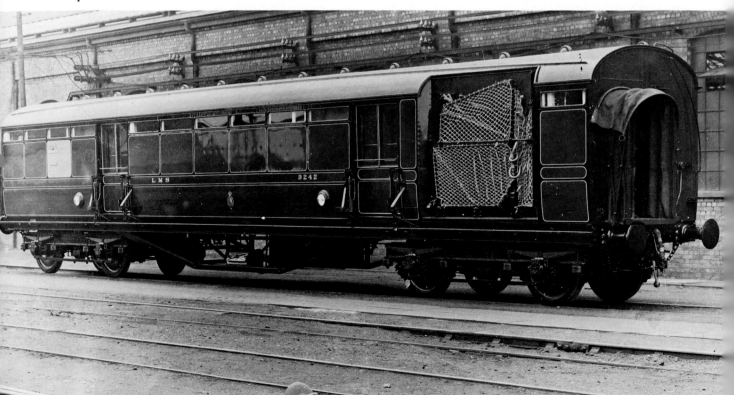

D1883 was built in 1933 and was a 42ft vehicle. In some respects it was similar to the 42ft luggage/parcels van of the same vintage except that D1883 had gangway connections and tumblehome sides rather than end loading doors and flat sides. D1867 of the same year was also a little odd. This was a six-wheel full brake but it had no interior fittings at all and no gangwayed connection. Both these unusual coaches were 'one-offs' and no reason for their very marked deviation from standard practice can be adduced. The LMS did not even distinguish them with the title of Stowage Van—they were simply 'Vans'.

Although the 1932/3 renumbering placed GPO vehicles in the 30200-30399 series, a quick perusal of the tables will indicate that there was no logic in the numbering of individual coaches. Some carried the numbers of the vehicles they replaced which would have been logical if universally applied but this was not so. For example 30307-8 eventually replaced 30261-2!

The only other point to make in this general discussion on GPO coaches is the very late date at which LMS design vehicles in this category were emerging. D2193 has, it is believed, the highest LMS series lot number to be issued for a passenger rated vehicle.

Many LMS design GPO vehicles outlived their passenger carrying contemporaries and it is conceivable that, pro-rata, more GPO type coaches survived to receive the BR blue/grey livery than any other group of LMS design coaches.

## TABLE 14d: SUMMARY TABLE OF LMS STANDARD GPO VEHICLES

*Note:* This table should be read in conjunction with the list of standard dimensions and details on page 62.

| Type | Diag | Lot | Qty | Date | Built | Dimensions (L×W×H) (see Footnote) | Weight | Period | Running Numbers | Withdrawals First | Last | Remarks |
|---|---|---|---|---|---|---|---|---|---|---|---|---|
| POS | 1794 | 472 | 1 | 1929 | Wolverton | 57'×8'8"×12'5½" | 31T | II | 30232 | | | The 'standard' LMS pattern GPO sorting coach. Change to simple livery came with Period III Lot 772. Lots 502/611/877 did not have a toilet. These coaches were often plated as 9'10" wide (presumably measured over the pick-up equipment). 30250/51 had the pick-up equipment removed at least by 1957 and several more followed suit. |
| POS | 1792 | 502 | 3 | 1930 | Wolverton | | 32T | II (Flush) | 30233-30235 | | | |
| | | 564 | 3 | 1931 | Wolverton | | 33T | II (Flush) | 30266-30268 | | | |
| | | Part 611 | 3 | 1931 | Wolverton | | 32T | II (Flush) | 30213-30215 | 8/48 | | |
| | | Part 611 | 3 | 1931 | Wolverton | | 32T | II (Flush) | 30246-30248 | | | |
| | | 612 | 1 | 1931 | Wolverton | 60'×8'8"×12'4¾" | 33T | II (Flush) | 30314 | | | |
| | | 772 | 3 | 1934 | Wolverton | | 32T | III | 30216-30218 | | | |
| | | 773 | 1 | 1934 | Wolverton | | 32T | III | 30219 | | | |
| | | 877 | 3 | 1935 | Wolverton | | 32T | III | 30220-30222 | 5/48 | | |
| | | 987 | 1 | 1936 | Wolverton | | 34T | III | 30230 | | | |
| | | 1059 | 3 | 1937 | Wolverton | | 33T | III | 30249-30251 | | | |
| | | 1197 | 3 | 1939 | Wolverton | | 33T | III | 30289-30291 | | | |
| POS | 1908 | 774 | 1 | 1934 | Wolverton | 57'×8'8"×12'4⅝" | 30T | III | 30204 | | | Basically a 57' version of D1792 but no lavatory. |
| POS | 1970 | 1052 | 2 | 1937 | Wolverton | 60'×8'8"×12'4⅝" | 33T | III | 30223-30224 | | | A genuine Period III version of D1792 but with slightly altered interior. |
| POS | 2043 | 1238 | 1 | 1939 | Wolverton | 60'×8'8"×12'4⅝" | 32T | III | 30225 | | | As for D1970 but without lavatory. |
| POS | 2175 | 1443 | 2 | 1947 | Wolverton | 60'×8'8"×12'4⅝" | 31T | III | 30292-30293 | | | Lot 1443 originally listed on D2043. Not fitted with pickup apparatus. |
| | | 1606 | 1 | 1950 | Wolverton | | 31T | III | 30281 | | | |
| POS | 2140 | 1488 | 3 | 1948 | Wolverton | 60'×8'8"×12'4⅝" | 31T | III | 30294-30296 | | | Virtually as for D2043 but slightly altered interior fittings. 30277 replaced 30294. |
| | | 1604 | 2 | 1950 | Wolverton | | 32T | III | 30277-30278 | | | |
| POS | 2167 | 1507 | 2 | 1949 | Wolverton | 60'×8'8"×12'4⅝" | 32T | III | 30269-30270 | | | As for D2140 but fitted with lavatory. |
| | | 1559 | 3 | 1950 | Wolverton | | 33T | III | 30271-30273 | | | |
| | | 1560 | 1 | 1950 | Wolverton | | 33T | III | 30274 | | | |
| | | 1619 | 3 | 1950 | Wolverton | | 32T | III | 30297-30299 | | | |
| POS | 2185 | 1620 | 3 | 1954 | Wolverton | 57'×8'8"×12'4⅝" | 30T | III | 30300-30302 | | | No pickput gear but fitted wardrobe and lavatory. |
| POS | 2188 | 1673 | 1 | 1954 | Wolverton | 60'×8'8"×12'4⅝" | 30T | III | 30303 | | | Fitted extra tables plus heating stove and oven. No pickup gear but fitted with lavatory. |
| POS | 2191 | 1674 | 2 | 1954 | Wolverton | 60'×8'8"×12'4⅝" | Not known | III | 30307-30308 | | | Coaches had recesses for pickup nets but the latter were not fitted. |
| POS | 2193 | 1689 | 2 | 1957* | Wolverton | 57'×8'8"×12'4⅝" | 33T | III | 30309-30310 | | | Basically a 57' design with both pickup apparatus and lavatory. BR type top lights. |
| POT | 1793 | 479 | 3 | 1930 | Wolverton | 50'×8'6"×12'4¾" | 28T | II (Flush) | 30210-30212 | 8/48 | | Recessed side but no net. Mail delivery apparatus fitted. Fitted shelves and 2 sliding doors each side. 30211 had nets by 1958. |
| POT | 1937 | 883 | 1 | 1935 | Wolverton | 50'×8'6"×12'4⅝" | 27T | III | 30341 | | | Completely empty interior but lavatory at Right Hand end looking at corridor side of vehicle. |
| POT | 2052 | 1297 | 1 | 1940 | Wolverton | 50'×8'6"×12'4⅝" | 25T | III | 30280 | | | As for D1937 but wardrobe in place of lavatory. 30280 built for M & NEJPS. |
| | | 1433 | 1 | 1946 | Wolverton | | 25T | III | 30282 | | | |
| POT | 2172 | 1561 | 1 | 1950 | Wolverton | 60'×9'2¼"×12'4⅝" | | III | 30275 | | | Fitted with lavatory and guard's compartment. Width quoted over handles as this was a normal profile diagram rather than the standard Post Officed type. |
| | | 1603 | 1 | 1950 | Wolverton | | 29T | III | 30276 | | | |
| | | 1672 | 1 | 1954 | Wolverton | | | III | 30306 | | | |
| POT | 2176 | 1605 | 1 | 1950 | Wolverton | 60'×8'6"×12'4⅝" | 30T | III | 30279 | | | Fitted with net, wardrobe, sink, oven and folding tables. |
| POT | 2187 | 1671 | 1 | 1954 | Wolverton | 57'×9'3"×12'4⅝" | Not known | III | 30305 | | | Empty interior except for water boiler and wardrobe. Normal profile vehicle and width is quoted over handles. |
| VAN | 1853 | 662 | 1 | 1933 | Wolverton | 42'×8'6"×12'4⅝" | 25T | III | 30304 | | | Probably full livery when new. No interior fittings at all. |
| VAN | 1867 | 703 | 1 | 1933 | Wolverton | 31'×8'9"×12'4¾" (six-wheel) | 16T | III | 30391 | | 12/65 | No gangway—probably full livery when new. To parcels van (12/52). |

*Note:* In this table, width is quoted over **body** (excluding projections) unless otherwise stated in 'Remarks' column. Most LMS Post Office coaches were 8'6" at waist plus a 2" projection on the sorting side giving an overall 8'8" dimension.

\* Official Date. The coaches actually appeared in 1958 and were given the last LMS series numbers to be allocated.

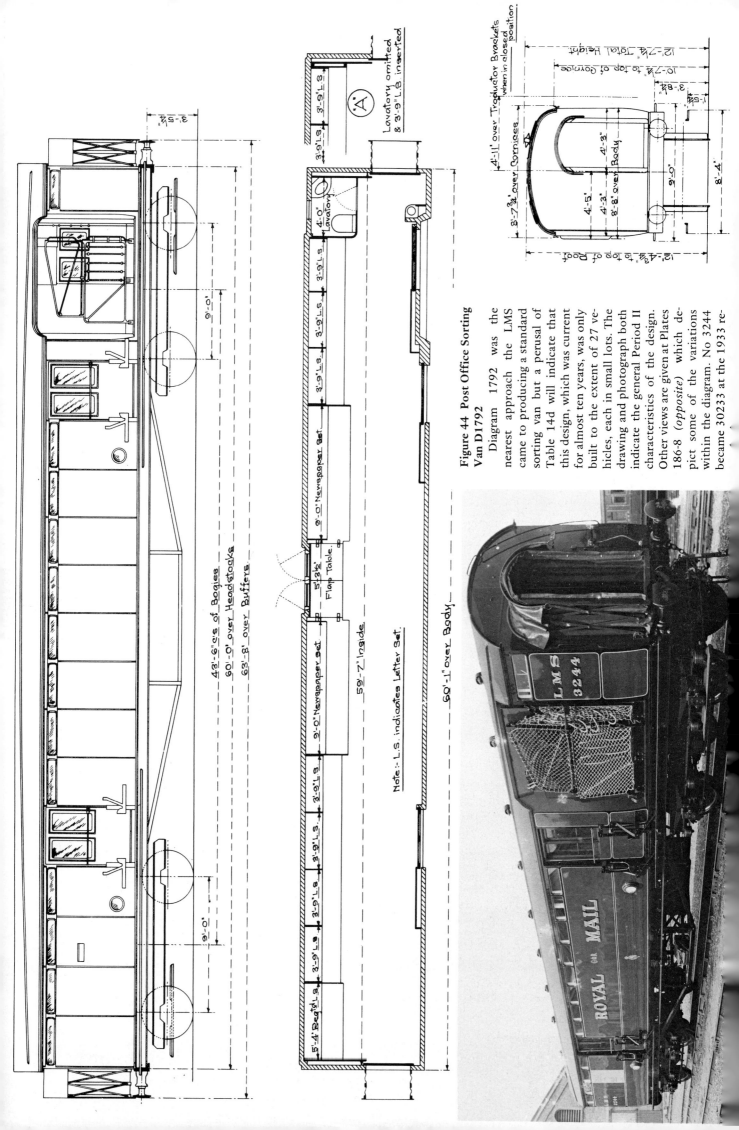

### Figure 44 Post Office Sorting Van D1792

Diagram 1792 was the nearest approach the LMS came to producing a standard sorting van but a perusal of Table 14d will indicate that this design, which was current for almost ten years, was only built to the extent of 27 vehicles, each in small lots. The drawing and photograph both indicate the general Period II characteristics of the design. Other views are given at Plates 186-8 (opposite) which depict some of the variations within the diagram. No 3244 became 30233 at the 1933 re-

Note:- L.S. indicates Letter Set.

43'-6" c's of Bogies
60'-0" over Headstocks
63'-8' over Buffers

9'-0'
9'-0'
3'-5⅛'

5'-4'Reg'd L.S. · 3'-9'L.S · 3'-9'L.S · 3'-9'L.S
9'-0'Newspaper Set
5'-3½'
Flap Table.
59'-7" Inside
60'-1" over Body

3'-9'L.S · 3'-9'L.S · 3'-9'L.S · 3'-9'L.S
9'-0'Newspaper Set
"A"
4'-0'
Lavatory
Lavatory omitted & 3'-9"L.S inserted

4'-11" over Traductor Brackets when in closed position
12'-7¾" Total Height
10'-7¾" to top of cornice
3'-8¼"
8'-7¾' over Cornices
9'-0'
8'-8' over Body
4'-5"
4'-3"
4'-3'
8'-4'
12'-4¾' to top of Roof

**Plate 186.** Opposite side view of No 3244 (Figure 44) showing the letter sorting 'bulges'.

**Plate 187.** POS No 3241, later 30314 to D1792 shows an example built without pick-up nets or traductor brackets but still with the recessed side where the net would be fitted. It is not known if nets were fitted later.

**Plate 188.** This view of POS No 3251 (later 30266) shows the sorting side view of a D1792 post office when fitted with toilet compartment. No 3241 (Plate 187) was of this type. Pictures indicate that toilets were often fitted to those coaches without pick-up nets but whether this was a standard distinction is not known.

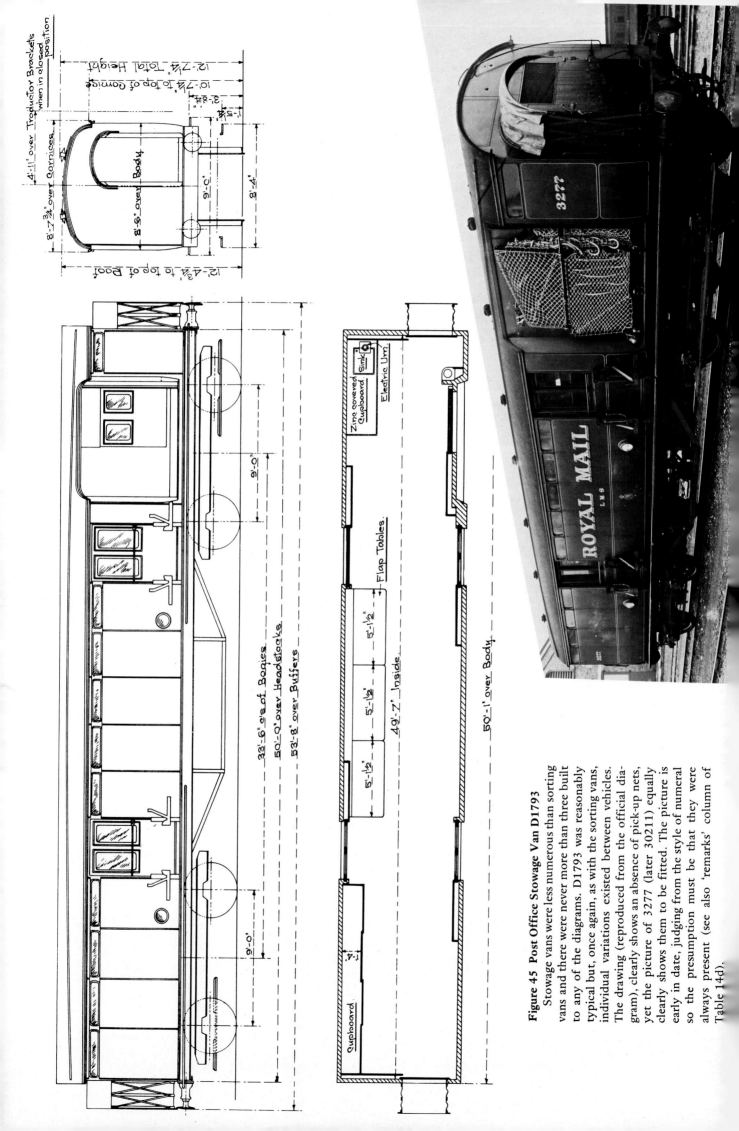

**Figure 45 Post Office Stowage Van D1793**

Stowage vans were less numerous than sorting vans and there were never more than three built to any of the diagrams. D1793 was reasonably typical but, once again, as with the sorting vans, individual variations existed between vehicles. The drawing (reproduced from the official diagram), clearly shows an absence of pick-up nets, yet the picture of 3277 (later 30211) equally clearly shows them to be fitted. The picture is early in date, judging from the style of numeral so the presumption must be that they were always present (see also 'remarks' column of Table 14d).

*Dimensions shown on the drawing:*

4'-11" over Troductor Brackets when in closed position

12'-7¾" Total Height

10'-7¾" to top of cornice

3'-8¼"

1'-6" 8'-4"

4'-11" over Cornices

8'-7¾"

8'-6" over Body

6'-0"

12'-4¾" to top of Roof

9'-0"

33'-6 c's of Bogies

50'-0" over Headstocks

53'-8" over Buffers

9'-0"

1'-4"

Cupboard

Zinc covered Cupboard

Sink

Electric Urn

Flap Tables

5'-1½" 5'-1½" 5'-1½"

49'-7" Inside

50'-1" over Body

ROYAL MAIL
LMS

3277

Plate 189. Interior of sorting coach No 30224, photographed from the end fitted with pick-up apparatus. The coach itself (D1970) was a Stanier version of the standard sorting coach.

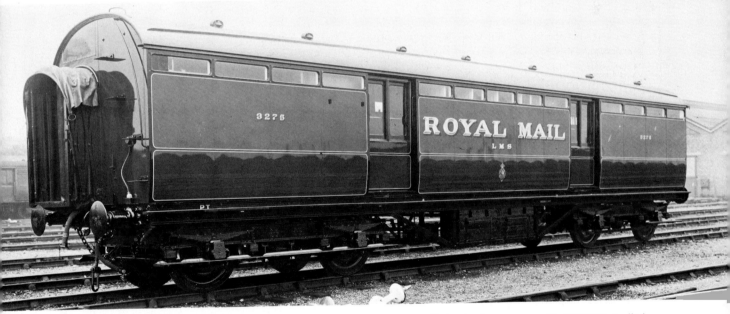

Plate 190 (above). This view of POT No 3275 (later 30210) shows the opposite side of D1793 to the view at Figure 45. This coach, the first example to the diagram, is thought not to have had pick-up nets.

Plate 191 (below). Stowage van No M30275, built in 1949 to D2172. This shows the general styling of Period III GPO vehicles.

# Chapter 15 - Special Saloons

*Introduction; Club Saloons; District Engineers' Saloons; Royal Saloons; Chairman's Saloons; Summary Table*

IT seems to have been almost a sacred doctrine of the British railway system that included amongst the oldest passenger vehicles owned by a railway company should be the bulk of its special saloons. This may have reflected a fondness for the traditional on the part of top management or possibly it was a realistic appraisal by the company officials that a special saloon ran a very low mileage and therefore took a long time to wear out! Be that as it may, the LMS followed the tradition and managed to make do with pre-group vehicles for a very long time after grouping. In fact, only two saloons, both travelling clubs, were built before the war. What was perhaps most surprising was the fact that the bulk of the special saloons which the LMS *did* build, entered service during the wartime period when most normal carriage construction had ceased in the national interest. Just how the LMS managed to get away with the building of these highly specialised vehicles at that time is not known and speculation is outside the scope of this book.

The saloons built by the LMS were few in number and are best considered by types in chronological order of building.

## CLUB SALOONS (OR CLUB CARS)

The travelling 'club' was a notable feature of railway working on parts of the LMS, particularly the North-West and both the LNWR and LYR had set aside special vehicles for this purpose. The LMS continued the practice and its activities took two forms, the conversion of older stock and the building of new coaches. Most conversion was of pre-group —for example some of the first class 65ft 6in coaches of the LNWR 'American Boat Train' sets—and only one example of the conversion of a standard coach has been traced. This was Period I vestibule first No. 3572 (original pre-1933 number) which was converted into a club saloon. It became 818 at the 1932/3 renumbering. As far as is known, it was little if any altered from its original state except that, being a club saloon, it would now be for the sole use of an exclusive clientele.

Only two club saloons were actually built as such by the LMS. These were 822 and 823, the latter being, of course, the 1939 'Coronation Scot' club car brake whose history is given in Chapter 13. Although this car seems to have been something of an after-thought, the same cannot be said of 822 which was a genuine type-designed vehicle for the pre-war Manchester—Blackpool service. It was built in 1935 to D1922 and was a 60ft Period III coach. Inside the car were three separate saloons, each equipped with individual armchairs and tables, and an attendant's compartment.

Club services never regained much popularity after the war and several LMS club cars and saloons found their way on to such services as the 'North Wales Land Cruise' where many of them served out their time. 818, 822 and 823 were among the coaches thus used.

## DISTRICT ENGINEERS' SALOONS

Some neat 50ft District Engineers' saloons were built during and after the war, all but the first to D2046. They had inspection saloons at each end which were connected by a side corridor which ran alongside the centre portion of the coach which was occupied by a lavatory, guard's compartment and a small kitchen/pantry. These coaches were preceded into service by the odd one out to D2045. This was probably a prototype for the D2046 version and the only significant difference was that this car was fitted with two lavatories.

No reason can be offered why so many, relatively speaking, of these saloons were built nor why they were allowed to be constructed during the war years.

**Plate 192.** LMS Club Car No 822 built in 1935 for the Manchester-Blackpool service. Note the supplementary wording adjacent to the doors and the distinctive roof board.

Plate 193. LMS District Engineer's saloon No 45026. Note the ascending steps below the guard's door.

## ROYAL SALOONS

The fact that King George V preferred the LNWR colours to those of the LMS and was thus instrumental in keeping the royal train in its traditional livery until the 1939—45 war is well known. Equally well known is the fact that the train was finally repainted in LMS livery to make it less conspicuous during the second world war. However, conspicuous or not, the magnificent LNWR saloons built originally for King Edward VII and Queen Alexandra were wood panelled and, therefore, highly vulnerable to air attack. Since safety of the monarch seems to have been the major consideration in the repainting of the train, it seems reasonable to assume that similar motives may have been the reason why the LMS was allowed to build new Royal saloons in 1941 with full armour plating. It is, of course, quite conceivable that the LMS would have wished to build new saloons anyway—although in all conscience it is hard to envisage much improvement on the LNWR pair—but no evidence has been located of any pre-war activity in this direction. The saloons built in 1941, are of course, still in existence.

Three vehicles were built on 12-wheel chassis. Two were the royal saloons themselves (798/799) and the third was a convertible sleeping, brake and power car. The chassis of the coaches are 67ft 6in over headstocks but the coaches are 69ft over the end panels since they have bowed ends. They were the only LMS built coaches to be constructed with drophead buffers, buckeye couplers and Pullman-type gangways. All three have slightly recessed end vestibule entrance doors. When new, the two royal saloons were fitted with armour-plated shutters over the windows but these features were later removed. The coaches were originally finished in standard LMS lake with a modified form of the simple lining. There was a waist line as on standard stock but this was taken round the entrance doors at the inner and upper edges. The LMS emblem appeared twice on each side of the coach. Windows on the coaches are mostly of standard Stanier 4ft 0in pattern but only a few are fitted with sliding ventilators. Side/end panel junctions are rounded off and the solebar is completely concealed by the lower bodyside panelling. All exterior grab handles etc. are of plated finish.

Plate 194. HM the King's Royal Saloon No 798 from the outside showing protective wartime armour plating.

**Plate 195.** HM The Queen's Saloon No 799 in LMS days without the armour plated shutters. The layout of the lining in this picture was faithfully copied when the saloon assumed the current Royal Claret colour during the 1950s.

The two royal saloons are almost identical except that the interior arrangements are opposite handed. Basically, each coach contains a suite of rooms (bedroom, bathroom and lounge) together with attendant's accommodation. The entrance vestibules are extremely wide and spacious as befits the nature of the coaches. It is believed that the coaches were designed to be marshalled with the two day saloons adjacent to each other. Needless to say, the interiors of these vehicles are sumptuous in the extreme. Just about every possible refinement was incorporated into the design and mere words cannot do justice to them. They were and are fit in every way to replace the original LNWR coaches although it could be argued that the fashion style of the 1940s compares unfavourably with the pre-group designs which they replaced.

The LMS royal saloons, together with the brake and power car are now finished in the royal train livery, described as claret, but which is, in fact a dark purple lake shade very close to the old LNWR colour. The lining style is still the same as in LMS days but rendered in vermilion and black rather than yellow and black. The royal saloons remained in use until 1977 when replaced by new BR Mk III vehicles. When finally withdrawn, they had been in service for almost as long as the pair they replaced of LNWR origin. The two Chairman's saloons, 45005/6 were also still in use in 1977 as sleeping cars in the Royal Train.

**Plate 196.** Interior view of HM The King's Lounge of Royal Saloon No 798

# CHAIRMAN'S SALOONS

In 1942, two identical Chairman's saloons were built to D2066. The interior of these 60ft coaches is given at Fig. 46 and the coaches were orthodox Period III styled vehicles. It is not known why they were allowed to be built during the war unless it was to act as mobile headquarters in connection with some aspect or other of wartime railway administration. At the same time it must be stated that there were surely enough pre-group saloons for this purpose if it was the reason. Thus, their origin is something of a mystery.

The saloons did not survive for long in their original state, being altered in 1948 into combined sleeping-cum-day saloons is also indicated in Fig. 46. Presumably in 1948, the continued existence of a 'Chairman's' saloon was something of an anachronism! The cars still survive in their rebuilt form, however, and are frequently employed in the royal train whose livery they now carry. They replaced some of the elderly ex-LNWR coaches which continued to be part of the royal train long after the newer royal saloons had been replaced by the 1941 LMS vehicles and were originally converted for the use of HRH The Princess Elizabeth and the Duke of Edinburgh.

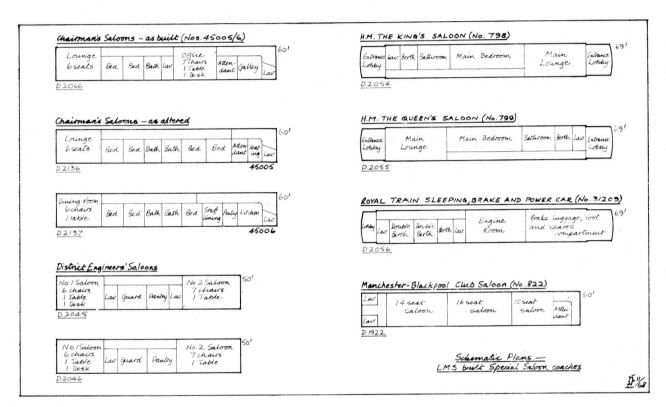

*FIGURE 46 LMS built special saloons—sketch plans* (Drawn by D. Jenkinson)

## TABLE 15: SUMMARY OF LMS BUILT SPECIAL SALOONS

| Type | Diag | Lot | Qty | Date | Built | Dimensions (L×W×H) | Weight | Running Numbers | Withdrawals First | Withdrawals Last | Remarks |
|---|---|---|---|---|---|---|---|---|---|---|---|
| Club | 1922 | 851 | 1 | 1935 | Derby | 60'×9'3"×12'4⅝" | 32T | 822 | — | 4/63 | |
| Club | 2020 | 1164 | 1 | 1939 | Derby | 59'5½"×9'2⅝"×12'2⁹⁄₁₆" | 31T | 823 | — | 4/63 | 'Coronation Scot' Car |
| District Engineer | 2045 | part 1221 | 1 | 1940 | Wolverton | 50'×9'3"×12'4⅝" | 31T | 45043 | — | 8/66 | |
| District Engineer | 2046 | part 1221 | 2 | 1940 | Wolverton | | 31T | 45044-5 | | | |
| | | 1264 | 3 | 1941 | Wolverton | | 31T | 45046-8 | | Some extant (1977) | |
| | | 1327 | 3 | 1942 | Wolverton | 50'×9'3"×12'4⅝" | 30T | 45028-30 | | | |
| | | 1356* | 3 | 1944 | Wolverton | | 31T | 45020/1/6 | 1968 | | |
| | | 1432* | 2 | 1947 | Wolverton | | 31T | 45035-6 | 8/66 | | |
| King's Saloon | 2054†1167 | | 1 | 1941 | Wolverton | 69'×9'0"×12'10⅞" | 56T | 798 | | | Quoted height for Royal Saloons is the overall value. |
| Queen's Saloon | 2055†1168 | | 1 | 1941 | Wolverton | 69'×9'0"×12'10⅞" | 57T | 799 | | | |
| Brake & Power | 2056 | 1229 | 1 | 1941 | Wolverton | 69'×9'0"×12'8½" | 52T | 31209 | | | |
| Chairman's (as built) | 2066 | 1323 | 1 | 1942 | Wolverton | 60'×9'3"×12'4¼" | 38T | 45005 | | All extant (1977) | |
| | | 1331 | 1 | 1942 | Wolverton | | 38T | 45006 | | | |
| Chairman's (altered) | 2136 | 1323 | 1 | 1948 | Wolverton | 60'×9'3"×12'4¼" | 39T | 45005 | | | 45005/6 built on secondhand underframes from war damaged coaches. |
| Chairman's (altered) | 2137 | 1331 | 1 | 1948 | Wolverton | 60'×9'3"×12'4¼" | 41T | 45006 | | | |

* Recessed door handles on these lots and only 9'2" wide.

† When the steel shutters were removed the saloon diagrams were renumbered 2054A and 2055A respectively.

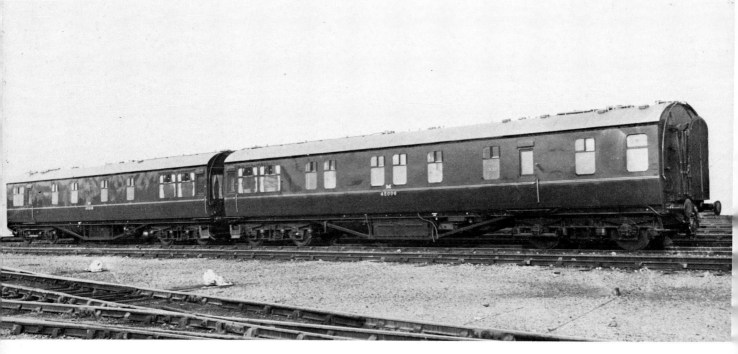

**Plates 197-198.** Exterior and interior views of the Chairman's Saloons 45005/6 taken at the time of conversion to their current (1976) form in 1948. These vehicles then became regular constituents of the London Midland Region Royal Train.

# Chapter 16 - Self-Propelled Vehicles

*Introduction; London Suburban Electric Stock; Liverpool-Southport Electric Stock; MSJA Electric Stock;*
*Mersey-Wirral Electric Stock; Steam Railcars; Internal Combustion Vehicles*

THE self-propelled vehicles listed in the LMS diagram book fall into convenient self-contained categories which will be taken as the basis for this discussion. In summary, the types to be considered were as follows:

*Electric multiple-unit stock*

London suburban stock — all compartment type
Liverpool-Southport stock — a mixture of compartment and open types
MSJA stock — all compartment type
Mersey-Wirral stock — all open type

*Other self-propelled stock*

Steam Railcars
Internal Combustion vehicles

The electric multiple-unit coaches accounted for the bulk of the vehicles built in term of overall quantity.

## LONDON SUBURBAN ELECTRIC STOCK

The London electrified lines of the LMS consisted of the former LNWR routes between Broad Street and Richmond and between Euston and Watford with their associated links and branches. The electrification was initiated in 1911 and was in large measure completed some two months before the grouping with the electrification of the Croxley Green branch. It was built and remained for many years a 630V dc four-rail system and its history is very well recorded already in *London's North Western Electric* by Atkinson and Adams, published in 1962 by the Electric Railway Society. Interested readers are referred to this very excellent account.

By the time the LMS came into existence, the North Western Electric already possessed a considerable number of vehicles composed of Siemens and Oerlikon centre corridor open types but the expansion of services necessitated further provision of stock at a fairly early stage after 1923. Not surprisingly, this was of standard LMS non-corridor style and the first batches entered service in 1927..

Three varieties of coach were provided: 17 third class driving motor coaches, 12 composite trailers and 12 third class driving trailers. They ran as three-car sets with five spare motor cars, but the stock was never kept in regular formations. All coaches were steel panelled but carried full Period I LMS livery (i.e. with painted waist panel). The motor coaches were 59ft over headstocks, a unique dimension for LMS standard stock with an equally unique bogie centre dimension of 39ft 6in (Fig. 47). The electrical equipment, by GEC, was based on that of the LNWR Oerlikon sets with which the LMS coaches were designed to run in multiple, when necessary. The motor cars had four 280 HP traction motors each. The trailers were of standard 57ft length and in every way similar to the contemporary locomotive hauled stock.

**Plate 199.** Close up of the composite trailer, No 5717, later 29608, from the three car set at Figure 47.

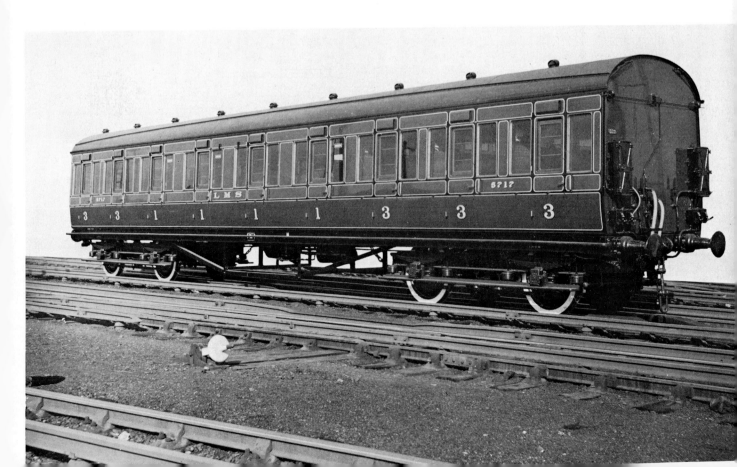

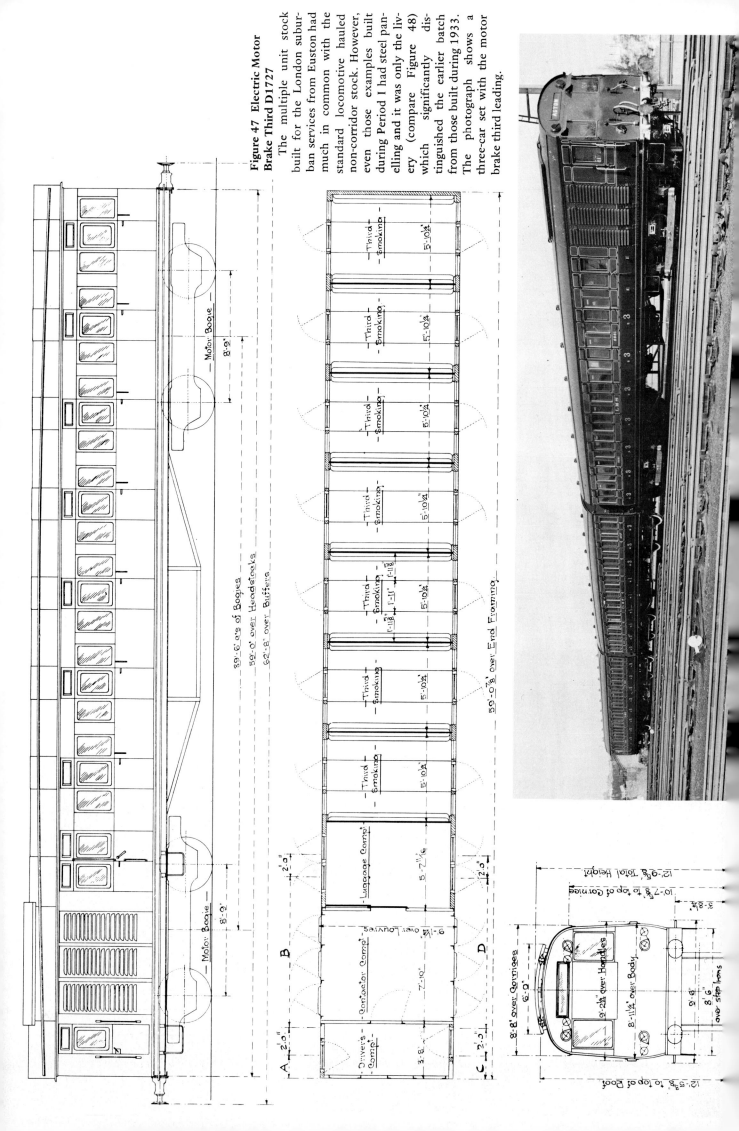

**Figure 47 Electric Motor Brake Third D1727**

The multiple unit stock built for the London suburban services from Euston had much in common with the standard locomotive hauled non-corridor stock. However, even those examples built during Period I had steel panelling and it was only the livery (compare Figure 48) which significantly distinguished the earlier batch from those built during 1933. The photograph shows a three-car set with the motor brake third leading.

In 1929, this initial batch of LMS design coaches was supplemented by a fourth type—this time a third class non-driving trailer of which 10 were supplied. These were used to make up some seven-car trains by being placed either 'inside' a three-car set or between two three-car sets. The coaches were again orthodox 57ft LMS types with fully lined livery.

The last batch of LMS stock for the North Western Electric system was a repeat order in 1932 for the first three types of coach; the electric traction motors were now, however, 320 rather than 280hp. This new stock, again in full livery but this time without waist 'panel', made it possible to dispense with some of the seven-car trains by running a more frequent service with six-car formations. The number of coaches provided was slightly variable, 13 driving trailers being built but only eight motor cars. Since there were five spare motors from the 1927 batch, 13 sets could be formed. However, instead of ordering 13 composite trailers to go with the driving ends, only 10 were provided, three of the 1929 third class trailers (now no longer needed for seven-car sets) being converted to make up the 13 new three-car sets. The conversion was confined to re-upholstery of the firsts and all nine compartments remained the same size. One more third class trailer of the 1929 batch was transferred to the MSJA system in 1939 which left six of the original 10 still running as thirds on the London lines. These too became surplus when seven-car trains ceased to run in 1941 (coincident with the abolition of first class on the system) but were not actually withdrawn until the advent of BR stock in 1957. Although LNWR saloon stock was gradually withdrawn after this date, the LMS compartment stock survived more-or-less intact until it too, was withdrawn en bloc when time-table rationalisation rendered it redundant in 1963. It is interesting to recall that plans issued in 1933 foreshadowed the use of sliding door stock on the London area lines. In the event it was not built but the idea was adopted later for the Southport and Wirral lines.

## TABLE 16a: SUMMARY OF LONDON SUBURBAN ELECTRIC STOCK

| *Type* | *Diag* | *Lot* | *Qty* | *Date* | *Built* | *Dimensions (L×W×H)* | *Running Numbers* | *Withdrawals First* | *Withdrawals Last* |
|---|---|---|---|---|---|---|---|---|---|
| Motor Brake Third | 1727 | Part 235 | 17 | 1927 | Met. C & W | 59'×9'2¼"×12'5⅜" | 28001-28017 | 6/62 | 11/63 |
| | 1847 | 636 | 8 | 1933 | Wolverton | 59'×9'2¼"×12'4¾" | 28018-28025 | 11/63 | 11/63 |
| Composite Trailer* | 1691 | Part 237 | 12 | 1927 | Clayton Wagons Ltd. | 57'×9'2¼"×12'5⅜" | 29600-29611 | 2/57 | 11/63 |
| | 1846 | 622 | 10 | 1933 | Wolverton | 57'×9'2¼"×12'5⅜" | 29612-29621 | 11/63 | 11/63 |
| Driving Trailer Third | 1728 | Part 236 | 12 | 1927 | Midland Ry C & W Ltd | 57'×92¼"×12'5⅜ | 28800-28811 | 11/63 | 11/63 |
| | | 623 | 13 | 1933 | Wolverton | | 28812-28824 | 11/63 | 11/63 |
| Third Trailer† | 1684 | 464 | 10 | 1929 | Wolverton | 57'×9'2¼"×12'5⅜" | 29400-29409 | 2/57 | 11/63 |

* Downgraded to third in 1941.

† Subsequent history as follows:

29400/7/8 altered to composite becoming 29622-4 in order (2/33).
29401 transferred to MSJA becoming MSJA 153 in 1939.

*Note:* In all probability, the three coaches of D1684 which were altered to composite never carried their 1933 series **third** class numbers since the conversion approximately coincided with the 1932/3 renumbering.

**Plate 200** *(right)*. Close-up of the end of a third class trailer from the 1929 batch — see also Plate 12.

**Plate 201** *(below)*. Motor bogie from one of the London area sets.

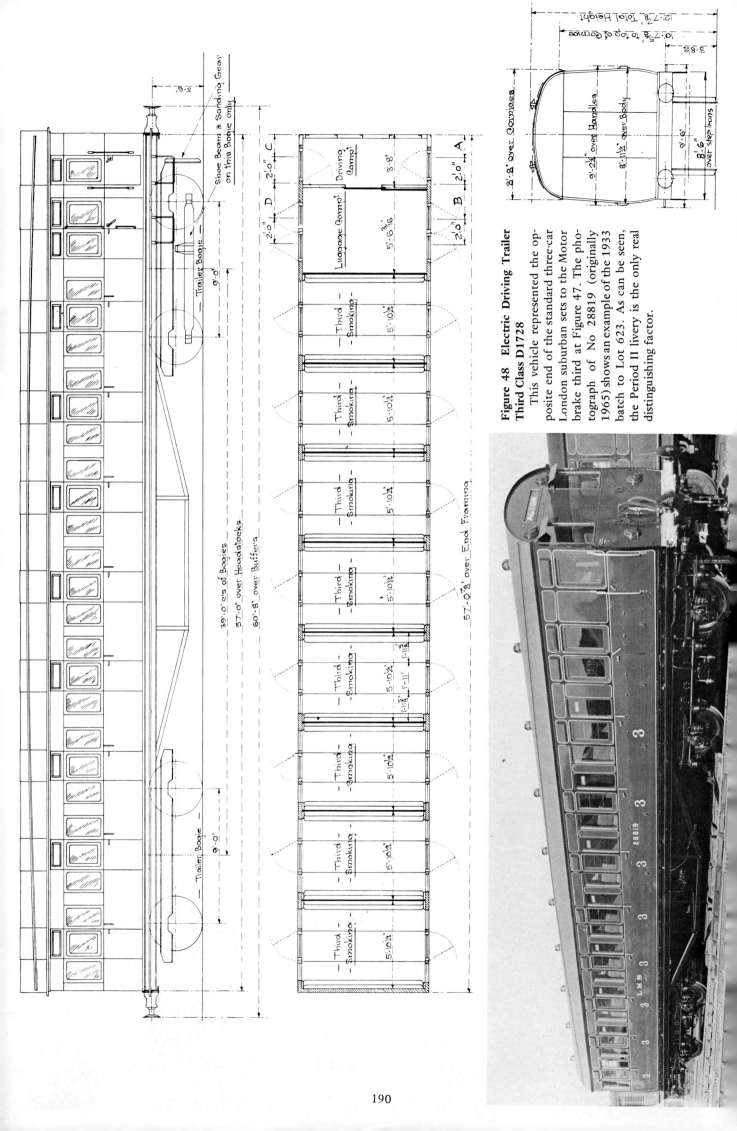

**Figure 48 Electric Driving Trailer Third Class D1728**

This vehicle represented the opposite end of the standard three-car London suburban sets to the Motor brake third at Figure 47. The photograph of No 28819 (originally 1965) shows an example of the 1933 batch to Lot 623. As can be seen, the Period II livery is the only real distinguishing factor.

190

## LIVERPOOL-SOUTHPORT ELECTRIC STOCK

The Liverpool-Southport line was originally electrified on the 550V dc system, later altered to the more common 630V dc supply; apart from this, the first LMS coaches built for use on the line were compartment vehicles identical to those provided in 1927 for the London suburban area. In fact the coaches were built at the same time to the same diagram and lot numbers. Eleven three-coach sets (motor brake third/composite trailer/driving trailer third) were provided plus an extra composite trailer. Five of the non-driving trailers were later transferred to the MSJA system as all thirds in 1939— presumably they could be spared as a result of the large scale building of open stock for the Southport line. In 1953, one each of the motor thirds and driving trailer thirds were converted at Derby as baggage cars for use on the system, part of the electrical equipment and traction motors being transferred from the motor coach to the driving trailer to form a second motor coach.

In 1939, the first of a considerable order for open stock was placed in service on the Southport line with English Electric equipment. These were very long coaches (66ft 6in) and moreover were 9ft 3in wide over body and 9ft 7in overall since the Liverpool-Southport line loading gauge was more generous than elsewhere, indeed the original L&Y stock for the line was 10ft wide. Four varieties were produced: motor brake thirds, trailer thirds, trailer composites and driving trailer composites of which the driving coaches were bow-ended at the driving end. The motor coaches were fitted with four 180 hp traction motors. The 1939 Liverpool-Southport stock was of lightweight all-steel welded construction in which the car body from underframe to roof forms a single girder structure; motor coaches for example weighed only 41 tons and trailer cars 24 tons compared with 56 tons and 28 tons respectively of 1927/33 stock.

The driving trailer composites were an insertion of a type not allowed for in the 1932/3 LMS block numbering scheme and, in consequence, their numbers were allocated at the end of the non-driving composite series. When new, the coaches were finished in a modified form of the simple LMS coach livery. They were painted all crimson with a yellow/black/ yellow line along the waist but *no* lining above the windows. Insignia was of standard LMS pattern. The driving coaches also carried the coach number on the front as indeed did most Liverpool area electric stock.

**Plate 203.** Electric baggage car No 28497. This coach was originally Liverpool-Southport driving trailer third No 29106.

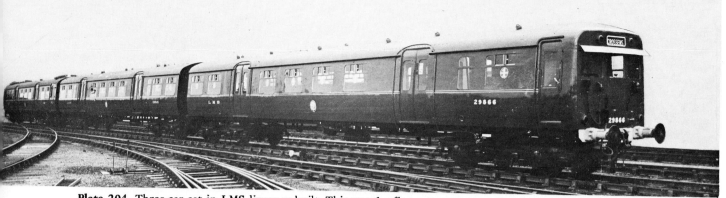

**Plate 204.** Three-car set in **LMS** livery as built. This was the first set to enter service; later ones were given the 1940-style scroll pattern running numbers. The leading vehicle is a driving trailer composite (29866) and the centre car a trailer third (29545).

**Plate 205.** Motor brake third No. M28315 in BR livery—unlined green.

**Plate 206.** Interior view of the first class seating area of driving trailer composite No 29885.

The quantities of each type built—see Table 16b—allowed for the formation of 34 three-car sets (motor third/trailer third/driving trailer composite) and 25 two-car sets consisting of a motor third plus trailer (16 thirds and nine composites). It will be appreciated therefore that not all sets had the same number of first and third class seats.

It may have been this imbalance between the seating accommodation which caused the somewhat confusing post-war rebuilding of the nine trailer composites (29812-20). Six were rebuilt as trailer thirds (29812-7) and, at a later stage, the other three were rebuilt as driving trailer composites (29818-20) along with one of the six which had already become 'all third'. Curiously, no diagrams were ever issued for these conversions. At the completion of this conversion operation, the final tally of coaches was as follows:

| | |
|---|---|
| Motor thirds | – 59 (all as built) |
| Trailer thirds | – 55 (50 as built plus five downgraded trailer composites) |
| Driving trailer composites | – 38 (34 as built plus four ex-trailer composites) |

By 1968, five motors and two non-driving trailers had been withdrawn from this total and the remaining stock was formed into 38 three-car sets, 15 two-car sets and a spare motor. The sets remained permanently formed almost in their original 1939 formations.

The open coaches seat two each side of the gangway in the first class sections and have a three-and-two arrangement in the thirds (now seconds). They also have a proportion of longitudinal seats adjacent to the entrance which are of sliding door type opening on to a reasonably sized passenger standing area. Except in respect of the surviving two-class accommodation, the interior arrangement is reminiscent of the London Transport Metropolitan and District line sets. The exterior styling is, of course rather different and is shared only with the Mersey-Wirral sets—see page 197.

### TABLE 16b: SUMMARY OF LIVERPOOL—SOUTHPORT ELECTRIC STOCK

| *Type* | *Diag* | *Lot* | *Qty* | *Date* | *Built* | *Dimensions** *(L×W×H)* | *Running Numbers* | *Withdrawals First* | *Withdrawals Last* | *Remarks* |
|---|---|---|---|---|---|---|---|---|---|---|
| *Compartment Stock* | | | | | | | | | | |
| Motor Brake Third | 1727 | Part 235 | 11 | 1927 | Met. C & W | $59' \times 9'2\frac{1}{4}'' \times 12'5\frac{3}{8}''$ | 28300-28310 | 3/53 | 7/63 | see footnotes |
| Composite Trailer† | 1691 | Part 237 | 12 | 1927 | Clayton Wagons Ltd. | $57' \times 9'2\frac{1}{4}'' \times 12'5\frac{3}{8}''$ | 29800-29811 | 1939 | 7/63 | |
| Driving Trailer Third | 1728 | Part 236 | 11 | 1927 | Midland Ry C & W Ltd. | $57' \times 2\frac{1}{4}'' \times 12'5\frac{3}{8}''$ | 29100-29110 | 4/53 | 7/63 | |
| Baggage Car | 2178 | Part 236 | 1 | 1953 | Derby | $57' \times 9'2\frac{3}{8}'' \times 12'5\frac{3}{8}''$ | 28497‡ | — | 2/66 | |
| | 2179 | Part 235 | 1 | 1953 | Derby | $59' \times 9'2\frac{3}{8}'' \times 12'5\frac{3}{8}''$ | 28496§ | — | 2/66 | |
| *Open Stock* | | | | | | | | | | |
| Motor Brake Third | 2012 | 1073 | 59 | 1939 | Derby | $66'5\frac{1}{4}'' \times 9'3'' \times 11'5''$ | 28311-28369 | see footnotes | | The open stock was actually delivered to service during the 1939-43 period. |
| Composite Trailer‖ | 2009 | 1076 | 9 | 1939 | Derby | $66'5\frac{1}{4}'' \times 9'3'' \times 11'5''$ | 29812-29820 | | | |
| Third Trailer | 2011 | 1074 | 50 | 1939 | Derby | $66'5\frac{1}{4}'' \times 9'3'' \times 11'5''$ | 29545-29594 | | | |
| Driving Trailer Composite | 2013 | 1075 | 34 | 1939 | Derby | $66'5\frac{1}{4}'' \times 9'3'' \times 11'5''$ | 29866-29999 | | | |

* Width of open stock is quoted over **body**. Over handles it was almost 9'7".
† The following coaches transferred to MSJA in 1939: 29800/2/3/8/11 becoming MSJA 154-8.
‡ Originally 29106 (D1728).
§ Originally 28300 (D1727).
‖ Subsequent rebuilding as follows:
29812-7 rebuilt to all third and renumbered 29595-9; 29544 in same order.
29818-20 rebuilt to driving trailer composite becoming 29863-5 in same order.
29597 (originally 29814) rebuilt to driving trailer composite and numbered 29862.

*Note:* The withdrawn coaches by 1968, all as a result of damage, were as follows:
Motor brake thirds (now seconds): 28320/1/5/9/46.
Third trailers (now seconds); 29576; 29544 (ex-29817).

**Plate 207.** Third class seating in third class trailer No 29545.

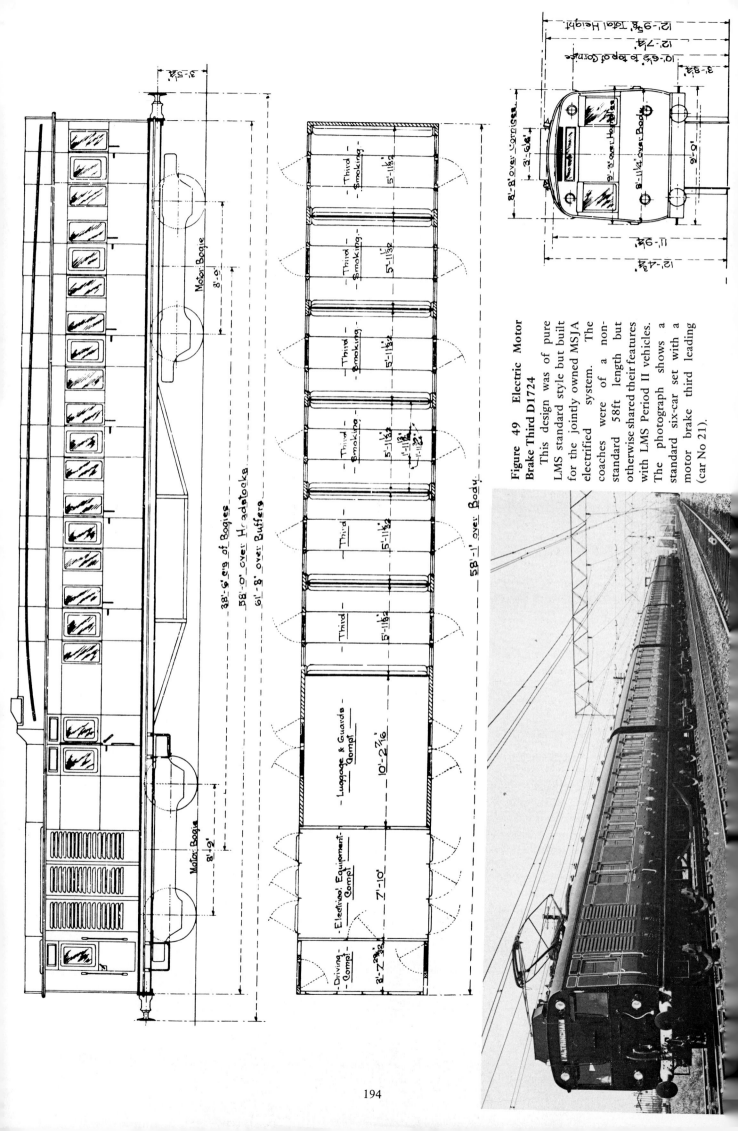

**Figure 49 Electric Motor Brake Third D1724**

This design was of pure LMS standard style but built for the jointly owned MSJA electrified system. The coaches were of a non-standard 58ft length but otherwise shared their features with LMS Period II vehicles. The photograph shows a standard six-car set with a motor brake third leading (car No 21).

**Side elevation dimensions:**

3'-5⅜"

8'-0" Motor Bogie

38'-6" c'rs of Bogies

58'-0" over Headstocks

61'-8" over Buffers

8'-2" Motor Bogie

**Plan dimensions:**

Third Smoking — 5'-11½"

Third Smoking — 5'-11½"

Third Smoking — 5'-11½"

Third Smoking — 5'-11½" / 5'-11½"

Third — 5'-11½"

Third — 5'-11½"

Luggage & Guards Compt — 10'-2⅜"

Electrical Equipment Compt — 7'-10'

Driving Compt — 8'-7 29/32"

58'-1" over Body.

**End elevation dimensions:**

12'-9⅝" Total Height

12'-7⅜"

10'-6⅝" to top of Cornice

3'-3⅛"

8'-8" over Cornices

3'-6¼"

9'-3" over Handrails

8'-11¼" over Body

2'-9'

11'-9¾"

12'-4¾"

**Plate 208.** Motor brake third No M28575 as running in BR livery without louvres on the side doors (MSJA No 5).

## MSJA ELECTRIC STOCK

The Manchester South Junction & Altrincham Railway was nominally an independent concern until 1947. It was owned jointly by the LMS and LNER and when it was electrified in 1931, it became the first line to be converted to the 1500V dc overhead system.

The stock for running the electrified services was of LMS standard style but, uniquely, all three varieties of coach were built on 58ft underframes—the only LMS diagrams of this length. The stock was built by Metropolitan-Cammell with Metrovick equipment and presented an orthodox Period II non-corridor appearance except for the lowered roof where the pantographs were fixed; 22 three-car sets were built (motor brake third/composite trailer/driving trailer third) plus two spare motors. All the motor cars were equipped with four 330hp traction motors. All the stock was given MSJA numbers and livery. The latter employed a mid-green body colour which was lined in LMS Period II style (i.e. full lining but no waist panel). The coaches also carried the MSJAR monogram and coat of arms. In 1948, the coaches were numbered into the LMS (now LMR) 1932/3 block series and both these and the MSJA numbers are given in the summary table.

In 1939, a decision was made to strengthen some of the peak trains to seven cars and for this purpose, eight trailer thirds were acquired. Two were built for the task at Wolverton, one came from the London suburban area and five from the Liverpool-Southport line. In style, all matched the original MSJA stock—except that they were 57ft long—and they were repainted and renumbered in the MSJA series. The experiment was not successful and the eight coaches had a mixed history afterwards. One was converted to a driving trailer (No. 74) to replace an accident victim (No. 57). No diagram was issued although the coach was 57ft not 58ft long. Six of the remaining seven were stored out of use for a long time while the seventh acted as a spare coach. In 1954, six were converted to locomotive-hauled coaches, renumbered and transferred away from the MSJA area. One of the latter even turned up in Euston-Bletchley-Northampton local set for a time.

A driving motor (28575) and a composite trailer (29664) were withdrawn in 1963 following a collision but apart from these, the stock remained virtually unchanged until late 1966 when the number of three-car sets was reduced to 16. These remained in service throughout the 1960s and gave to the railway enthusiast his last opportunity of regularly riding in pure pre-war LMS type compartment stock. Two survive in private ownership, converted for locomotive haulage.

**Plate 209.** Third class trailer No 151 (MSJA series) showing the MSJA livery. This was one of two cars built at Wolverton in 1939 to supplement those transferred from the London and Liverpool areas. In spite of the late date of building it was given full lining and Period II styling. The body colour was light green and the coaches carried the MSJAR monogram and crest.

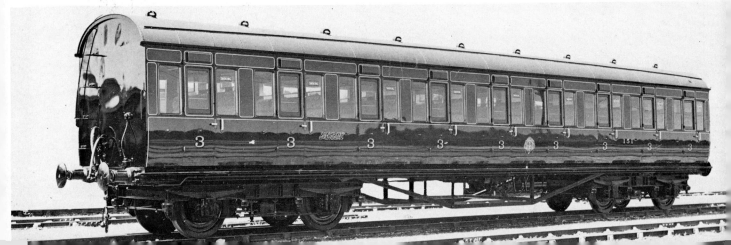

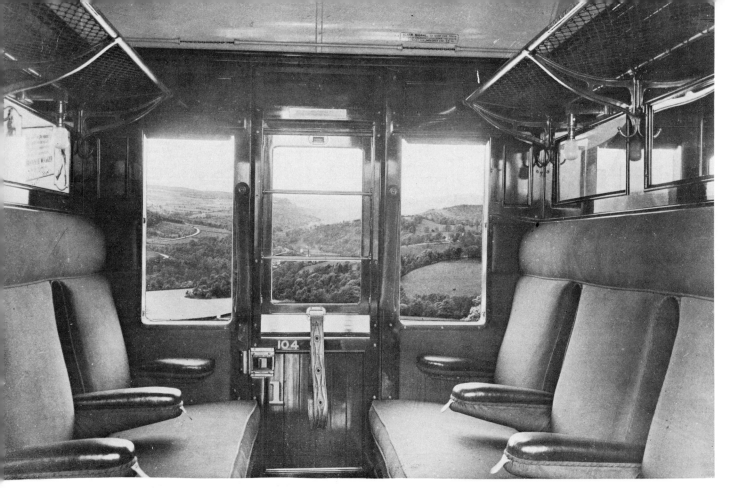

**Plate 210.** First class compartment interior of MSJA trailer composite No 104.

### TABLE 16c: SUMMARY OF MSJAR ELECTRIC STOCK

| Type | Diag | Lot | Qty | Date | Built | Wt | Dimensions (L × W × H) | MSJA Nos | LMS Series Numbers | Withdrawals First | Last |
|------|------|-----|-----|------|-------|----|------------------------|----------|--------------------|-------------------|------|
| Motor Brake Third | 1724 | 504 | 24 | 1931 | Met-Camm | 57T | 58' × 9'3" × 12'4¾" | 1-24 | 28571-28594 | 12/63 | not known |
| Composite Trailer | 1726 | 505 | 22 | 1931 | Met-Camm | 30T | 58' × 9'3" × 12'4¾" | 101-122 | 29650-29671 | 12/63 | not known |
| Driving Trailer Third* | 1725 | 506 | 22 | 1931 | Met-Camm | 31T | 58' × 9'3" × 12'4¾" | 51-56<br>57<br>58<br>59-72 | 2931-29236<br>Accident<br>29237<br>29239-29252 | 13/48 | not known |
| Trailer Third† | 1684 | 1158 | 2 | 1939 | Wolberton | 28T | 57' × 9'2¼" × 12'5⅝" | 151-152 | 29390-29391 | See Note 1 | |

* One more driving trailer (MSJA 74) rebuilt from trailer third No. 153 (below) and renumbered 29238 in 1948.

† Six more trailer thirds as follows: 153 was ex-London Suburban No. 29401 and later became driving trailer 74. 154-8 were ex-Liverpool-Southport composite trailers 29800/2/3/8/11 (D1691). In 1948, these five became 29392-29396.

*Note:* 1. In 1954, trailer thirds Nos. 29390-5 (ex-MSJA 151/2/4-7) were altered to locomotive hauled stock and renumbered 12278-83 in the LMS series non-corridor third class number block. 29396 withdrawn period 7/66.

2. All the renumbering of the MSJA stock into the LMS block series took place after nationalisation so the coaches were given the appropriate 'M' prefixes and suffixes with effect from the renumbering date.

**Plate 211.** LMS-built three-car set when new. Note the non-standard LMS insignia and absence of lining above the window. The waist lining was carried on a raised beading strip. The picture shows a driving trailer third leading.

**Plate 212.** BR-built three car set with motor brake third leading. Note by comparison with Plate 211 the absence of waist beading and the outward facing solebar channel.

## MERSEY-WIRRAL ELECTRIC STOCK

This system of suburban electrification, on the 650V dc third rail system, originated as two separate concerns which made an end-on junction at Birkenhead Park. East of this location and below the river to Liverpool, the lines belonged to the Mersey Railway while the remainder was LMS (ex-Wirral Railway) property. The Mersey Railway was electrified in 1903 but the Wirral lines to West Kirby and New Brighton were not converted until 1938. Both halves of the system lost independent identity in 1948.

The new stock for the 1938 electrification built by the LMS to supplement existing Mersey Railway stock took the form of 19 three-car sets (motor brake third/composite trailer/driving trailer third). The motor thirds had four 135hp traction motors. The coaches were all of open pattern with styling almost identical to that exhibited by the 1939 Liverpool-Southport stock (above). In fact, it is possible that the Mersey-Wirral stock set the pattern for the coaches built for the Southport line. There were, however, a few differences worthy of note. The Mersey-Wirral coaches were much shorter than the Southport vehicles being 58ft over headstocks (driving coaches) or 56ft over headstocks (non-driving trailers). Like the Southport stock, but was given non-standard sans-serif insignia edged in black. The coaches were assembled in sets in seats each side of the gangway (third class) or two-and-one seating (first class). The overall width over foot boards, however, was no less than 9ft 11in. Like the Southport sets the Wirral stock was of lightweight construction, motor coaches taring 36 tons and trailers only 20 tons. The coaches had sliding doors and longitudinal seating adjacent to the entrance area. The combination of shorter body and narrower width made a considerable difference to the seating capacity compared with the Southport coaches.

The stock was finished in the same modified version of the simplified LMS livery as described for the Liverpool-Southport stock, but was given non-standard sans-serif insignia edged in black. The coaches were assembled in sets in correct number order but two driving trailers and two non-driving trailers were destroyed at Birkenhead during the war.

In 1956-7, the ex-Mersey Railway stock was scrapped and replaced by 24 further sets of the LMS type. The main differences between these and the 1938 coaches were in external detail. The 1956 stock had slight detail changes in the windows, no raised beading strip along the waist and was built with an *outward* facing solebar channel. The passenger-open push-buttons for the sliding doors were on the doors themselves on 1938 stock but on the bodysides on the 1956 stock. Along with the 24 new sets, opportunity was also taken to replace the war losses mentioned above. Unlike the LMS sets, the formation of the BR built sets, although normally remaining unchanged, is not in any particular order of running numbers. The actual running numbers of the 1956 sets do not run consecutively with the LMS-built coaches but are in the correct number blocks.

The building of the Mersey-Wirral open stock was a joint venture between the Birmingham Railway Carriage & Wagon Company and Metropolitan-Cammell. The former firm built the driving trailers, Metro-Cammell the motors and the two works shared the non-driving trailers.

**Plate 213.** First class interior of one of the LMS-built composite trailers.

**Plate 214.** Third, now second class interior of BR-built motor brake third No 28371.

## TABLE 16d: SUMMARY OF LMS DESIGN MERSEY-WIRRAL ELECTRIC STOCK

| Type | Diag | Lot | Qty | Date | Built | Wt | Dimensions* (L × W × H) | Running Numbers |
|------|------|-----|-----|------|-------|-----|----------|---------|
| Motor Brake Third | 2004 | 1009 | 19 | 1938 | Met-Camm | 36T | 58' × 9'1" × 11'5" | 28672-28690 |
| | | 1685 | 24 | 1956 | Met-Camm | 37T | | 28371-28394 |
| Composite Trailer Trailer | 2005 | 1012 | 11 | 1938 | Birimingham | 20T | 56' × 9'1" × 11'5" | 29702-29712 |
| | | 1010 | 8 | 1938 | Met Camm | 20T | | 29713-29720 |
| | | 1682 | 10 | 1956 | Birimingham | 20T | | 29821-29830 |
| | | 1684 | 2 | 1956 | Birmingham | 20T | | 29831-29832† |
| | | 1686 | 14 | 1956 | Met-Camm | 20T | | 29833-29846 |
| Driving Trailer Third | 2006 | 1011 | 19 | 1938 | Birmingham | 21T | 58' × 9'1" × 11'5" | 29271-29289 |
| | | 1681 | 24 | 1956 | Birmingham | 22T | | 29131-29154 |
| | | 1683 | 2 | 1956 | Birmingham | 22T | | 29155-29156† |

\* Width is quoted over handles. Over footboards the stock measured 9'1" and over body it was 8'8".

† These lots built as replacements for wartime losses as follows :
   Composite trailers: 29708; 29717 (which ran with motors 28678; 28687).
   Driving trailers: 29277; 29286 (which ran with motors 28678; 28687).

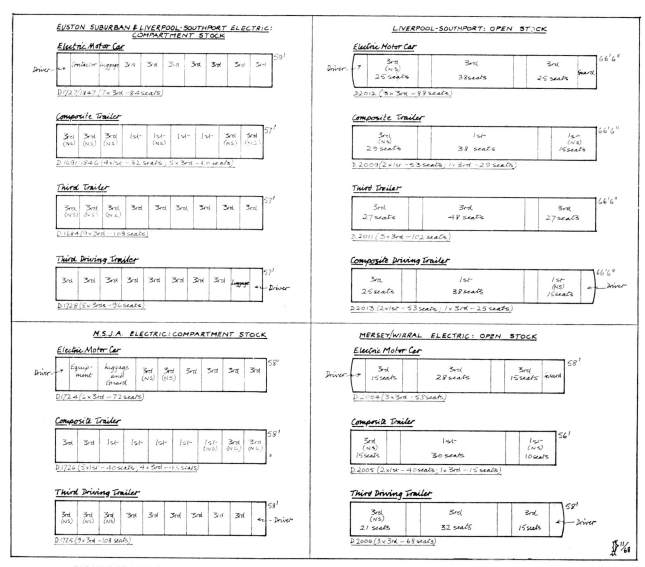

*FIGURE 50 LMS design electric multiple unit stock as originally built—sketch plans* (Drawn by D. Jenkinson)

## STEAM RAILCARS

The LMS experimented with steam railcars for about 10 years but does not seem to have found them as useful as did the LNER. One could argue that a steam railcar is a locomotive but the LMS inserted its examples in the passenger stock diagram book and numbered them in the coach series—thus their inclusion in this book.

There were 14 steam railcars built for the LMS of which 13 were to one design (D1779) and the last one to be acquired to D1842. All were of the Sentinel type and double ended. D1779 was chain driven and had the motive power end articulated to the passenger saloon (see Fig. 51), but D1842 was a rigid vehicle with shaft drive. Both versions were the same length and the main difference in layout was that the luggage compartment of D1842 was at the powered end of the car. The interior saloon of both types of railcar seated 44 passengers in seats arranged two each side of the gangway. The cars were third class only.

Unlike the LNER the LMS bestowed neither special livery nor distinctive names to the Sentinel railcars and all were turned out in standard full lined livery and insignia. They were allotted 29XXX series numbers in 1932/3 but it is not possible to say if all carried these numbers since most were withdrawn around 1935.

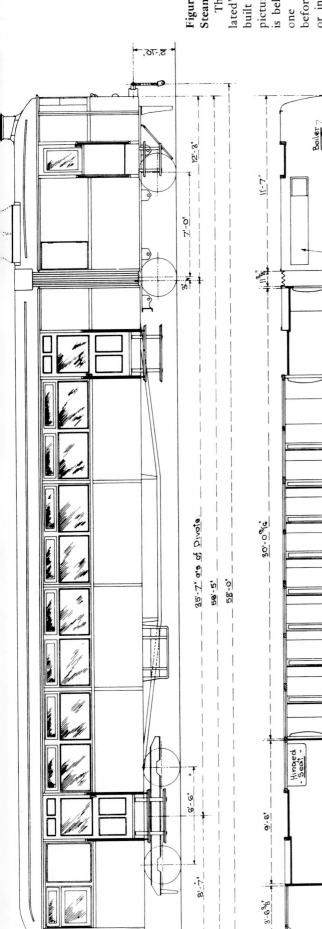

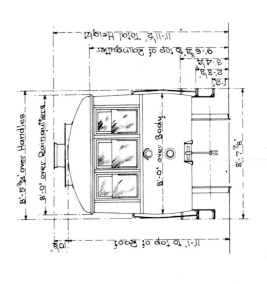

**Figure 51 Sentinel-Cammell Steam Railmotor D1779**

Thirteen of these 'articulated' steam railmotors were built for the LMS and the picture appended on this page is believed to be of the first one delivered (No 29900) before receiving LMS livery or insignia. When fully painted, the cars were broadly similar to the rigid railcar illustrated at Plate 215.

**Plate 215.** Rigid steam railcar No 4349, later 29913 (D1842). This picture shows the style of livery adopted with all the steam railcars.

Little contemporary evidence has survived about the use to which the LMS put its Sentinels other than pictures which show them to have operated as far afield as Strathpeffer and Highbridge. It seems reasonably clear that they were an attempt to stem the tide of the motor omnibus in the more remote areas of the system.

### Prototype Details

D1779 — Articulated steam railcar.
13 built in 1926/7 to Lot 312 by the Sentinel Wagon Works and Metro-Cammell. Allocated numbers 29900-12 in 1932/3. Weight: 21T.
All withdrawn in 1935 except 29910 (1937). 29900 was a prototype and ran on hire for several years.

D1842 — Rigid steam railcar.
One built in 1930 to Lot 576 by Sentinel Wagon Works and Metro-Cammell. Weight 25T. Given number 29913 in 1932/3 and withdrawn 13/39.

## INTERNAL COMBUSTION VEHICLES

The remaining self-propelled vehicles built by the LMS were, like the steam railcars, somewhat experimental designs of the 1930s. The first to be considered were three Leyland four-wheel railcars built to D2132 in 1933 and in some ways akin to the BR railbuses of 25 years later. One suspects from the Diagram number that it was allocated some time after the cars were in service possibly after some modification. Their appearance is best appreciated by the perusal of pictures—a sort of cross breed between the contemporary Leyland Titan double-deck bus and a single deck Blackpool tram. Their Lot number was 760, they weighed just over 10 tons and were numbered 29950-2.

They seated 40 third class passengers—all in pairs of seats either side of the gangway—in two saloons either side of the centre entrance. The seats faced outwards from the centre of the car and the driver sat in a small compartment at the left hand side facing forward. The livery is not known with certainty but the light bands of colour at waist and skirt level were probably cream, with LMS red as the base colour.

The Leyland railcars are recorded as having entered service in mid-1934 and initially worked in the Accrington, Blackburn, Lower Darwen, Preston and Hamilton districts in turn. Their subsequent history is not known but they were withdrawn in 1951.

**Plate 216.** Leyland railcar No 29950 to D2132. Note the general resemblance to the maker's contemporary omnibus designs.

**Plate 217.** Diesel articulated unit coach 80000 leading. Later, the sheeting between the bogies was removed and the driving cab windows slightly altered by fitting with external wire 'screens'. The LMS crest was placed on each unit in the plain panel to the side of the entrance doors about half way between waist and cantrail.

The final unit to be considered in this chapter is the experimental three-car articulated Diesel train of 1938 to D1996. This design was the prototype for the 'LMS' system of articulation by means of a double pivot alluded to on p. 23, but it was also yet another attempt to combat growing road competition over shorter distances. Little is known of the train since it entered revenue service only six months before the 1939-45 war and was stored during the latter event. In its few months of service it was allocated to Bedford.

The design was very distinctive and very much in the 'streamline' image of the 1930s. Its markedly rounded nose was very reminiscent of more recent Continental stock and its livery was somewhat striking—bright red and cream with a dividing band of black and probably a silver roof. The overall length over body was 182ft, the end components of the set being 64ft long and the centre portion 52ft long. Bogie centres were 52ft 6in—53ft—52ft 6in. Bogies were of a new design and the set was powered by six 125hp engines mounted under the floor (two per car), each driving a single axle via a torque converter. Bodyside panels were carried down between the bogies in the manner of the 1939 'Coronation Scot' train which toured America although in the case of the railcar, these panel extensions seem to have been cut back at an early stage.

The outer cars each seated 54 third class passengers in two saloons. The endmost saloon seated 26 and contained a small lavatory while the inner saloon seated 28. Most seats were transverse with reversible seat backs. Between the passenger saloons and the driver was a small luggage and brake compartment. Entry was gained by air operated sliding doors at the centre of the car only. The middle vehicle of the set was a composite. At one end was a 30 seat third class saloon with lavatory and luggage racks and at the other end was a 24 seat first class saloon. The two were separated by the entrance vestibule. The third class seats in the centre vehicle all had reversible seat backs but the LMS diagram shows the firsts to have been arranged in varied fashion, some facing each other and others as for the thirds. In all parts of the train, the seats were arranged in pairs on each side of the gangway. The driving cab was very capacious and the driver was centrally placed.

It is not possible to say whether the LMS intended to multiply the design*. It anticipated in many respects the present day DMU style of vehicle but no evidence has been located by the authors which would indicate whether or not enough data was obtained about the experiment to lead to any valid conclusions. It remained out of use until 1949 when it was converted to a two-car maintenance train for the MSJA electric line. The two outer ends were articulated on one bogie, the roof was flattened and the driving cabs were also given flat ends. All passenger seats were removed and semi-standard buffers were fitted. All but two engines were removed but the method of propulsion was unchanged. The set moved to Longsight in 1959 and was still there, derelict, in late 1967.

When new, the articulated set weighed 73 tons and was numbered 80000/1/2. After conversion, the two outer ends (80000/2) tared 54 tons and were renumbered M19885/6 in the departmental stock series.

*Another set *was* marked on the diagram but was never built.

# Chapter 17- Non-Passenger Coaching Stock

*Introduction; Livestock Vehicles; Covered Combination Trucks; Fruit and Milk Vans; Luggage, Parcels and Scenery Vans; Vehicles for Perishable Traffic (excluding fruit and milk); Milk Tanks; Open Carriage Trucks; Non-passenger Stock Livery*

AT first sight, the term 'non-passenger coaching stock' could be taken to refer to all vehicles which did not actually carry passengers. However, this literal interpretation would not be strictly accurate since the LMS divided its non-passenger stock into those coaches which were included in the passenger diagram book (full brakes and GPO vehicles) and those which it placed in the official 'non-passenger' diagram book. It is this latter group with which this chapter is concerned. By one of those paradoxes which only railway management can explain, the non-passenger diagram book also includes some vehicles which would be more at home in the freight stock book. However, we have taken the non-passenger book as the yardstick for this chapter. All the information is based upon the surviving official records, but it must be made clear that there is only space to give a very general resumé of the vehicles concerned and it is not possible to go into great detail about the many minor changes which must have taken place.

Since the vehicles to be covered do not readily fall into the Period I/II/III classification adopted in most previous chapters, the treatment of the non-passenger stock will be by generic groups as listed in the LMS Diagram book. Summary tables are appended for each type after the narrative section rather than place them at the end of the chapter. Finally, a brief definition of the requirements for non-passenger coaching stock seems called for. Basically, vehicles could run in passenger trains if they were fitted with automatic brake or 'through pipe' and had running gear, axle journals, oil boxes, springs, drawgear etc. compatible with the speed at which they would run in service.

## LIVESTOCK VEHICLES

The LMS built only two types of non-passenger livestock vehicles, namely horseboxes, of which there were seven varieties and prize cattle vans for which two diagrams only were raised. All were four wheel vehicles.

The first LMS horse box was to D1878 and was characteristic of MR designs. It had a fully panelled exterior with matchboard ends and was given full livery. The interior arrangement set the style for all subsequent diagrams. There was a half compartment for the groom at one end, a luggage compartment at the opposite end and between the two was the accommodation for the horses, of which three could be carried.

D1878 was succeeded by a series of diagrams of almost identical appearance but with varying arrangements of such matters as brakes and lighting which was the reason for the many diagrams (D1879/1952/1956/1972). All shared the same basic body shape as D1878 and retained the 12ft 6in wheelbase. However, on all four diagrams, the body style exhibited horizontal planking rather than the panelling of D1878. All had matchboard ends.

In 1938, an example from D1972 was converted to 16ft 0in wheelbase and this seems to have been the prototype for D2125, a post-nationalisation diagram which was built with the new longer wheelbase. It continued to have the 21ft long fully planked body of its predecessors and the standard LMS horse box profile. The final diagram (D2181) was a complete break from the previous types. It is difficult in some ways to see why this Diagram was included in the LMS book at all for the running numbers were in the LNER series and basically the design emanated from the LNER to ER Diagram 9. The first 25 were built at York in 1954 but 120 were built at Earlestown in 1955.

**Plate 218.** The first LMS-design horsebox to D1878 No 545, later 42000. Note the general resemblance to contemporary coaching practice and the fully lined livery.

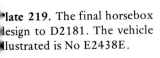

**Plate 219.** The final horsebox design to D2181. The vehicle illustrated is No E2438E.

Prize cattle vans, sometimes referred to as Special cattle vans, were very similar to horse boxes but unlike the majority of horseboxes, the first LMS prize cattle vans to D1876 were built with straight sides. Dimensionally they were very similar to the horse boxes but had no luggage space—the cattle compartment being correspondingly longer. The second diagram for this category of livestock (D1877) was identical in layout to D1876 but had the horse box profile with horizontal side planking and matchboard ends. One batch of this version was built as late as 1952. These were 24ft vehicles running on 15ft 6in wheelbase.

### TABLE 17a: SUMMARY OF LIVESTOCK VEHICLES

**Horse Boxes:**—For variations in brakes/lighting, etc., see notes at foot of table. All had 12'6'' wheelbase unless noted otherwise.

| Diag | Lot | Qty | Date | Built | Wt | Dimensions (L×W×H) | Running Numbers | Withdrawals First | Last |
|---|---|---|---|---|---|---|---|---|---|
| 1878 | 232 | *49 | 1926 | Derby | 10T | 21'×8'6½''×12'0⅛'' | 42000-42048 | 2/54 | 10/61 |
| 1879 | 436 | 60 | 1929 | Derby | 10T | | 42099-42158 | 12/57 | 13/62 |
| | 493 | 100 | 1930/1 | Derby | 10T | 21'×8'6½''×12'0⅛'' | 42159-42258 | 11/58 | 13/62 |
| | 584 | 100 | 1931/2 | Derby | 10T | | 42259-42358 | 1/59 | 10/62 |
| | 657 | 50 | 1932/3 | Derby | 10T | | 42359-42408 | 1/59 | 13/62 |
| 1952 | part 854 | 3 | 1935 | Derby | 10T | 21'×8'6½''×12'0⅛'' | 42521-42523 | 9/62 | 13/62 |
| 1956 | 317 | 50 | 1927/8 | Derby | 10T | | 42049-42098 | 6/56 | 8/61 |
| | 696 | 50 | 1933 | Derby | 10T | | 42409-42458 | 3/62 | 13/62 |
| | 748 | 25 | 1934 | Derby | 10T | 21'×8'6½''×12'0⅛'' | 42459-42483 | 10/62 | 13/62 |
| | 749 | 25 | 1934 | Derby | 10T | | 42484-42508 | 9/62 | 13/62 |
| | part 854 | 12 | 1935 | Derby | 10T | | 42309-42520 | 9/62 | 13/62 |
| 1972 | 1040 | 20 | 1937 | Derby | 10T | 21'×8'6½''×12'0⅛'' | 42524-42543† | 12/62 | 3/66 |
| | 1088 | 30 | 1938 | Derby | 10T | | 42544-42573 | 5/63 | 3/66 |
| 2125 | 1452 | 20 | 1948 | Derby | 10T | | 42574-42593 | 12/63 | 3/66 |
| | 1534 | 30 | 1948/9 | Derby | 10T | 21'×8'6½''×12'0⅛'' | 42594-42623 | 7/63 | — |
| | 1502 | 40 | 1950 | Derby | 10T | (16'0'' wheelbase) | 42624-42663 | 1/64 | 3/66 |
| | 1582 | 26 | 1950/1 | Derby | 10T | | 42664-42689 | 2/64 | — |
| 2181 | 1662 | 70 | 1954 | Earlestown | 12T | | 2391-2460‡ | | |
| | 1664 | 30 | 1955 | Earlestown | 12T | 24'×8'3''×12'3'' (16'0'' wheelbase) | 2461-2490‡ | not known | |
| | 1675 | 20 | 1955 | Earlestown | 12T | | 2491-2510‡ | | |

\* Possibly 50 built but only 49 renumbered—the only panelled horseboxes.

† 42536 converted to 16'0'' wheelbase in 1938.

‡ Many of these were allocated off the London Midland Region with the appropriate regional prefixes, etc. An LNER design with LNER series number.

**Diagram differences, other than dimensional:**

D1878   Gas lit, automatic vacuum and hand brake, Westinghouse through pipe.
D1879   Oil lit, automatic vacuum and hand brake, Westinghouse through pipe.
D1952   Electrically lit (Stones inductor alternator system), automatic vacuum and hand brake only.
D1956   Gas lit, automatic vacuum and hand brake only.
D1972   Electrically lit (Stones Lilliput single battery system), automatic vacuum and hand brake only.
D2125   Electrically lit (Stones O.L. system), automatic vacuum and hand brake only.
D2181   Electrically lit, automatic vacuum and hand brake only.

**Prize Cattle Vans:**—All with automatic vacuum and handbrake and all fitted with Westinghouse through pipe.

| Diag | Lot | Qty | Date | Built | Wt | Dimensions (L×W×H) | Running Numbers | Withdrawals First | Last | Remarks |
|---|---|---|---|---|---|---|---|---|---|---|
| 1876 | 227 | 27 | 1926 | Ntn. Heath | 10T | | 43800-43819 | 5/55 | 12/60 | All gas lit. |
| | 318 | 15 | 1927 | Derby | 10T | 21'×8'0''×11'8⅛'' (12'6'' wheelbase) | 43820-43834 | 7/56 | 8/61 | |
| | 377 | 15 | 1928 | Derby | 10T | | 43835-43849 | 6/57 | 1/61 | |
| 1877 | 463 | 10 | 1930 | Derby | 10T | | 43850-43859 | 5/59 | 13/62 | All oil lit except Lot 855 (gas). |
| | 598 | 10 | 1931 | Derby | 10T | 24'×8'6½''×12'0⅝'' (15'6'' wheelbase) | 43860-43869 | 4/61 | 13/62 | |
| | 855 | 5 | 1935 | Derby | 10T | | 43870-43874 | 12/63 | 3/65 | |
| | 1638 | 25 | 1952 | Ealrestown | 10T | | 43875-43899 | 12/63 | — | |

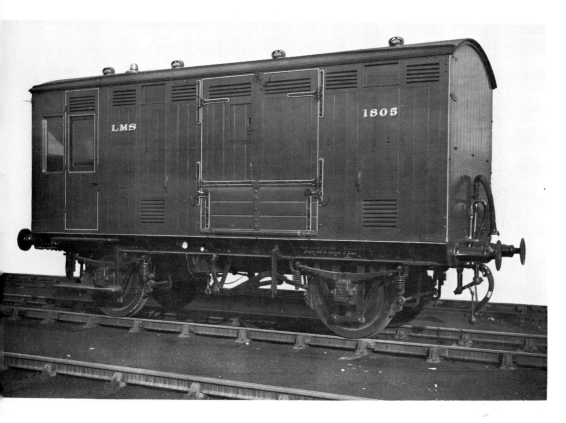

## COVERED COMBINATION TRUCKS

This family of mainly four and six-wheel vehicles embraces stock which was variously called 'motor car van' and 'aeroplane van' in the diagram book as well as the normal CCT reference. With odd exceptions, most of the vehicles were around 30ft long over headstocks, there being variations of a few inches, and were carried either on six-wheel or very long wheelbase four-wheel chassis. The principal exception was one diagram issued as an 'Aeroplane Van' which was a bogie vehicle (see below).

Two six-wheel diagrams were issued under the CCT reference (D1871/1872). D1871 was a 30ft vehicle on a 21ft 6in wheelbase chassis while D1872 was a 30ft 5in design on a 21ft 0in wheelbase chassis. Later lots of D1872 had 30ft 1in bodies but retained the 21ft wheel base. Both varieties were outside framed and bore a strong resemblance to the Midland design from which they must have originated.

Other than the dimensional differences, the two diagrams seem to have differed only in the chassis. Both are shown with identical body framing and end door arrangement. However, some, at least of D1872 seem to have been given more old fashioned underframes if pictorial evidence is any guide. They had longer leaf springs than D1871 and there were round section tie rods connecting the lower part of the axle boxes. Further tie rods were taken diagonally from the outer axle-boxes to the outer leaf spring hangers.

Many of these vehicles, of both diagrams, were later converted to departmental use and this went along with slight modifications to the bodywork. Outside steps were removed, end doors were boarded up and so forth. They were prohibited from passenger train use in February 1959 and this instruction probably heralded their general downgrading for other purposes.

**Plate 222.** Four-wheel CCT to D1929 No M35556.

The third CCT diagram in the LMS diagram book was D1929. This was a 30ft 5in four-wheel vehicle with 19ft 0in wheelbase. One hundred and twenty-five were built during the middle 1930s and the vehicles presented a cleaner external appearance. Unlike the six-wheel CCTs, they were vacuum fitted only. Curiously, however, the diagram book rates them at 8T carrying capacity rather than the 6T of the six-wheel designs.

The bulk of the remaining vehicles in this section were classified as motor car vans. The first of these was D2032 which was a variant of the D1872 CCT considered above. Twenty-five were built and they were 30ft 1in vehicles with a high arch roof and 20ft 0in wheelbase, six-wheel chassis. These vehicles were built in 1925 as part of the same lot as some of the D1872 CCTs.

The next motor car van was a hideously ugly experimental design which appeared in 1925 to D1868 (later altered to D2042). One only was built, of steel construction and, judging from the fact that it was not repeated, one must presume that it was not successful.

The most numerous LMS design motor car van was D2026. These vehicles first appeared in 1938 and some were built as late as 1956. They were 30ft 5in vehicles on a 19ft 0in wheelbase four-wheel chassis. They have a sort of GWR 'Fruit D' appearance and one naturally speculates if Stanier had any influence on the design. The design was classified CCT by British Railways.

The final design to be considered here is the above-mentioned 'aeroplane van'. Six were built to D1880 at Derby and Wolverton on second-hand underframes. From the bogie style and other features, the underframes were clearly of Midland origin. The design was extremely distinctive and built to the extreme limit of the loading gauge. The lettering on the solebar indicated that the wheels must not exceed 3ft 6in diameter on the tread—one is not entirely surprised!

**Plate 223.** Bogie Aeroplane Van to D1880 No 4853, later 44302. Note the rather simple lining confined mainly to the extreme edges of the main panels. The high arch roof was a distinctive feature of this design.

**Plate 224.** Motor Car Van No 37000 to D2026 the prototype vehicle of the diagram; the use of freight-type insignia rather than passenger-type is interesting.

## TABLE 17b: SUMMARY OF COVERED COMBINATION TRUCKS AND ALLIED VEHICLES

| Diag | Lot | Qty | Date | Built | Wt | Dimensions (L×W×H) | Running Numbers | Withdrawals First | Last |
|------|-----|-----|------|-------|-----|---------------------|-----------------|-------------------|------|
| **Covered Combination Trucks** | | | | | | | | | |
| 1871* | 111 | 25 | 1926 | Wolverton | 12T | 30'0"×8'5¼"×12'4¼" | 35030-35054 | 2/57 | 4/63 |
| | 123 | 75 | 1926 | Wolverton | 12T | | 35055-35128‡ | 2/57 | 4/64 |
| 1872* | part 35 | 5 | 1925 | Wolverton | 12T | | 35025-35029 | 2/59 | 4/62 |
| | 363 | 20 | 1928 | Derby | 12T | | 35129-35148 | 9/56 | 7/62 |
| | 406 | 50 | 1928/9 | Wolverton | 12T | | 35149-35198 | 4/55 | 6/68 |
| | 532 | 50 | 1930 | Wolverton | 12T | 30'5"×8'5¼"×12'4¼" | 35199-35248 | 5/55 | 5/63 |
| | 594 | 100 | 1931/2 | Wolverton | 12T | | 35249-35348 | 2/55 | 5/65 |
| | 661 | 25 | 1932 | Wolverton | 12T | | 35349-35373 | 11/57 | 7/65 |
| | 746† | 50 | 1934 | Wolverton | 12T | | 35374-35423 | 12/56 | 6/66 |
| | 747† | 50 | 1934 | Wolverton | 12T | | 35424-35473 | 8/57 | 4/64 |
| 1929 | 860 | 100 | 1935 | Wolverton | 12T | 30'5"×8'7¾"×12'10" | 35474-35573 | 9/61 Some extant |
| | 999 | 25 | 1937 | Wolverton | 12T | | 35574-35598 | 4/65 early 1970s |

\* Fitted with automatic vacuum and hand brake, also Westinghouse through pipe.  Six wheel vehicles.
† 30'1" over headstocks.
‡ One withdrawn before 1933.

**Motor Car Vans**

| Diag | Lot | Qty | Date | Built | Wt | Dimensions (L×W×H) | Running Numbers | Withdrawals First | Last |
|------|-----|-----|------|-------|-----|---------------------|-----------------|-------------------|------|
| 2032 | part 35 | 25 | 1925 | Wolverton | 12T | 30'1"×8'5¼"×12'9½" (six-wheeled) | 35000-35024 | 4/54 | 4/64 |
| 1868 | 85 | 1 | 1925 | Derby | not known | 33'0"'×8'6½"×12'1¼" (four wheeled) | 37200* | — | 4/65 |
| 2026 | 1154 | 150 | 1938 | Met-Cammell | 12T | | 37000-37149 | 6/63 Many |
| | 1636 | 30 | 1951/2 | Earlestown | 12T | 30'5"×9'0⅞"×12'10" | 37298-37327 | 6/68 extant |
| | 1770† | 35 | 1956/7 | Swindon | 12T | 12'10" | 37200-37234 | 9/60 early 1970s |
| | 1773† | 10 | 1956 | Swindon | 12T | (four-wheeled) | 37235-37244 | — |

\* On conversion to D2042 the running number was altered to 34999.  Wheel-base was 17'6".
† GW not LMS series Lot numbers.

**Aeroplane Vans**

| Diag | Lot | Qty | Date | Built | Wt | Dimensions (L×W×H) | Running Numbers | Withdrawals First | Last |
|------|-----|-----|------|-------|-----|---------------------|-----------------|-------------------|------|
| 1880 | 299 | 1 | 1927 | Derby | 17T | 39'6"×9'1"×13'0" (bogie vehicle) | 44300* | — | 1/42 |
| | 407 | 5 | 1929 | Wolverton | 17T | | 44301-44305 | 6/45 | 6/68 |

\* Later allocated CCT No. 37067.

Plate 225. Covered Milk van to D1874 No 7419, later 40117, one of the Lot 304 examples renumbered into the 'Fish Van' series. Note the lining round the edges of the wooden framing.

## FRUIT AND MILK VANS

The three diagrams covered under this classification were all of six-wheel type and all but two of the vehicles concerned bore a close family resemblance to the six-wheel CCTs considered above.

The earliest design to D1873 was a developed version of a Midland design. They were slatted sided vehicles and 145 were built between 1923 and 1933. They shared the same profile as the six-wheel CCTs but, of course, did not have the end opening doors. In later years, many were classified 'Fish' and some of them had the slatted sides boarded up. The diagram refers to them as 'Fruit and Milk' whereas the next design to appear was subtly re-titled 'Covered Milk'. It shared the same size and profile as D1873 but the sides were solid from the outset with louvre vents in the upper portions (D1874). At the 1932/3 renumbering, the two lots to this diagram were renumbered separately, one into the fish van series (401XX) and the other into the milk series (385XX). This reflected a pre-1933 distinction between the two lots since only the later versions were actually lettered 'Milk' on the outside.

The final vehicles were two experimental 'Insulated Milk Vans' built to D1936 in 1935. These were austere looking vehicles with very plain exterior styling and the design was not repeated.

Plate 226. Covered Milk van to D1874 No 7316, later 38542, was one of the examples from this diagram renumbered into the correct post-1933 milk van series. Comparison with Plate 225 will reveal that below the side louvres, vans from the Wolverton series, of which 7316 is an example, had slatted sides rather than the fully boarded up variant of Plate 225.

**Plate 227.** Insulated Milk Van to D1936 No 38550. The transposition of letters and running numbers to the opposite ends of the vehicle was a little unusual.

### TABLE 17c: SUMMARY OF FRUIT AND MILK VANS

| Diag | Lot | Qty | Date | Built | Wt | Dimensions (L × W × H) | Running Numbers | Withdrawals First | Last |
|------|-----|-----|------|-------|----|-----|-----|-----|-----|
| 1873* | 112 | 15 | 1924 | Derby | 12T | | 38300-38314† | 11/46 | 6/61 |
| | 233 | 100 | 1926 | Wolverton | 12T | 30'5" × 8'5¼" × 12'4¼" | 10000-40099‡ | 5/57 | 12/63 |
| | 364 | 25 | 1928 | Derby | 12T | | 38500-38524 | 8/56 | 12/61 |
| | 663 | 5 | 1933 | Derby | 12T | | 38545-38549 | 10/58 | 7/63 |
| 1874 | 304 | 25 | 1927 | Derby | 11T | 30'5" × 8'5¼" × 12'4¼" | 40100-40124‡ | 6/57 | 11/61 |
| | 442 | 20 | 1929 | Wolverton | 11T | | 38525-38544 | 7/53 | extant (1969) |
| 1936 | 887 | 2 | 1935 | Derby | 16T | 31' × 8'8" × 11'10⅛" | 38550-38441 | 2/58 | 7/66 |

\* Fitted with Westinghouse through pipe as well as vacuum brake.
† Originally 38000-14.
‡ These numbers are in the 'Fish Van' series.
All types were six-wheeled with 21'0" wheelbase.

---

**Plate 228.** The standard 42ft LMS luggage and parcels van to D1870 No 37714. This is an early example from the diagram and was given full livery. Note the general resemblance to passenger coaching stock and the 'standard' placing of the insignia. The 42ft D2023 version was similar but with a higher roof profile.

## LUGGAGE, PARCELS AND SCENERY VANS

With the exception of the aeroplane van mentioned on p. 205, this group contains all the end door *bogie* vehicles built to LMS diagrams. In fact, it would be more logical for the LMS to have included its one aeroplane van diagram in the luggage/parcels van section of the diagram book since this latter section includes one diagram annotated as 'suitable for aeroplane traffic'. However, this was not the case.

Seven LMS diagrams are covered under the general heading of luggage, parcels and scenery. All were bogie vehicles and in terms of general styling, only two variants were to be seen; semi-flush sided steel panelled types and outside framed wooden bodied designs. Those described as 'luggage and parcels' were all of the steel panelled type while the scenery vans were wood bodied. There were three diagrams for each type and the seventh diagram to be considered was another wooden bodied vehicle, this time called simply 'parcels' van.

The luggage and parcels vans all post-dated Stanier's arrival on the LMS scene and, in consequence, shared a great deal in common with the gangwayed full brakes of contemporary age. They had fairly orthodox Period III features but there was no tumblehome and, of course, no gangway connection to the adjacent vehicles. They did have the raised metal beading strips along the bodyside which were mentioned in connection with Stanier full brakes on p. 171.

The standard design was D1870. This was a 42ft vehicle and was extensively multiplied between 1933 and 1937, eventually totalling 240 units. The early examples were given full livery and with their generally coach-like styling, looked very much at home in passenger trains. One of these coaches (37706) was altered in 1937 by fitting steel floor, stronger springs and tethering hooks for the conveyance of elephants! A less light-hearted version of the design was the D2023 version which was built to 13ft 0in height and annotated not to exceed 3ft 6in wheels. Ten of these were built and were rated as suitable for aeroplane traffic.

The final luggage and parcels van was D1933. This was a 45ft version of the standard 42ft vehicle for the simple reason that the coaches were built on the 45ft frames of ex-LNWR open scenery trucks.

The bogie parcels van diagram and the three theatrical scenery diagrams can be considered together since they shared a common exterior styling which resembled the six-wheel CCTs—page 204. All four diagrams also shared another feature, namely an utterly bewildering variety of lengths. Normally, the LMS issued a new diagram for a different length of vehicle

**Plate 229** *(above).* Theatrical scenery truck No 6516 later 37530 to D1875, a 44ft 5in vehicle on an ex-MR underframe.

**Plate 230** *(below).* Theatrical scenery truck No 250,

later 37546, also to D1875, a 54ft vehicle again utilising an ex-MR underframe. The overall style is very similar to Plate 229 but it is difficult to see how the two could have been built to the same drawings!

but in these cases, several lengths found their way onto one diagram. Some of the vehicles are officially recorded as having second hand underframes and it is the authors' belief that all, in fact were built on older underframes. Further confusing the matter is the fact that the diagrams themselves do not seem to indicate any logical pattern to the segregation into four separate 'designs', except in the matter of overall height where there was some consistency.

The so called 'parcels vans' were four in number to D1869. Three separate lengths were involved (!) and the vehicles do not seem to have differed a great deal from the three 'Theatrical Scenery Truck' diagrams (D1875/1881/1882). The latter three were all much alike but two were annotated as Westinghouse fitted as well as vacuum braked. Seven different lengths appear on D1875 and two each on the other two theatrical diagrams. It is not even possible to generalise very much about the styling of the vehicles since all were a little different. Two coaches from D1875 are illustrated and the diagram of these vehicles infers that both were built to the same drawing—how this could be is anyone's guess!

An attempt has been made in Table 17d to cover all these variations but, as will be apparent, there is little pattern to any of it.

### TABLE 17d: SUMMARY OF LUGGAGE, PARCELS AND SCENERY VANS

| Diag | Lot | Qty | Date | Built | Wt | Dimensions (L×W×H) | Running Numbers | Withdrawals First | Last |
|---|---|---|---|---|---|---|---|---|---|
| **Luggage and Parcels Vans** | | | | | | | | | |
| 1870 | 690 | 50 | 1933 | Wolverton | 24T | | 37700-37749 | 12/64 | |
| | 750 | 25 | 1934 | Wolverton | 24T | | 37750-37774 | 12/65 | |
| | 751 | 25 | 1934 | Wolverton | 24T | | 37775-37799 | 2/65 | Many |
| | 848 | 50 | 1935 | Derby | 24T | 42′×8′6″×12′4⅝″ | 37800-37849 | 11/65 | extant |
| | 863 | 25 | 1935 | Wolverton | 24T | | 37850-37874 | 3/66 | (1969) |
| | 864 | 25 | 1935 | Wolverton | 24T | | 37875-37899 | 4/66 | |
| | 1050 | 40 | 1937 | Wolverton | 24T | | 37900-37939 | 3/64 | |
| 2023 | 1051 | 10 | 1938 | Wolverton | 22T | 42′×8′6″×13′0″ | 44306-44315* | 11/65 | 11/67 |
| 1933 | 793 | 15 | 1934 | Wolverton | 25T | 45′×8′6″×12′4⅝″ | 38253-38267† | 4/64 | extant (1969) |

\* Numbered as aeroplane vans.

† Converted from ex-LNWR open scenery trucks.

**Parcels Van**

| Diag | Lot | Qty | Date | Built | Wt | Dimensions (L×W×H) | Running Numbers | Withdrawals First | Last |
|---|---|---|---|---|---|---|---|---|---|
| 1869 | 250 | 4 | 1926 | Derby | see below | see below | 34500-34503 | 10/54 | 7/56 |

**Theatrical Scenery Trucks**

| Diag | Lot | Qty | Date | Built | Wt | Dimensions (L×W×H) | Running Numbers | Withdrawals First | Last |
|---|---|---|---|---|---|---|---|---|---|
| 1875 | 134 | 10 | 1925 | Derby | see below | see below | 37500-37506 | 4/42 | 6/55 |
| | | | | | | | 37530-37532 | 2/54 | 5/56 |
| | 160 | 20 | 1925/6 | Derby | see below | see below | 37507-37512 | 1/52 | 7/54 |
| | | | | | | | 37538-37540 | 5/55 | 10/57 |
| | | | | | | | 37543-37553 | 10/53 | 4/62 |
| 1882 | 308 | 9 | 1927 | Derby | see below | see below | 37513-37519 | 1/52 | 4/55 |
| | | | | | | | 37541-37542 | | 2/54 |
| 1881 | 400 | 15 | 1929 | Derby | 17T | see below | 37420-37529 | 10/53 | 7/56 |
| | | | | | | | 37533-37537 | 12/44 | 11/58 |

**Diagram differences, etc., for Parcels and Theatrical Vehicles**

| Running Number | Diagram | Dimensions (L×W×H) | Wt | Other remarks |
|---|---|---|---|---|
| 34500-1 | 1869 | 42′5″×8′5¼″×12′4¼″ | 16T | |
| 34502 | 1869 | 44′5″×8′5¼″×12′4¼″ | 17T | All four rated 8T capacity and vacuum fitted only. |
| 34503 | 1869 | 53′5″×8′5¼″×12′4¼″ | 21T | |
| 37500-12 | 1875 | 42′5″×8′5¼″×12′4¼″ | 16T | Vacuum fitted only. |
| 37513-19 | 1882 | 42′5″×8′5¼″×12′6¾″ | 16T | Dual fitted. |
| 37520-9 | 1881 | 42′9″×8′5¼″×12′11″ | 17T | Dual fitted. |
| 37530-2 | 1875 | 44′5″×8′5¼″×12′4¼″ | NK | Vacuum fitted only. |
| 37533-7 | 1881 | 44′5″×8′5¼″×12′1¼″ | 17T | Dual fitted. |
| 37538-9 | 1875 | 47′5″×8′5¼″×12′4¼″ | NK | Vacuum fitted only. |
| 37540 | 1875 | 49′5″×8′5¼″×12′4¼″ | NK | Vacuum fitted only. |
| 37541-2 | 1882 | 53′5″×8′5¼″×12′6¾″ | 21T | Dual fitted. |
| 37543-9 | 1875 | 54′0″×8′5¼″×12′4¼″ | 21T | Vacuum fitted only. |
| 37550-2 | 1875 | 57′0″×8′5¼″×12′4¼″ | 21T | Vacuum fitted only. |
| 37553 | 1875 | 57′11″×8′5¼″×12′4¼″ | 21T | Vacuum fitted only. |

**N.K.** Weight not known. D1875 gives 16T and 21T as the weight for these vehicles but there were several intermediate weights between the two extremes.

## VEHICLES FOR PERISHABLE TRAFFIC (EXCLUDING FRUIT AND MILK)

The next vehicles to be considered were for perishable traffic of various kinds and fall into two natural groups. The first of these groups contains exclusively four-wheel vehicles which would be more at home, stylistically at all events, in the freight stock book. However, they were given the passenger livery and listed in the passenger book. They were used for the carriage of meat or fish. The second group was more variable and contained four, six and eight wheeled vehicles, mostly for the sausage traffic but also including two coaches rejoicing in the name of 'Cream Vans'.

Dealing first with the meat/fish van group, nine diagrams were involved, all concerning standard 17ft 6in long four wheel goods van type vehicles. Two diagrams concerned meat vans, the remainder were variations of design in vehicles for fish traffic.

The meat vans were all initially built to D1883 as ventilated refrigerator vans. They were orthodox tidy looking vehicles and, other than their passenger rating, they differed little from contemporary freight vehicles. At a later stage (believed c. 1950), all were altered to D1883A which was a modification involving the removal of the refrigeration equipment which gave a larger interior load space. They were then reclassified ventilated insulated vans and although retained in the passenger book, it is thought they were given the BR fitted freight bauxite livery. They had 9ft 0in wheelbase.

Plate 231. Ventilated refrigerator van for meat traffic No 6372, later 38705 (D1883) in plain red livery with passenger style insignia.

The fish vans exhibited quite a number of detail changes as time went by and are best considered in diagram order. The first vans were to D1884 which was a slatted type van. Some were fully fitted, others merely carried a through pipe and, in addition, the diagram only involved part of one lot (105). The remainder of the vans to Lot 105 were built to D1885 (below). The D1884 vans were transferred to the wagon stock as Banana Vans in 1937 and finally to Ale Wagons in 1944.

The next fish van diagram (D1885) introduced solid sides which remained standard for all future construction to LMS design. The style is illustrated and needs little further description save to remark that as with D1884, some were fully fitted and others had a through pipe only. These vans evolved into the D1886 version which dispensed with the side louvre vents and diagonal side strapping but had louvre vents at both sides of both ends. Again there were fully fitted and 'piped only' examples and this diagram saw an increase in wheelbase from 9ft 0in to 10ft 0in.

With D1887, the side vents re-appear, this time at the expense of the end louvres. All of this batch were fully fitted and retained the 10ft 0in wheelbase.

During the evolution of these designs, which took place during the period 1924-31, there was introduced a rather different fish van design to D1982 which first appeared in 1929. These were, outwardly, orthodox ventilated vans with side strapping, vertical planking, roof-top torpedo ventilators and no louvre vents at all. They are recorded as having been built with 9ft 0in wheelbase, later converted to 10ft 0in—date of conversion not known.

The final LMS four wheel fish van diagrams were D2059 and D2107. They appeared in 1941 and 1945 respectively and were identical save for the wheelbase (10ft 0in and 10ft 6in respectively). The exterior of these vehicles was completely devoid of strapping apart from strengthening plates at the corners and doors. They were given neither louvres nor roof vents which, in view of the traffic carried, must be considered a little unusual.

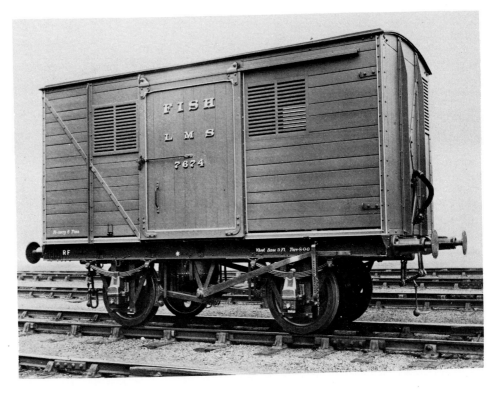

Plate 232. Fish van to D1885 No 7674, later 39114, with simplified version of the full lining.

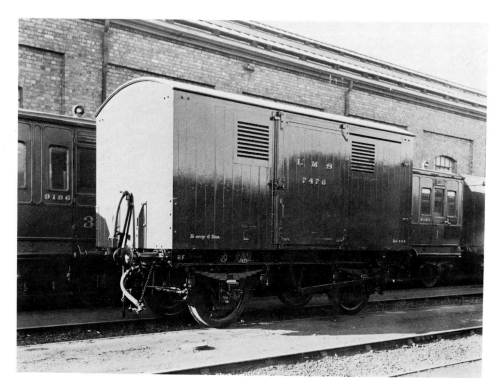

The final group of perishable vehicles to be considered were of more orthodox non-passenger coaching stock design. The first to be considered is the six-wheel 'Express Fish' van (D2115) introduced in 1947. Although taken out of date sequence, this design forms a logical conclusion to the above description of LMS four-wheel fish vans since its body style was all but identical to that of the final four-wheel diagrams. Moreover it was rated at the same carrying capacity (6T) as the four-wheel designs.

The remaining vehicles were the colourful vans built mainly for the sausage trade during the later 1930s. Four types were involved but all carried the high distinctive Palethorpes livery. In diagram order, the first design was a six-wheel vehicle (D1955) bearing a marked similarity to the contemporary insulated milk vans. The main difference was the presence on the sausage vans of end ladders and roof hatches. A bogie equivalent was built at about the same time to D1957. It was 50ft long but shared the same style of body with roof hatches and end ladders.

A second bogie design to D2001 was introduced in 1938. These vehicles were unusual for non-passenger coaching stock in that they were given gangway connections. The interior space was arranged in side-corridor fashion. The corridor side elevation contained three standard Period III 4ft 0in windows between the two pairs of double doors and another 4ft 0in window between each double door and the extreme end of the vehicle. Double doors opposite those on the corridor side led into the van from the side corridor while the van side itself presented the same austere aspect as the non-corridor equivalent with but two pairs of double doors to relieve the completely flat sided exterior. Like the non-gangwayed version, the D2001 coaches had completely flat sides.

**Plate 235.** Four-wheel insulated sausage van No 38731 to D1958. The livery and style of all Palethorpes' sausage vehicles were similar.

Two all but identical 50ft gangwayed vans were built to D2002 at the same time as D2001. These were annotated 'Insulated Cream Vans' and rated at 10½T capacity rather than the 6T of the gangwayed sausage vans.

The four-wheel sausage van was to D1958 and was contemporary with the six and eight-wheel designs. It had but one pair of double doors and was rated at 3T capacity. During 1956, the two examples of the type were converted to 'Passenger Vans'.

## TABLE 17e: SUMMARY OF PERISHABLE STOCK

| Diag | Lot | Qty | Date | Built | Wt | Dimensions* (L×W×H) | Running Numbers | Withdrawals First | Last |
|---|---|---|---|---|---|---|---|---|---|
| **Ventilated Refrigerator Van (Meat)** | | | | | | | | | |
| 1883† | 133 | 30 | 1927/8 | Derby | 10½T | 17'6"×8'0"×12'2¼" | 38700-38729 | 5/56 | 5/64 |
| **Fish Vans** | | | | | | | | | |
| 1884 | part 105 | 53 | 1924/5 | Derby | 8T | 17'6"×7'8"×11'10½" | 39021-39073 | to wagon stock 1937 | |
| 1885 | 66 | 20 | 1926 | Wolverton | 8T | | 39000-39019 | 11/52 | 6/61 |
| | part 105 | 47 | 1925 | Derby | 8T | 17'6"×7'8"×11'10½" | 39020 39074-39119 | 5/56 | 7/61 |
| | 336 | 50 | 1928 | Ntn Heath | 8T | | 39120-39169 | 3/48 | 4/61 |
| | 399 | 50 | 1929 | Ntn Heath | | | 39170-39219 | 2/55 | 9/63 |
| 1982 | 456 | 60 | 1929 | Ntn Heath | 8T | 17'6'×7'8"×11'10¼" | 39220-39279 | 2/53 | ‡ |
| 1886 | 589 | 66 | 1931 | Wolverton | 9½T | 17'6"×7'8"×11'10¼" | 39280-39345 | 9/58 | ‡ |
| | 592 | 34 | 1932 | Wolverton | 9½T | | 39346-39379 | 4/59 | 5/64 |
| 1887 | 660 | 20 | 1932 | Wolverton | 9½T | 17'6"×8'0"×11'10¼" | 39380-39399 | 5/59 | ‡ |
| | 691 | 40 | 1933 | Wolverton | 9½T | | 39400-39439 | 9/59 | 9/64 |
| 2059 | 1299 | 75 | 1041 | Earlestown (bodies built at Derby) | 9T | 17'6"×8'0"×11'10¼" | 39440-39514 | 2/59 | ‡ |
| 2107 | 1390 | 35 | 1945 | Wolverton | 9T | 17'6"×8'0"×11'10¼" | 39515-39459 | 11/58 | ‡ |
| 2115 | 1428 | 50 | 1946/7 | Wolverton | 17T | 31'0"×8'0"×12'1" (six wheel) | 40200-40249 | 4/64 | ‡ |
| | 1445 | 50 | 1949 | Wolverton | 17T | | 40250-40299 | 7/66 | ‡ |
| | 1509 | 40 | 1949 | Wolverton | 17T | | 40300-40339 | 10/65 | ‡ |
| **Insulated Sausage Vans/Cream Vans** | | | | | | | | | |
| 1955 | 986 | 4 | 1936 | Wolverton | 17T | 31'0"×8'0"×12'2⅜" | 38732-38735 | 6/66 | 10/66 |
| 1957 | 984 | 2 | 1936 | Wolverton | 28T | 50'0"×8'0"×12'2⅜" | 38877-38878 | 6/67 | 6/67 |
| 2001 | 1125 | 3 | 1938 | Wolverton | 29T | 50'0"×8'0"×12'2⅜" | 38874-38876 | 5/67 | 6/67 |
| | 1157 | 1 | 1938 | Wolverton | 29T | | 38873 | — | 3/65 |
| 1958 | 985 | 2 | 1936 | Wolverton | 11T | 21'0"×8'0"×12'3" | 38730-38731 | 10/67 | — |
| 2002 | 1156 | 2 | 1938 | Wolverton | 29T | 50'0"×8'0"×12'2⅜" | 38998-38999§ | extant (1969) | |

\* Width is given over body.

† Rebuilt to D1883A retaining original numbers but reclassified 'Ventilated Insulated Van (Meat)'.

‡ Survivors to wagon stock (c.1965) and some possibly still in service (1976).

§ These two vehicles classed as 'Insulated Cream Vans'.

Plate 236. Four-wheel milk tank No 638, built to Lot 357 in the 1920s (diagram number not known). Rebuilt to six-wheel diagram D1993 in 1937 and renumbered 44000.

Plate 237. Standard LMS six-wheel milk tank to D1994 No 1999, later 44179, pictured in 1932. The solebar seems to be the same colour as the tank.

Plate 238. Open carriage truck No 41216 to D2027.

# MILK TANKS

The rail-carried milk tanks listed in the LMS non-passenger coaching stock are something of a mystery since in some cases the identical lot numbers are also listed in the freight stock book but with different diagram numbers! This section will deal with those examples which were officially classified as passenger rated.

Eight diagrams were involved, six being genuine milk tanks and the other two being underframes for carrying road milk tank trailers. All the six milk tank diagrams differ in slight detail although sharing a common six-wheel chassis, 20ft 6in over headstocks with a 13ft 0in wheelbase. Some of the six-wheel diagrams were issued to cover the conversion of the pioneer milk tanks from four-wheel chassis. The earliest examples were built in this way but in 1937 it was decided to convert all tanks to a six-wheel chassis and the old diagrams were removed from the book. Hence, only the six-wheel diagrams can be quoted in this work. The only logical way to deal with them is diagram by diagram. Running numbers were mixed up amongst the diagrams and are therefore given in Table 17f. Most other details are given in the narrative.

*D1992* This diagram was issued in 1937 to cover the conversion to six-wheel chassis of the original 2000 gallon four-wheel tanks. Fourteen vehicles were involved from various pre-1937 lots but the rebuilding was given a fresh Lot number, being classed as part of Lot 1077. All were liveried for 'United Dairies'. This was the only 2000 gallon milk tank diagram. The tanks on these vehicles were quite small being 15ft 9in x 5ft 3in diam.

*D1991* This was an early 3000 gallon diagram being issued in 1931. It contained three vehicles only to Lot 613, all of which were built for Nestles. Tank size was 17ft $2\frac{1}{8}$in x 6ft $3\frac{1}{8}$in.

*D1993* These were virtually identical to D1991 except that the tank size was 16ft 9in x 6ft 3in. They were, like D1992 (above) ex four-wheel tanks to various pre-1937 lots and the batch of 25 concerned in the rebuilding was also classed as part of Lot 1077. Some were 'United Dairies' and some were 'Nestles'. The conversion took place in 1937.

*D1994* This was the earliest 3000 gallon diagram and dated from 1931. It contained an impressive number of different lots but none totalled very many vehicles. All are listed in Table 17f. This diagram was again similar to D1991 but had a tank dimension of 18ft $0\frac{1}{2}$in x 6ft 1in. Both new vehicles and converted ex-four wheel tanks were included on the diagram which was, in a sense, the LMS 'standard' milk tank. The tanks were built for many companies and an 'Express Dairy' version is illustrated.

*D2173* D1994 continued to be current until 1946 and was superseded by D2173 which was introduced in 1950. Again a 3000 gallon diagram, these tanks differed from all their forerunners in having the tank hatch and access ladder offset to one end of the tank. Tank dimensions were almost identical to D1994 (actually half an inch longer!).

*D2170* This was another 1950 diagram and the last to be listed in the LMS book. It had a centre hatchway type tank but only six vehicles were built. The style was virtually identical to D1994 but this time with a half inch shorter tank and some changes to the tank supporting structure.

The two road milk tank diagrams (D1989/D1990) seem to have been very similar. In D1989 the chassis was a fairly conventional six-wheel structure, identically dimensioned to that of the milk tanks proper. Both types were designed to carry 2000 gallon road trailers but D1990 was designed to carry a six-wheel as opposed to a four-wheel road trailer and, in consequence, was built to a greater length (24ft 6in) over headstocks and had a longer wheelbase (16ft 0in).

As stated above, the milk tanks were numbered indiscriminately although all were in the 44XXX series. It is believed that the railway owned the underframe only, the tank belonging to the dairy concerned. As far as can be deduced, the 1932/3 renumbering system for milk tanks took account of the owning dairy and number blocks were allocated to each company. New tanks were placed in the appropriate series by ownership rather than by taking the lowest available number in a continuous series. The allocations as listed in the diagram book were as follows:

| | |
|---|---|
| 44000–74: | United Dairies |
| 44075–139: | Nestles |
| 44140–69: | Co-operative Wholesale Society |
| 44170–249: | Express Dairy |
| 44250–2: | Cow & Gate |
| 44295–8: | H. Edwards & Son |
| 44253–94/9 | ⎤ |
| 44500 upwards | ⎦ Not listed as allocated to a particular owner—many were railway owned. |

*NOTE: For full list of milk tanks built see Table 17f (overleaf)*

# OPEN CARRIAGE TRUCKS

At the grouping, the LMS acquired more than enough open carriage trucks to satisfy its needs for almost 20 years. Most of the time, these vehicles would be standing waiting for traffic anyway. The only LMS diagram of the type was for a four-wheel design (D2027) which was somewhat longer than most pre-group four-wheel types although not as long as some of the six and eight-wheel pre-group examples. It is thought that the diagram may have arisen to accommodate wartime traffic in army vehicles: 40 vehicles were built at Derby to two Lots (1185 and 1263) in 1939 and 1940 respectively. Lot 1185 was numbered 41200–24 and Lot 1263 was numbered 41225–39. The trucks were 28ft 0in over headstocks by 8ft 6in wide with a central well 15ft 0in x 8ft 0in. Wheelbase was 20ft 0in.

| Diag | Lot | Qty | Date | Built | Running Numbers | Withdrawals First | Last | Remarks |
|------|-----|-----|------|-------|-----------------|-------------------|------|---------|
| 1992* | part 1077 | 14 | 1937-8 | Derby | 44006-11; 44016-9; 44032-5 | 7/41 | | |
| 1991 | 613 | 3 | 1931 | Derby | 44091-2; 44096 | | | |
| 1993 | part 1077 | 25 | 1937-8 | Derby | 44000-5; 44012-5; 44020-31; 44075-7 | 1/65 | | |
| 1994 | 596 | 3 | 1931 | Derby | 44087-9 | 6/64 | | |
| | 599 | 5 | 1931 | Derby | 44090; 44171-2; 44174-5 | 4/61 | | |
| | 615 | 6 | 1931 | Derby | 44093-5; 440097-8 plus one scrapped before renumbering? | | | |
| | 631 | 2 | 1931 | Derby | 44180-1 | 6/61 | 2/66 | |
| | 632 | 2 | 1931 | Derby | 44170; 44173 | | | |
| | 633 | 6 | 1932 | Derby | 44036-41 | | | |
| | 640 | 6 | 1932 | Derby | 44099-104 | 9/58 | 1/68 | |
| | 651 | 3 | 1932 | Derby | 44105-7 | 6/65 | | |
| | 656 | 4 | 1932 | Derby | 44176-9 | 9/62 | | |
| | 668 | 3 | 1932 | Derby | 44250-2 | | | |
| | 705 | 12 | 1933 | Derby | 44182-93 | 1/64 | | |
| | 727 | 2 | 1933 | Derby | 44042-3 | | | |
| | 781 | 3 | 1934 | Derby | 44194-6 | | | |
| | 782 | 1 | 1934 | Derby | 44197 | | | |
| | 791 | 3 | 1934 | Derby | 44253-5 | 2/67 | | |
| | 812 | 6 | 1934 | Derby | 44044-9 | 4/61 | | |
| | 874 | 5 | 1935 | Derby | 44276-80 | 6/56 | | |
| | 875 | 4 | 1935 | Derby | 44281-4 | 3/61 | | Withdrawal details are not entirely complete but many examples ran on into the 1970s. |
| | 881 | 3 | 1935 | Derby | 44198-200 | | | |
| | 882 | 1 | 1935 | Derby | 44201 | | | |
| | 893 | 3 | 1935 | Derby | 44050-2 | | | |
| | 936 | 1 | 1935 | Derby | 44285 | | 3/61 | A number of the railway owned vehicles have been renumbered into the 'dairy' series to replace withdrawals during the 1960s. |
| | | 12 | 1937 | Derby | 44078-86; 44150-2—these 12 were rebuilt ex-four wheel | 12/56 | | |
| | 1067 | 5 | 1937 | Derby | 44053-7 | 2/66 | | |
| | 1068 | 1 | 1937 | Derby | 44058 | | | |
| | 1129 | 2 | 1937 | Derby | 44059-60 | | | |
| | 1172 | 3 | 1938 | Derby | 44061-3 | | | |
| | 1232 | 2 | 1939 | Derby | 44256-7 | | | |
| | 1306 | 6 | 1941 | Derby | 44064-9 | | | |
| | 1328 | 4 | 1942 | Derby | 44258-61 | | | |
| | 1378 | 4 | 1944 | Derby | 44562-5† | | | |
| | 1434 | 6 | 1946 | Derby | 44230-5 | 5/67 | | |
| 2173‡ | 1580 | 10 | 1950 ⎫ Derby and | | 44500-9 | | | |
| | 1614 | 2 | 1950 ⎬ Earlestown | | 44510-1 | | | |
| | 1640 | 50 | 1950-1 | Derby | 44512-61 | 2/61 | | |
| 2174 | 1641 | 6 | 1950 | Derby | 44263-8 | 7/67 | | |
| 1989* | 878 | 3 | 1935 | Derby | 44297-9 | | | |
| | 931 | 1 | 1935 | Derby | 44296 | | | |
| | 932 | 1 | 1935 | Derby | 44295 | | | |
| 1990* | 1008 | 5 | 1936 | Derby | 44104-4 | 6/56 | | |
| | 1240 | 2 | 1939 | Derby | 44153-4 | 7/61 | 6/64 | |
| | 1491 | 1 | 1947 | Derby | 44155 | | | |

\* 2000 gallon types, the remainder being 3000 gallon.

† These four vehicles were built in 1943/4 on behalf of the Ministry of War Transport for Messrs. Libby, McNeil and Libby Ltd. When built they were never given LMS series numbers nor taken into LMS stock. The numbers quoted are those which were allocated when the vehicles were finally taken into stock in 1951.

‡ United Dairies owned some, at least, of these 445xx series vehicles and probably most of them.

# NON-PASSENGER STOCK LIVERY

With the exception of the rail carried milk tanks, all LMS passenger rated vehicles were given crimson lake livery. Until the introduction of the simplified lining style on normal coaching stock, the non-passenger stock was given a fully lined treatment. It is not possible to generalise about the lining adopted since so much depended on the type of vehicle involved. Thus, the fully panelled horseboxes were given what amounted to the complete passenger livery (probably lined in yellow rather than gold), whereas such vehicles as outside framed milk vans or the theatrical scenery vans were given yellow lining at the edge of the raised framing but the black seems to have been omitted. In some cases, no lining was applied and in others, a very simple form of lining was adopted. In all cases, underframes and running gear were black and roofs most probably grey.

The insignia adopted during the first 10 years or so seems to have generally matched that given to conventional coaches. The 3in scroll numerals were vitually universal and the seriffed 'LMS' was usually of matching height rather than the 4in version used on passenger coaches.

From about 1934, all lining was discontinued on non-passenger stock and in many cases, the running number was applied in sans-serif characters. The 4in LMS lettering was also used from time to time. Luggage and parcels vans were usually given simple lining.

It is not possible to generalise about the placing of insignia. The pictures illustrating this chapter show some of the variations but it is felt most probable that there were other schemes as well.

The principal exceptions to the above very general outline were the milk tanks. These carried the distinctive owning company liveries on the tank itself, the underframe being black and lettered in white. The sausage vans were finished in LMS red with yellow lettering and a coloured representation of the Palethorpes sausage advertisement on the side. It should also be mentioned that it was not uncommon in later years for non-passenger coaching stock to be turned out with varnish and lettering applied *direct* to the undercoat colour, thus giving a rather brown appearance to the vehicle.

# APPENDIX I STANDARD CODES FOR COACHING STOCK

The BR system of coding coach types is based on the old LNER system and following parts of it are relevant to LMS standard coaches discussed in this book, the LMS codes being given for comparison:

| | BR Code | LMS Code |
|---|---|---|
| **Dining and Kitchen Vehicles** | | |
| First Class Kitchen/Dining car | RF | 1st RKC |
| Composite   „   „ | RC | Compo RKC |
| Third Class   „   „ | RT | 3rd RKC |
| Unclassified   „   „ | RU | Common RKC |
| Kitchen/Buffet car | RB or RKB | BRC |
| Kitchen only car | RK | KC |
| First Class vestibule dining coach | RFO | QL (Dining) |
| Composite   „   „   „ | RCO | VC (Dining) |
| Third Class   „   „   „ | RTO | QF (Dining) |
| Unclassified   „   „   „ | RUO | — |
| **Sleeping Cars** | | |
| First Class | SLF | SC |
| Composite | SLC | CSC |
| Third Class | SLT | SCT |
|   „   „   (twin berth) | SLT (T) | — |
| **Vestibule Stock** | | |
| Vestibule First Class | FO | QL |
|   „   Composite | CO | VC |
|   „   Third Class | TO | QF |
|   „   Third Class Brake | BTO | VH |
| Semi-open First Class (Corridor/Vestibule) | Semi-FO or Semi-RFO | CQL |
| Semi-open Third Class (Corridor/Vestibule) | Semi-TO or Semi-RTO | — |

| | 3R Code | LMS Code |
|---|---|---|
| **Corridor Stock** | | |
| First Class | FK | CL |
|   „   „   Brake | BFK | E |
| Composite | CK | CBC |
|   „   Brake | DCK | CBB |
| Third Class | TK | CF |
|   „   „   Brake | BTK | CH |
| **Non-corridor Stock** | | |
| First Class | F | L |
|   „   „   (with lavatory) | FL | LM |
| Composite | C | BC |
|   „   (with lavatory) | CL | L&C |
| Third Class | T | F |
|   „   „   Brake | BT | H |
|   „   „   „   (with lavatory) | BTL | LH |
| **Other Coaching Stock** | | |
| Passenger full brake with gangway | BG | CBR |
| 6 wheel passenger full brake with gangway | BGZ | CR |
|   „   „   „   „   without gangway | BZ | R |
| Post Office Sorting Van | POS | POR |
| Post Office Tender (Stowage Van) | POT | PPR |

*Note:* 1. Articulated stock is prefaced by the word 'Twin' or 'Triple' in the BR system.

2. Codes exist for multiple unit stock but have not been employed in this book.

# APPENDIX II THE 1932/3 LMS COACH RENUMBERING SCHEME

The 1932/3 renumbering scheme grouped all coaching stock (pre- and post-grouping) into systematic number blocks according to coach type. Within the pre-group allocations, the numbering order was generally as follows: LNWR (which carried the lowest numbers); MR; LYR; FR; CR; GSWR; HR (which carried the highest numbers). Generally speaking the LMS standard coaches were numbered consecutively upwards from the start of the block and the pre-group coaches were numbered backwards from the end of the block. The pre-group numbers were allocated in such a way that the complete pre-group block of coaches generally occupied the last and highest numbers in any series. This usually left a gap between the end of the LMS standard block and the start of the pre-group block which was available for new construction. In some cases the 1932 planners underestimated the size of the number blocks they would need and certain coaches overflowed into the other blocks—these are annotated below.

**1-99 First Class Kitchen/Dining Cars**
- 1-44 LMS Standard types
- 45-58 Vacant
- 59-99 Pre-group types

**100-199 Third Class Kitchen/Dining Cars and Buffet Cars**
- 100-148 LMS Standard types
- 147-199 Pre-group types (including first 147/8)

**200-299 Composite Kitchen/Dining Cars**
- 200-221 Ex-Pullman cars (mostly Scottish)
- 222-252 LMS Standard types
- 253-270 Sundry post-1947 cafeteria conversions of LMS coaches
- 241-299 Original pre-group allocation

**300-499 First Class Sleeping Cars**
- 300-402 LMS Standard types
- 403-437 Vacant
- 438-496 LNWR (with a few gaps)
- 497-499 Vacant

**500-699 Third Class Sleeping Cars**
- 500-599 LMS Standard SLT
- 600-624 LMS type SLT(T)
- 625-699 Vacant

**700-799 Composite Sleeping Cars**
- 700-724 LMS Standard types
- 725-789 Vacant
- 790-799 LNWR—note second 798/9 later given to HM The King's and HM The Queen's Saloons

**800-999 Special Saloons—mainly pre-group varieties**

**1000-1199 Corridor Firsts and Semi Open Firsts**
- 1000-1128 LMS Standard types
- 1128-1199 Pre-group types (including first 1128)

**1200-3399 Corridor Thirds**
- 1200-2516 LMS diagrams
- 2235-3399 Pre-group types (including first 2235-2516)

**3400-3499 Push pull conversions of older gangwayed stock—both pre-group and LMS Standard types** (some of the pre-group examples were built new as push pull vehicles)

**3500-4999 Corridor Composites**
- 3500-4514 LMS Standard types
- 4357-4999 Pre-group types (including first 4357-4514)
- 2nd 4800-4899 LMS Standard types

**5000-5199 Corridor First Brakes and Open First Brakes**
- 5000-5004 LMS Standard Lounge (open) brakes
- 5005-5077 LMS Standard BFKs
- 5078-5144 Vacant
- 5145-5199 Pre-group types

**5200-6599 Corridor Third Brakes**
- 5200-6038 LMS diagrams
- 5990-6599 Pre-group types (including first 5990-6038)

**6600-7399 Corridor Composite Brakes**
- 6600-6876 LMS Standard types
- 6877-6956 Vacant
- 6957-7399 Pre-group types

**7400-7599 Vestibule Firsts (both FO and RFO)**
- 7400-7575 LMS Standard types (Note: First 7465-89 were later downgraded and the numbers in part used again for later standard coaches)
- 7556-7599 Pre-group types (including first 7556-7575)

**7600-9699 Vestibule Thirds (both TO and RTO)**
- 7600-9518 LMS Standard types
- 9519-9561 Vacant
- 9562-9699 Pre-group types

**9700-9799 Vestibule Composites (both CO and RCO)**
- 9700-9758 LMS Standard types
- 9759-9791 Vacant
- 9792-9799 Ex-LYR

**9800-9999 Vestibule Brake Thirds**
- 9800-9999 LMS Standard types
- 9971-9999 Pre-group types—first coaches with these numbers

*Note:* This concluded the initial allocation of numbers for passenger carrying non-articulated gangwayed stock. Extra batches built after the number series filled up were as follows:

Corridor Thirds: 12750-13184
Corridor Composites: 24500-24739

Corridor Brake Thirds: 26100-27095 ⎫ Some of these also originally used
Vestibule Thirds: 27100-27449 ⎬ to renumber pre-group gangwayed stock to clear the original
Vestibule Third Brakes: 27900-27956 ⎭ series for standard construction.

**10000-10699 Non-corridor Firsts**
- 10000-10131 LMS Standard types
- 10132-10308 Vacant
- 10309-10699 Pre-group types

**10700-15799 Non-corridor Thirds**
- 10700-12267 LMS Standard types
- 12268-12277 Downgraded composites from 160xx series
- 12278-12283 Ex-MSJA trailers (converted 1954)
- 12284-13610 Vacant (12750-13184 used for overflow numbering of TKs and 13610 downwards used for various downgraded vehicles)
- 13611-15799 Pre-group types

*Number list continues overleaf*

**15800-15999 Non-corridor Thirds—Motor Fitted**
15800-15857   Pre-group types
15858-15906   LMS Standard types
15907-15996   Vacant
15997-15999   LMS Standard types (converted)

**16000-17899 Non-corridor Composites**
16000-16325   LMS Standard types (16000-16006 originally compo. seconds)
16326-16330   Vacant—allocated initially to 17900-4 (Push-Pull version)
16331-16796   LMS Standard types
16797-16876   GWR designs built post-1947 and given LMS series numbers
16850-16937   Originally part of the vacant series but later used in part (post-1947) for ex-CLC stock and marked down pre-group firsts
16938-17899   Pre-group types

**17900-17999 Non-corridor Composites—Motor Fitted**
17900-17942   LMS Standard types
17943-17957   Vacant but some later used for conversions
17958-17999   Pre-group types

**18000-18199 Non-corridor Lavatory Firsts**
18000-18029   LMS Standard types
18030-18161   Vacant
18162-18199   Pre-group types

**18200-18999 Non-corridor Lavatory Thirds**
No LMS Standard designs built but 18614-18999 were pre-group coaches

**19000-19999 Non-corridor Lavatory Composites**
19000-19199   LMS Standard types
19200-19386   Originally Vacant but 19377-86 were given to non-lavatory Cs to Lot 1450 (Motor fitted coaches—D1921A—see p 84)
19387-19999   Pre-group types, also first 19385/6

**20000-24399 Non-corridor Third Brakes**
20000-21251   LMS Standard types
21252-22214   Vacant (22196-202 later used for ex-North London area LMS Standard brake seconds and 22203-14 for other down graded coaches)
22215-24399   Pre-group types (24317-31 later used again for Push-Pull driving trailers—1950)

**24400-24499 Non-corridor Driving Trailer Thirds**
24400-24459   LMS Standard types
24460-24499   Pre-group types and LMS standard conversions

**24500-24799 Non-corridor Composite Brakes**
24500-24717   Vacant (no LMS designs) but later used for overflow numbering of Period III CKs 24500-24739
24718-24799   Pre-group types (including first 24718-24739)

**24800-24899 Non-corridor Driving Trailer Composites**
24800-24895   Vacant (No LMS Standard types)
24896-24899   Ex-MR and Ex-LYR

**24900-24999 Non-corridor Second Brakes**
24900-24906   LMS Standard designs for North London sets—later downgraded and renumbered 22196-202
24907-24999   Vacant but 24989-99 later used for marked up BTs (pre-group) which were later marked down again

**25000-25699 Non-corridor Lavatory Third Brakes**
25000-25272   LMS Standard types
25273-25507   Vacant
25508-25699   Pre-group types

**25700-25999 Non-corridor Lavatory Composite Brakes**
25700-25777   Vacant (No LMS Standard designs)
25778-25999   Pre-group types

**26000-27999 Pre-group four/six wheel passenger carrying coaches—all types**
*Note:* Survivors of this block again renumbered 26000-99 when the 'overflow' numbering began

**28000-29899 Electric Multiple Unit Stock**
The number allocation in these blocks was a little complex and is best appreciated by studying Chapter 16.

**29900-29999 Miscellaneous Railcars, etc.**

**30000-30199 Kitchen Cars**
30000-30106   LMS Standard types
30107-30196   Vacant
30197-30199   Ex-LNWR

**30200-30399 Post Office Vehicles**
The numbers in this group were completely haphazard—see Chapter 14

**30400-32899 Bogie Corridor Full Brakes**
30400-32019   LMS Standard types and LMS built conversions from other coaches. There were vacant numbers—see Chapter 14, Tables 14a-c
32020-32899   Pre-group types built as full brakes

**32900-33499 Six Wheel Corridor Full Brakes**
32900-33019   LMS Standard types
33020-33441   Vacant
33442-33499   Pre-group types

**33500-44999 Non-passenger carrying coaching stock—see Chapter 17**

**45xxx numbers Chairman's and Engineer's Saloons** (total of 16 to LMS design)—see Chapter 15

**50000 Upwards Articulated coaches—see Chapters 12 and 13**